ELIAS RIVERA

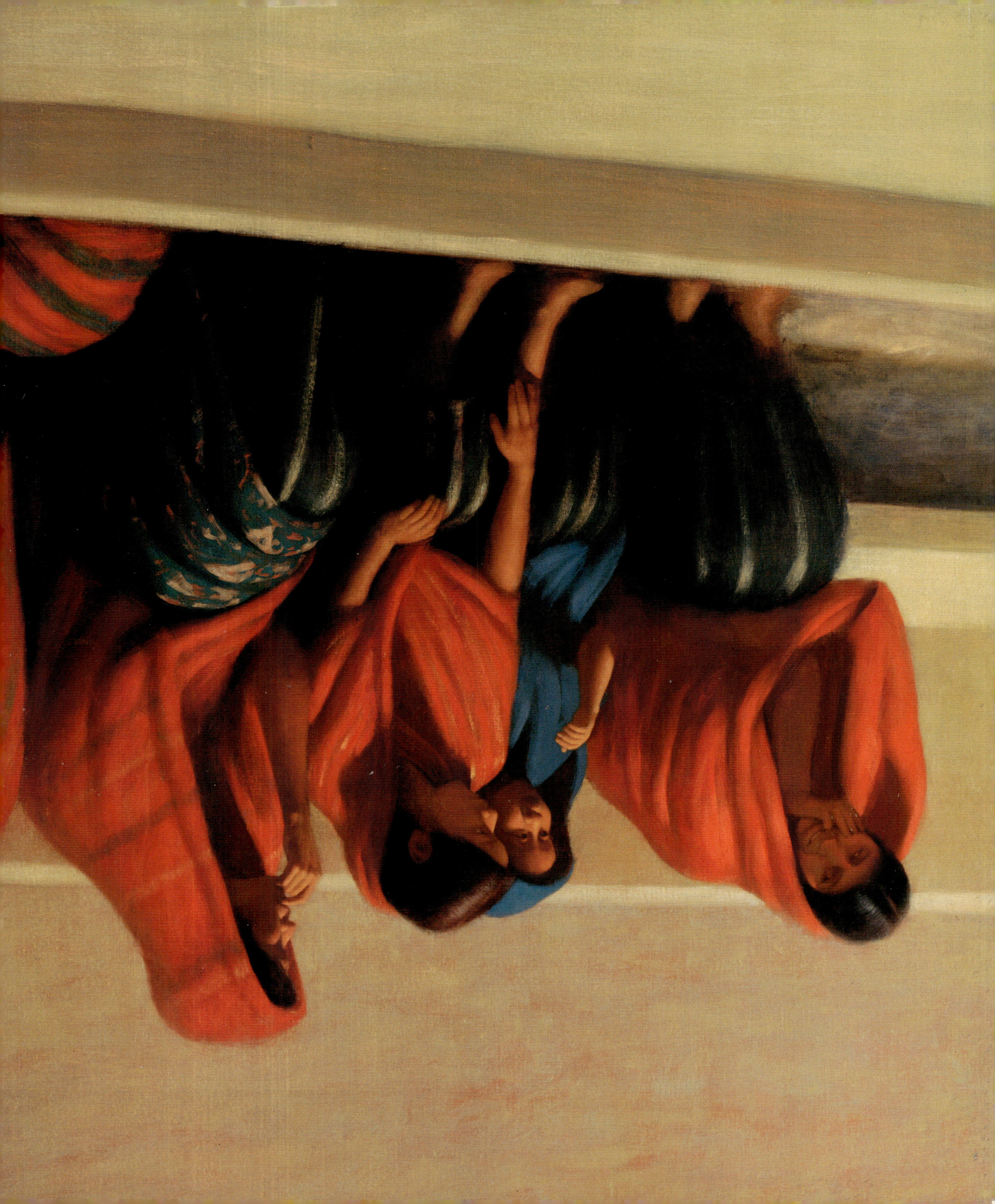

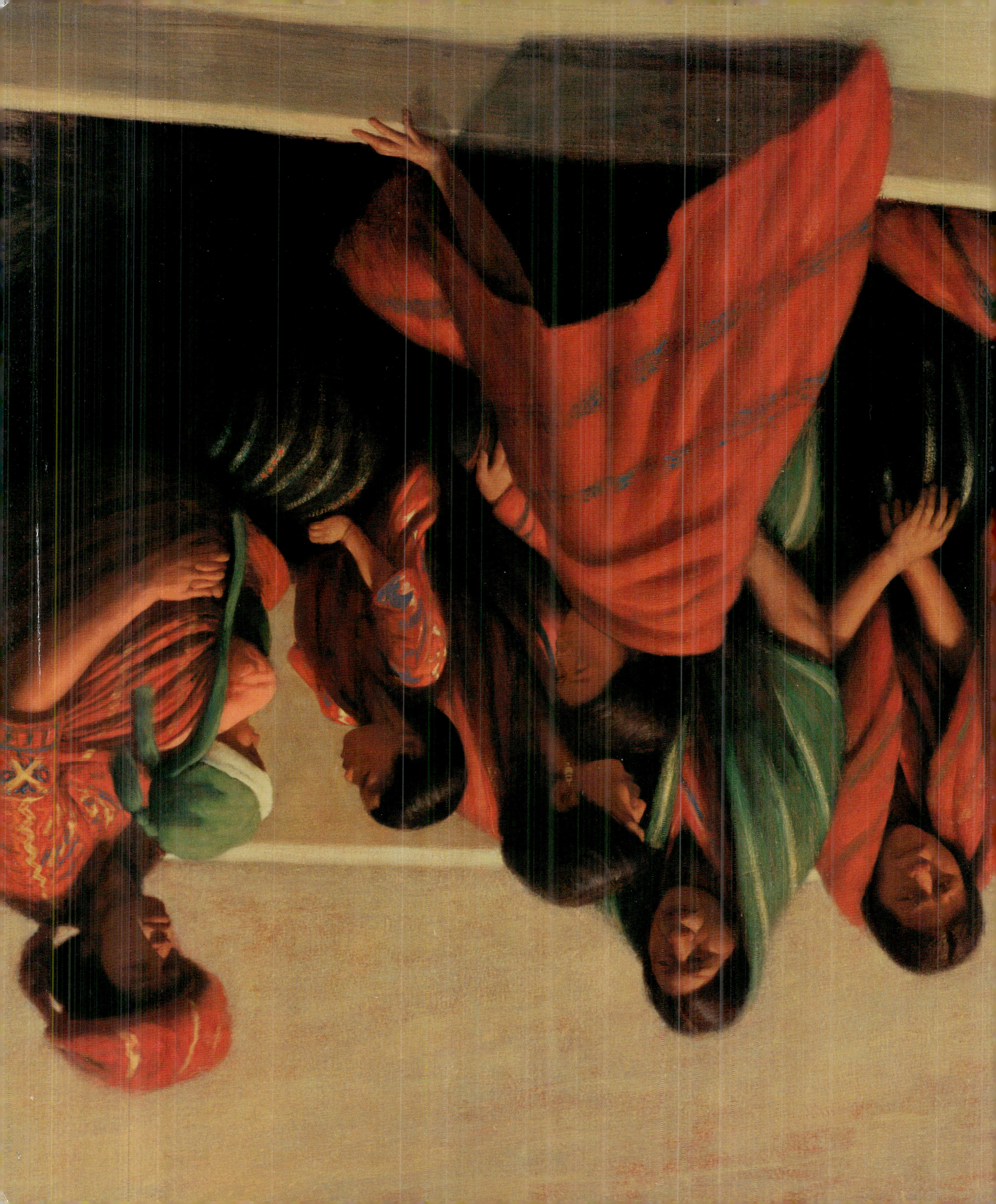

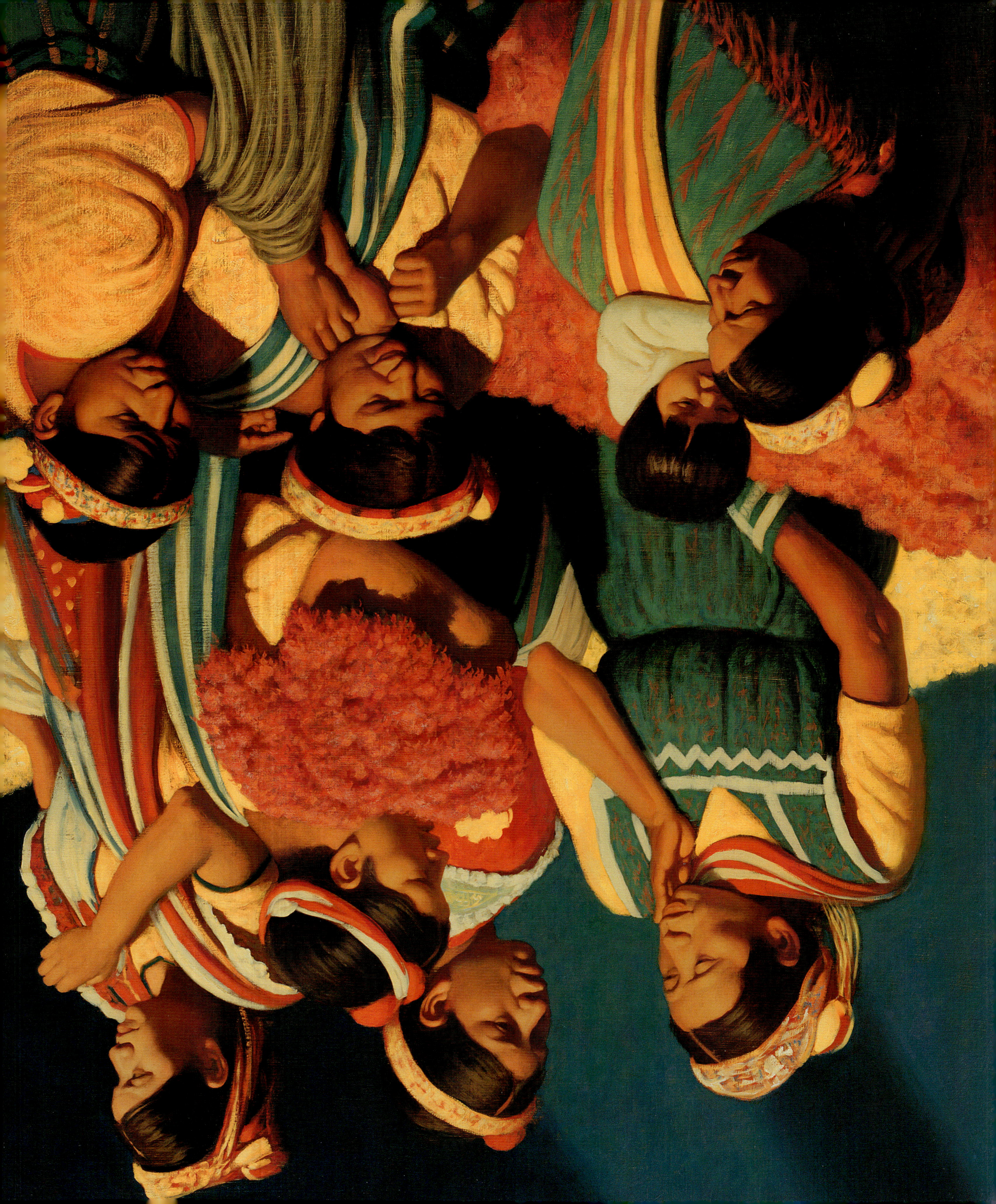

ELIAS RIVERA

EDWARD LUCIE-SMITH

FOREWORD BY GENE HACKMAN

HUDSON HILLS PRESS
NEW YORK AND MANCHESTER

In celebration of this publication and the work of Elias Rivera,
an exhibition will be held at the Riva Yares Gallery, Santa Fe, New Mexico, August, 2006.

First Edition

Published in the United States by Hudson Hills Press LLC, 74-2 Union Street, Manchester, Vermont 05254.
Distributed in the United States, its territories and possessions, and Canada by National Book Network, Inc. Distributed in the United Kingdom, Eire, and Europe by Windsor Books International.

Co-Directors: Leslie van Breen and Randall Perkins
Founding Publisher: Paul Anbinder
Editor: Laura Addison
Designer: David Skolkin/Skolkin + Chickey, Santa Fe, NM
Production Manager: David Skolkin/Skolkin + Chickey, Santa Fe, NM

Color separations by Pre Tech Color, Wilder, Vermont
Printed and bound by Mondadori Printing, Inc., Verona, Italy

Library of Congress Cataloging-in-Publication Data
Lucie-Smith, Edward.
Elias Rivera / by Edward Lucie-Smith ; foreword by Gene Hackman.— 1st ed.
p. cm.
ISBN 1-55595-267-4 (alk. paper)
1. Rivera, Elias, 1937— Themes, motives. I. Rivera, Elias, 1937- II. Title.
ND237.R569A4 2006
759.13—dc22

2006001160

Photography credits: Richard Di Liberto, black-and-white photographs from the New York period. Lynn Lown and Susan Contreras, color photographs. Herb Lotz, plate 49.

pg. ii–iii: *The Longest Bench* (diptych), 1995, oil on canvas, 60 × 132 inches.
Frontispiece: Detail of *Flowers of the Mind #4*, 2001, oil on canvas, 60 × 50 inches.
pg. viii: Detail of *Fiesta at Santa Fe*, 1985, oil on canvas, 20 × 30 inches. Collection of the Museum of Fine Arts, MNM, Department of Cultural Affairs.
pg. x: Detail of *A Whimsical Moment*, 1994, oil on canvas, 48 × 36 inches.
pg. xii: Elias Rivera, photograph by Susan Contreras.

CONTENTS

AN APPRECIATION by Governor Bill Richardson
ix

FOREWORD by Gene Hackman
xi

ELIAS RIVERA by Edward Lucie-Smith
1

PLATES
15

ACKNOWLEDGMENTS
231

CHRONOLOGY
233

SELECTED EXHIBITIONS & COLLECTIONS
239

SELECTED BIBLIOGRAPHY
243

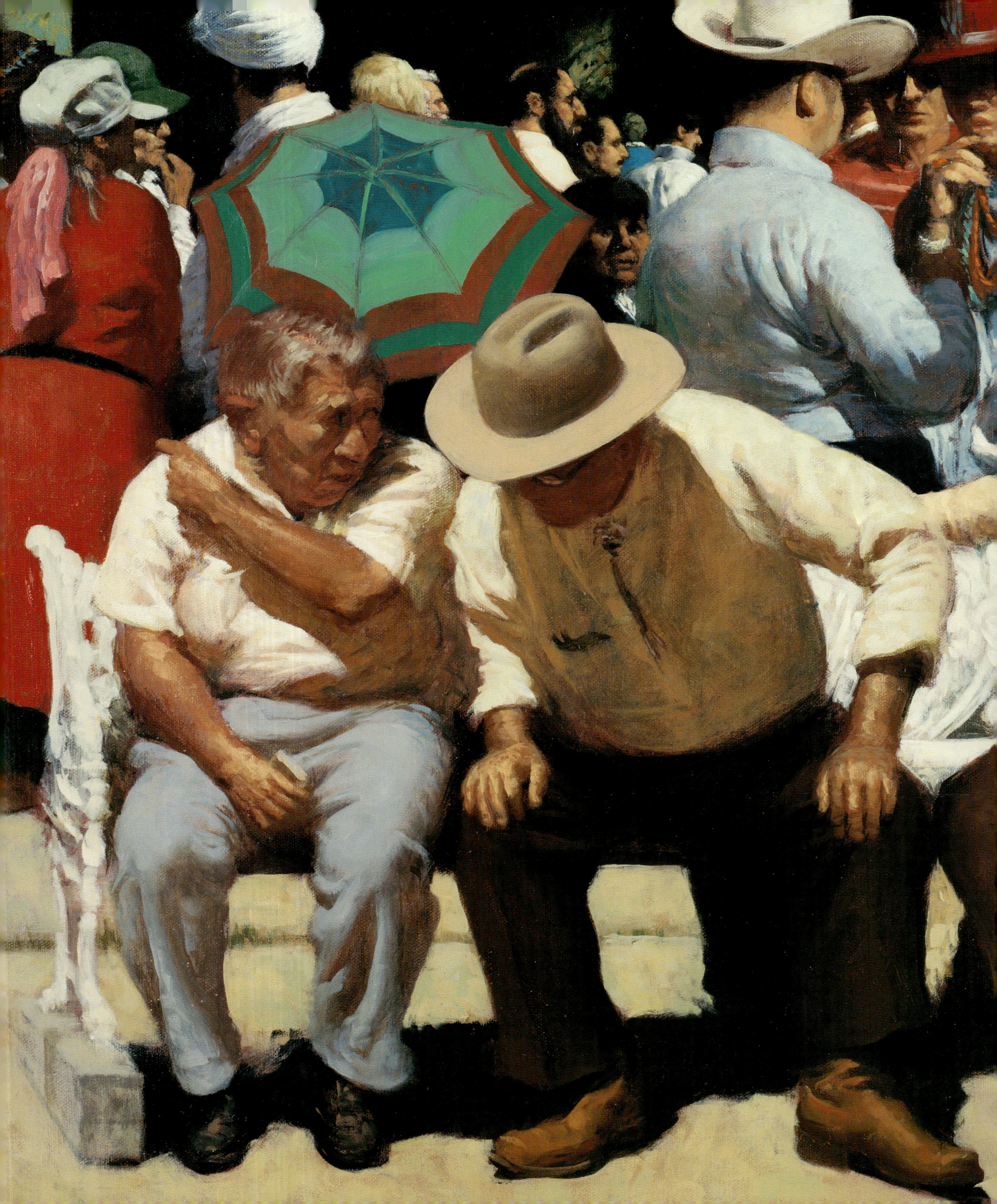

AN APPRECIATION

GOVERNOR BILL RICHARDSON

New Mexico is home to beautiful natural treasures, a rich heritage, diverse peoples, and a history marked by vibrant multicultural expression. We are fortunate to have been blessed by these influences, and we are proud of the many talented artists who display them with compassion and humanity in their work.

One of those artists stands out in particular: Elias Rivera. More than twenty years ago, Rivera moved from his native New York to New Mexico, where his unmatched talents blossomed, and he became a world-class painter. His work is featured in the collections of the state's Museum of Fine Arts and the State Capitol. Anchored by his affiliation with the Riva Yares Gallery, he has had successful solo exhibitions in many museums and galleries around the world.

Rivera shows us vivid depictions of Latin American culture filled with warmth and passion. His work captures the dynamic spirit of the Latino people, and his skilled technique and use of color embolden the senses and bring the images to life. Literal descriptions fail to fully express the mastery and excellence of his art; the paintings have to be seen.

In New Mexico, we have made special efforts to foster and encourage artistic development. From visual arts to music, dance, opera, and, recently, film, we have invested time, attention, and resources to preserve, protect, and promote the rich artistic heritage found in the Land of Enchantment.

We are honored to have a timeless artist such as Elias Rivera make his home in New Mexico. We are proud of his representations of Latino culture, his depictions of family and community, and his excellence in portraying the beauty and virtue of the people.

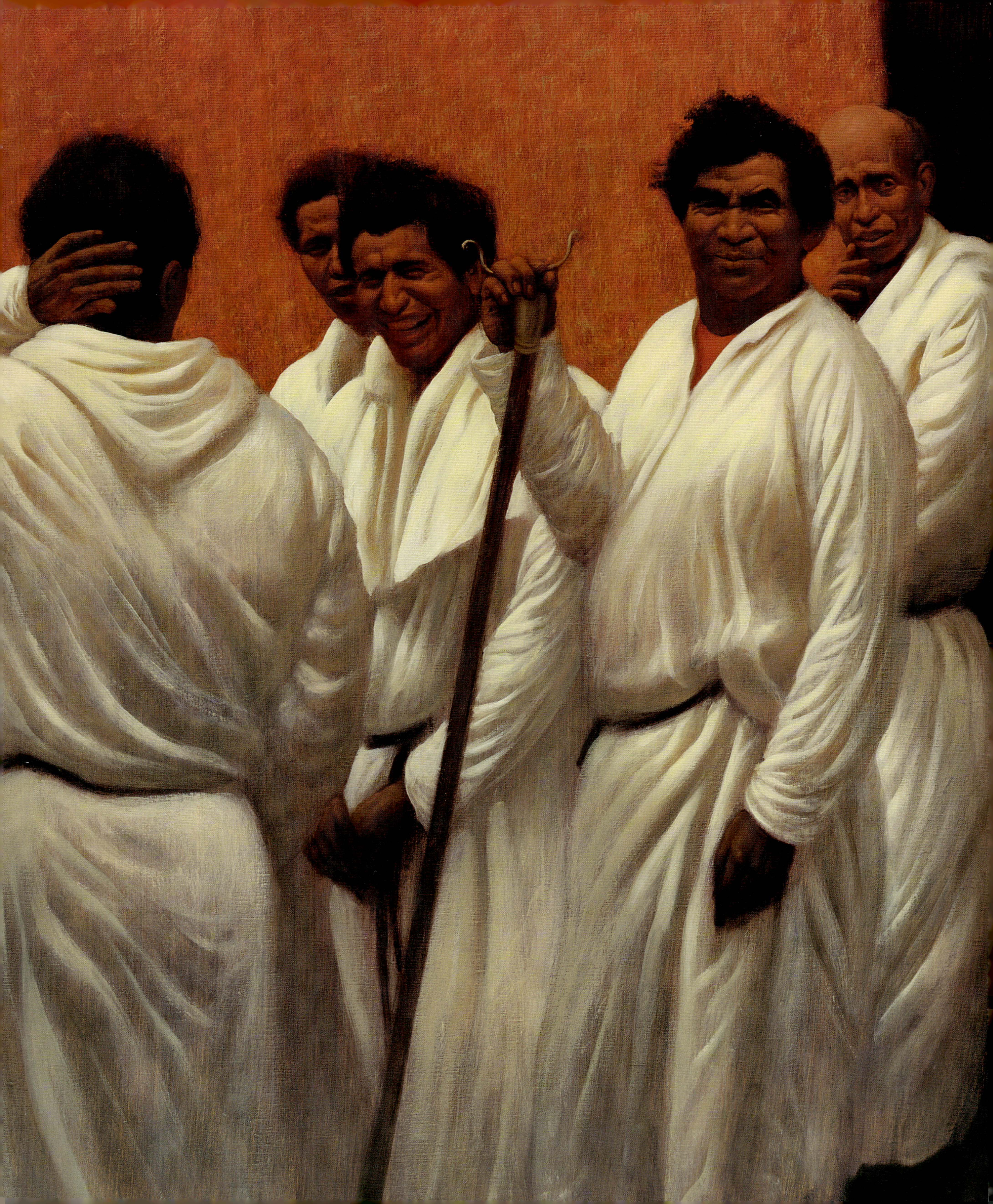

FOREWORD

GENE HACKMAN

THE IDEA OF A PAINTING reflecting a moment in time, a thought, or feeling, seems to be an attractive abstraction in which my friend Elias Rivera thrives. Caring and tenderness are whispered thoughts across his canvas that, for whatever reasons, carry us, and him, as active participants in painterly passages, colorful and full of form. Whether we feel the same as Elias is not as important as being aware that we have become just that tiny bit more human. Our sense of "what is beauty" has been questioned; we are curious, aroused, and enlightened by his sensitive work.

By strange coincidence, we both attended the Art Students League in New York City and were students of Frank Riley at the same time. Much to my regret, we didn't actually meet until some forty years later in Santa Fe. At the League, Elias was privileged to have been taught by both Riley and the brilliant Frank Mason. Mason, an iconoclastic, rough-edged true artist, mentored the young Rivera. Five decades later, the former student and teacher still communicate.

The early sixties found Elias chronicling the New York street scene from subways to colorful automats. His vibrant civil-rights canvases came alive with the artist's passion for minority rights. Elias's recent signature works transform a mere market scene from Latin America into a colorful landscape of form and figure. We see the lives of marketers, the gossip of shoppers, the simple beauty of the everyday. He allows us into their lives. With a lifetime of work behind him, Elias continues to search, finding in the small towns of

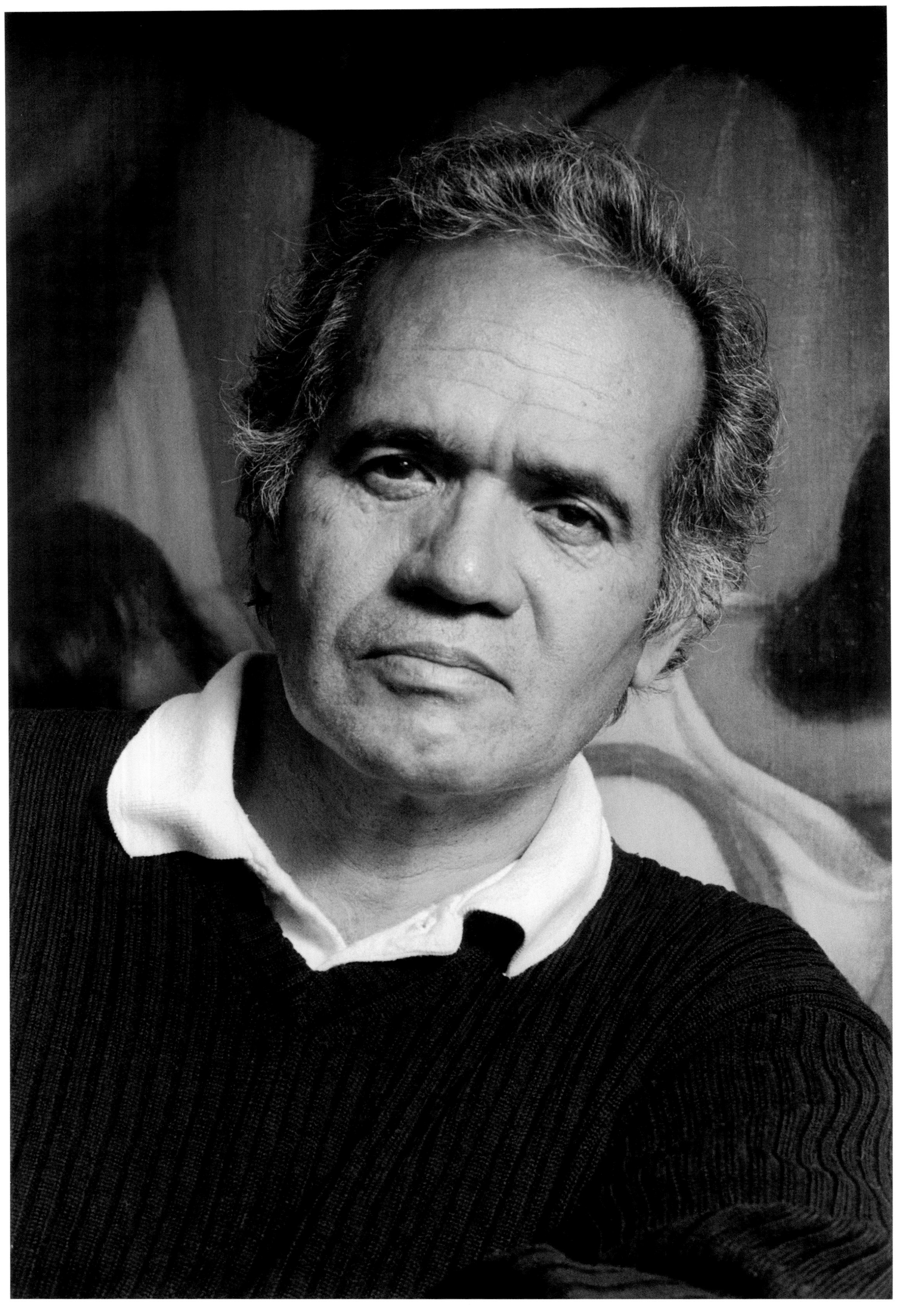

Guatemala an amalgamation of the simple sellers of produce and shoppers merging into beautifully animated canvases.

In years to come, Elias Rivera's work will certainly stand the test of time for it is work of remarkable love, not only for his subject matter but for his craft, his art, his life. I am, indeed, privileged to call him a friend.

—Santa Fe, 2005

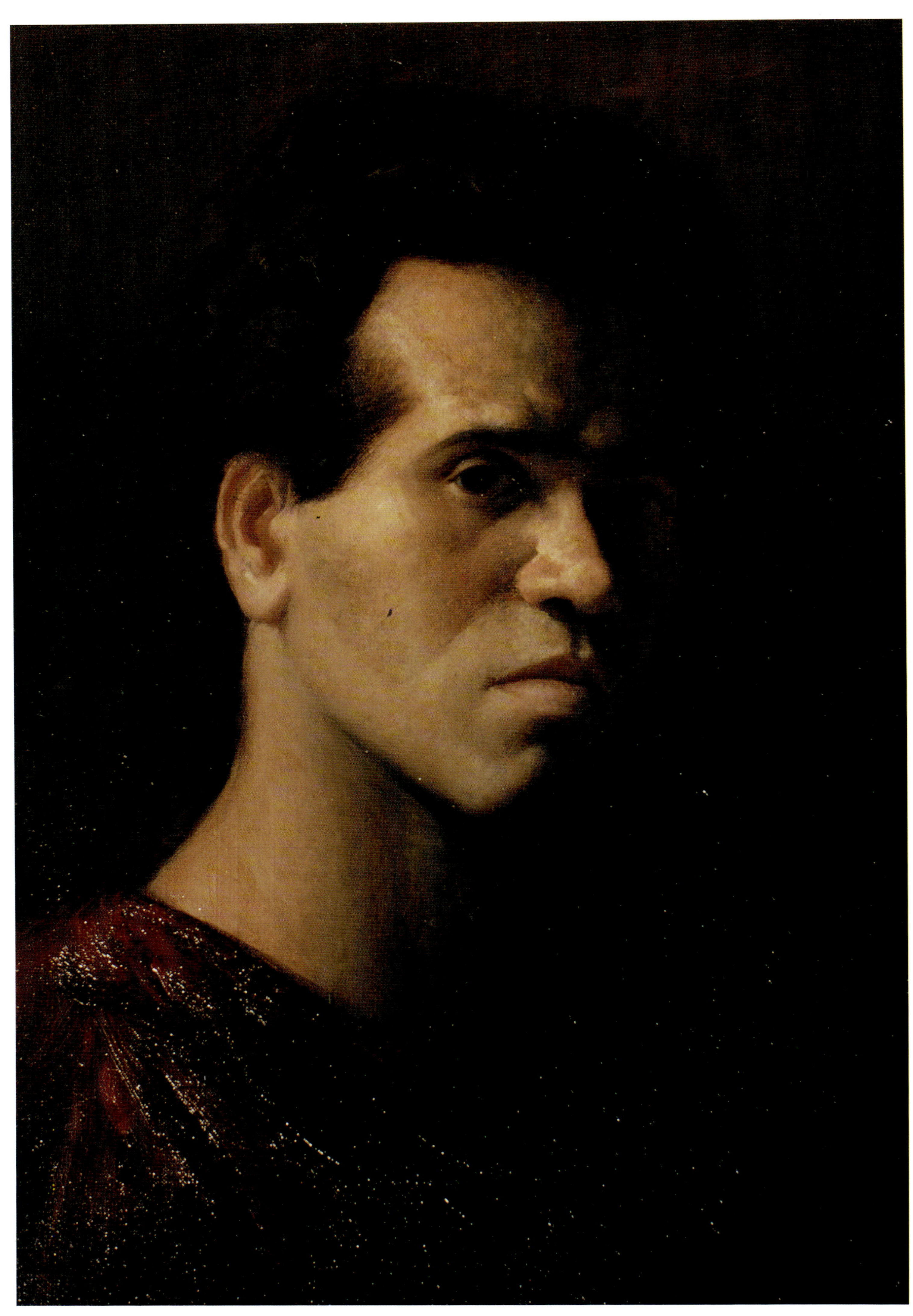

1. SELF-PORTRAIT
1958, oil on canvas, 18 × 12 inches

ELIAS RIVERA

BY EDWARD LUCIE-SMITH

Elias Rivera is of Puerto Rican origin, but he was born in the Bronx, and brought up in New York. His first exposure to the idea of art came thanks to a childhood illness, which kept him bedridden for two weeks. To keep him amused, his mother bought him some modeling clay. He started making little figures with this, and was immediately hooked. As he now says, "I knew what my destiny was."

Rivera's initial training was at the Art Students League, which he entered in 1955 at the age of eighteen. Founded in 1875 in a loft on the lower reaches of Fifth Avenue and later housed in much more spacious premises on West Fifty-seventh Street, the Art Students League is an integral part of the history of American painting, particularly its rise to a dominant position in world art. Founded by and for artists, the school offers open-ended courses. A list of those who have attended includes Winslow Homer, Georgia O'Keeffe, Mark Rothko, and Jackson Pollock. Former instructors include Thomas Eakins, William Merritt Chase, George Grosz, Reginald Marsh, Hans Hofmann, and Roy Lichtenstein.

Not surprisingly Rivera initially felt somewhat overwhelmed by this new milieu. Although New York offered an enormous range of experiences in the visual arts as well as the best in literature, music, and the theater, this was not a world that Elias accessed in his youth. He grew up with very little in the way of intellectual or artistic culture, a situation he would voraciously amend throughout his adult life. What would prove to offset this initial modest upbringing, however, was an unshakable faith in his own technical ability. He also had a very strong work ethic. His original intention was to work as an illustrator, but he soon found he preferred something more ambitious — figurative painting.

The years Rivera spent at the Art Students League (1955–61) corresponded with those of the Eisenhower presidency. It was a time when Abstract Expressionism seemed to be everywhere triumphant as the quintessential American style—a conspicuous and immensely prestigious representative of the worldwide triumph of American culture.

In more sophisticated terms, the period has often been portrayed as a time when mainstream conformism was being increasingly confronted by new and radical kinds of artistic endeavor. The cultural historians of the period spoke of challenges to tradition and of new ways of making art—assemblages, environmental installations, and performance art—and of a fascination with what was temporary and disposable rather than permanent. The general assumption was, nevertheless, that freeform abstraction would remain dominant in the American art world for the foreseeable future. Many second-, third-, and fourth-generation Abstract Expressionists staked their careers on this, often with disastrous results.

Despite, or perhaps even because of, his cultural naiveté, Rivera remained stubbornly unaffiliated with any of these tendencies. What he wanted to be was a figurative painter who belonged to an artistic tradition that had existed long before the rise of twentieth-century modernism, and which still seemed—to him at least—to possess its own validity. His *Self-portrait* (1958; pl. 1), painted at the age of twenty-one when he was still at the Art Students League, shows a young man who is simultaneously timid and determined, gazing out from the midst of a Rembrandtesque chiaroscuro. It is a touchingly direct and honest depiction of character.

Three paintings made a little later—one of the artist's studio and two backyard views—reflect the humble circumstances in which he was then living; however they have other things to tell us as well. The studio interior, *My Studio* (1963; pl. 2), shows the influence of Dutch seventeenth-century still-life painting, not only in the careful arrangement of objects, but in the use of light to model their forms. The backyard views (both 1963; pl. 3, 4) have strong links to the work of members of the Ashcan School, who worked in New York just before World War I. These paintings can be thought of, for instance, as less complex versions of a well-known work by George Bellows, *Cliff Dwellers*, painted in 1913.

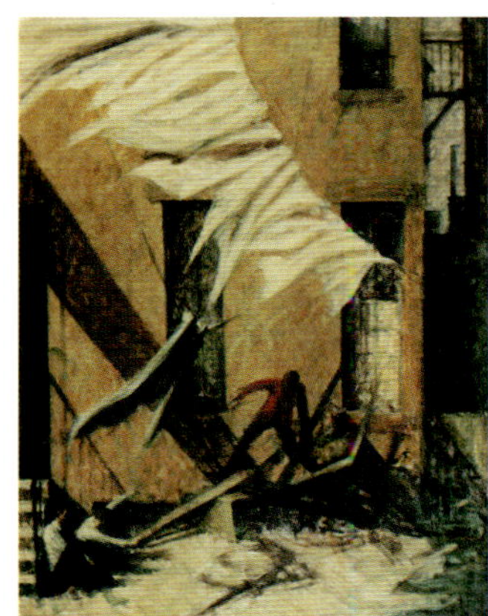
Backyard, 1963

There is a continuity that runs from Bellows to the work of the three Soyer brothers—Moses (1898–1973), Raphael (1898–1987), and Isaac (1902–1981)—to these early works by Elias Rivera. In addition, these three paintings reveal other not-so-easily detected influences: the rhythmic swing of the backyard paintings was in part the product of his part-time occupation as a dance instructor.

The 1960s were a period of political and social agitation in America. Many people, including artists, were involved in the campaign for civil rights and the agitation against the Vietnam War. Some of Rivera's works of this period are directly related to these events—for example the large and ambitious *Birmingham* (1964; pl. 5), which shows the Birmingham, Alabama, police using dogs against civil-rights demonstrators. Rivera remembers that this was painted in a tiny railroad flat—an apartment so small that it was difficult to get very far away from the canvas.

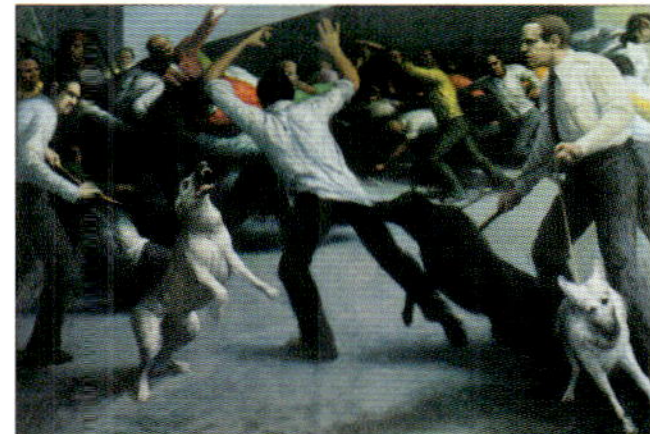

Birmingham, 1964

The more generalized paintings of this time, such as *Rescue* (1966; pl. 6), often have a striking resemblance to the French realist art of the mid-nineteenth century, particularly certain canvases by Daumier. They are also rooted in the striking news photographs of the 1960s. Examples are *Vietnam* (1966; pl. 8), an image of a wounded soldier being carried away by his comrades, and *Pursuit* (1966; pl. 7), which shows a traitor to the ANC being beaten up by the inhabitants of a South African township. Their photographic sources were never copied directly. Another source for *Vietnam* (thought the artist may not have been conscious of this when the painting was made) is clearly Raphael's *Baglione Entombment* (1507), which shows an arrangement of figures that is closely similar, but in reverse. It is even possible to detect a less exact parallel between the fleeing traitor in *Pursuit*, and the figure of Joseph in Rembrandt's etching *Joseph and Potiphar's Wife* (1634). Another source may be the hauntingly similar half-naked figure of the would-be seductress that appears in a painting, now in the British Royal Collection at Windsor Castle, of the same subject by Rembrandt's older contemporary Orazio Gentileschi.

These links demonstrate how rapidly and thoroughly Rivera absorbed the "high culture" that had been denied him during his childhood and adolescence. He made use of source material from very different genres. *Automat* (1970; pl. 10) owes something to Edward Hopper, but even more to the Swedish filmmaker Ingmar Bergman. *Piano Man* (1973; pl. 11) is a tribute to the Billy Joel song of the same title:

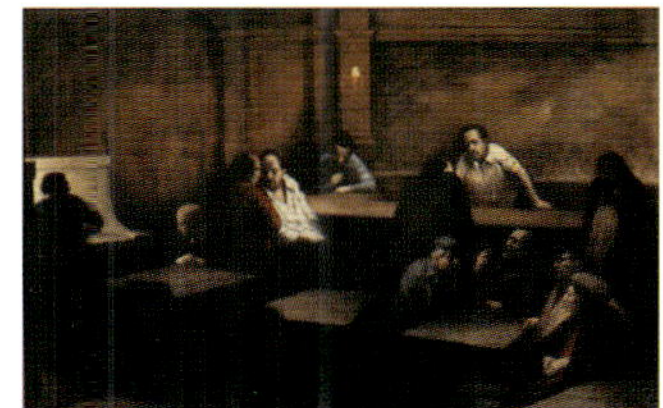

Piano Man, 1973

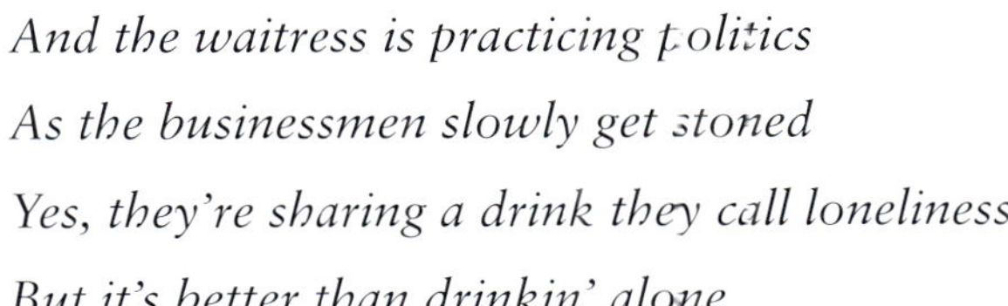

And the waitress is practicing politics
As the businessmen slowly get stoned
Yes, they're sharing a drink they call loneliness
But it's better than drinkin' alone

It is also a reference to one of Eugene O'Neill's great dramas, *The Iceman Cometh*, with its barroom setting.

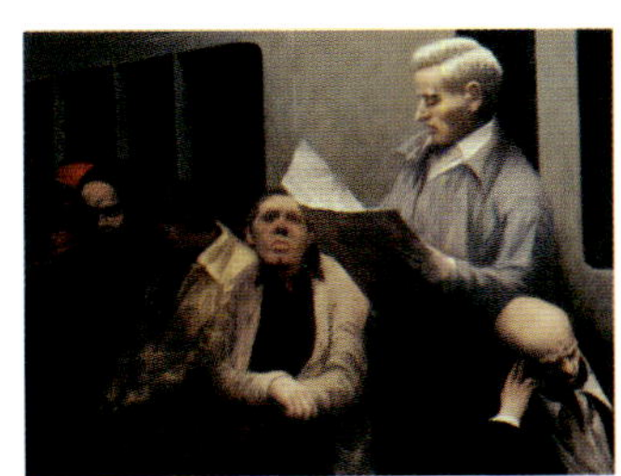

Subway #2, 1975

Throughout this early period, Rivera was keenly interested in the urban life he saw around him in New York. His series of subway paintings (1975; pl. 15–18) references similar paintings of employment agencies and waiting rooms made by the Soyer brothers. They also seem to have links with a famous series of photographs made surreptitiously in the subways by the great American photographer Walker Evans. The pictures were taken between 1938 and 1941 but not published or exhibited until 1966, fewer than ten years before Rivera made his own series of paintings on this theme.

Rather similar in intention is a group of paintings that celebrates Minsky's (1977; pl. 19–21), then a popular restaurant in Brooklyn. These in turn can be linked to a number of other restaurant scenes painted at the same epoch, the mid-1970s. A number of these employ complex lighting systems. One of the Minsky's paintings, *Minsky's # 2* (pl. 20) offers no fewer than three different light sources, which have been blended to make a coherent whole. This interest in light also derives in part from his study of the Old Masters. *Lodge* (1975; pl. 14), a study of the interior of a ski lodge with people at tables, takes its inspiration from interior scenes by Pieter Bruegel the Elder.

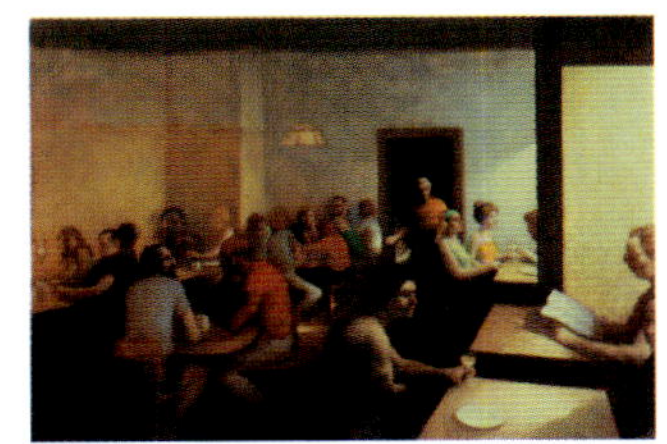

Minsky's #2, 1977

During these early New York years, Rivera found it very hard to make a living as a painter. Potential clients often told him that, while they admired his skills, they found his work depressing. A frequent comment was, "I can't live with that." Rivera says, "I was trying to create a career for myself in a world that thought I was a fly in the ointment, so that made me very miserable, very angry, very conflicted, very tortured. But I always had a sense of integrity about my work. I knew I was doing good painting, because I worked hard at perfecting my process. I knew it wasn't personal—I just didn't fit with the time."

In 1982 he made a life-changing decision. He decided to go to New Mexico to take a look at Santa Fe, a place he knew little or nothing about, except that he had a friend who had already moved there, and that it had long been a haven for artists. As soon as he arrived, he fell in love with this new environment.

His beginnings in Santa Fe were, in one sense, not auspicious. Almost immediately, he fell seriously ill with nephritis, which he now sees as a delayed reaction to "the toxicity of my anger and rage in New York." In other respects he had better luck. He met and fell in love with a local figurative painter, Susan Contreras. And at last, using the rental income from a Brooklyn brownstone he owned, he found he was able to devote himself to painting full time—his paintings began to sell.

One reason for this change in material fortune was his radical change of subject matter. Rivera had always been fascinated by what he saw around him. The subway paintings and restaurant paintings of the mid- and late 1970s were painstakingly built up from sketches and photographs. Now he had a whole new range of subjects, very different from anything he had observed in New York.

Some of these subjects were in his immediate environment in Santa Fe. For example, a series of paintings entitled Under the Portal (1986–1992; pl. 44–51) represents the vendors of Native American jewelry who each day spread out their wares in the arcade that runs along the south side of the Palace of the Governors. These vendors come from no fewer than forty-one different tribes, pueblos, chapters, and villages in New Mexico itself and also parts of Arizona.

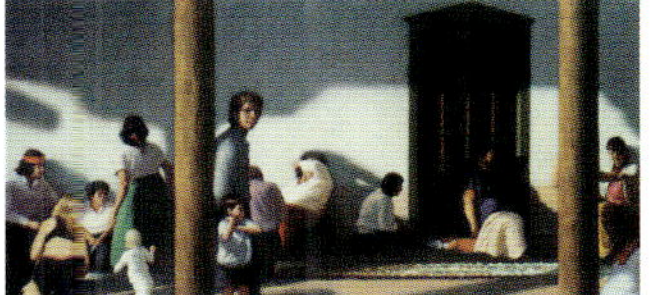
Under the Portal of Santa Fe, 1988

At this time, two characteristic elements began to show in Rivera's work. First, he seems to have found a significant element of "otherness" in these Native American figures. He was able to consider them in a cooler way than the personages presented in his New York subway and restaurant paintings.

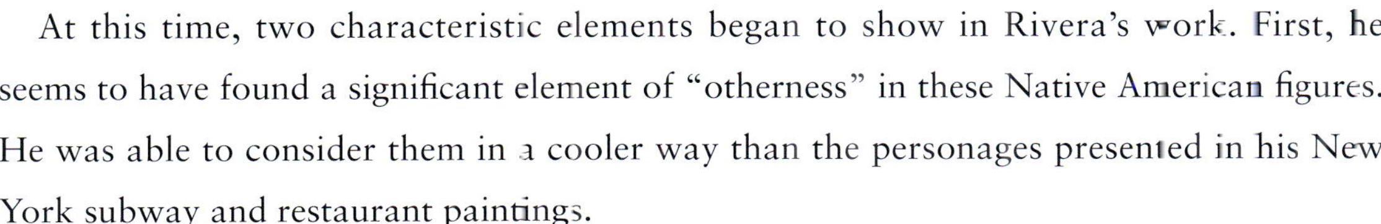

The other element is the use of a kind of frieze-like composition. An example is *Under the Portal of Santa Fe* (pl. 48). The *portal* is a very particular kind of space, wide and shallow, that lends itself to frieze-like compositions. These two elements would have a major impact on how Rivera's art developed in the future.

Two other subjects during this early time in Santa Fe were horsemen and the rodeo. *Gatesman at the Downs* (1984; pl. 39) shows grooms leading racehorses on to the Santa Fe Downs racecourse, which has since been closed. It is probably Rivera's most Degas-like picture, and hence a little divorced from the rest of his production. *Waiting at the Paddocks* (1984; pl. 40) is another scene of this sort, but with more importance to the human figures than the horses. The same emphasis on humans, rather than animals, can be found in a painting entitled *Galisteo Rodeo* (1986; pl. 42), which focuses on the spectators, although a bull is visible in the foreground. Here too the composition is frieze-like, with four rhythmically interlinked male figures all in the same plane.

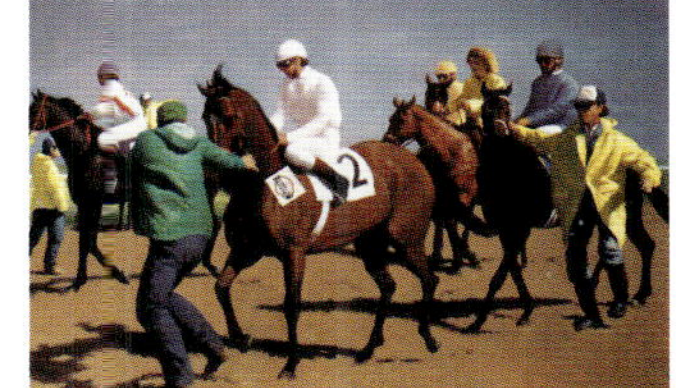
Gatesman at the Downs, 1984

In general, the 1980s were years of experiment and exploration for Rivera. He went to Mexico and was immediately fascinated by Oaxaca, particularly by its market, depicted in a series of paintings made in 1983 and 1984 (pl. 28–38). A rather different series, painted in 1986 and 1987, was devoted to depictions of Tarahumara Indians (pl. 52–56). The Tarahumara, who form the largest indigenous group in the Mexican state of Chihuahua, have chosen to live largely apart from modern Western culture. They live in caves during the winter months but move to small log cabins in summer. These people are celebrated for their colorful costumes and ritual dances, which are performed in the open air so that

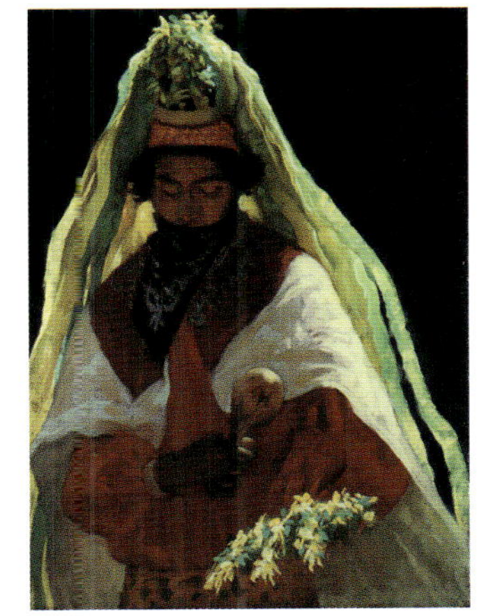
Tarahumara #1, 1986

the sun and moon can witness them. While the dances have a strongly religious element, they also have curative functions and are performed to drive out or ward off sickness.

Rivera made some multifigure compositions depicting these dances, and he also made paintings in which the Indians were seen close-up, half-length, or three-quarter length—occasionally singly, but most often in groups. Anyone who has some familiarity with pre-Modern art will recognize that these close-up groups have a distinguished ancestry in Baroque painting. Though not unknown during the later Renaissance, there are some paintings, chiefly double portraits by Titian and other sixteenth-century Venetian masters, which employ a similar formula. Compositions of this sort achieved their most characteristic form in the hands of Caravaggio, then Guercino and other leading Italian Baroque artists of the first half of the seventeenth century.

The aim of the Baroque masters seems to have been to create a greater sense of intimacy, especially when they were dealing with a sacred event. Examples are Caravaggio's *Betrayal of Christ* (1602–03), now in Dublin, and his *Doubting Thomas* (1602–03) in Potsdam. This, however, does not seem to have been Rivera's aim. Rather, he seems to be fascinated by the "otherness" of his subjects—their intrinsic strangeness and separation from Western life—even more so than by the same qualities as shown by the vendors of Indian jewelry plying their trade under the *portal* in Santa Fe.

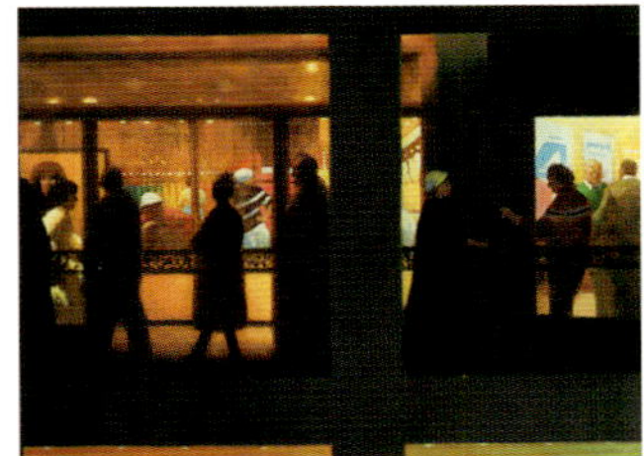

Georgetown Mall #2, 1988

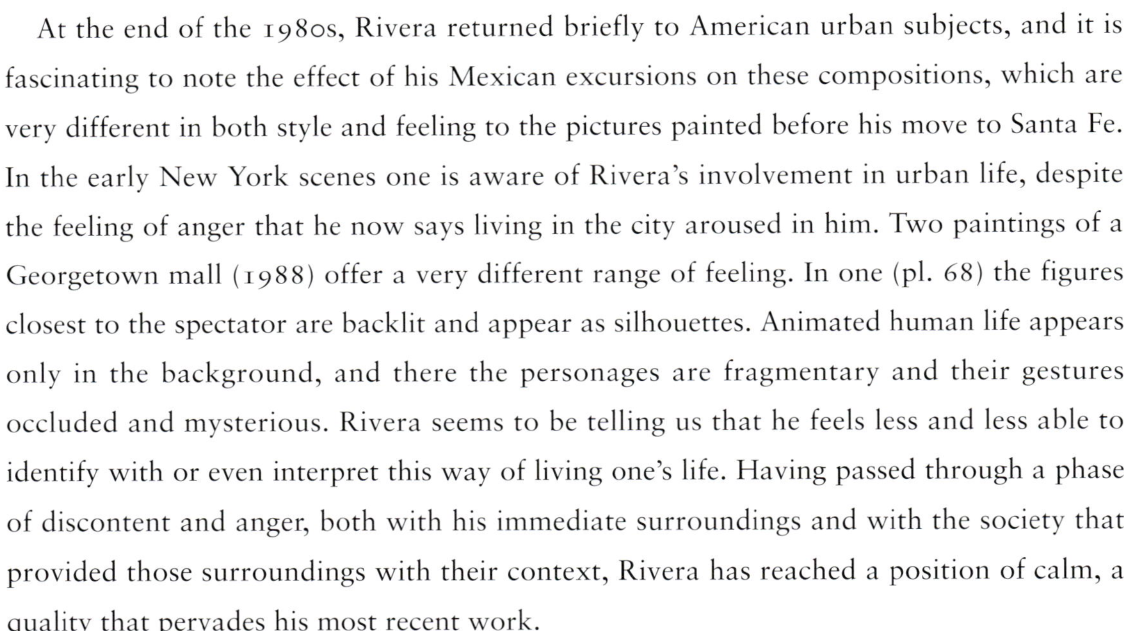

At the end of the 1980s, Rivera returned briefly to American urban subjects, and it is fascinating to note the effect of his Mexican excursions on these compositions, which are very different in both style and feeling to the pictures painted before his move to Santa Fe. In the early New York scenes one is aware of Rivera's involvement in urban life, despite the feeling of anger that he now says living in the city aroused in him. Two paintings of a Georgetown mall (1988) offer a very different range of feeling. In one (pl. 68) the figures closest to the spectator are backlit and appear as silhouettes. Animated human life appears only in the background, and there the personages are fragmentary and their gestures occluded and mysterious. Rivera seems to be telling us that he feels less and less able to identify with or even interpret this way of living one's life. Having passed through a phase of discontent and anger, both with his immediate surroundings and with the society that provided those surroundings with their context, Rivera has reached a position of calm, a quality that pervades his most recent work.

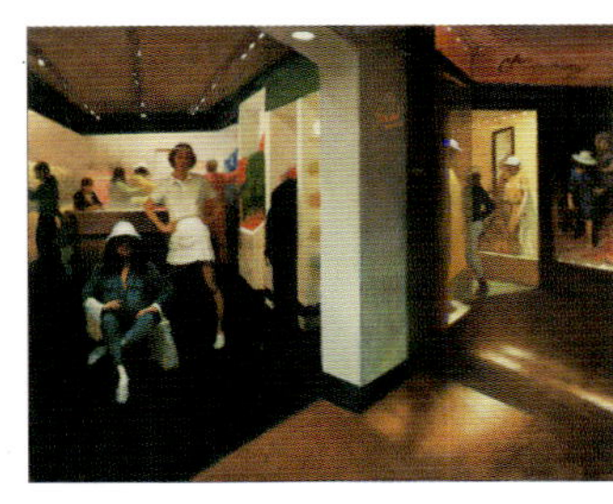

Georgetown Mall, 1988

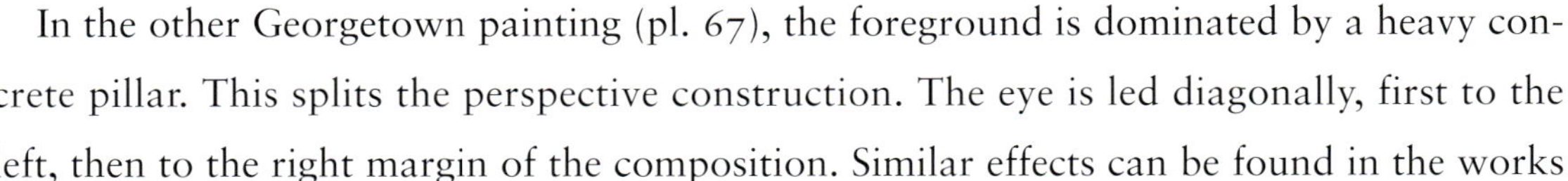

In the other Georgetown painting (pl. 67), the foreground is dominated by a heavy concrete pillar. This splits the perspective construction. The eye is led diagonally, first to the left, then to the right margin of the composition. Similar effects can be found in the works of the Old Masters, particularly in the church interiors painted by the seventeenth-century Dutch artist Pieter Jansz Saenredam (1597–1665). For example, Saenredam's *Interior of the Church of St Bavo at Haarlem* (1630), now in the Louvre, follows almost exactly the same perspective scheme. Although Saenredam's church interiors are sometimes spoken of as "tranquil" because of their rigorously stripped-down character, in fact they induce feelings of unease, because the split perspectives create a sense of physical instability. This is also the situation with Rivera's painting.

In compositions featuring the interior of the Trump Tower in New York (1988; pl. 69–71), Rivera makes sophisticated use of the escalators that fill the soaring interior entrance space. The figures perpetually gliding by, seemingly without any will of their own, suggest the famous scene of the "Whirlwind of Lovers" in Dante's *Inferno* (Canto V):

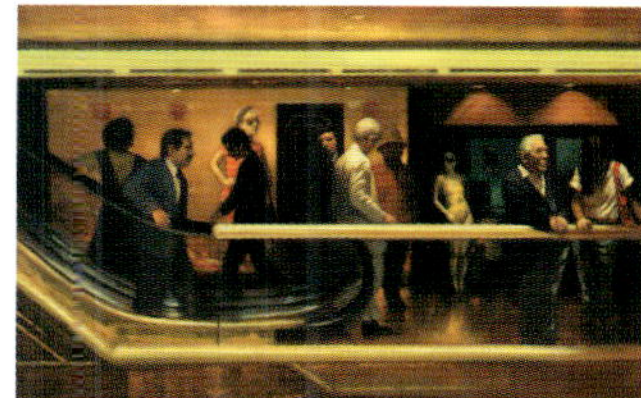

Trump Tower #1, 1988

And as the wings of starlings bear them on
In the cold season in large band and full,
So doth that blast the spirits maledict;
It hither, thither, downward, upward, drives them;
No hope doth comfort them for evermore,
Not of repose, but even of lesser pain.

Only very occasionally in the paintings of this group does Rivera return to the work of Edward Hopper, which is sometimes a strong presence in the New York paintings of the 1970s. When he does so, for instance in *Beverly Center* (1989; pl. 72), presumably an image of the famous upscale shopping mall of that name in Los Angeles, he infuses what he borrows with a strong sense of irony. *Beverly Center* features not the fashionable excesses of the upper three floors, where the "shopping opportunities" are to be found, but the rather ordinary pizza restaurant on the ground level, whose interior, seen distantly through a plate-glass window, is rendered in a fashion reminiscent of Hopper's iconic *Nighthawks* (1942). The image expresses palpable contempt for Hollywood glitz.

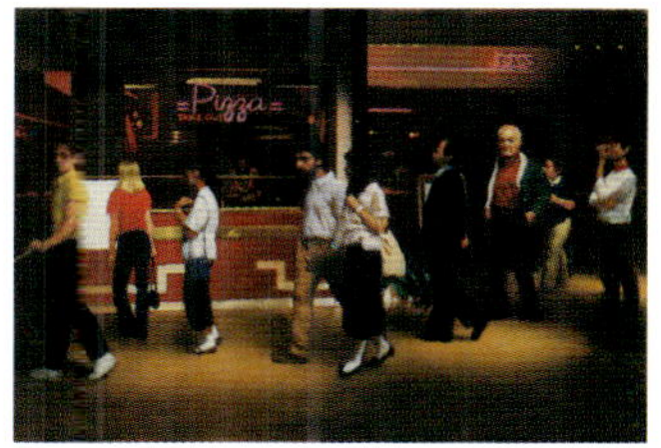

Beverly Center, 1989

In the early 1990s, Latin America became once again the focus of Rivera's paintings. His chosen subjects henceforth have been the market people of Mexico and Central America. He is fascinated by them as individuals and even more so by markets and other gathering places as social organisms. In a way, this represents an extension of the interests he had cultivated as a young painter in New York. A series of paintings made in the early 1990s focuses on the city of Antigua, Guatemala, founded by the Spanish in the early sixteenth century and largely destroyed by an earthquake in 1773. Antigua is famous for the impressive ruins that survived this earthquake, but these architectural elements play no part in the paintings Rivera dedicated to the place. He was interested only in its inhabitants, seen singly and in groups.

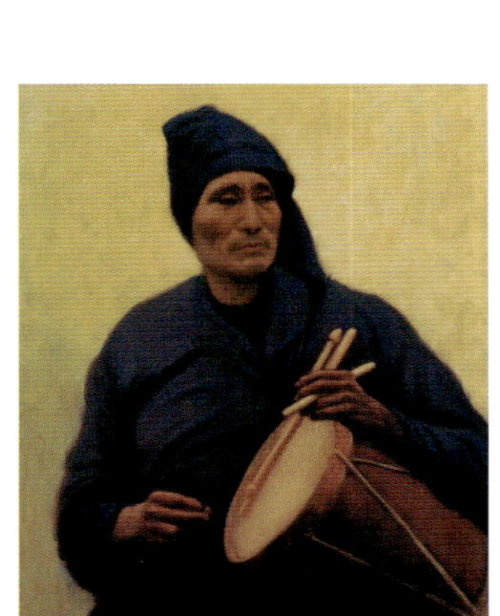

A Pause in the Procession II, 1993

The paintings of single figures, such as the impressive portrait called *A Pause in the Procession II* (1993; pl. 79), seem to owe a good deal to the Spanish Old Master tradition. One can see a link, for example, to the philosopher portraits painted by Jusepe de Ribera. Similarly, some paintings of groups, such as *A Whimsical Moment* (1994; pl. 82), show the influence of Zurbarán. Dressed in white, the subjects participating in an Easter procession are very clearly the descendants of the white-robed Carthusian monks portrayed by the great Spanish artist.

One major way the works of Rivera differ from those of Ribera is the color gamut. Ribera almost certainly would not have ventured the deep purple of the main garment in *A Pause in the Procession II*, especially when placed against a contrasting yellow ground. This intense, sonorous color was not conspicuously present in Rivera's early work. It seems to have been one of the gifts brought to him by the clear desert light of New Mexico and the rich, bright colors he found in Latin America.

It is in these Guatemalan paintings that Rivera at last fully exploited his gift for color. He says, indeed, that the reason he abandoned Mexico for Guatemala was that the colors of the local costumes were so much richer. For example, one can see how much he revels in the resonant blue that dominates the painting simply called *Blue Blanket* (1994; pl. 83).

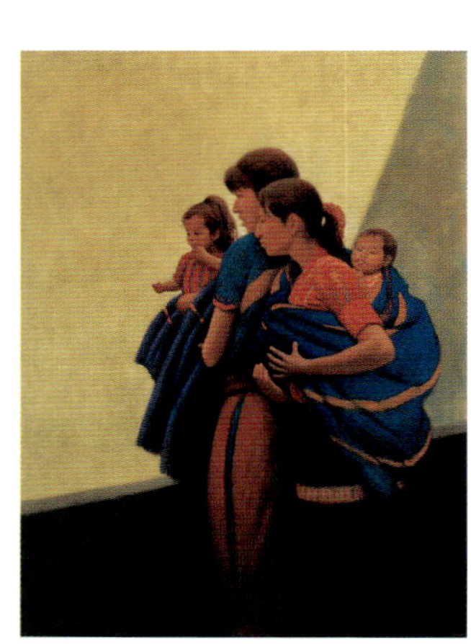

Blue Blanket, 1994

Other Guatemalan pictures made during the first half of the 1990s show scenes in Sololá and Patzún. Both of these places are famous for the beauty of their textiles, as well as for the fact that the inhabitants, who are of Mayan descent, continue to wear traditional costumes that have fallen out of use elsewhere.

A striking feature of the multifigure compositions of this period is that they usually show what can be described as "incomplete events"; that is, the figures seem placed on the margin of some activity that is not shown. Very often, their gazes are directed towards the left- or right-hand margin of the composition, as they might appear in a snapshot. Indeed, photography has accustomed modern spectators to compositions of this type. Looking at a photograph, we automatically and almost unthinkingly construe the whole from the part, if that is what the image demands. Rivera's paintings of figures grouped together find part of their ancestry in news and sports photographs, which offer single instants seized from a continuous stream of instants. We understand from the frozen moment not only what the camera actually saw when the photographer pressed the shutter release, but also what came immediately before and what happened afterwards.

Only occasionally does Rivera revert to more traditional formulations. *Simple Secrets* (1995; pl. 93), with its group of figures seated close together on a stone bench or parapet, is a composition that might have been invented by the Victorian academic Alma-Tadema. After a steep plunge in reputation, Alma-Tadema is fetching very high prices in the great auction rooms today, because collectors have once again learned to recognize his sophisticated skills as a picture maker. What Rivera has done here is to get rid of the need for fancy dress, for the self-conscious literary reference, that spoils the work of so many gifted nineteenth-century artists.

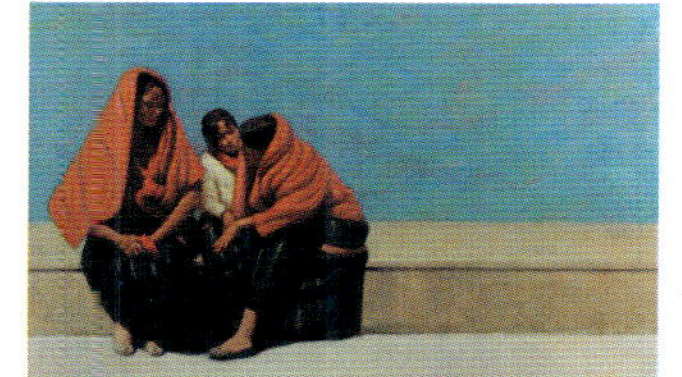
Simple Secrets, 1995

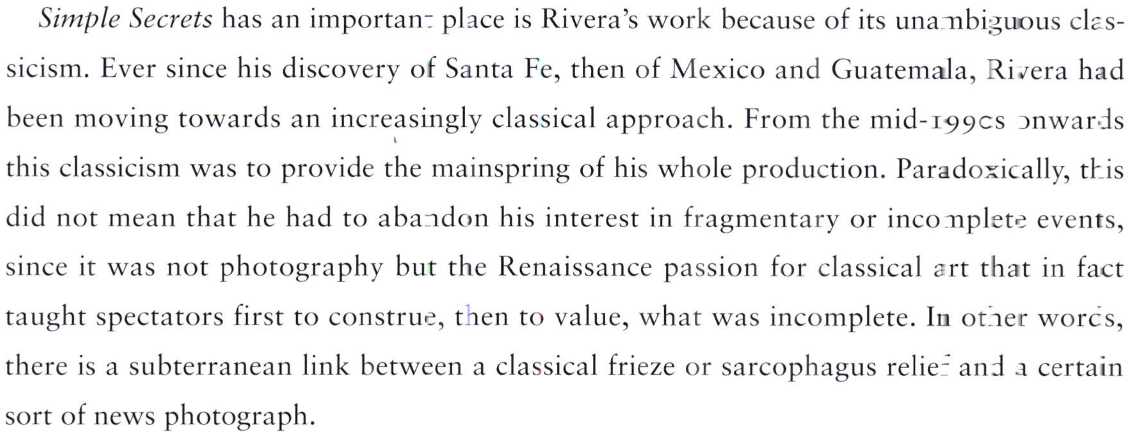

Simple Secrets has an important place is Rivera's work because of its unambiguous classicism. Ever since his discovery of Santa Fe, then of Mexico and Guatemala, Rivera had been moving towards an increasingly classical approach. From the mid-1990s onwards this classicism was to provide the mainspring of his whole production. Paradoxically, this did not mean that he had to abandon his interest in fragmentary or incomplete events, since it was not photography but the Renaissance passion for classical art that in fact taught spectators first to construe, then to value, what was incomplete. In other words, there is a subterranean link between a classical frieze or sarcophagus relief and a certain sort of news photograph.

Despite the evidence of the Parthenon frieze, with its many horses, people still tend to think of classicism as something whose primary concern is with the ennobled, usually nude, human figure. Elias Rivera deals with the figure, but his figures are invariably clothed. Because they are peasants and artisans who belong to a completely different culture from his own, he is able to examine them with detachment. His attitude is sympathetic, but he does not fully identify himself with what he sees, and in this sense the new work is very different from the polemical social-realist paintings he produced at the beginning of his career.

It is possible to relate what Rivera does to a branch of the nineteeth-century Latin American tradition *costumbrismo*, whose painters depicted local customs, with figures in national or regional dress. A similar school of painters flourished contemporaneously in Spain, its activity focused on Andalusia. Isolated painters of this sort are also to be found elsewhere—for example the Italian painter Agostino Brunias, who worked in the West Indies in the late eighteenth century, and the Swiss artist Joseph Reinhardt, who made images of Swiss peasants at about the same time. Neither of these artists ranks as a major figure, but both have attracted attention in the twentieth century—Brunias because he provided a record of a unique society, that of the "free people of color" existing uneasily between black slaves on the one hand and white plantation owners on the other; Reinhardt because of his influence over the young Balthus, visible in Balthus's most ambitious early painting, *The Street* (1933). What Brunias and Reinhardt have in common is that their work is curiously impassive. In some mysterious fashion they both seem to turn back to a much greater and much earlier master, Piero della Francesca, who was another of Balthus's early influences.

While his paintings are much more fluent and stylistically supple, Elias Rivera's mature work of the past decade is also marked by this quality. Although it is clear, for example, that the figures he depicts have relationships—they interact, they gesture, they converse with one another—these relationships are never the primary subjects. Instead, the subject matter, if one can call it that, is rhythm and color. In other words, in a real sense one can regard these paintings as abstract works in figurative disguise.

This brings me to what are perhaps the most important general topics in this book, the role of representation in contemporary art and Rivera's place within it. The story of modernism in art is, in part at least, the story not only of a struggle to accommodate the idea of abstraction but of a parallel struggle to find new ways of approaching the figurative. The influential art historians and critics of the very earliest years of the twentieth century explored radically new approaches, which increasingly tended to discard concerns with narrative, and, moving on from that, with subject matter in general. Some of the reasons for this were rooted in news technology. Photography throughout the nineteenth century increasingly seemed ready to take over tasks that were once entirely the business of painters. It recorded the actual appearance of things with seemingly greater accuracy than any painter could aspire to. At the same time, what had been a completely unitary education system, based on the Bible and the classics, began to diversify and at the same time to fragment itself.

One of the first people to take account of these phenomena was the great art historian Bernard Berenson. In his seminal essay "The Florentine Painters of the Renaissance," published in 1896, Berenson attempted to divert the attention of spectators from the narratives, the apparent *raison d'être* of the masterpieces produced by Giotto and his successors, to the formal qualities to be discovered in the same works. He put forward a theory of "tactile values" and encouraged an empathetic reaction not to the stories the paintings told, but to the rhythm of shapes and forms. This was a first step towards an aesthetic revolution that eventually, just less than two decades later, led to the birth of abstract art.

Berenson's theorizing was carried a step further by Clive Bell, a British critic closely associated with the Bloomsbury group of writers; he was, in fact, the brother-in-law of Virginia Woolf. In his book *Art*, published in 1914, Bell laid his cards on the table in the first chapter:

> *What quality is shared by all objects that provoke our aesthetic emotions? What quality is common to St. Sophia and the windows at Chartres, Mexican sculpture, a Persian bowl, Chinese carpets, Giotto's frescoes at Padua, and the masterpieces of Poussin, Piero della Francesca, and Cézanne? Only one answer seems possible—significant form. In each, lines and colors combined in a particular way, certain forms and relations of forms, stir our aesthetic emotions. These relations and combinations of lines and colors, these aesthetically moving forms, I call "Significant Form"; and "Significant Form" is the one quality common to all works of visual art.*

The names Berenson and Bell do not glitter particularly brightly today, because so much of what they said has now been painlessly and noncontentiously absorbed into our culture. Nevertheless, what has happened very recently is, to say the least, paradoxical. All those preoccupations that early modernist critics strove to uproot—the interest in narrative, the preoccupation with documentation, the use of art as an instrument for the discussion of political issues and moral values—have returned with a vengeance in the newest forms of artistic expression. The great difference from the Victorian epoch, when these ideas also flourished in art, is that their expression is not primarily visual. If one examines, for example, the work of the man who was probably the most influential artistic personage of the last three decades of the twentieth century, Joseph Beuys, one sees quasi-Victorian values expressed in largely nonvisual ways that make them seem completely innovative and radical. With Beuys it is the gesture, the personality, the charisma that count, not the creation of physical objects whose primary function is to be looked at.

So where does Elias Rivera fit into all of this? The experiments that he eschewed in the 1960s, when he was at the beginning of his career as an artist, have now become a new kind of orthodoxy, and it is painting, once central to the Western visual tradition, that is now in danger of being marginalized. Rivera is conscious of this; how could he fail to be? I think he is also conscious of the fact that the kind of art he wants to make has to combine what is secretly novel with what is outwardly traditional.

What does this novelty consist of? Basically, what Rivera does is to make abstract values primary, despite the fact that his painting is rigorously figurative. When I say "rigorously figurative" what I mean is that he does not distort in any way. There is no intrusive stylistic convention—no expressionist distortion, no cubist faceting. The Guatemalan peasants who figure in his recent work are shown—or so we feel when we first meet them—just as we would see them ourselves. It comes as no surprise to learn that the artist uses photographic documentation, made on the spot, as an aid in constructing his compositions and incorporated into a much more complex whole.

As a result, most people would classify Elias Rivera as a realist painter, in the fullest sense of the word. Unlike many twentieth- and early-twenty-first-century painters commonly described as realists, he never hectors. There is, to put it another way, no expressionist element in his work, with either a small or a large letter "E." We are not to empathize with anything that is taking place in his paintings; they are presented to us as purely visual, purely aesthetic events. In this sense, they are surprisingly cooler and less emotional than the work of an abstract artist such as Rothko, who once said that he wanted people to break down and cry when they stood in front of one of his paintings.

However, no sensible person would describe Rivera's compositions as photo-realist. Photo-realism is no longer simply a description; it has become a stylistic label whose characteristics are well understood—extreme sharpness of focus, all-over clarity without much interest in chiaroscuro or atmospheric events, a preference for monocular vision (seeing the way the camera sees) rather than for the way our own two eyes work in real life.

Rivera's most typical recent compositions, however, are frieze-like, as I have already mentioned. This means that they make the spectator's gaze shuttle from one side of the composition to the other. Looking at them is a process of repeated scanning, which is one reason why they hold our attention; it takes more than a moment to see what there is to be seen. We cannot simply look and pass on.

This certainly aligns what Rivera does with many elements in the Old Master tradition, as I have suggested in a number of comparisons made in this essay. Yet, with some exceptions, he does not really fit into this kind of 'revived Old Master' category, any more than he fits into the box labeled photo-realism.

In recent years there has been a considerable revival of classical imagery in painting—for example, in the hands of the artists who belong to the durable *pittura colta* group in Italy, which has been in existence since the end of the 1970s. *Pittura colta* differs from what Rivera does in a number of ways—the imagery is overtly classical and the intention is either ironic or quasi-surrealist, following the example to Giorgio de Chirico, who ended his long career in 1978, just as *pittura colta* was coming to birth. A similar irony pervades the mock-Stalinist classicism embraced in the 1980s by the Russian duo Komar and Melamid. Rivera has never been an ironist, and there is no trace of surrealism in his work.

It is at this point that I would like to introduce a perhaps unexpected name—that of the English eighteenth-century horse painter George Stubbs. Stubbs transformed the art of horse painting—regarded before his appearance on the scene as a lowly, quasi-artisanal branch of the painter's activity—by giving it an entirely novel classical structure. His frieze-like paintings of mares and foals, sometimes shown against a completely plain ground, are triumphs of abstract rhythm. Stubbs was able to demonstrate that classical principles of composition were applicable to any branch of representational art.

If we for a moment compare Stubbs to his near-contemporary Jacques-Louis David, the chief figure in late-eighteenth- and early-nineteenth-century neoclassicism, we immediately see both resemblances and vast differences. David's subject matter falls into three categories: portraits (which need not really concern us here); paintings glorifying the French Revolution or the Napoleonic regime that followed it, such as *Le Sacre* (1805–07) and *The Distribution of the Eagles* (1810); and paintings with overtly classical subjects (his most immediately influential works), such as *The Oath of the Horatii* (1784) and *Leonidas at Thermopylae* (1814). Stubbs painted a few—a very few—classical compositions of this sort, chief among them the different version of his *Phaethon*, none of which are on a heroic scale. He was in no sense a political artist, while David's whole existence was political.

Stubbs does nevertheless represent a particular set of intellectual attitudes that remains influential today. He is a typically Enlightenment figure, and his art has a unique calm rationality. Some of his paintings in which the human figure is more prominent than usual, *The Laborers* and *The Haymakers* (both 1785) for instance, offer very exact parallels to paintings by Rivera that portray everyday activities—for example, to *The Lone Potter*, a diptych from 1995 (pl. 94). These have a detached appreciation of the rhythms of human labor of a sort entirely in tune with the work of Stubbs.

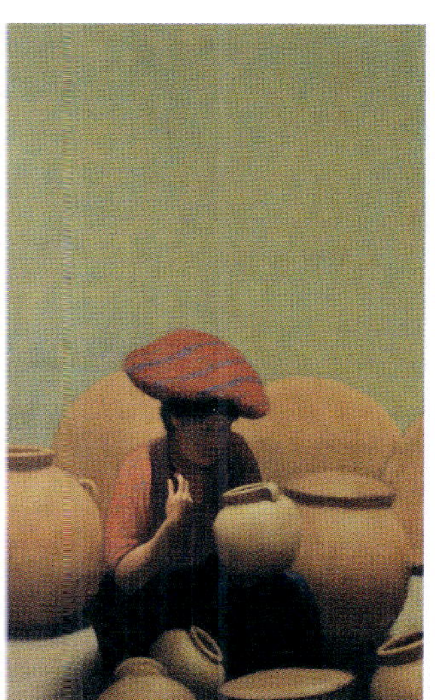

Detail of *The Lone Potter*, 1995

The difference between Rivera's situation and that of Stubbs is that Rivera inhabits a much more complex world. The complexity is of two kinds. The first is to do with art itself. For Stubbs, the relevance of painting as a legitimate means of creative expression was a "given." That is not the case now, when influential curators, theoreticians, and critics repeatedly call into question its relevance. In addition, the art of Stubbs's day had not yet experienced the seismic shocks of the modernist experiment or the plurality of styles that developed in its wake. It is very difficult for an artist to find equilibrium in these circumstances, especially when he insists on using a creative medium that is under strong theoretical assault.

The second kind of complexity is cultural and geographical. I have cited painters from the past who specialized in the idea of the exotic—Brunias is a case in point. However, the idea of "otherness" is really a modern invention that first surfaced fully formed in art when Picasso, Braque, and some of their contemporaries fell in love with the tribal arts of sub-Saharan Africa. "Otherness" has been a constantly recurring theme in the modern art of Latin America.

Despite the fact that he is of Puerto Rican origin, Rivera should not be considered as a Latin American artist. It is nevertheless significant that he is such a prominent figure in the art community of Santa Fe. The city and its surrounding region have long attracted artists who are fascinated by the plurality of New Mexican culture, simultaneously North American, Native American, and Hispanic. This plurality seems to have liberated Rivera into a new aesthetic freedom. His market figures exist with great physical solidity, but they also inhabit a distanced, magical realm. Their "otherness" liberates the painter, rather than constricting him. He is free to use their gestures, their garments, and their physical being as points of departure for daring experiments with rhythm and color, without being forced to distort the basic forms he is observing. The magic of Rivera's art is that it is simultaneously figurative and abstract, without having to compromise either aspect. From his beginnings as a social-realist painter, he has evolved almost to the opposite extreme, to become one who offers sensations that are focused on aesthetic experiences of a kind that Clive Bell would undoubtedly have recognized.

PLATES

Unless otherwise indicated, all works are in private collections.

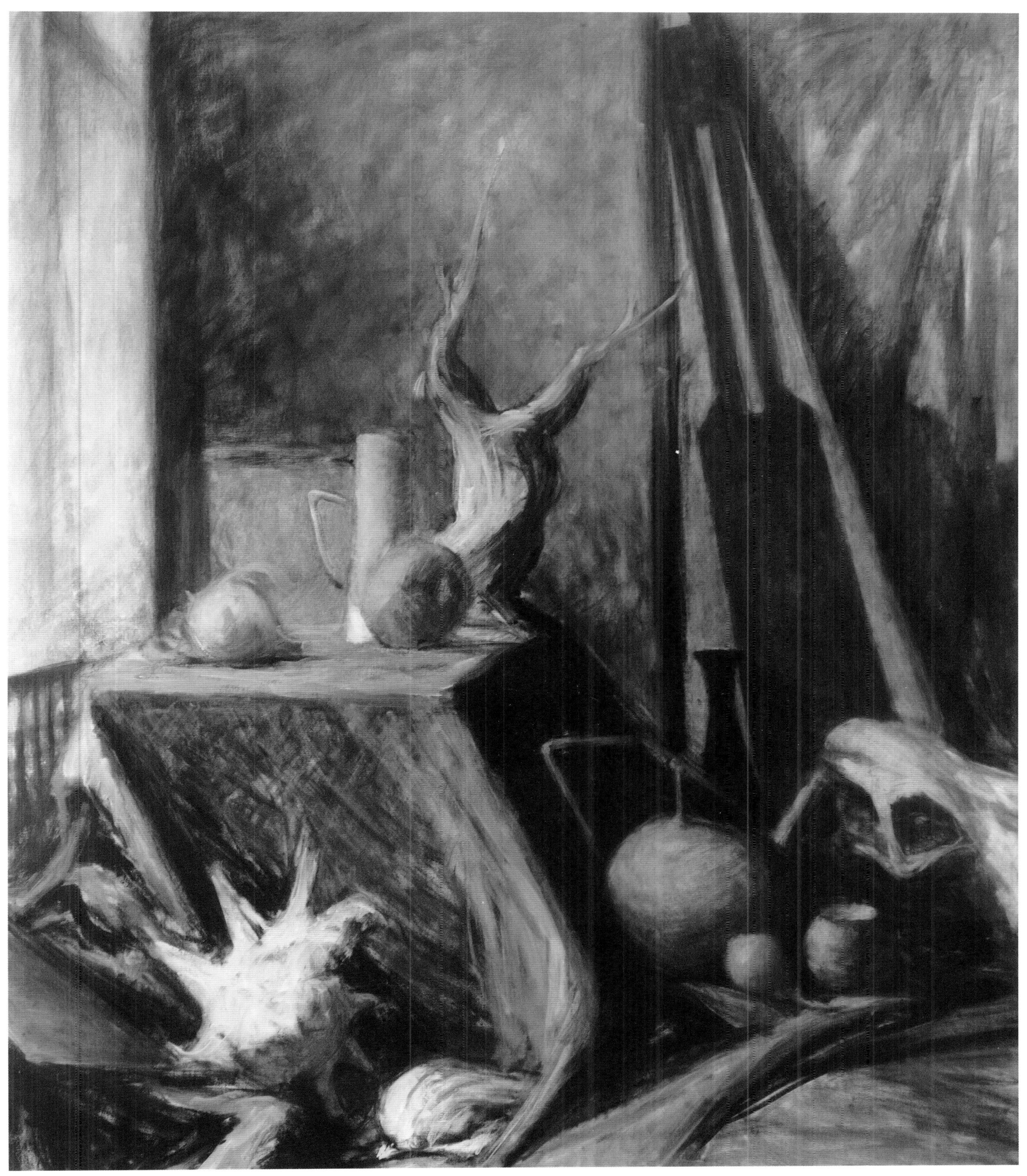

2. MY STUDIO

1963, oil on canvas, 40 × 30 inches

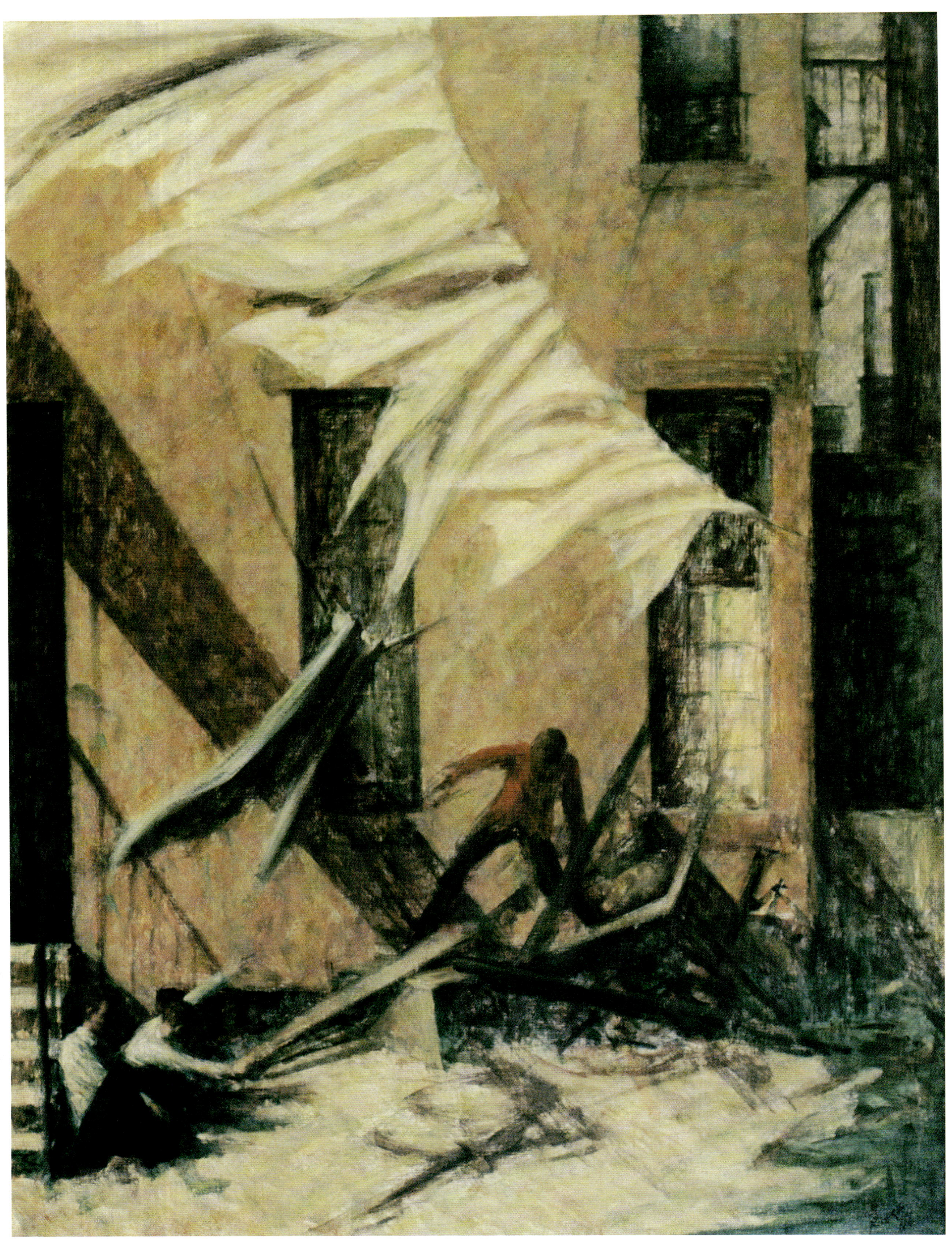

3. BACKYARD
1963, oil on canvas, 48 × 36 inches

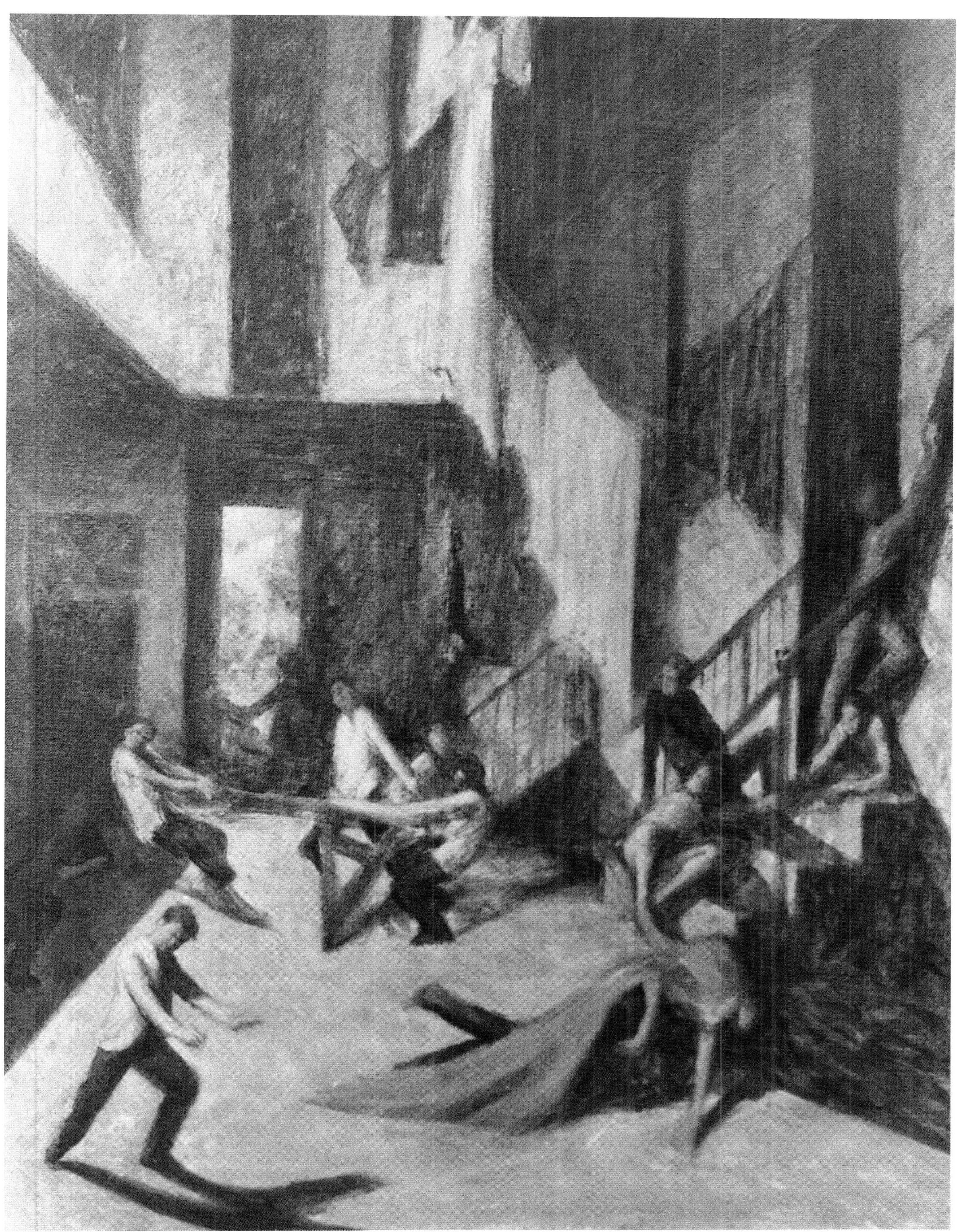

4. BACKYARD #2

1963, oil on canvas, 48 × 36 inches

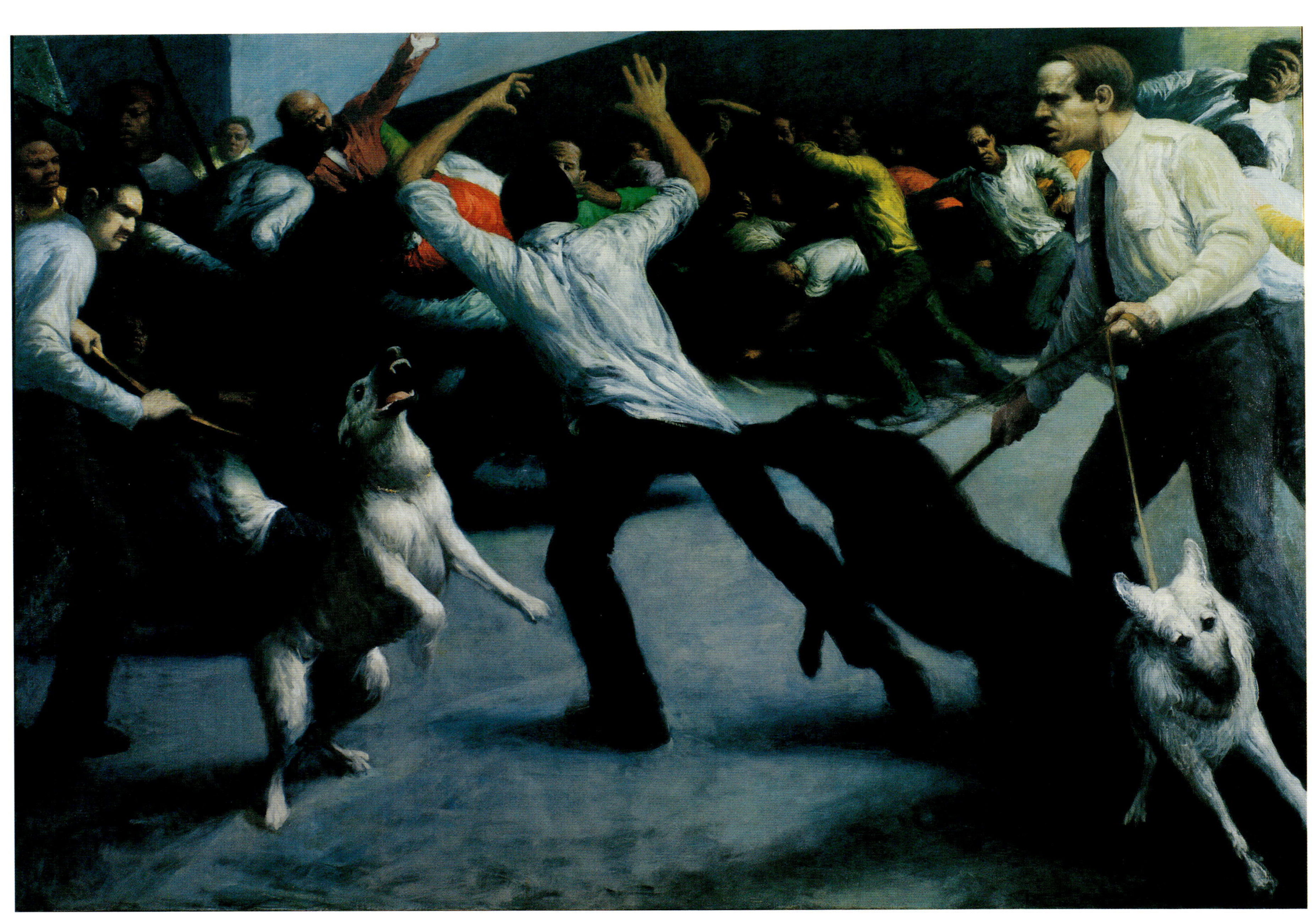

5. BIRMINGHAM
1964, oil on canvas, 69 ½ × 100 inches

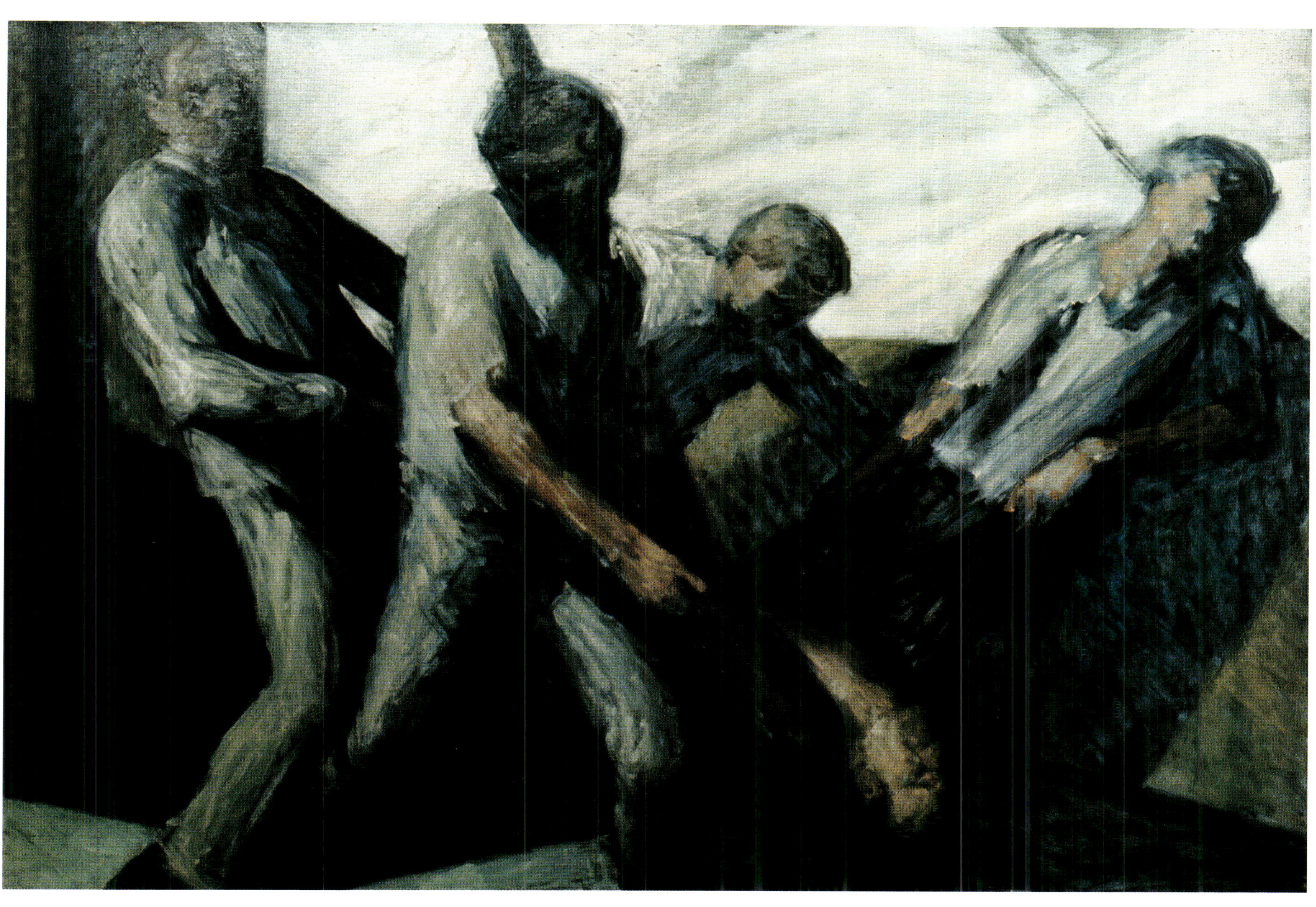

6. RESCUE

1966, oil on canvas, 54 × 72 inches

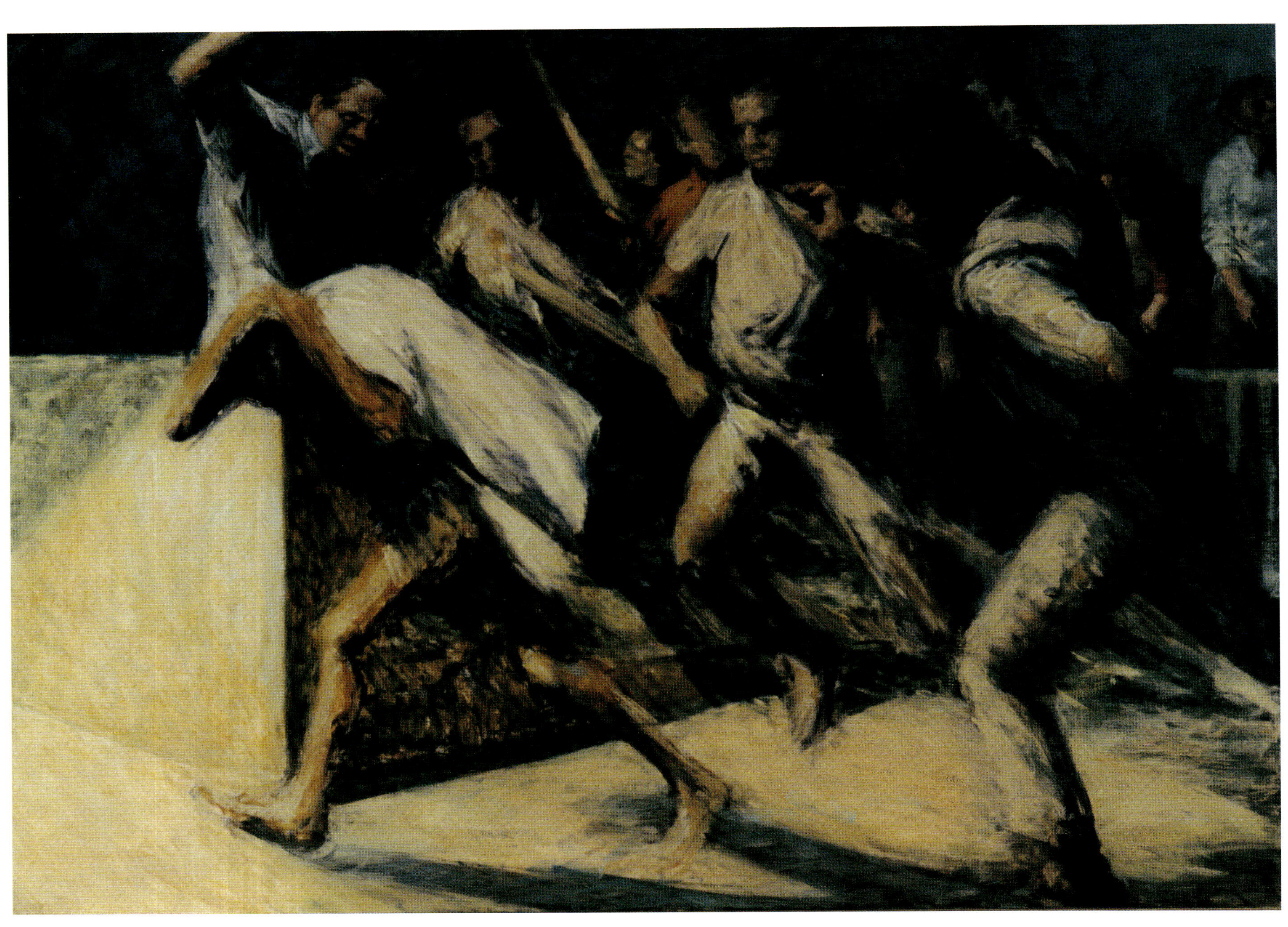

7. PURSUIT

1966, oil on canvas, 54 × 72 inches

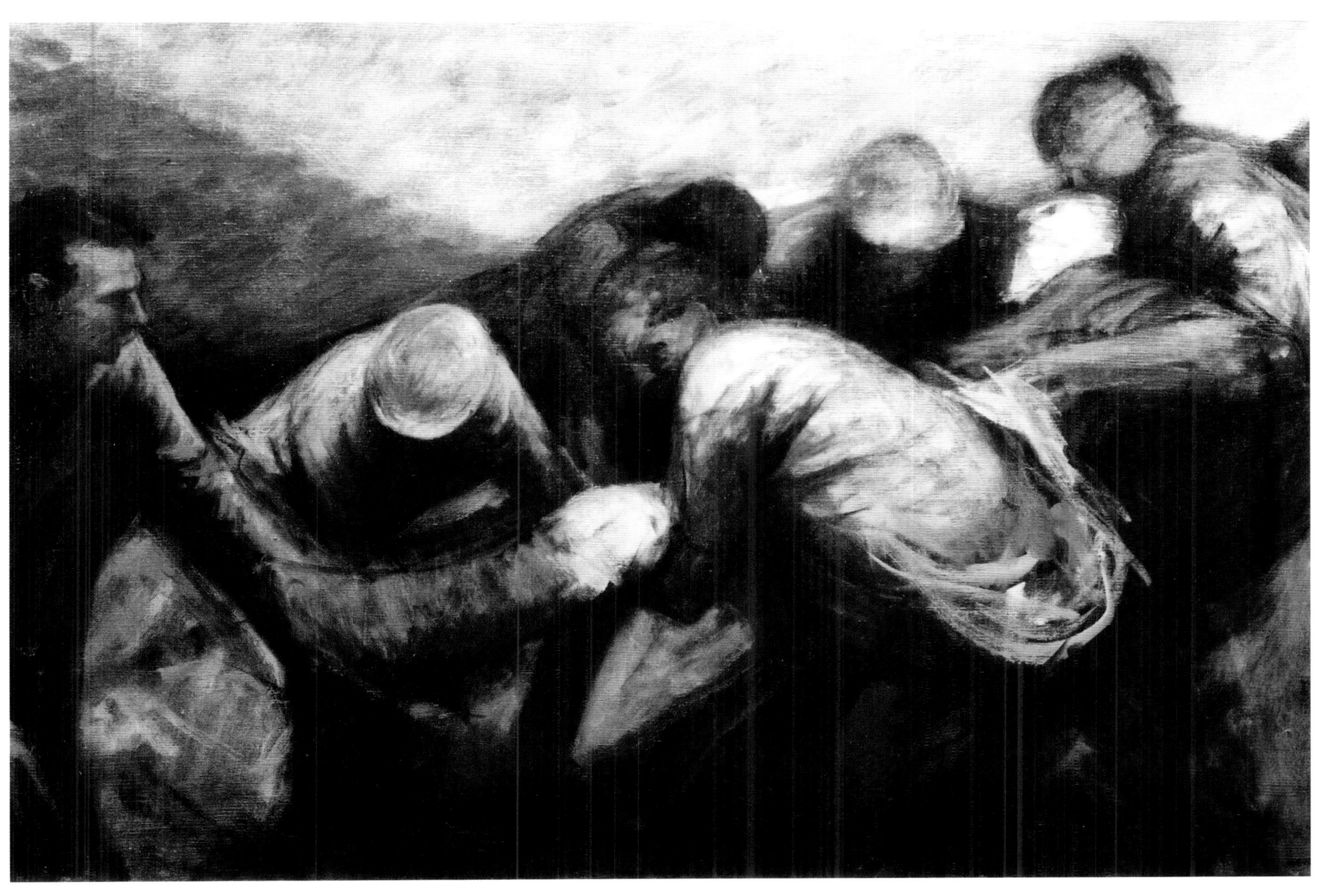

8. VIETNAM

1966, oil on canvas, 54 × 72 inches

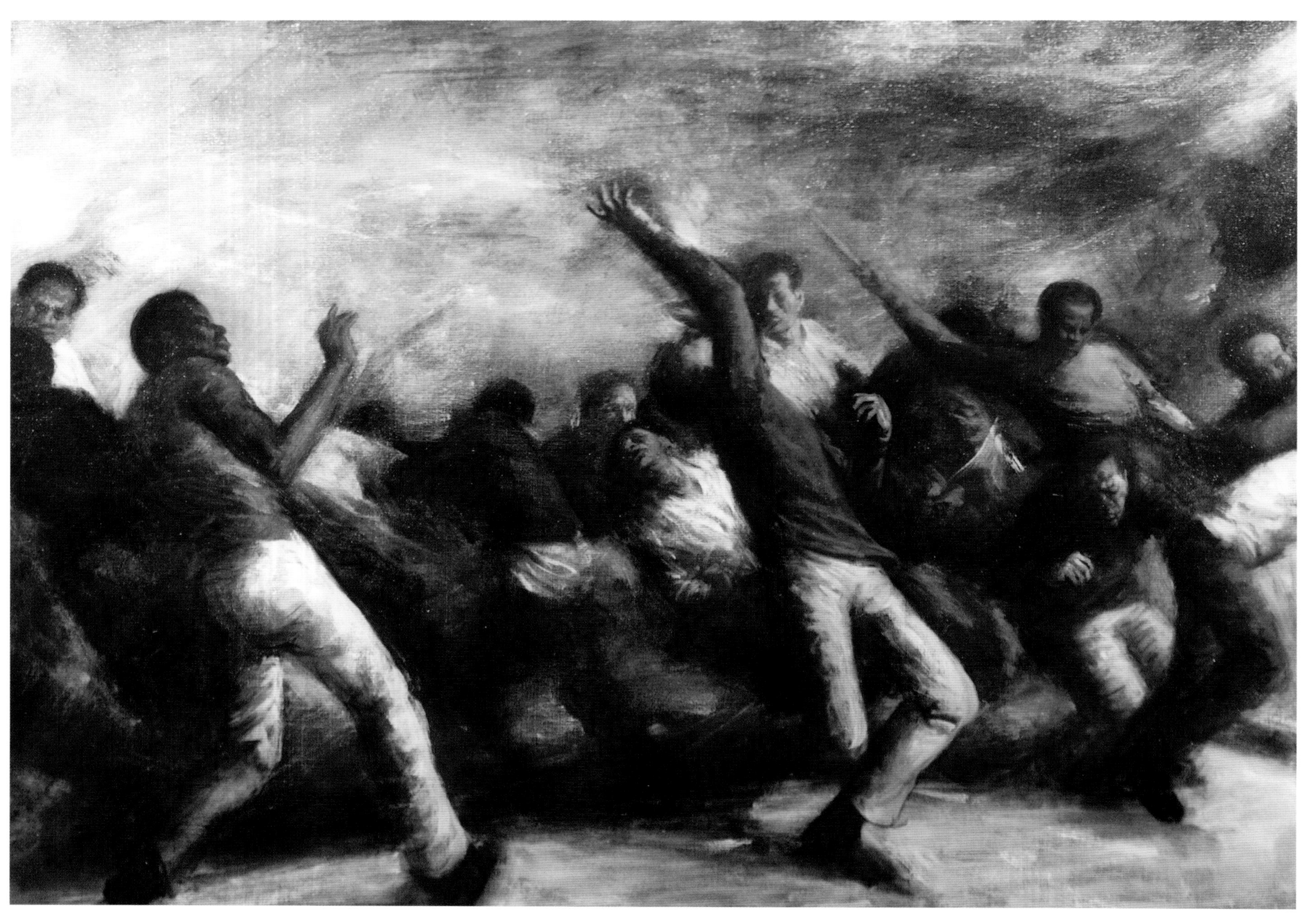

9. RIOT
1968, oil on canvas, 30 × 40 inches

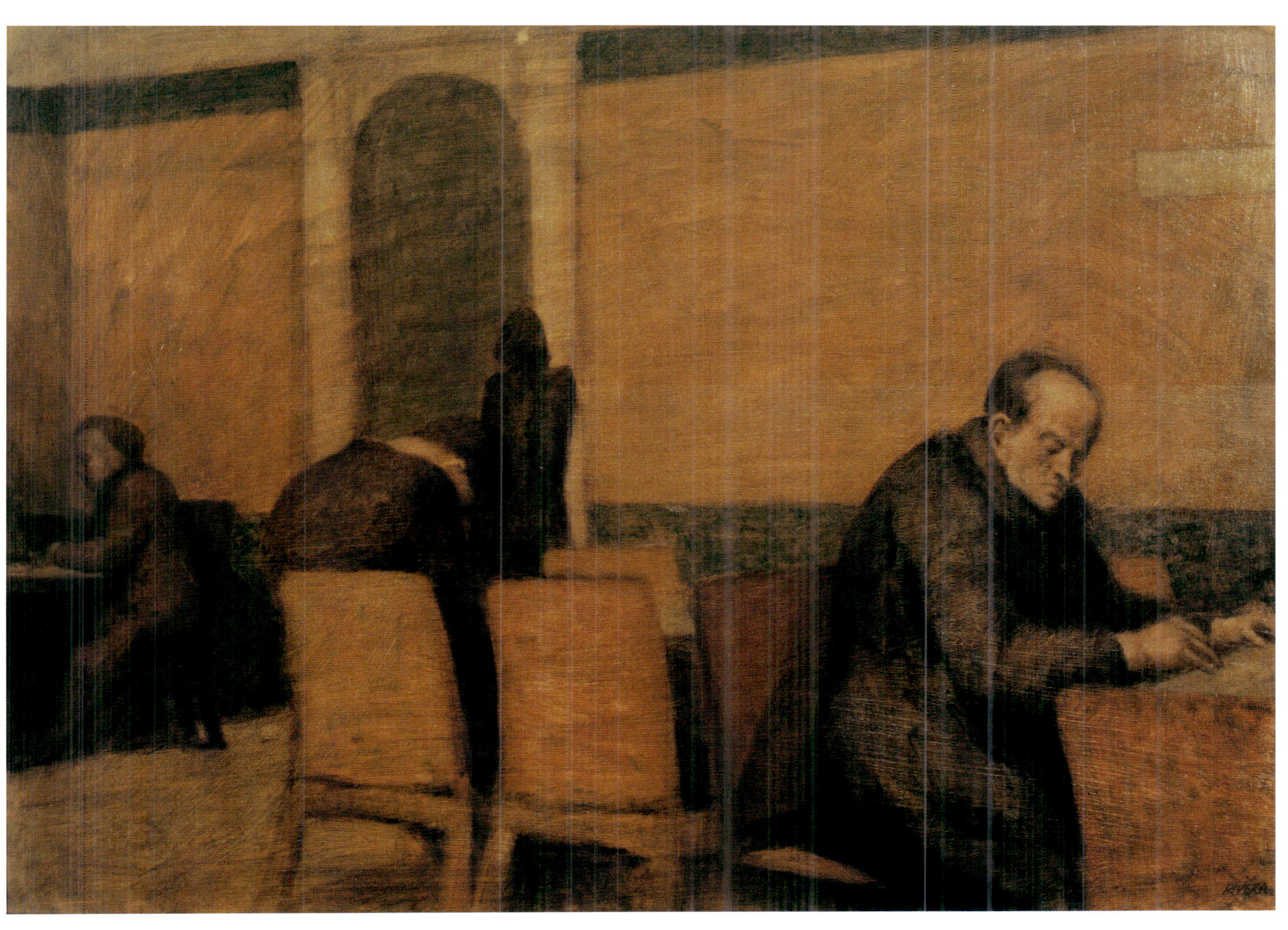

10. AUTOMAT

1970, oil on canvas, 15½ × 22½ inches

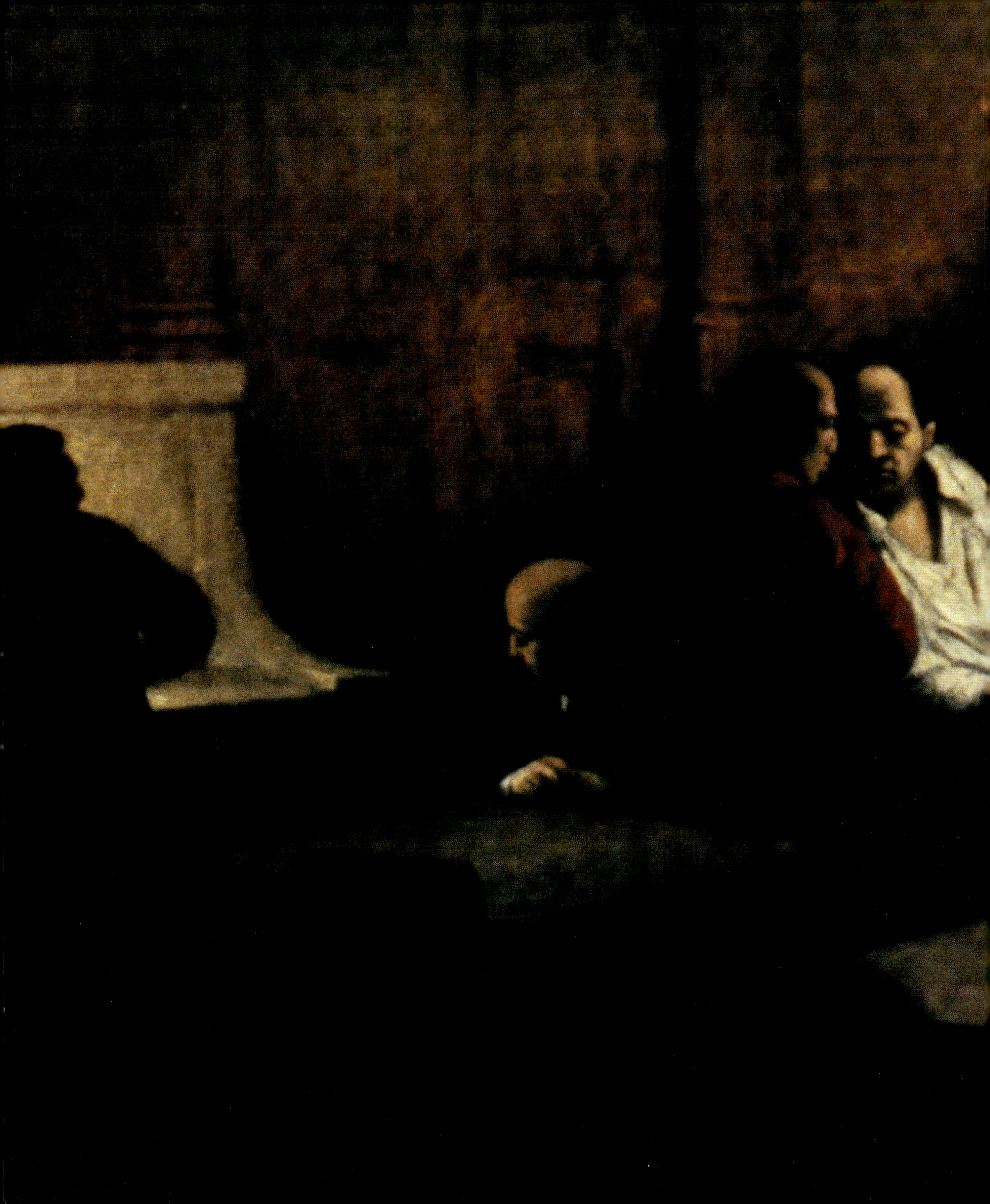

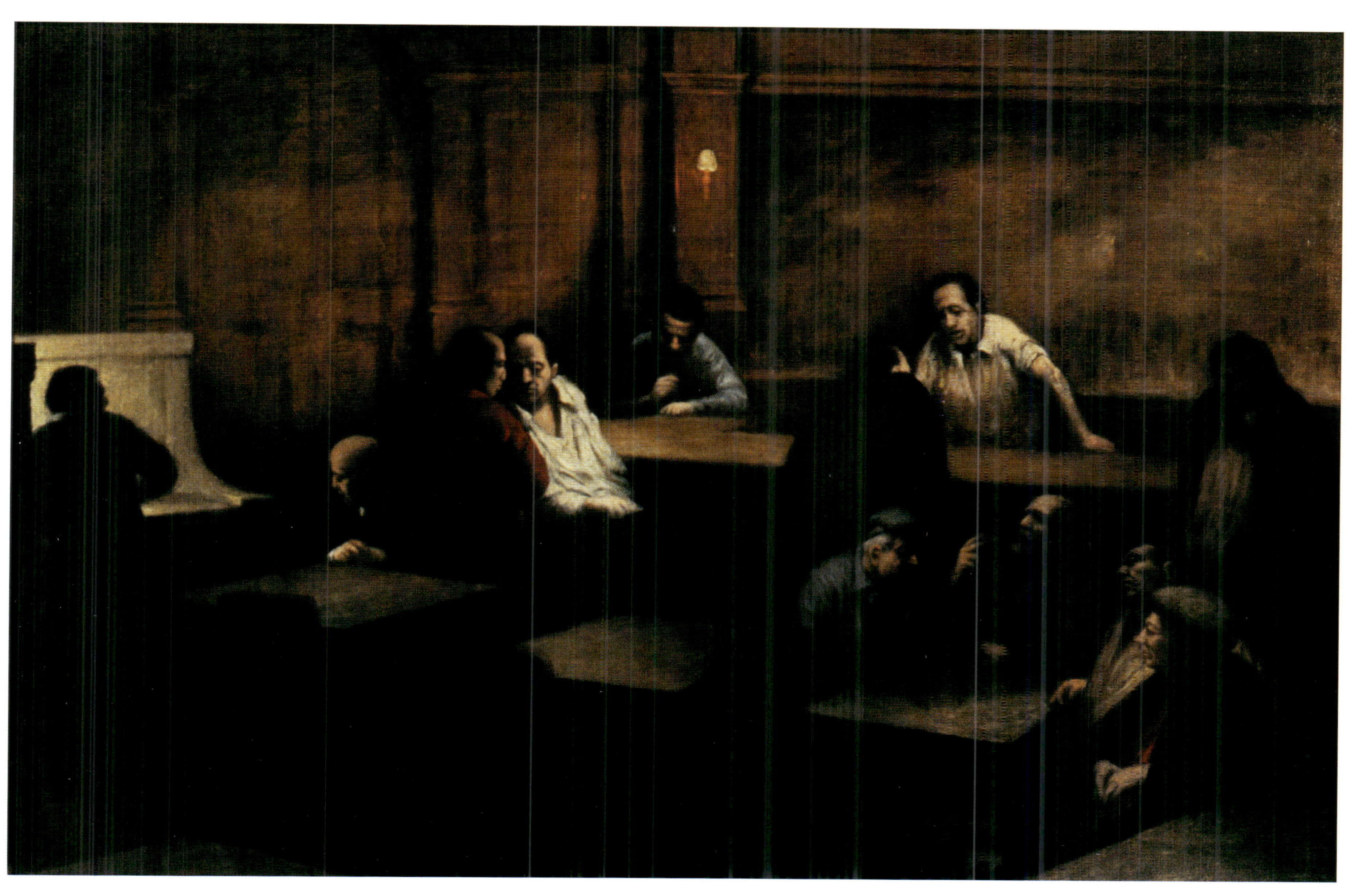

11. PIANO MAN

1973, oil on canvas, 30 × 40 inches

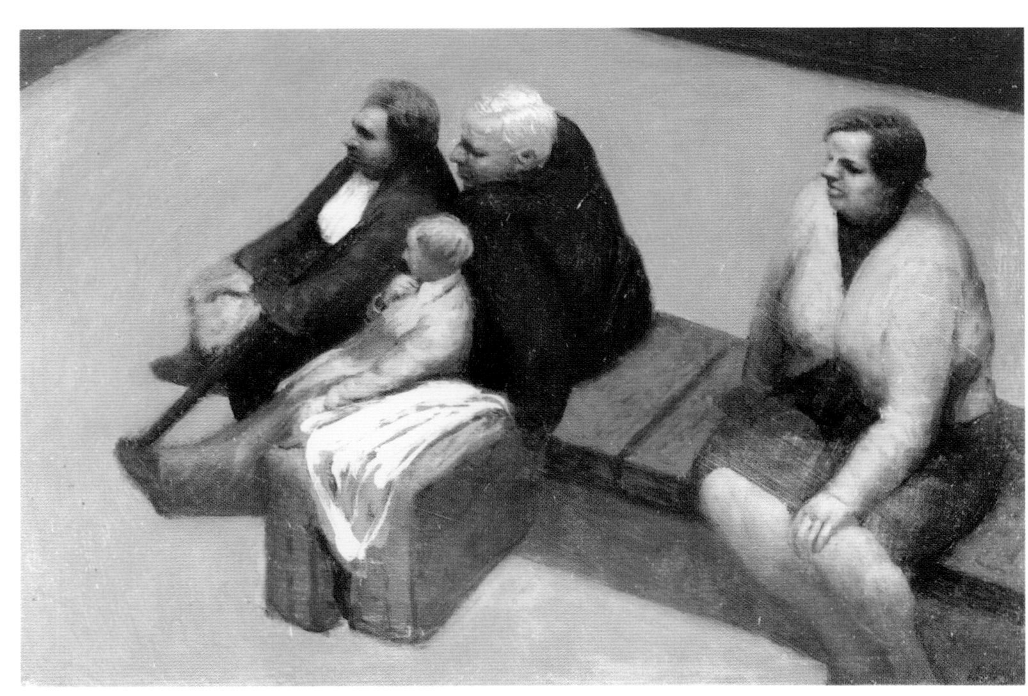

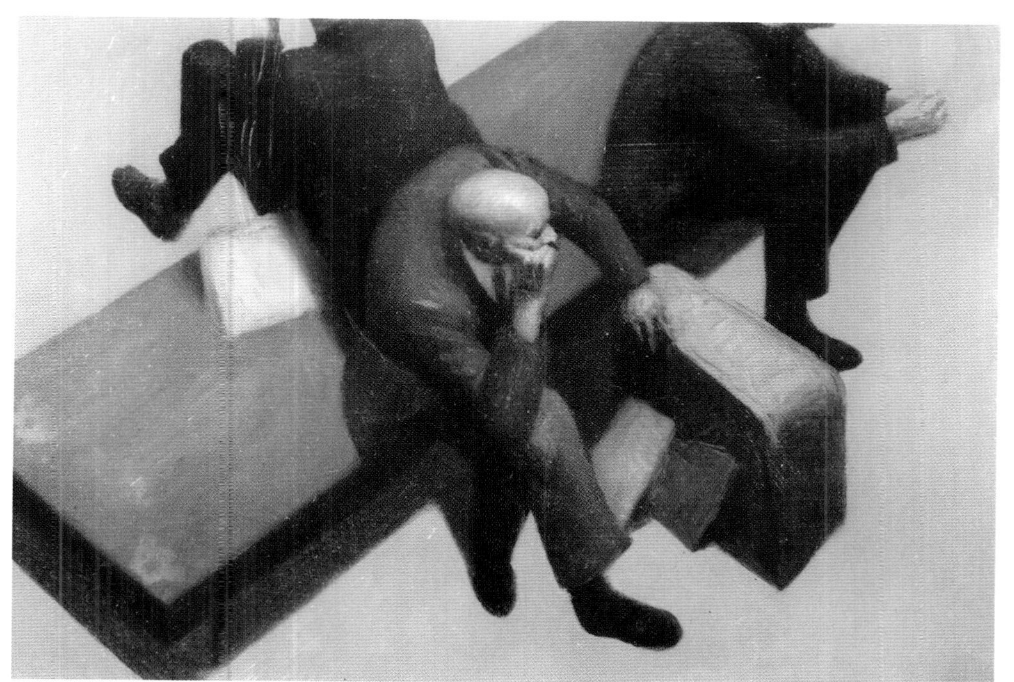

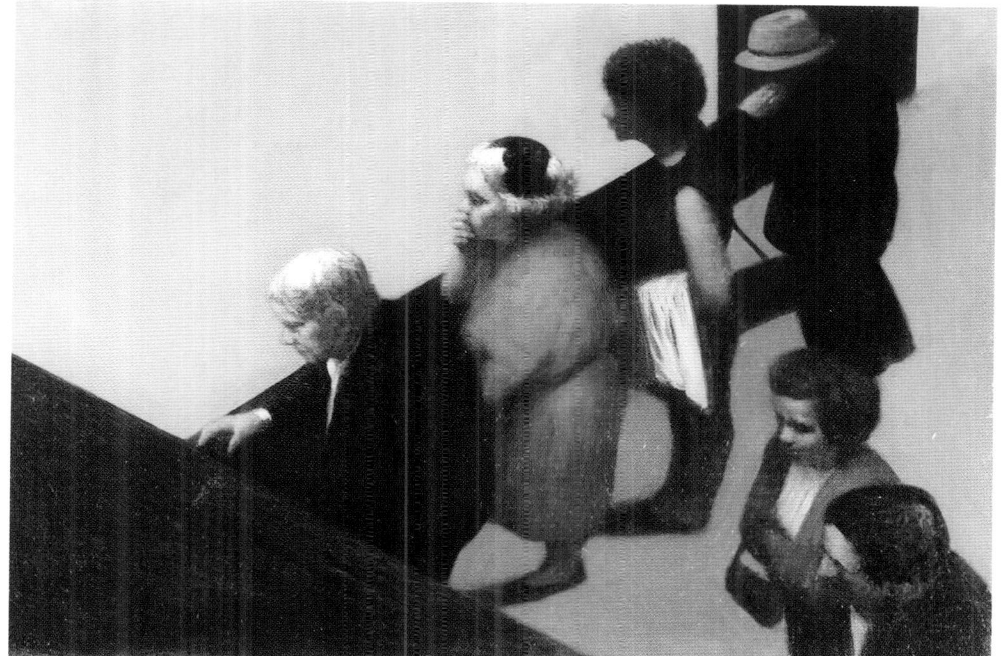

12. AIRPORT (triptych)
1975, oil on canvas, 10 × 14 inches each

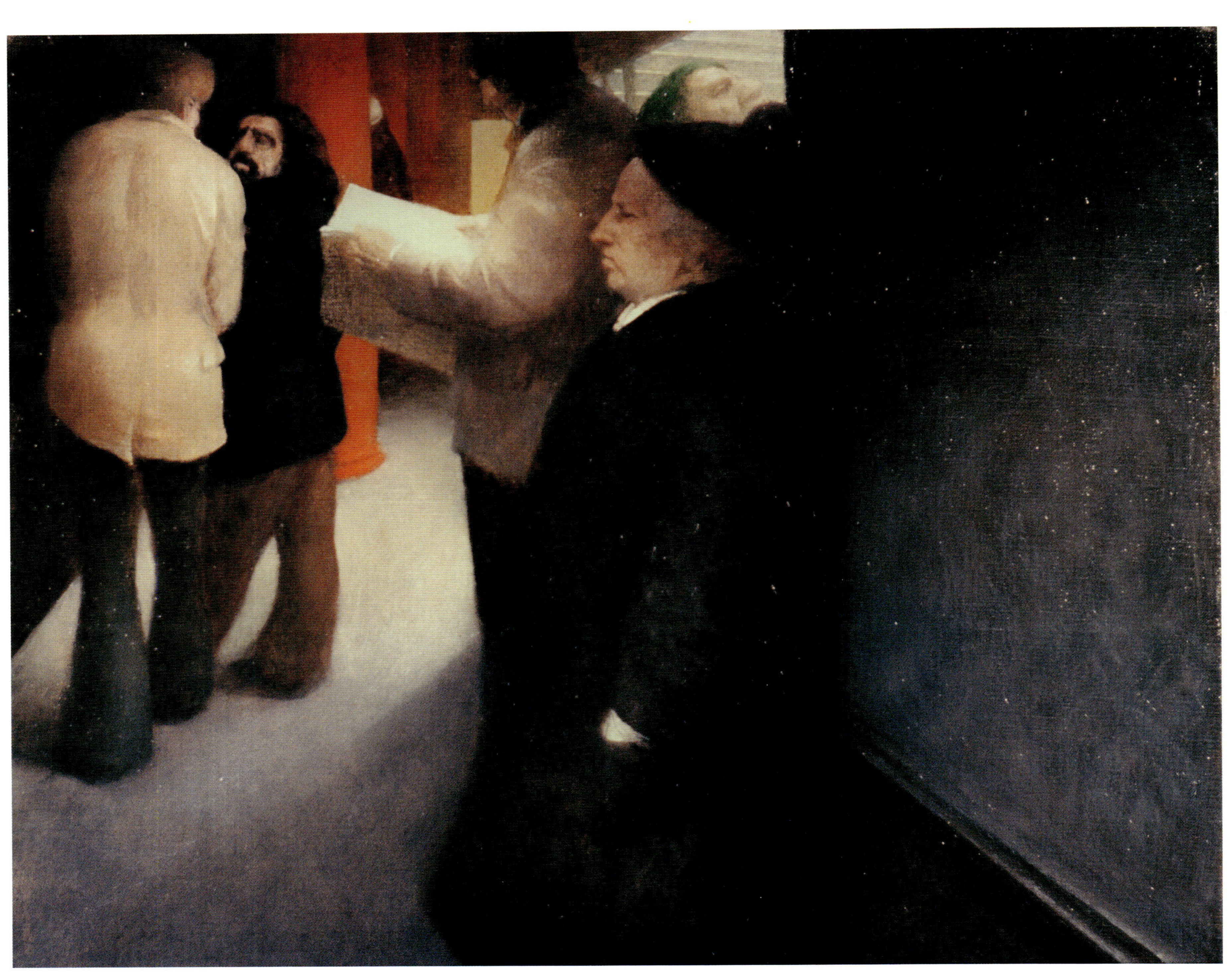

13. STATION
1975, oil on canvas, 16 × 20 inches

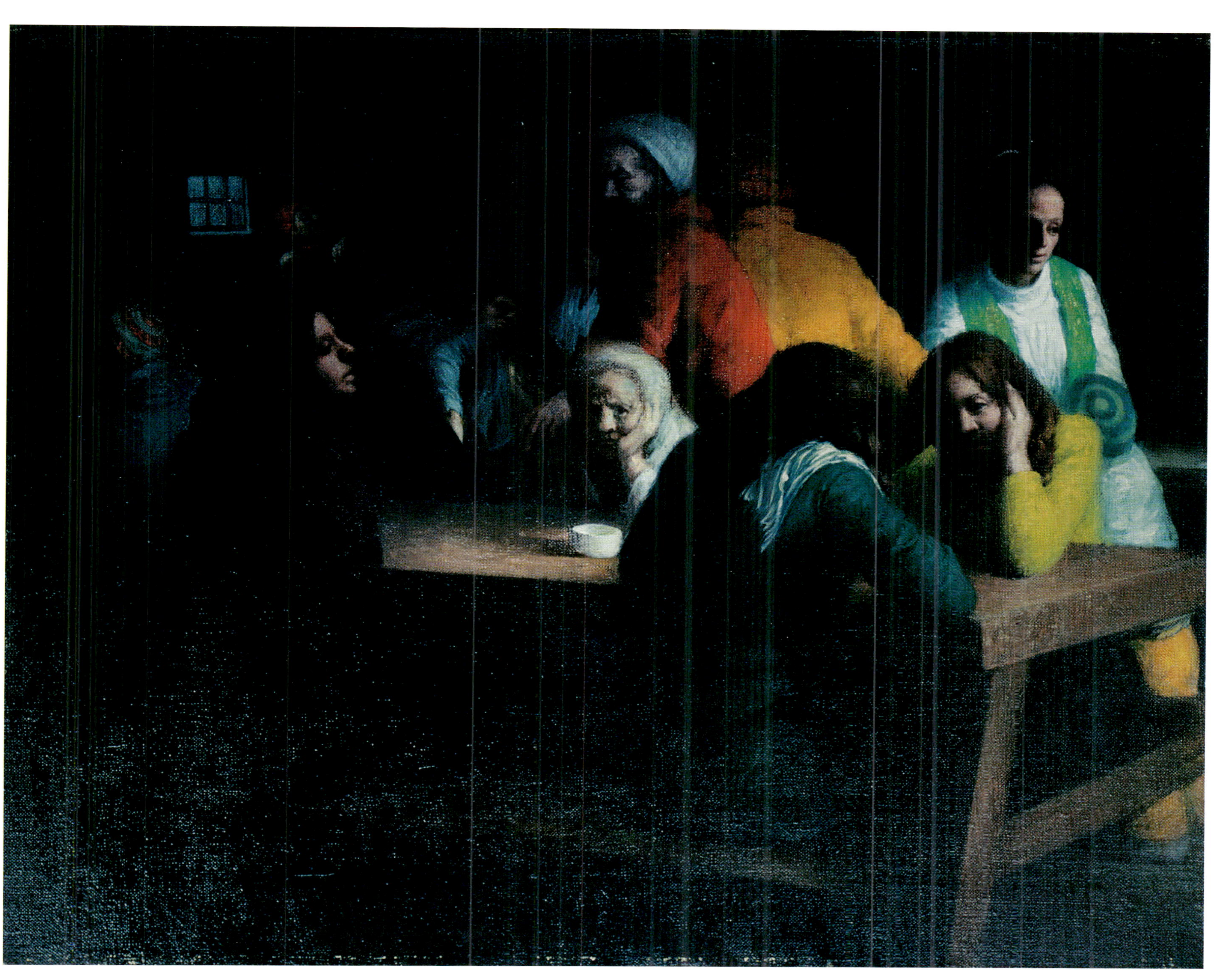

14. LODGE

1975, oil on canvas, 12 × 16 inches

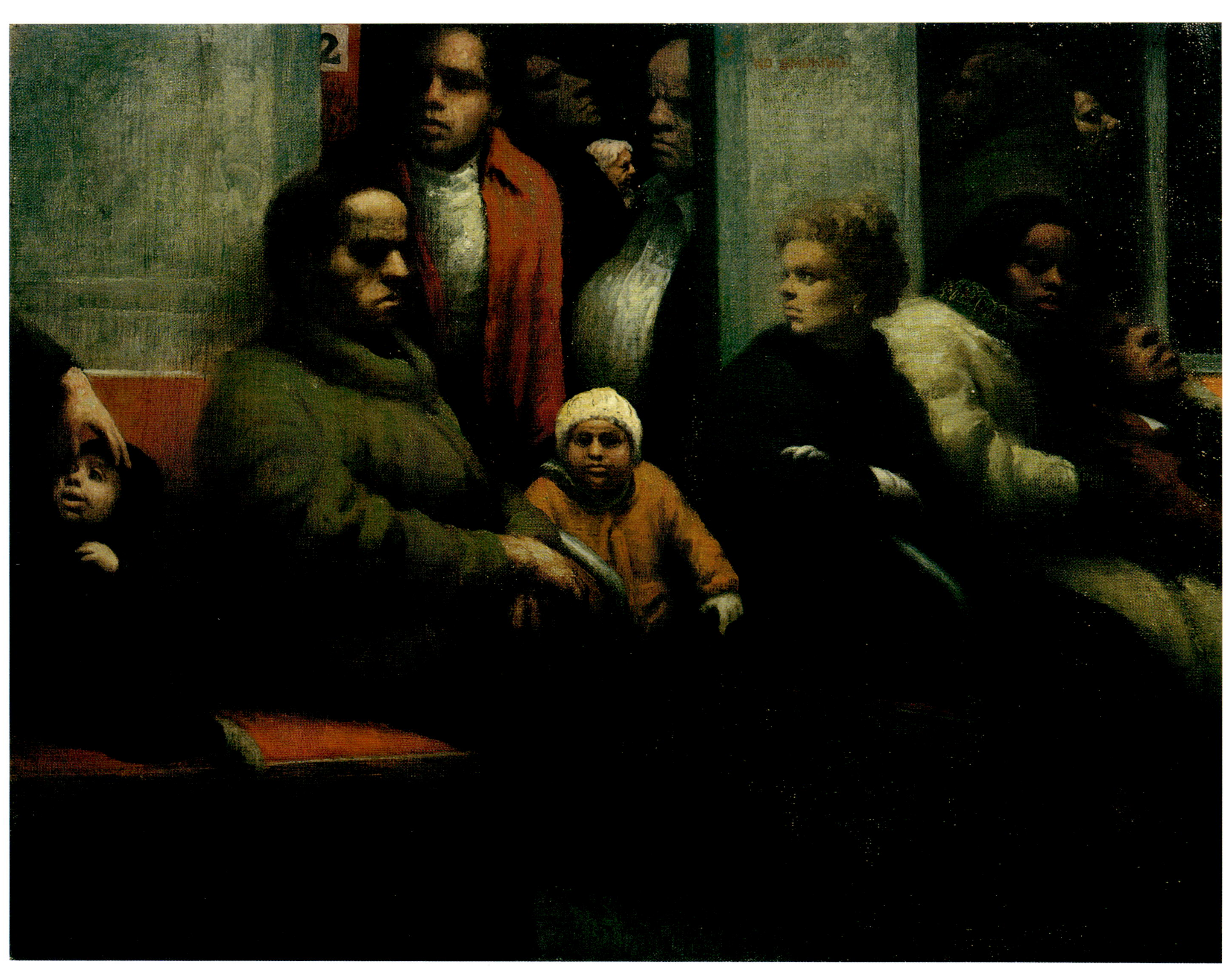

15. SUBWAY
1975, oil on canvas, 16 × 20 inches

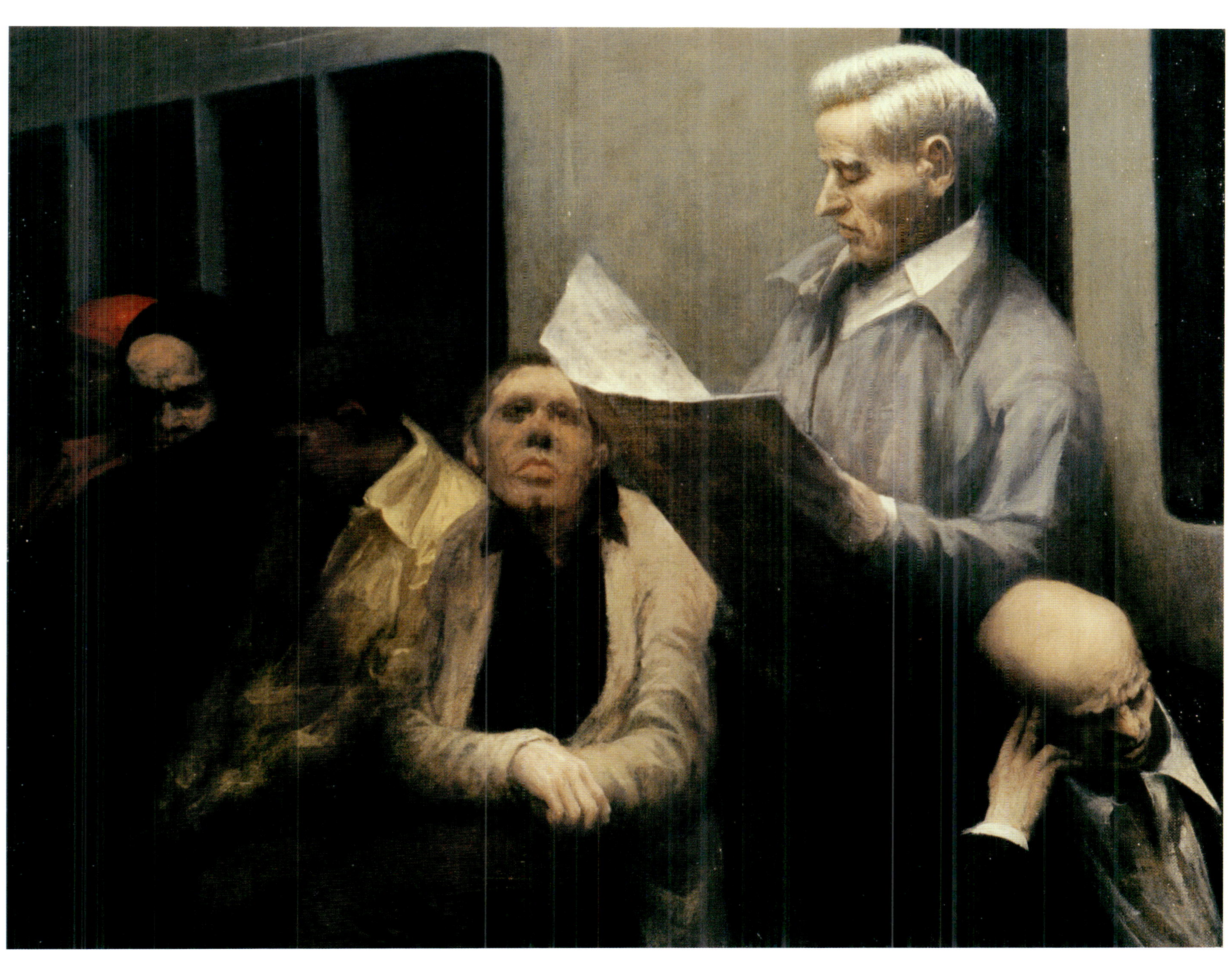

16. SUBWAY #2

1975, oil on canvas, 16 × 20 inches

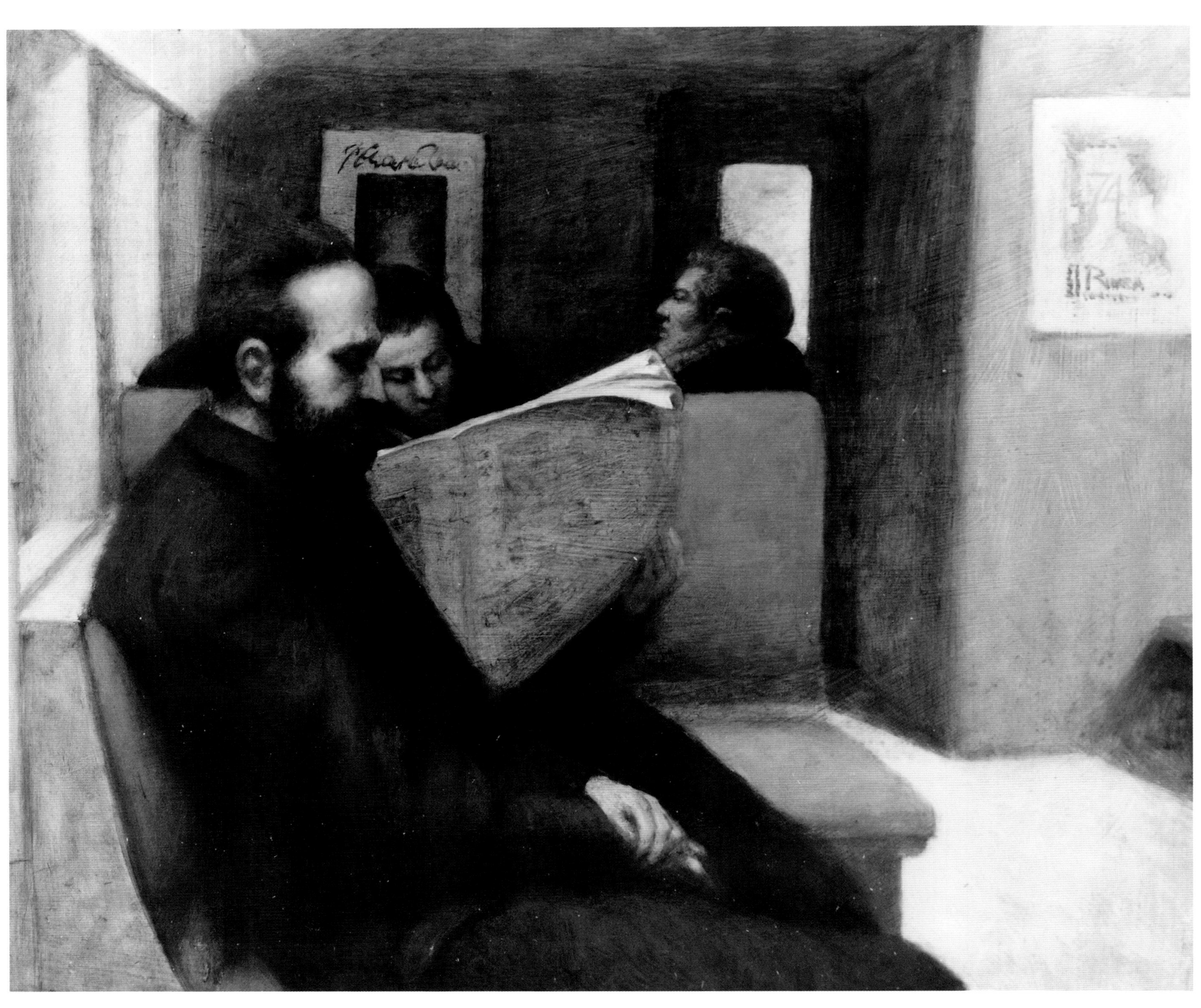

17. SUBWAY #3

1975, oil on canvas, 16 × 20 inches

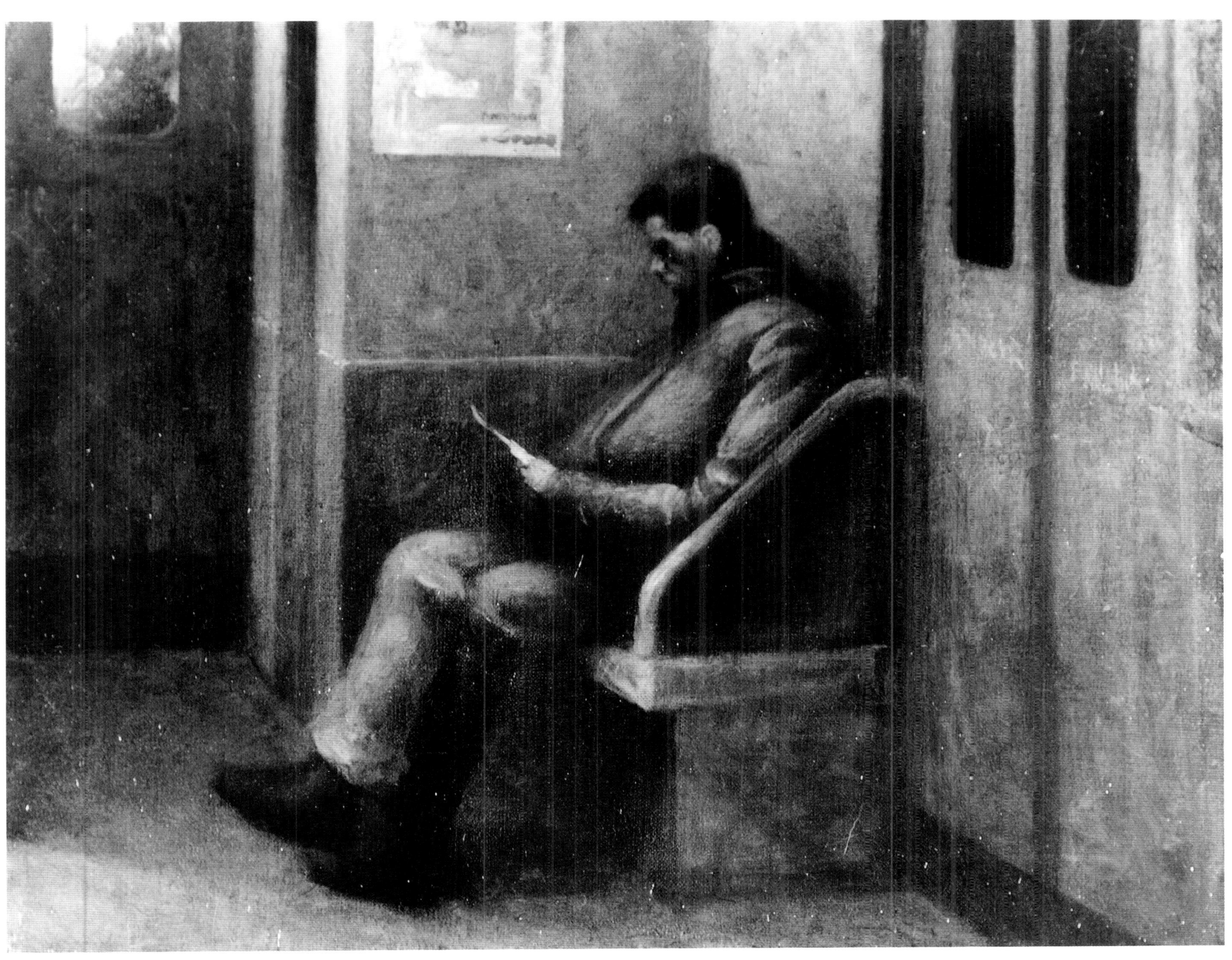

18. SUBWAY #4

1975, oil on canvas, 16 × 20 inches

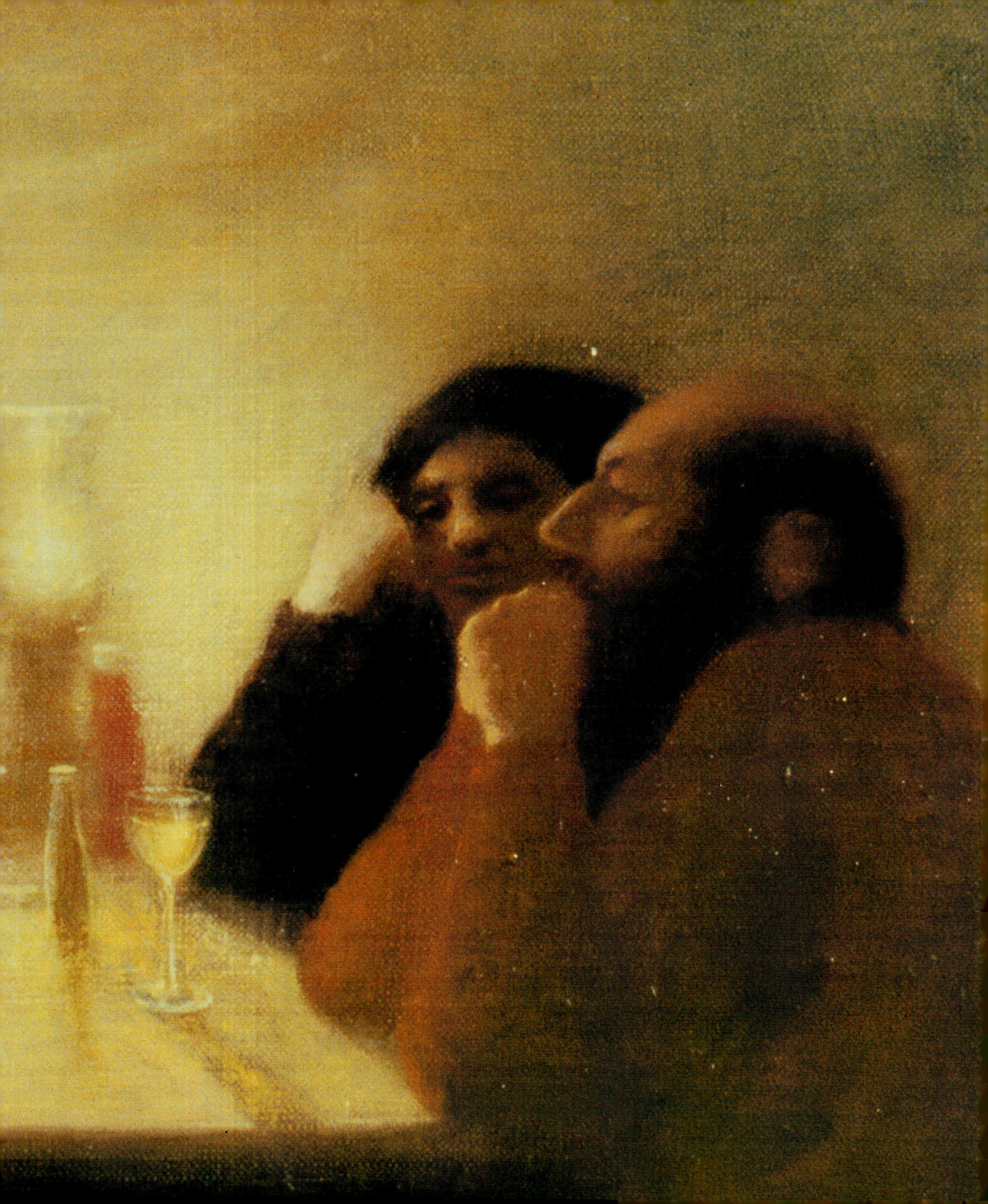

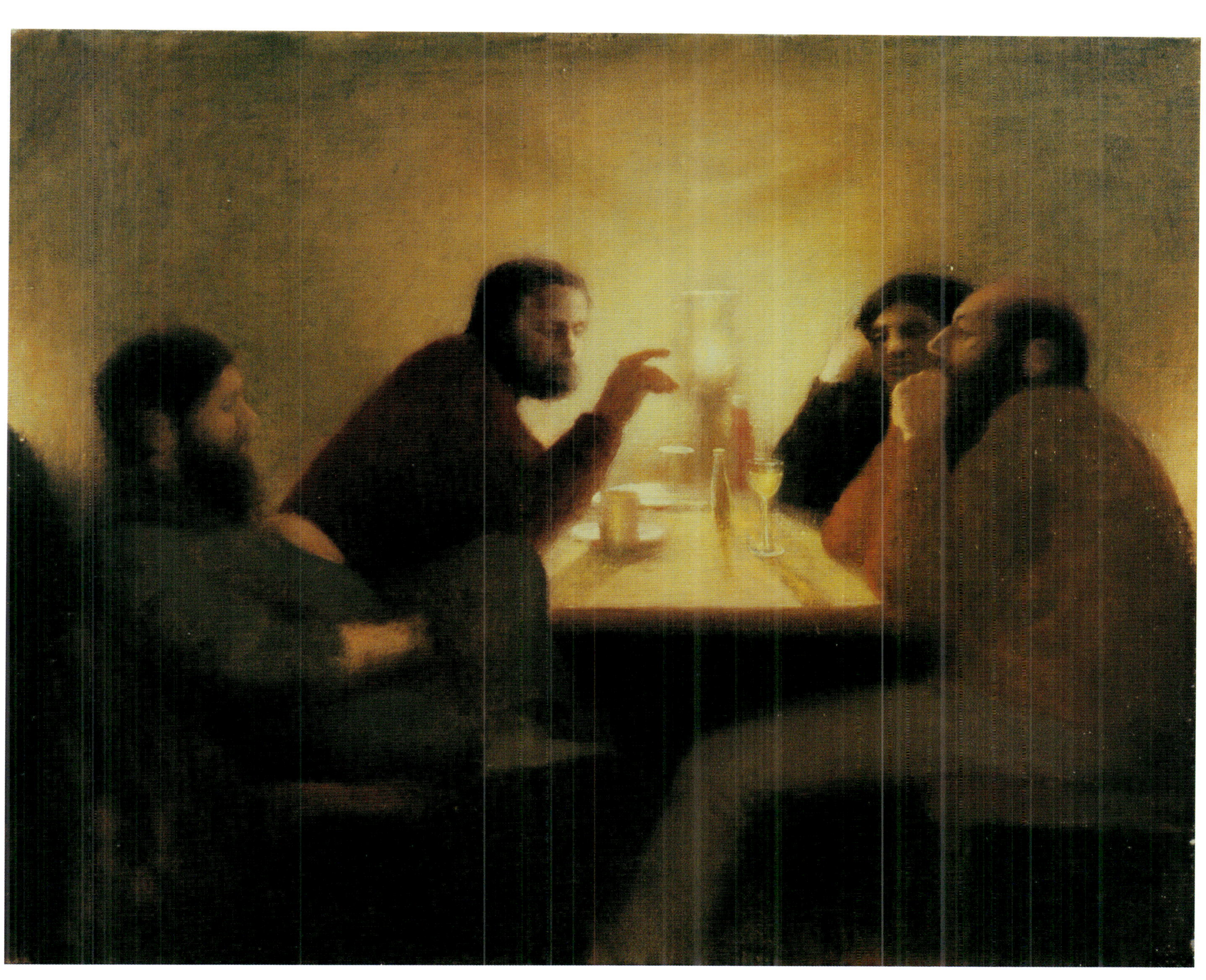

[illegible]9. MINSKY'S

1977, oil on canvas, 16 × 20 inches

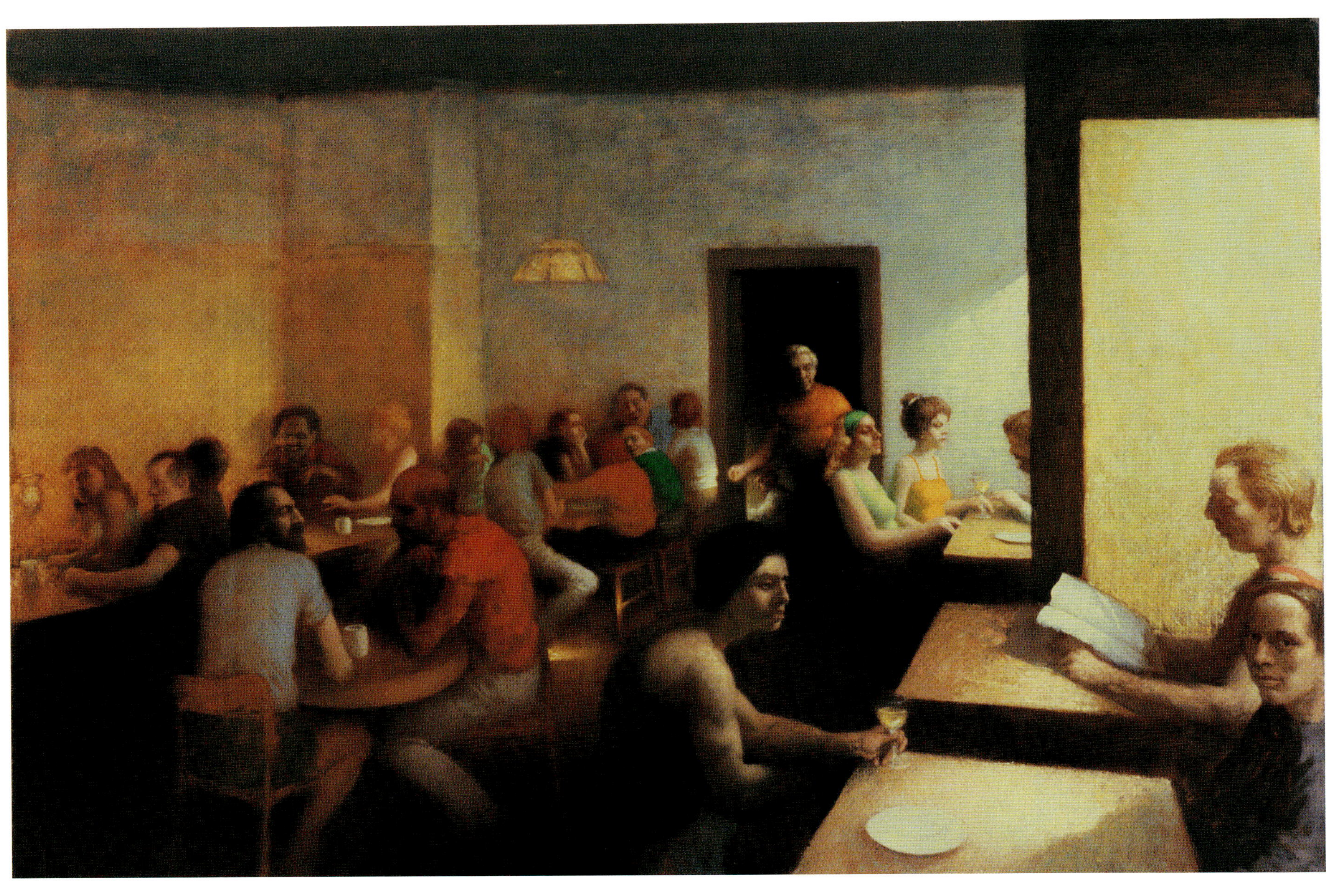

20. MINSKY'S #2

1977, oil on canvas, 30 × 40 inches

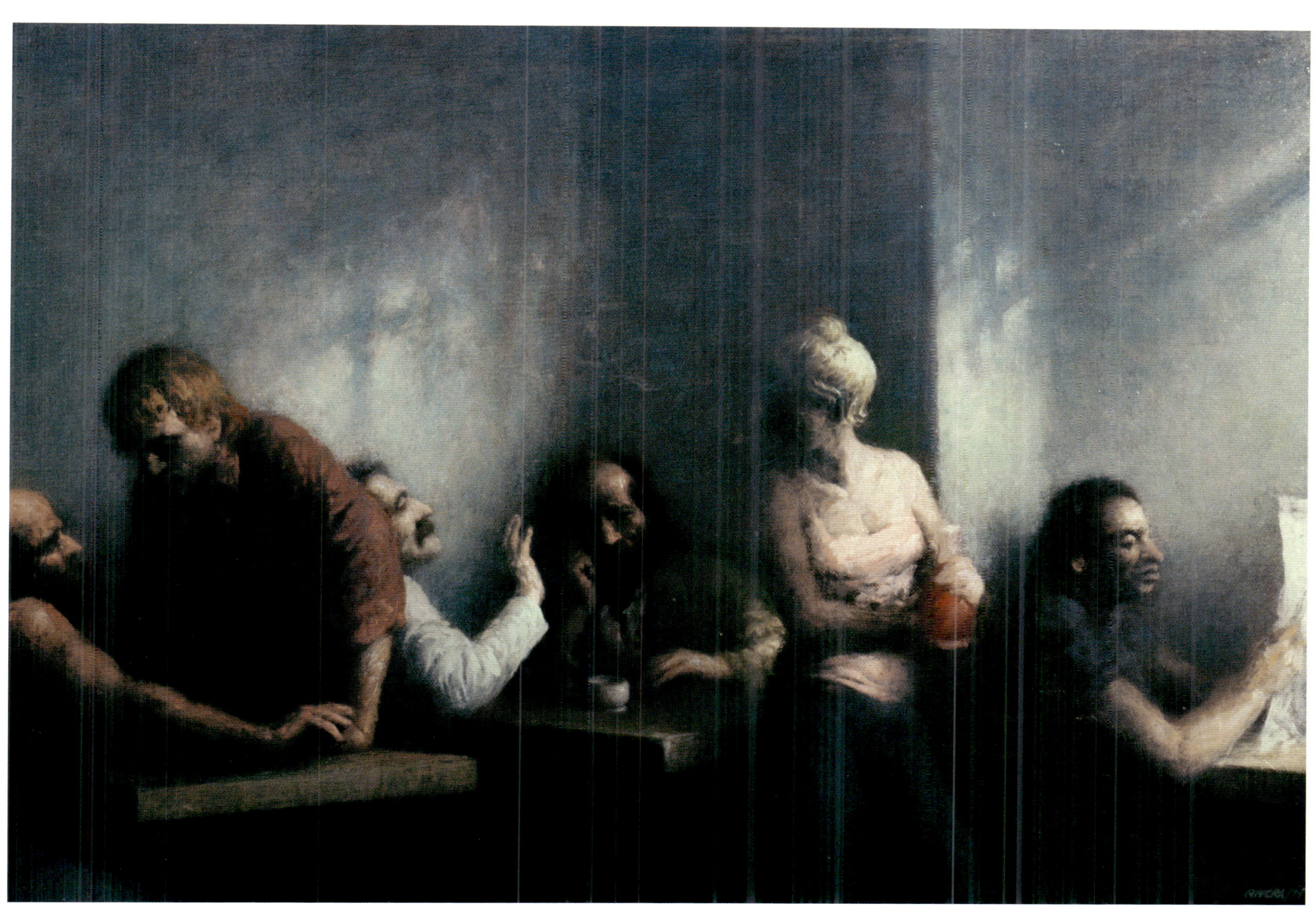

21. MINSKY'S #3

1977, oil on canvas, 16 × 20 inches

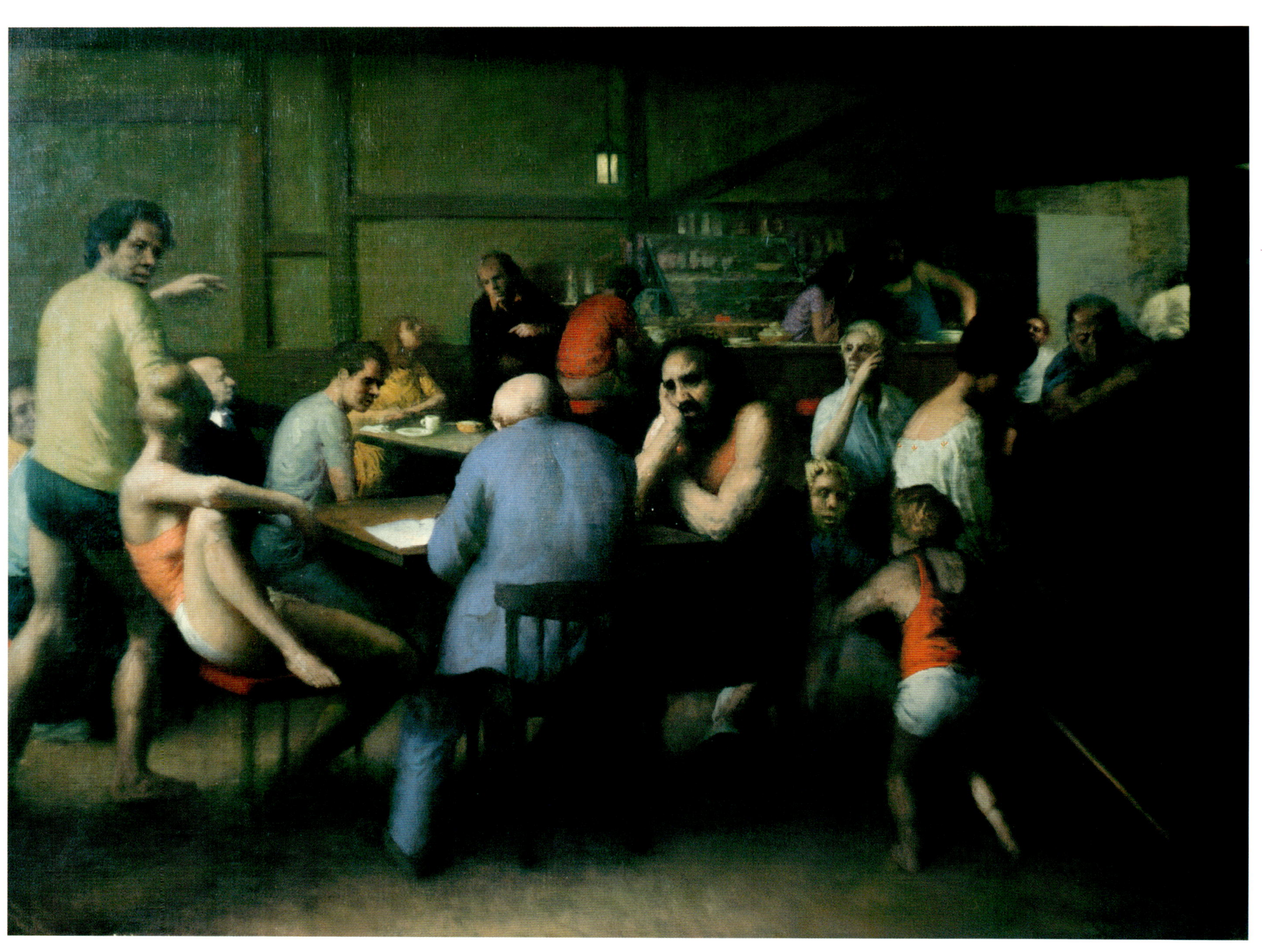

22. CAFE WOODSTOCKER

1977, oil on canvas, 30 × 40 inches

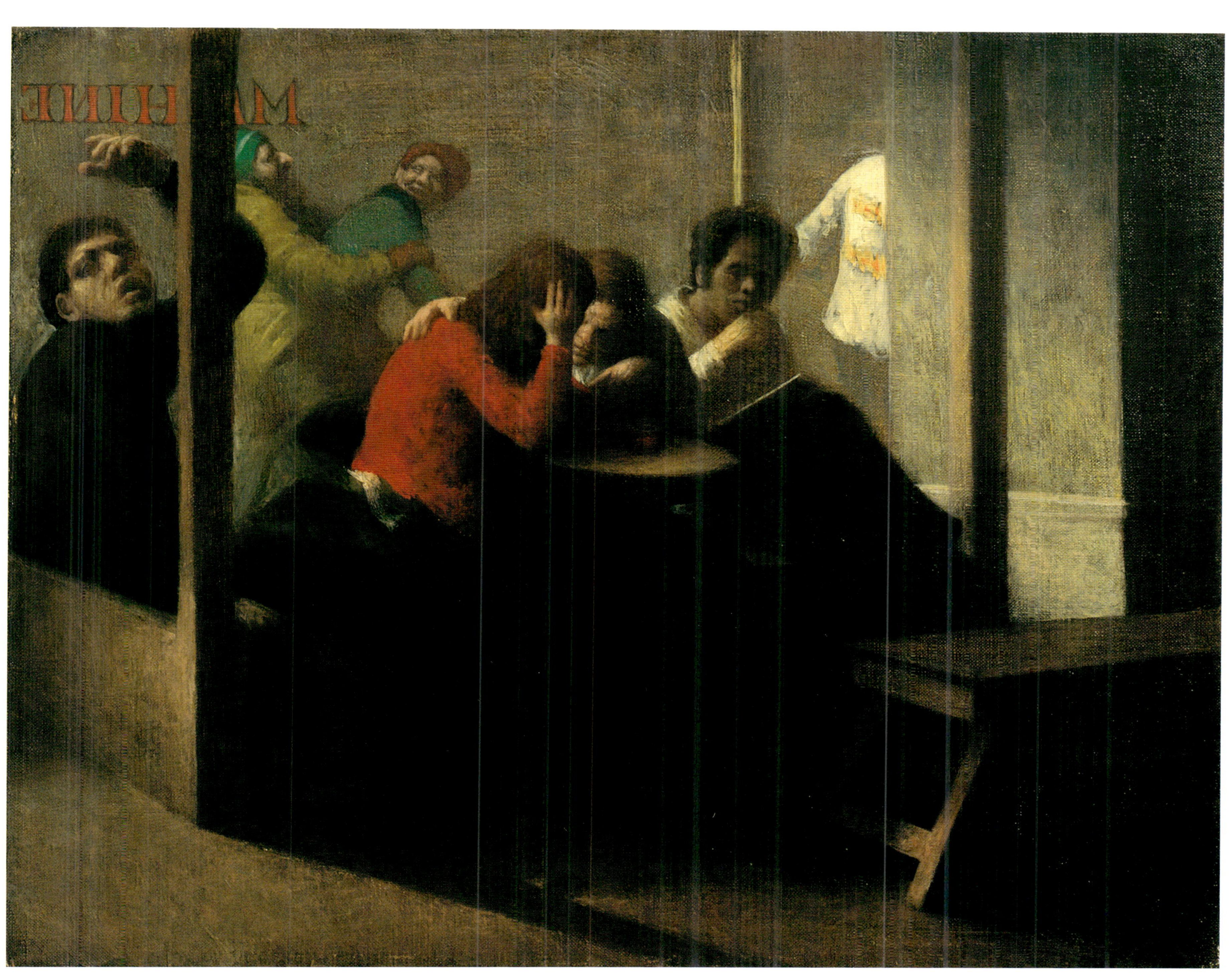

23. MACHINE COFFEEHOUSE

1978, oil on canvas, 16 × 20 inches

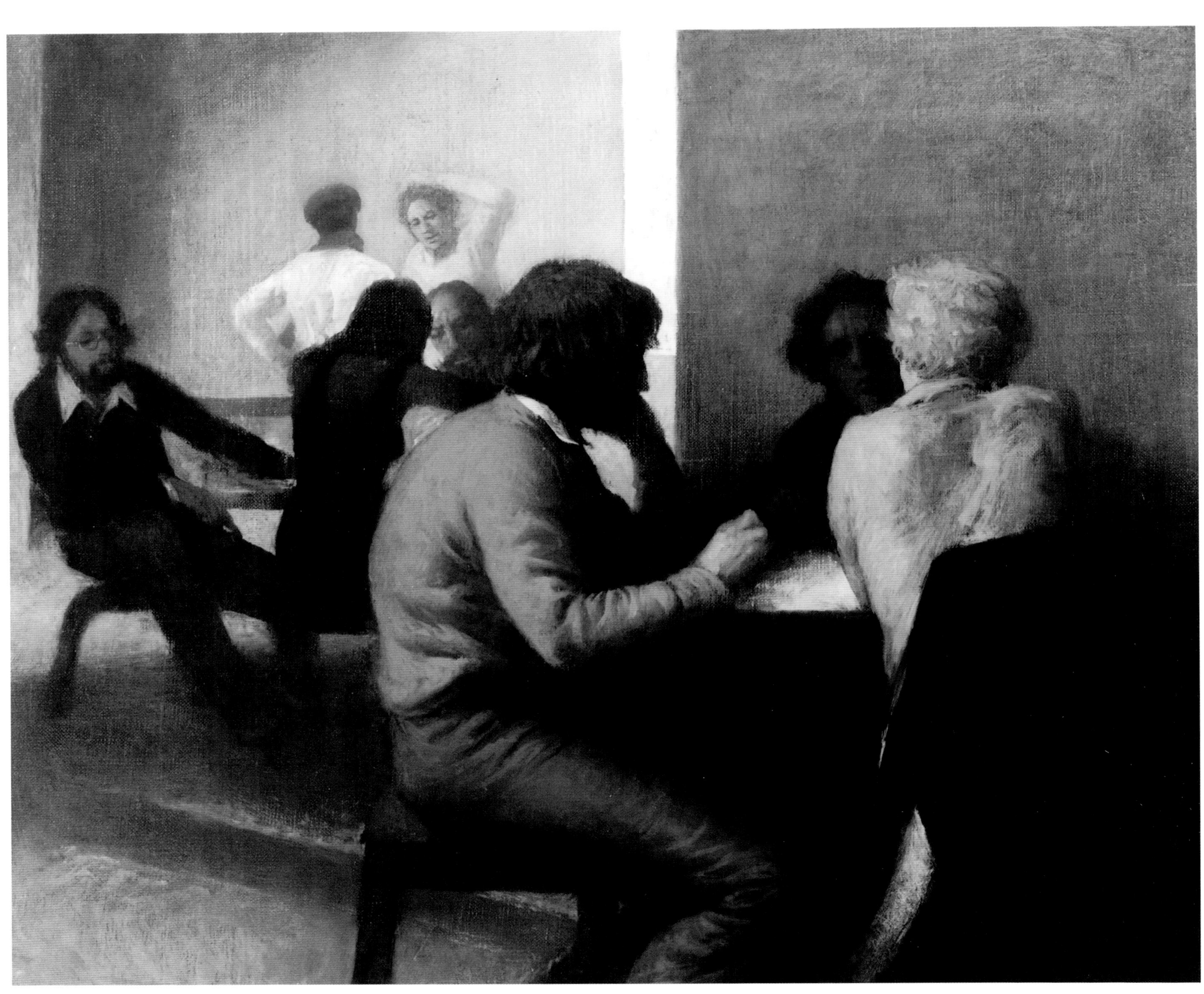

24. COFFEEHOUSE

1978, oil on canvas, 16 × 20 inches

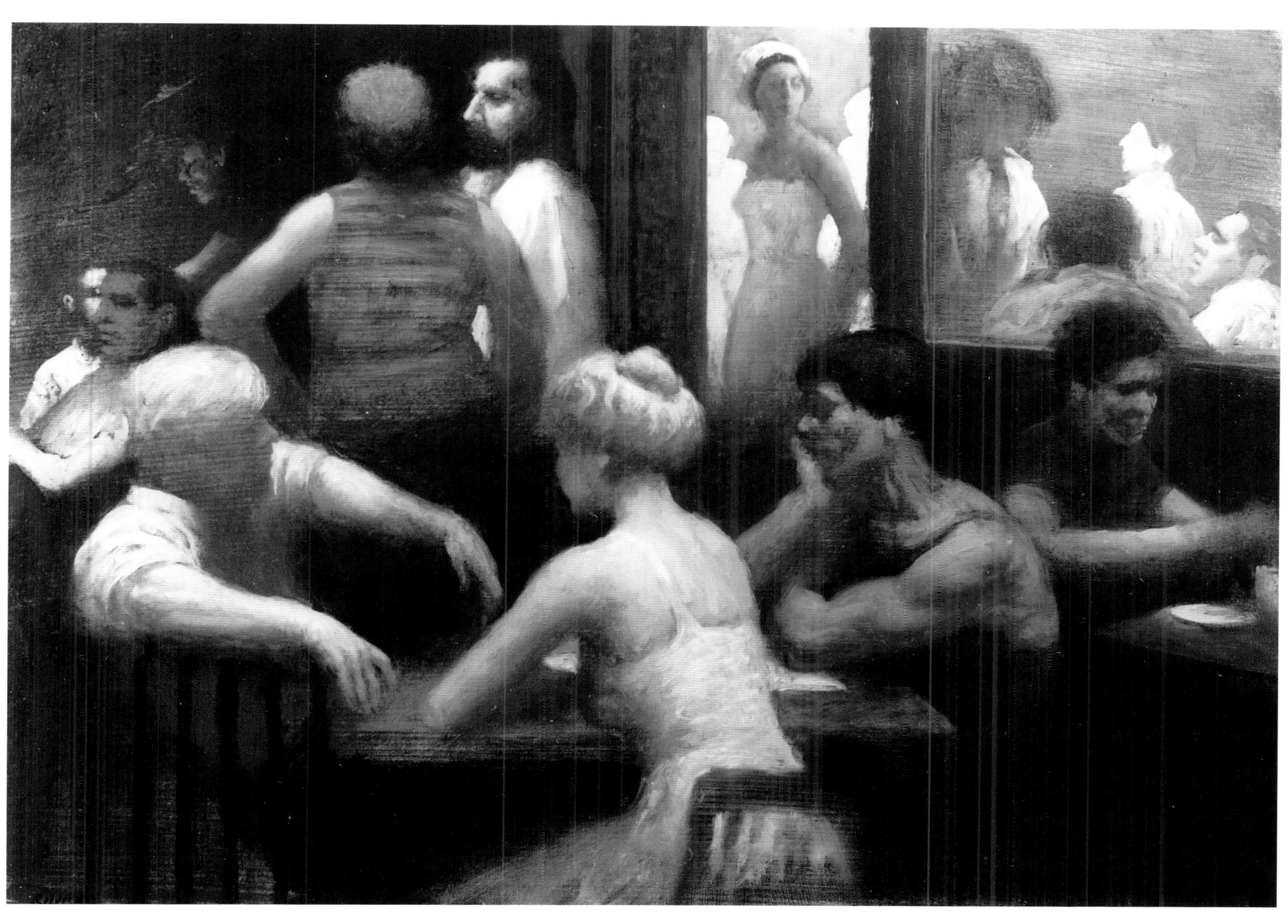

25. COFFEEHOUSE #2
1978, oil on canvas, 14 × 18 inches

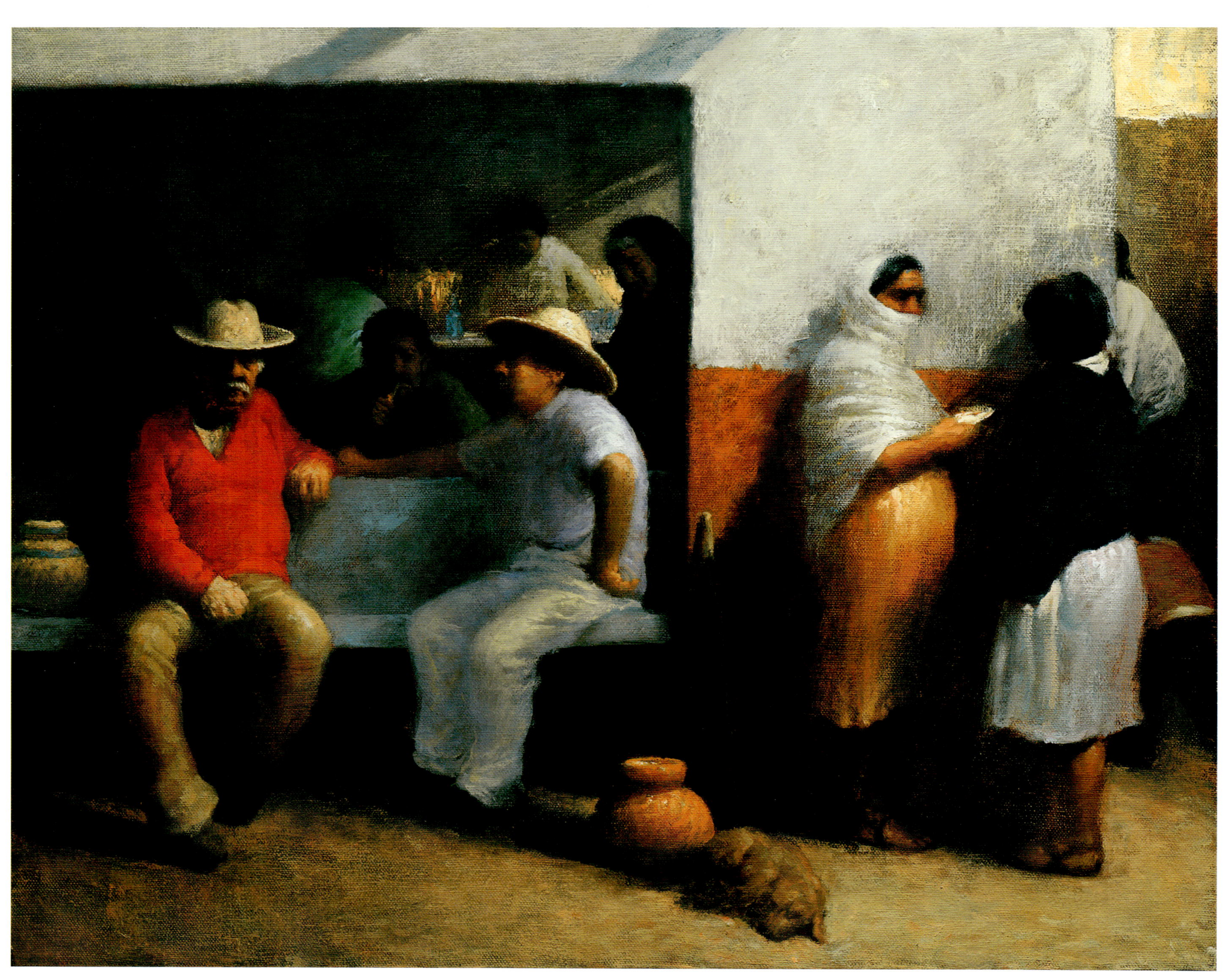

26. PATZCUARO

1982, oil on canvas, 16 × 20 inches

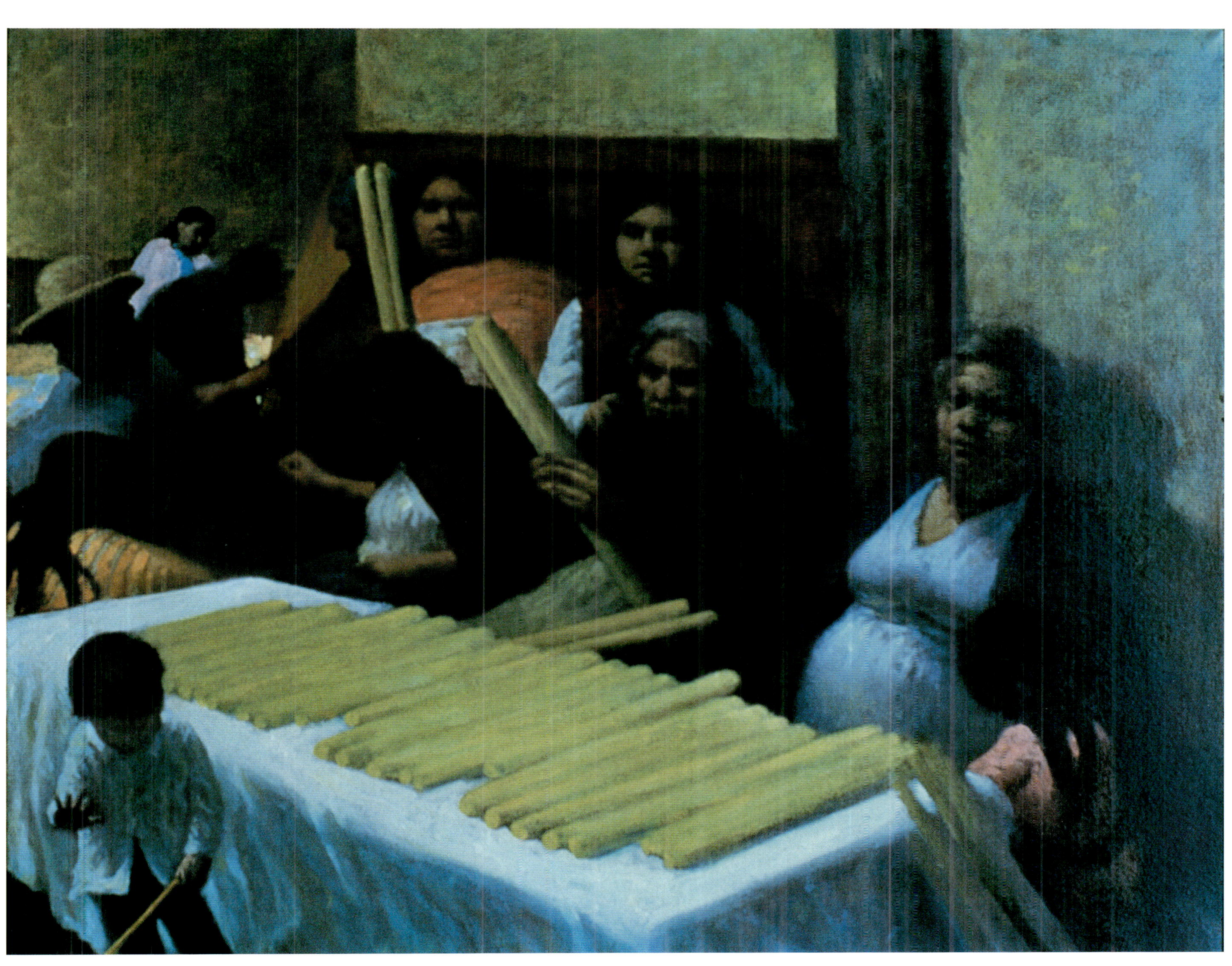

27. PATZCUARO #2

1982, oil on canvas, 16 × 20 inches

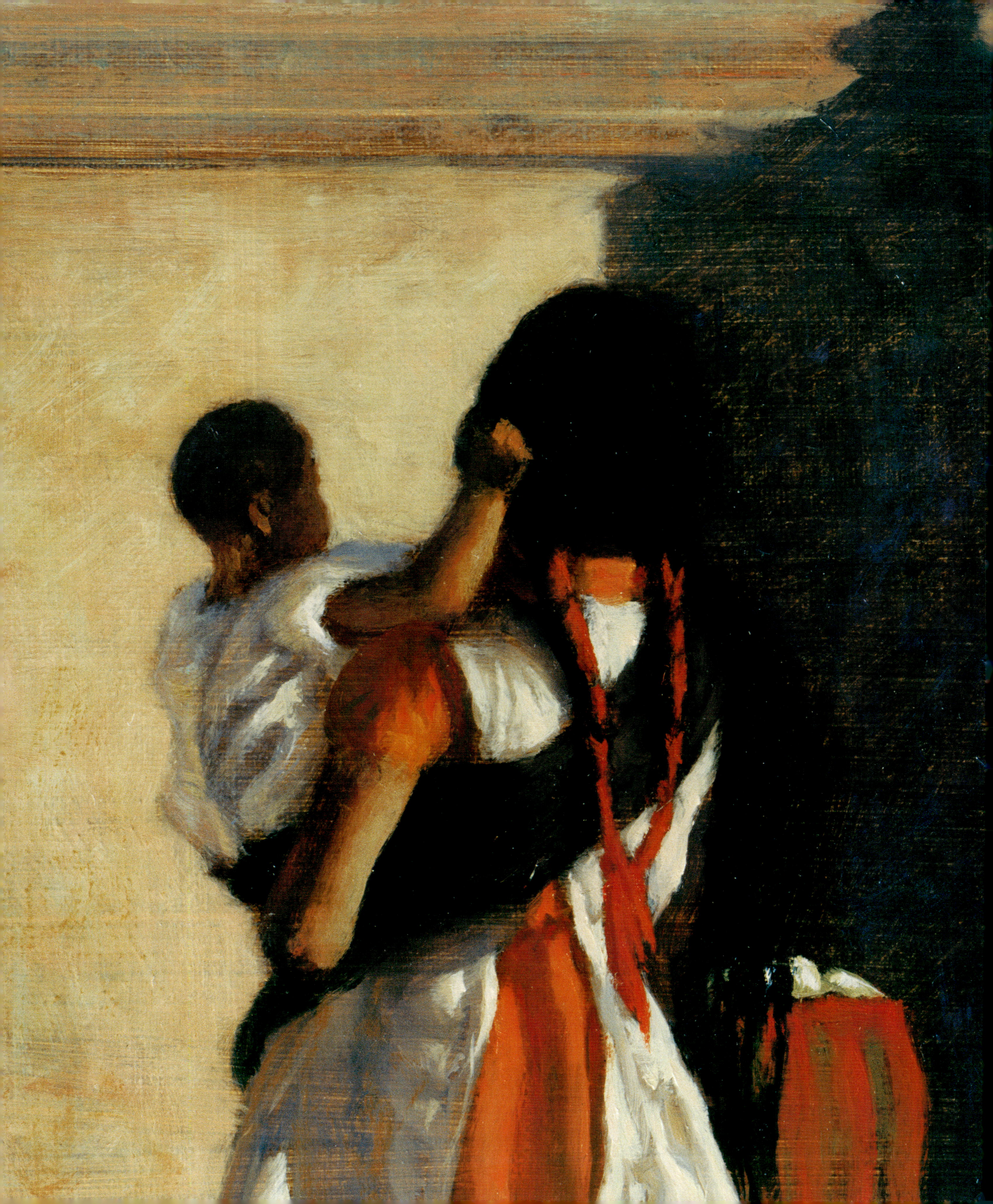

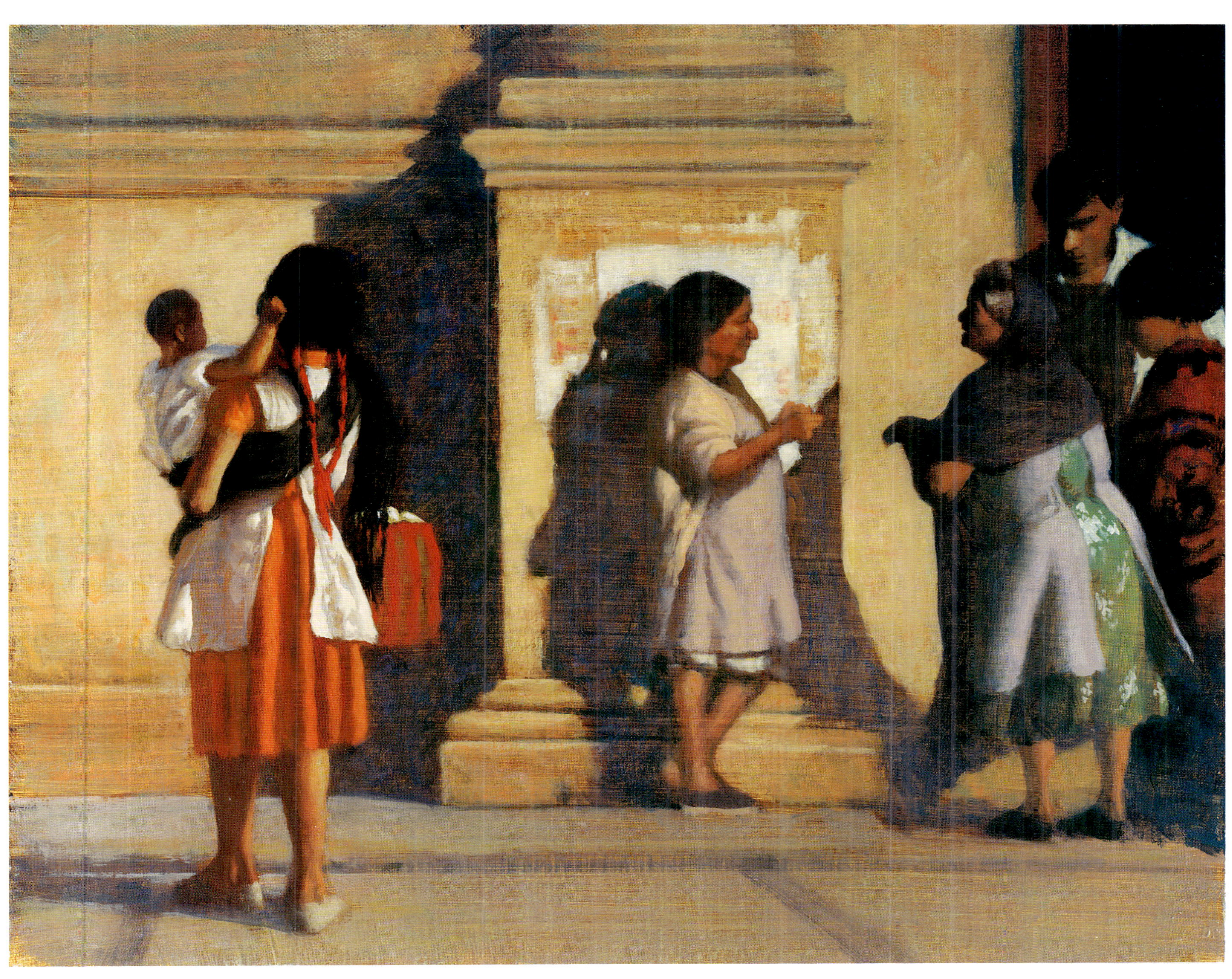

28. OAXACA #1

1983, oil on canvas, 16 × 20 inches

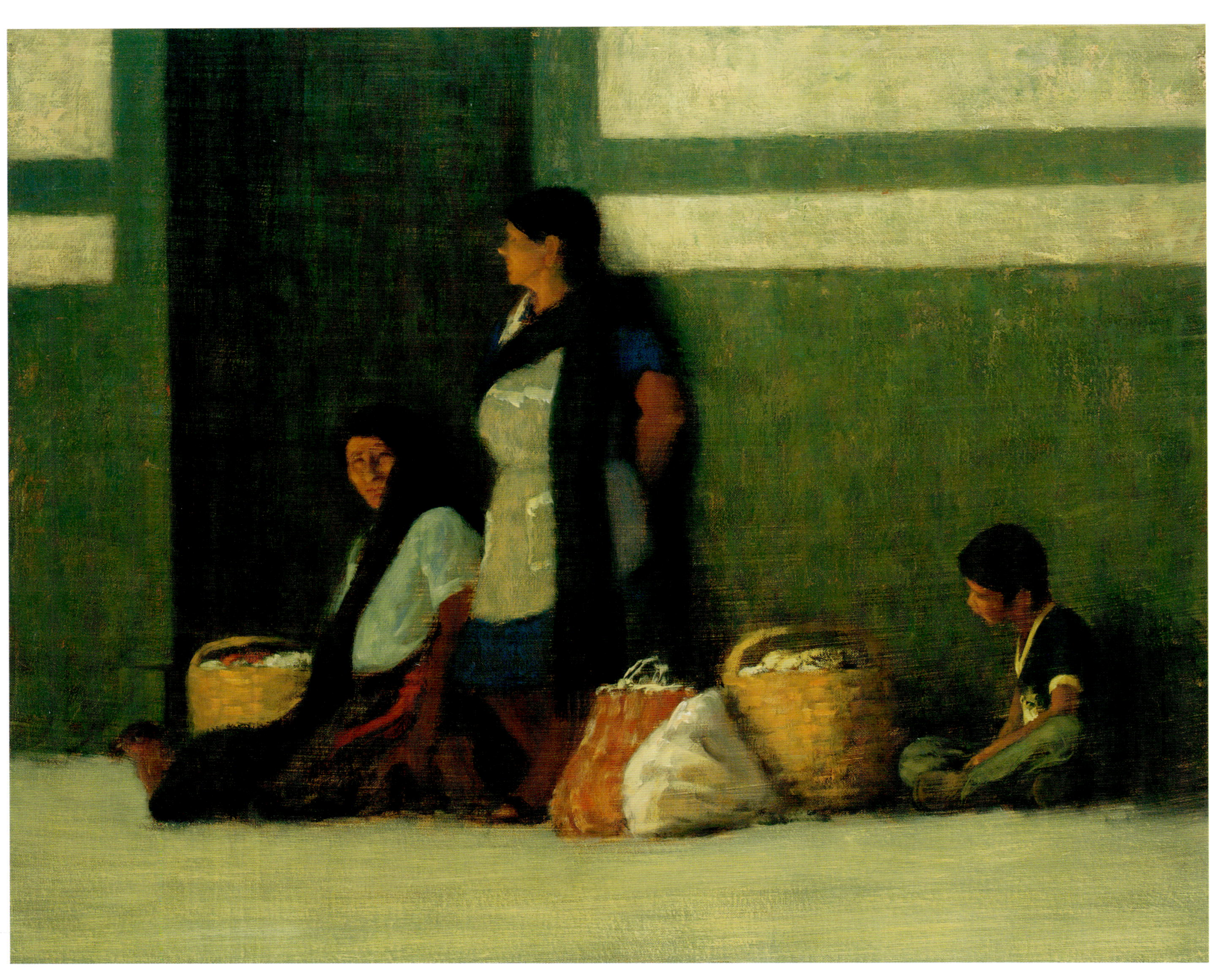

29. OAXACA #2

1983, oil on canvas, 16 × 20 inches

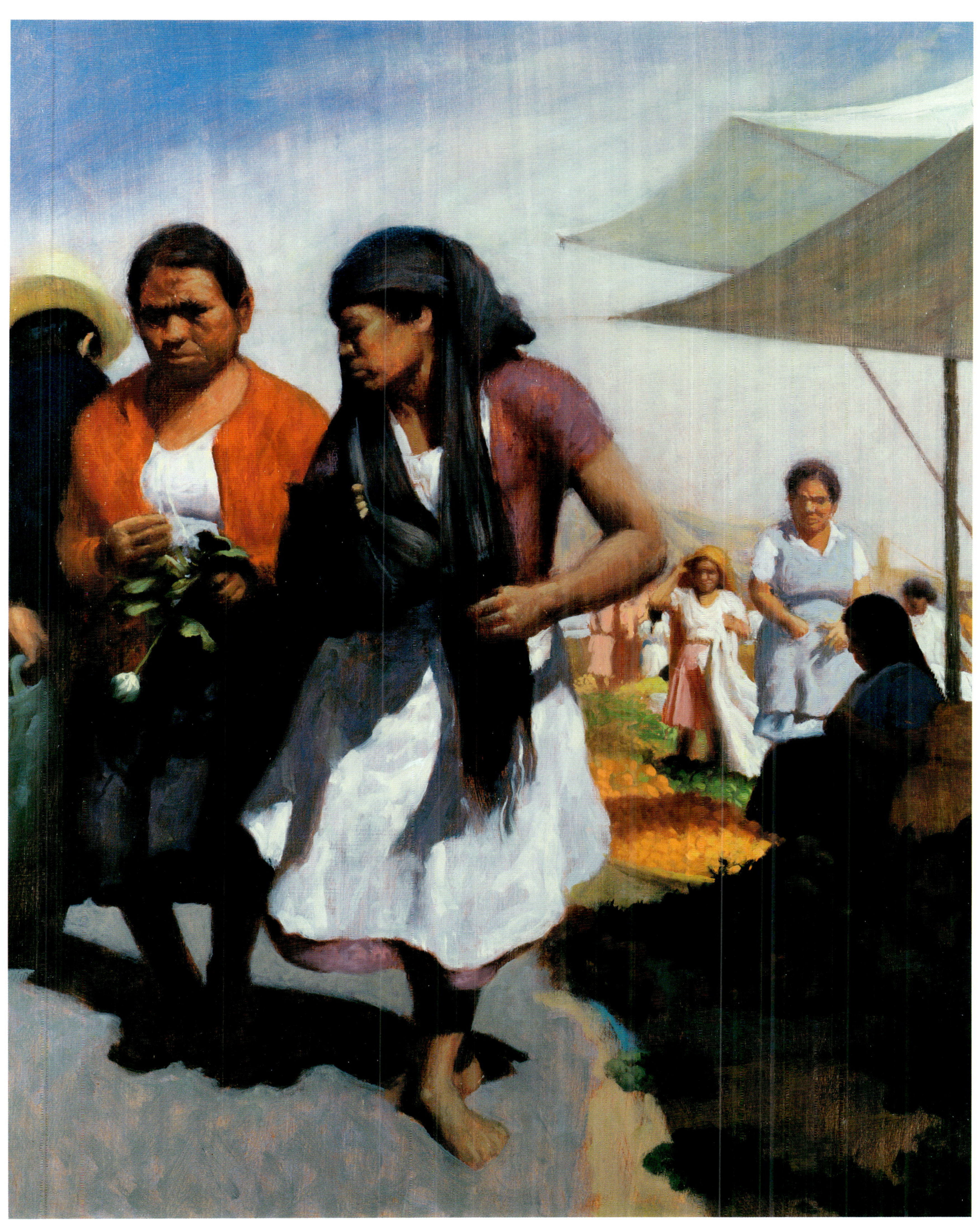

30. OAXACA MARKET #1
1983, oil on canvas, 20 × 16 inches

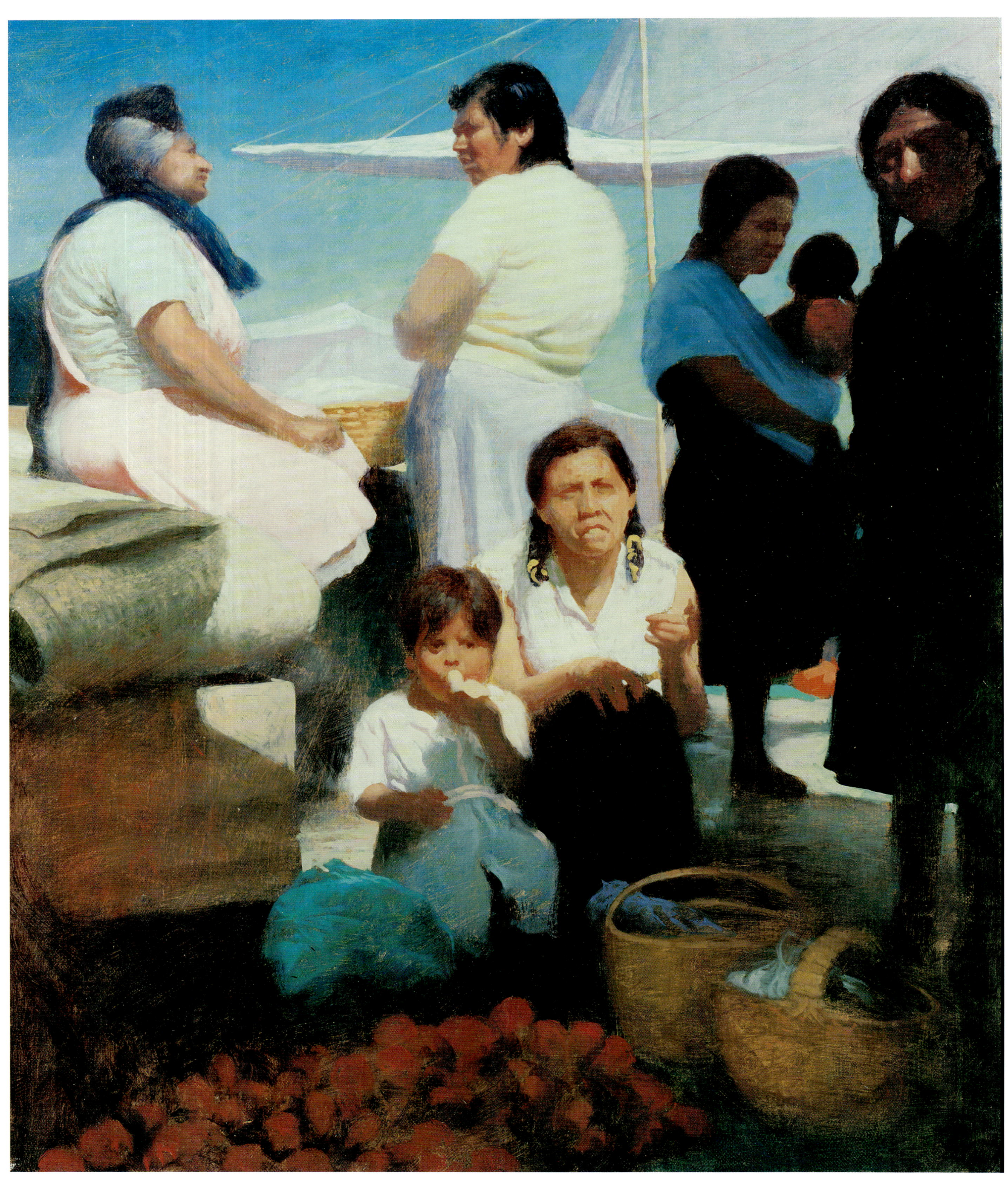

31. OAXACA MARKET #2
1983, oil on canvas, 20 × 16 inches

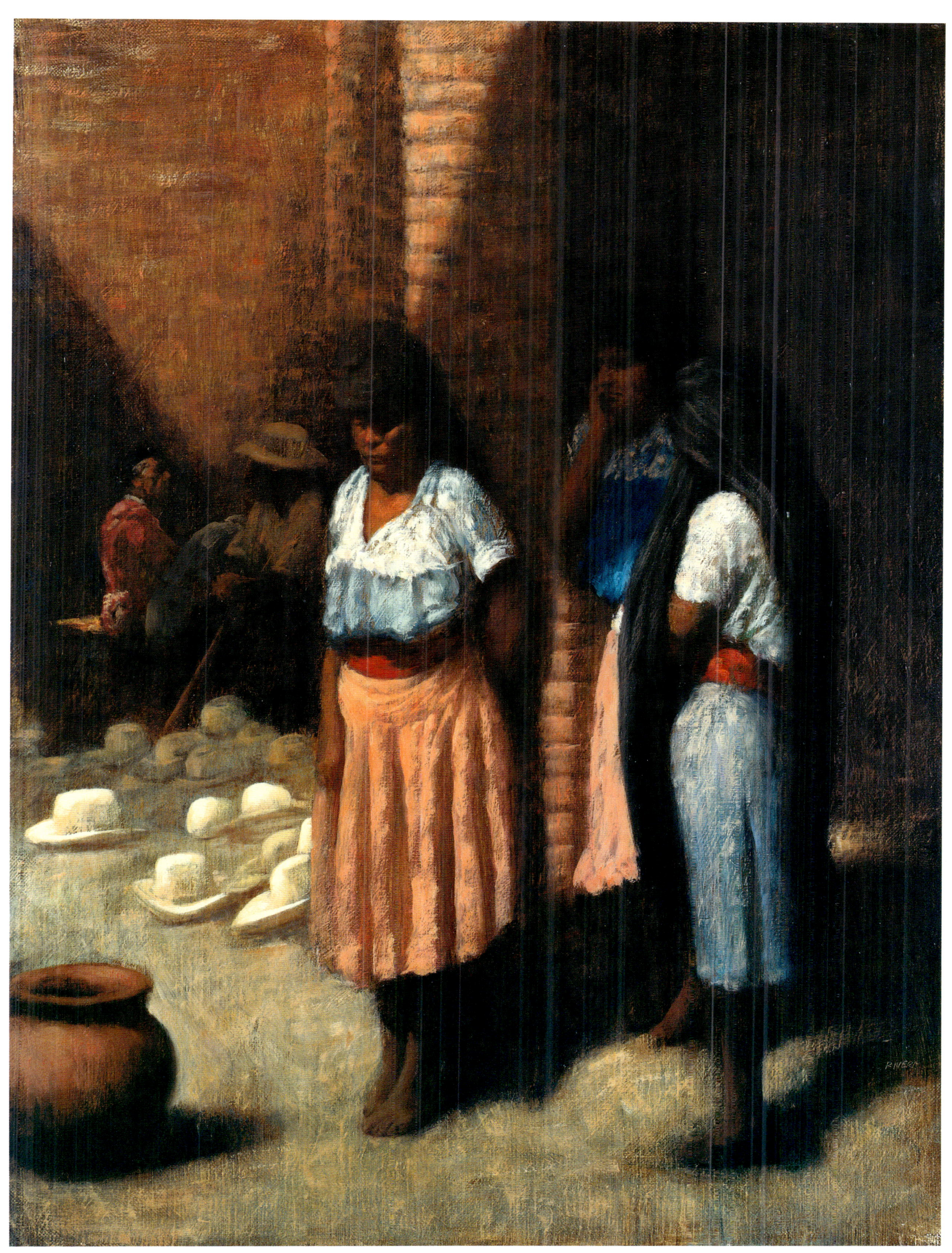

32. OAXACA MARKET #3

1984, oil on canvas, 20 × 16 inches

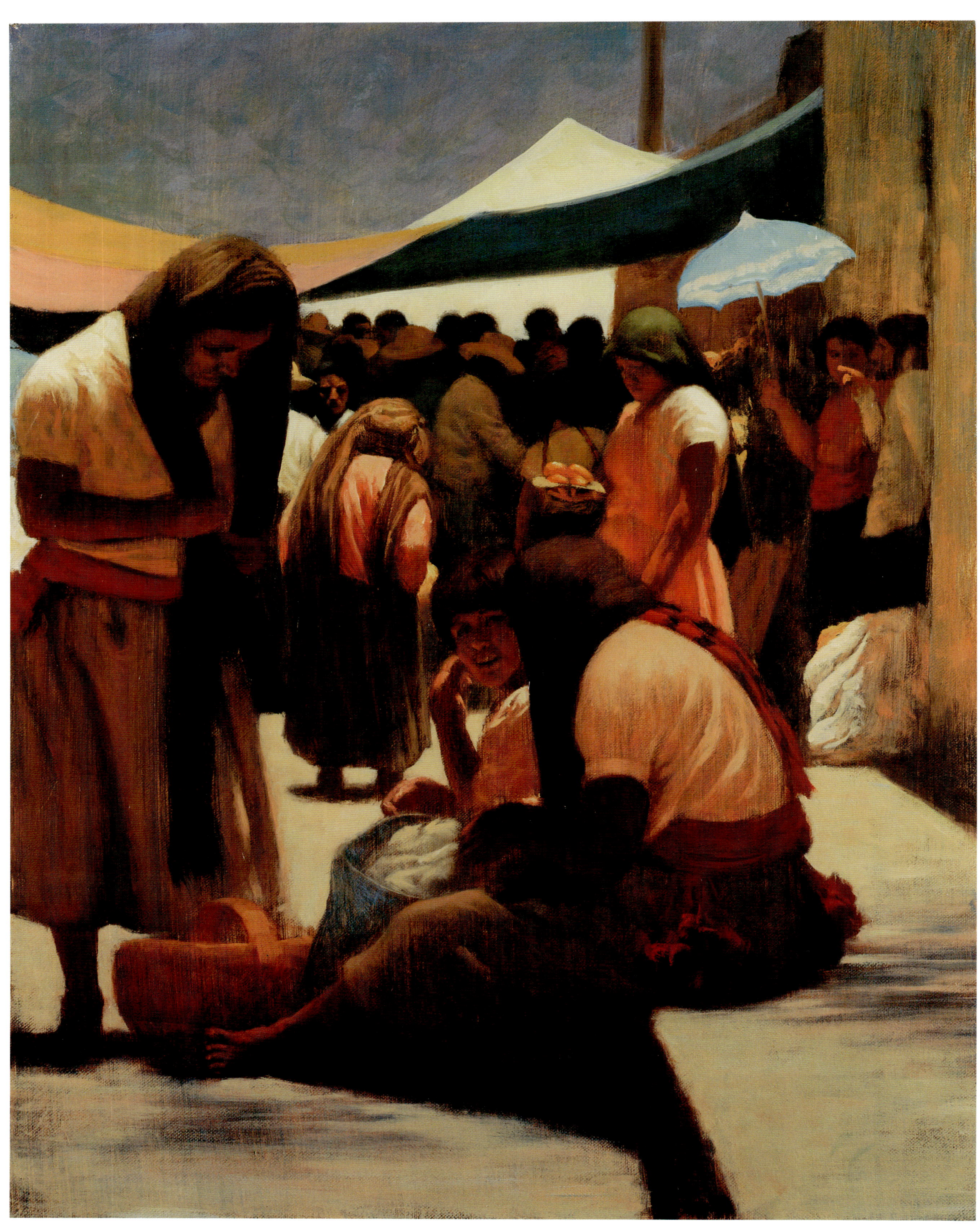

33. OAXACA MARKET #4
1984, oil on canvas, 20 × 16 inches

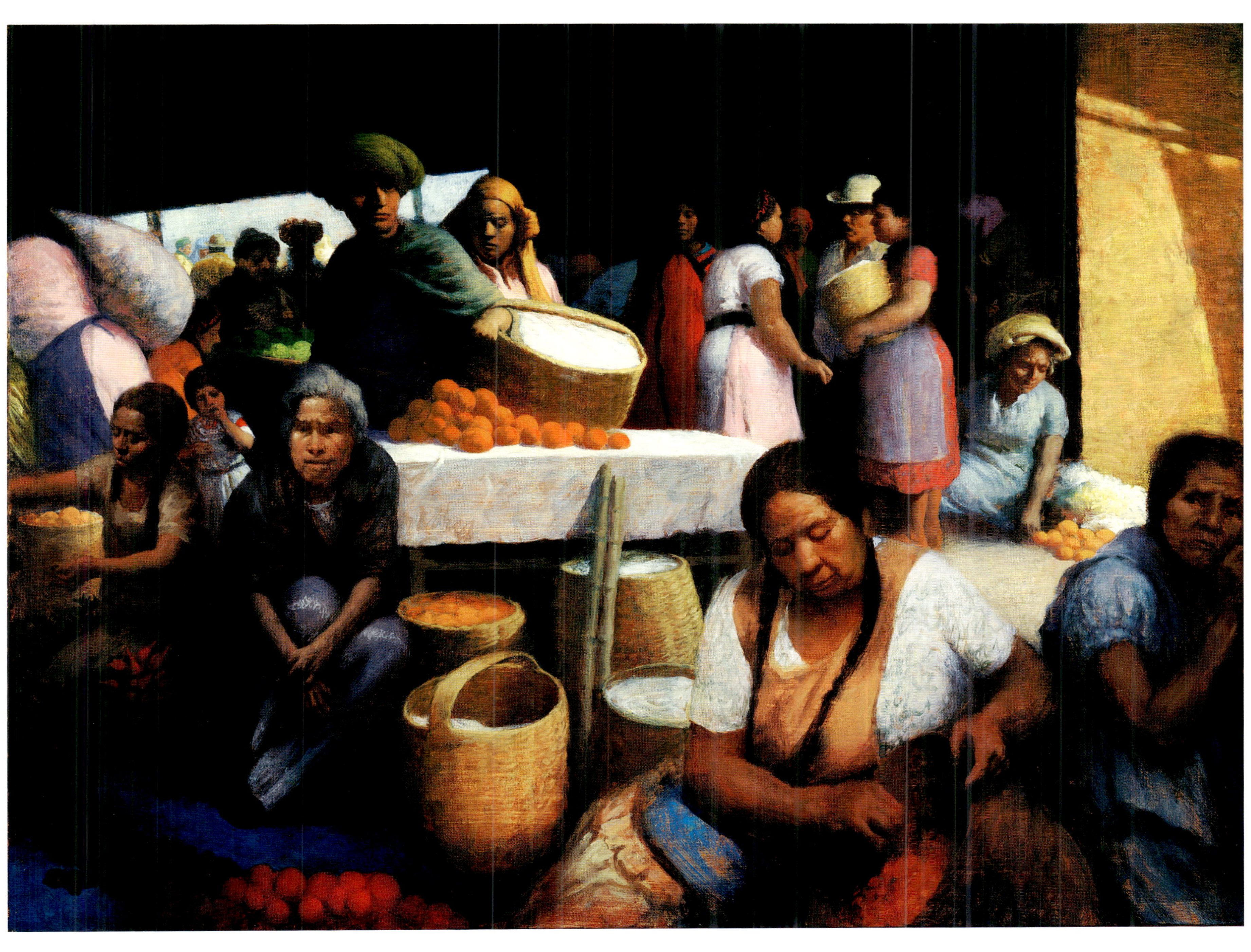

34. OAXACA MARKET

1984, oil on canvas, 30 × 40 inches

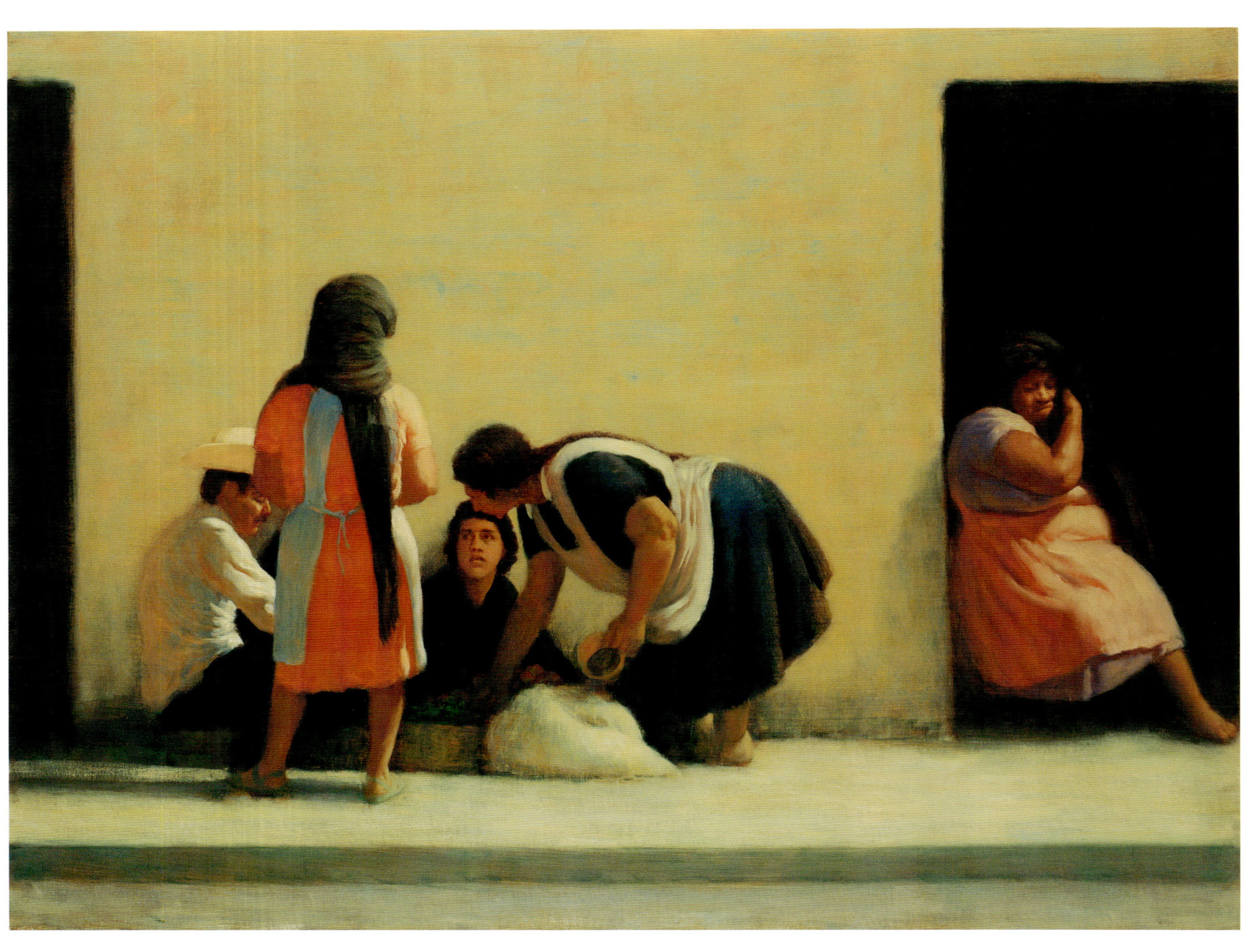

35. OAXACA #11

1984, oil on canvas, 16 × 20 inches

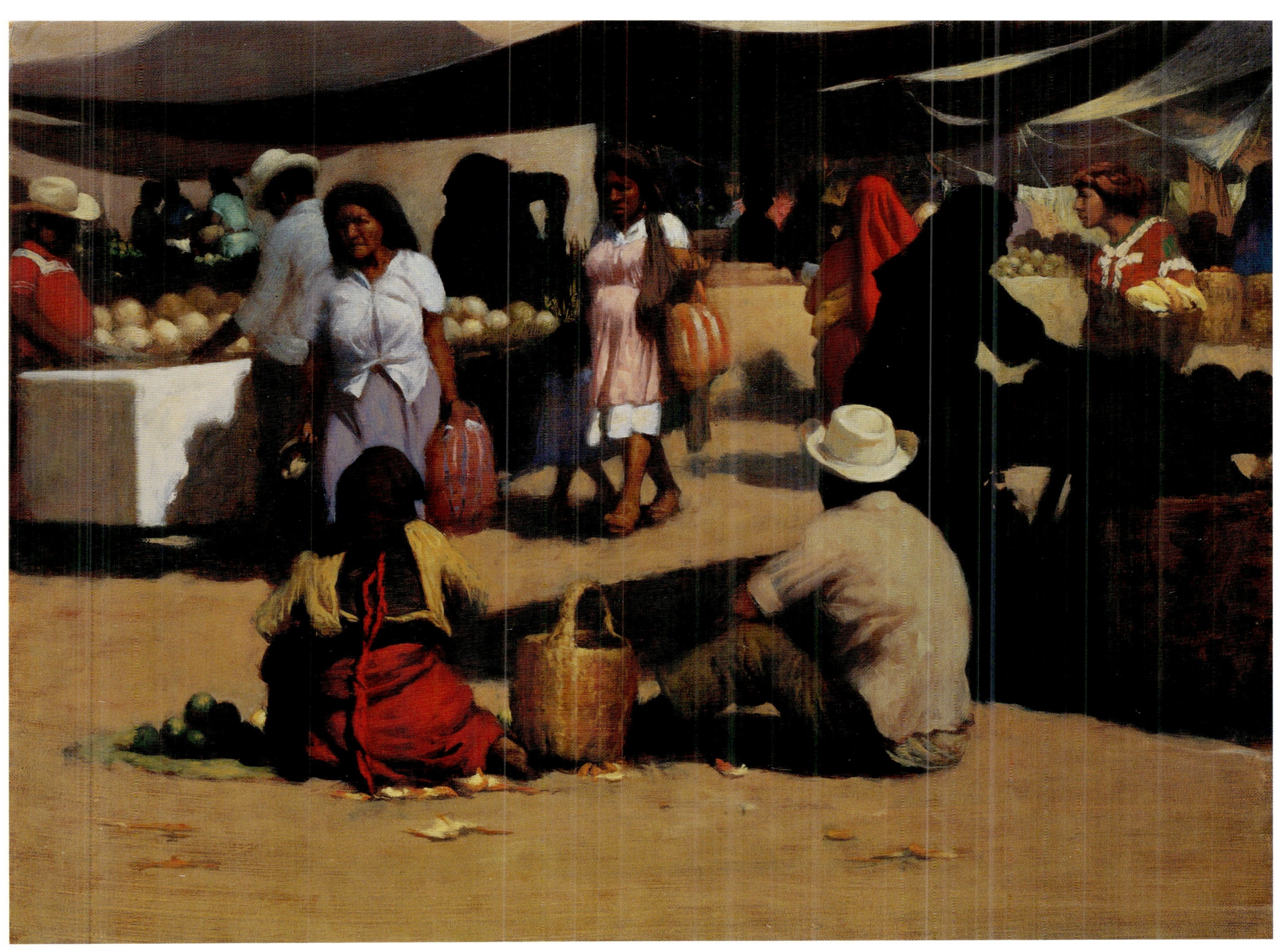

36. OAXACA #12
1984, oil on canvas, 20 × 24 inches

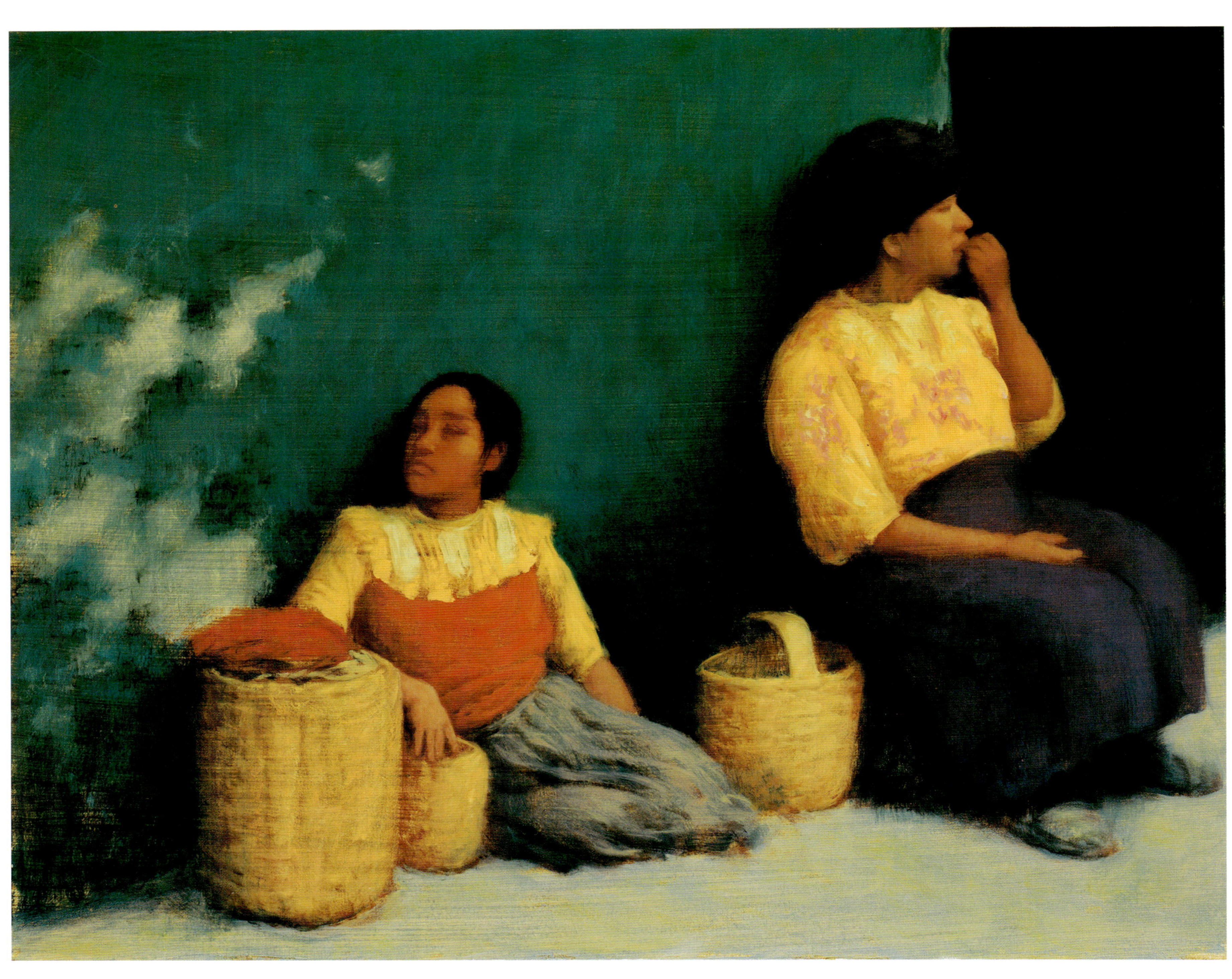

37. OAXACA #20

1984, oil on canvas, 16 × 20 inches

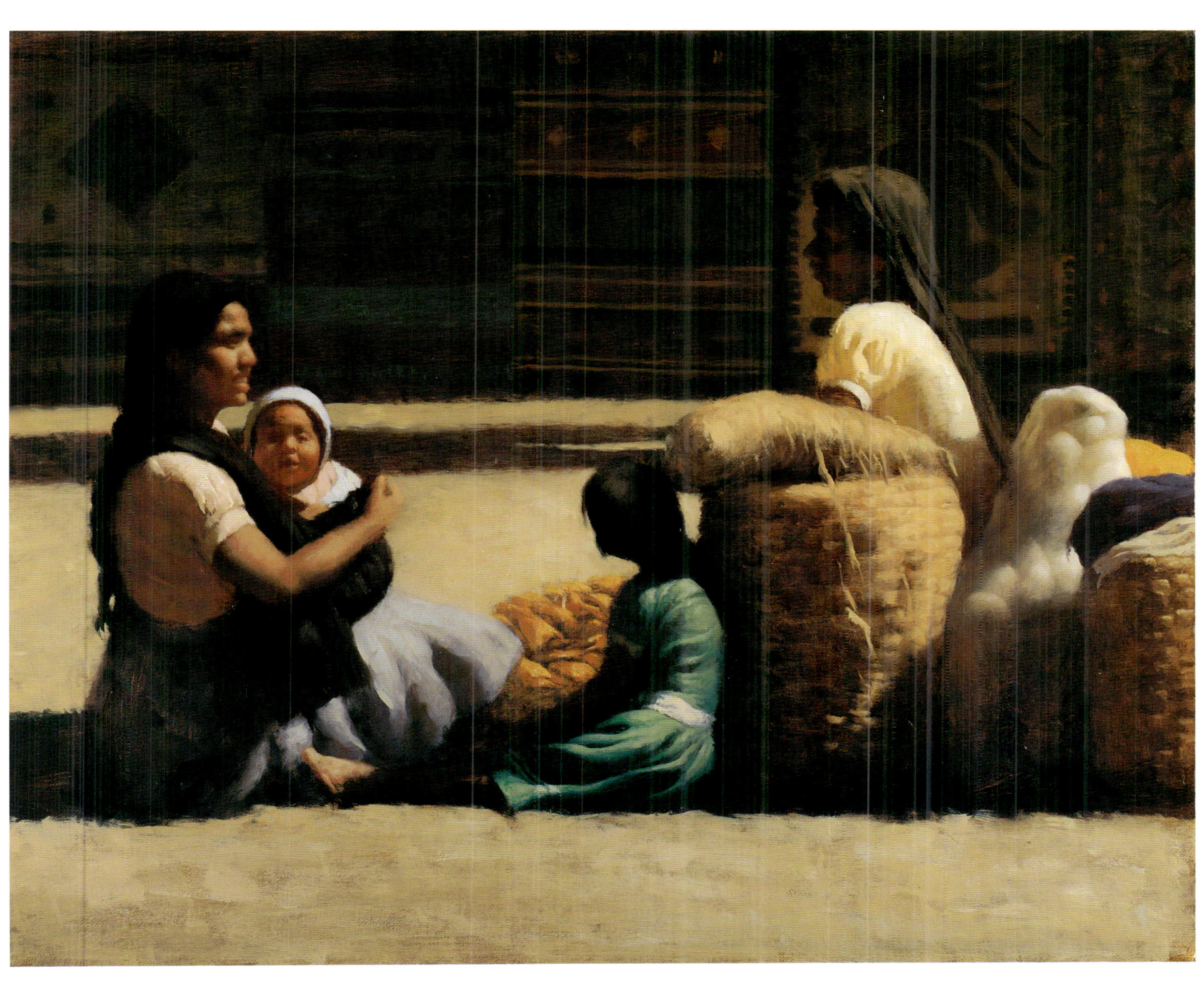

38. OAXACA #21

1584, oil on canvas, 16 × 20 inches

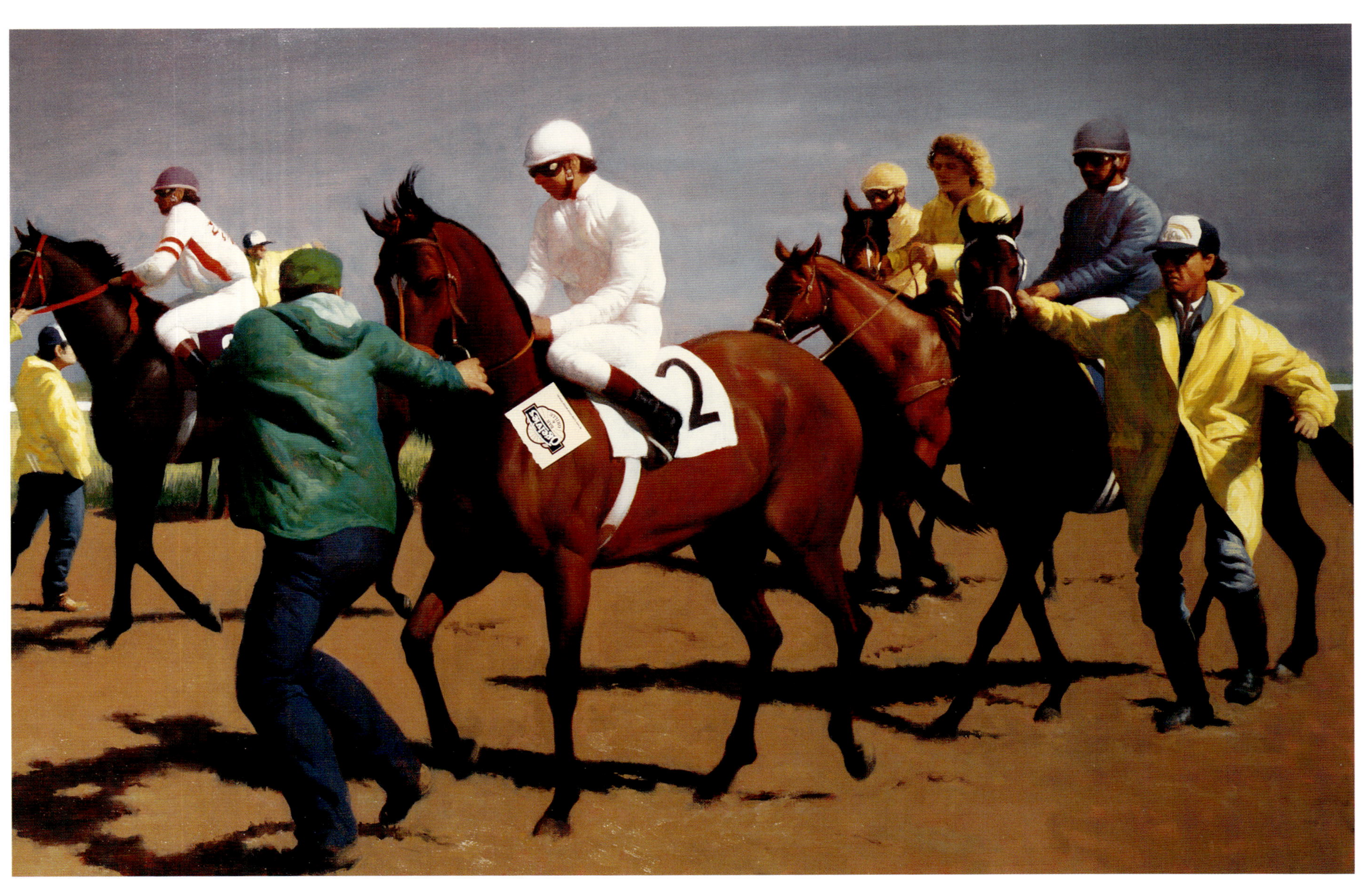

39. GATESMAN AT THE DOWNS

1984, oil on canvas, 26 × 40 inches

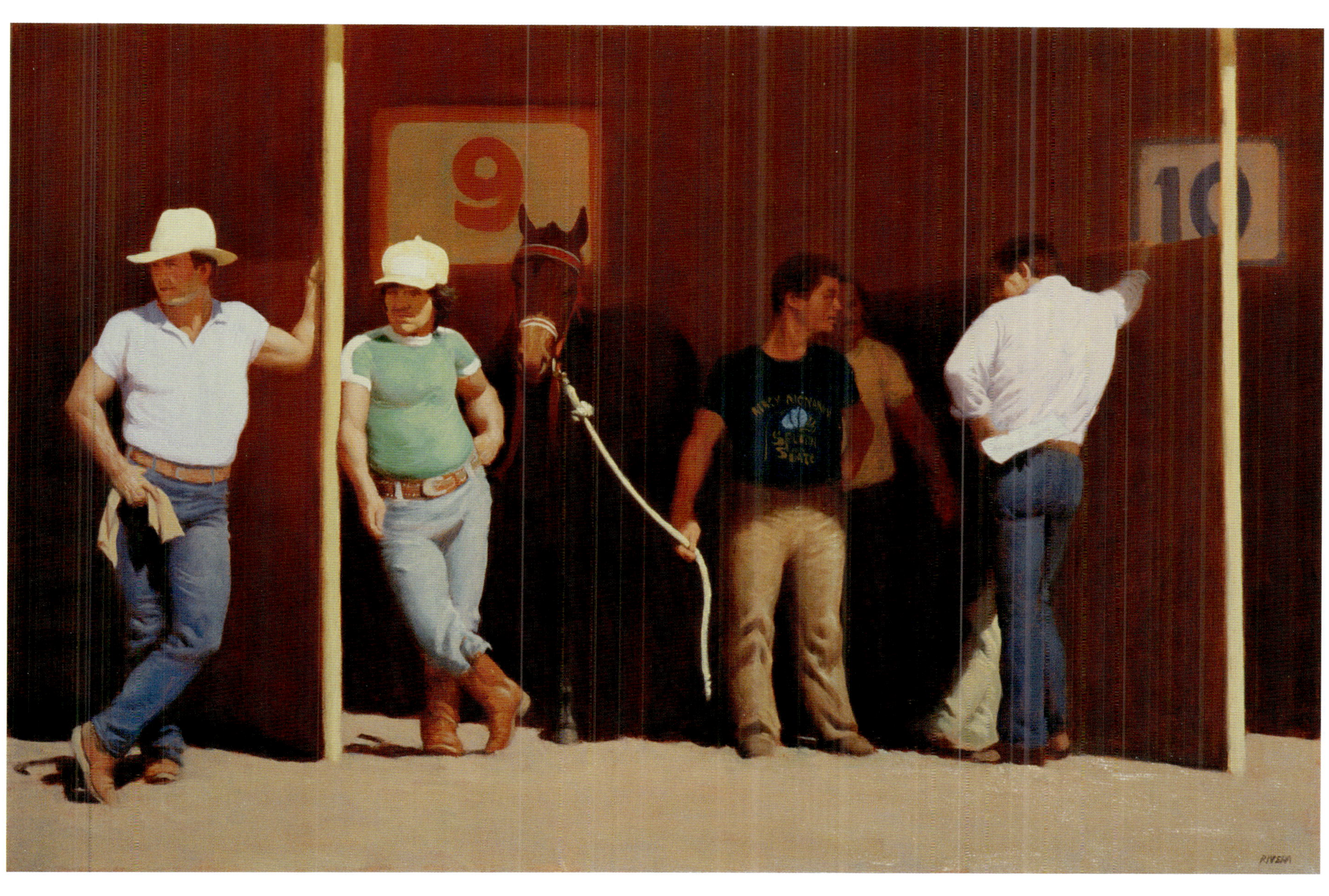

40. WAITING AT THE PADDOCKS

1984, oil on canvas, 20 × 30 inches

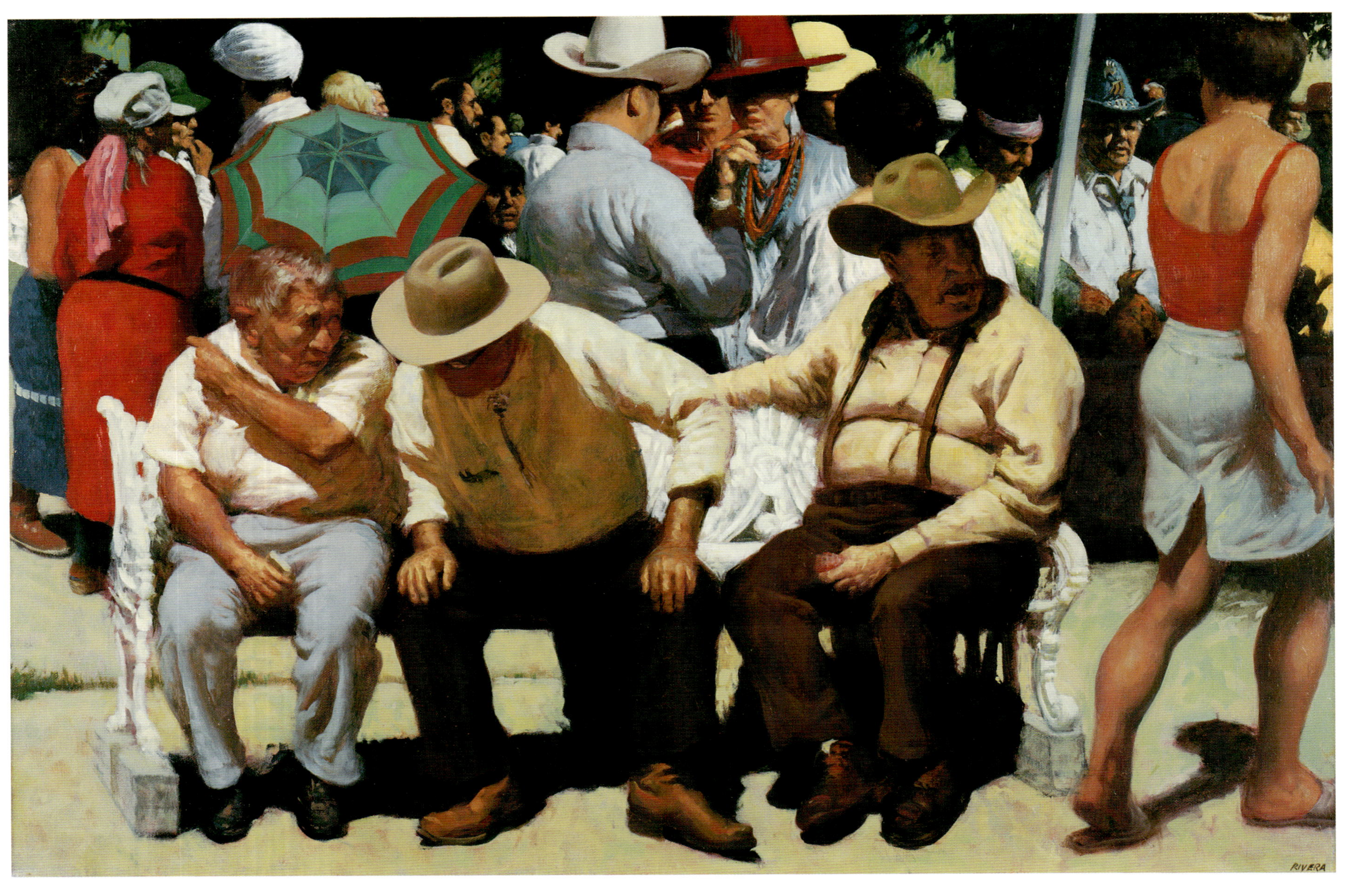

41. FIESTA AT SANTA FE

1985, oil on canvas, 20 × 30 inches

Collection of the Museum of Fine Arts, MNM, Department of Cultural Affairs

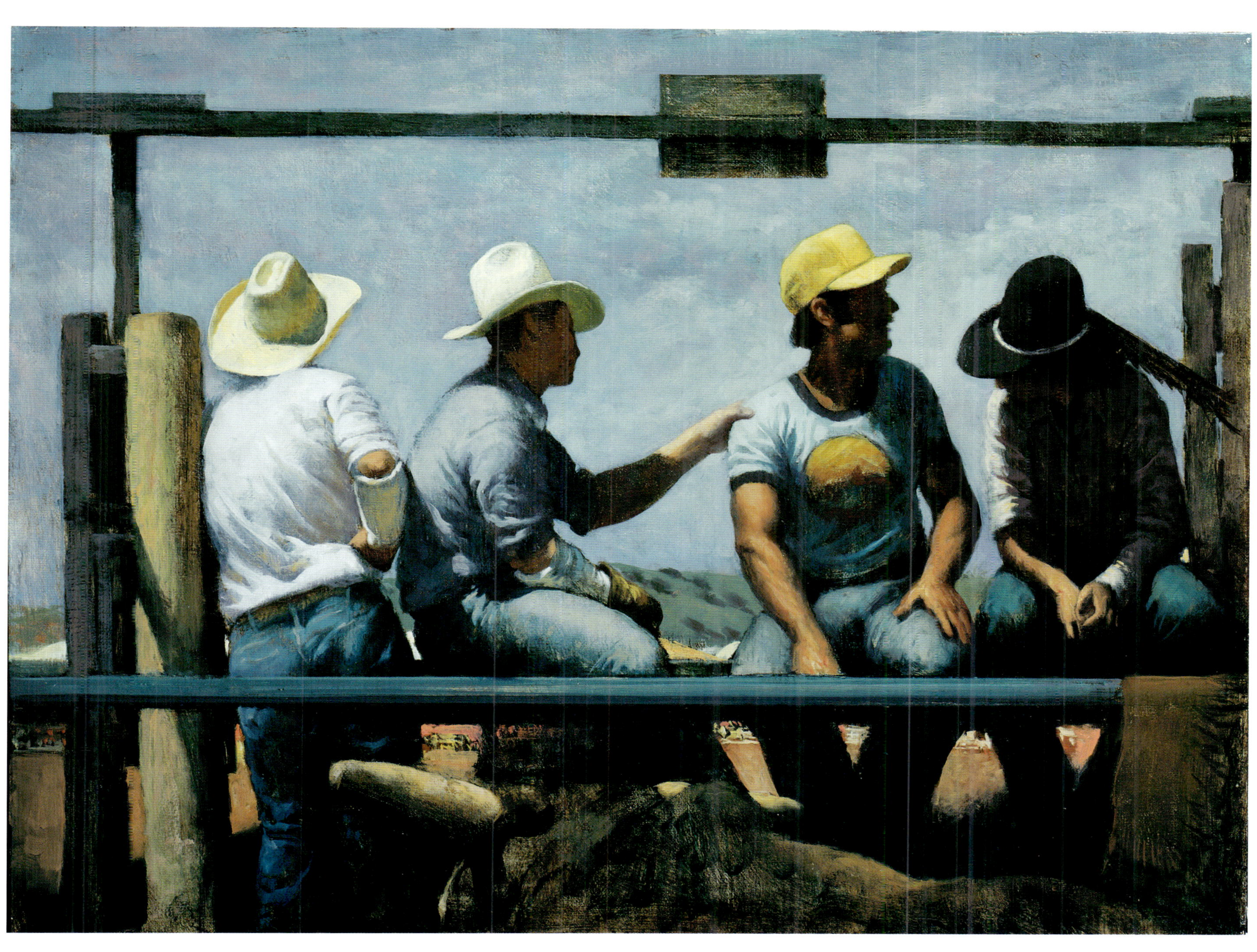

42 GALISTEO RODEO
1986, oil on canvas, 20 × 24 inches

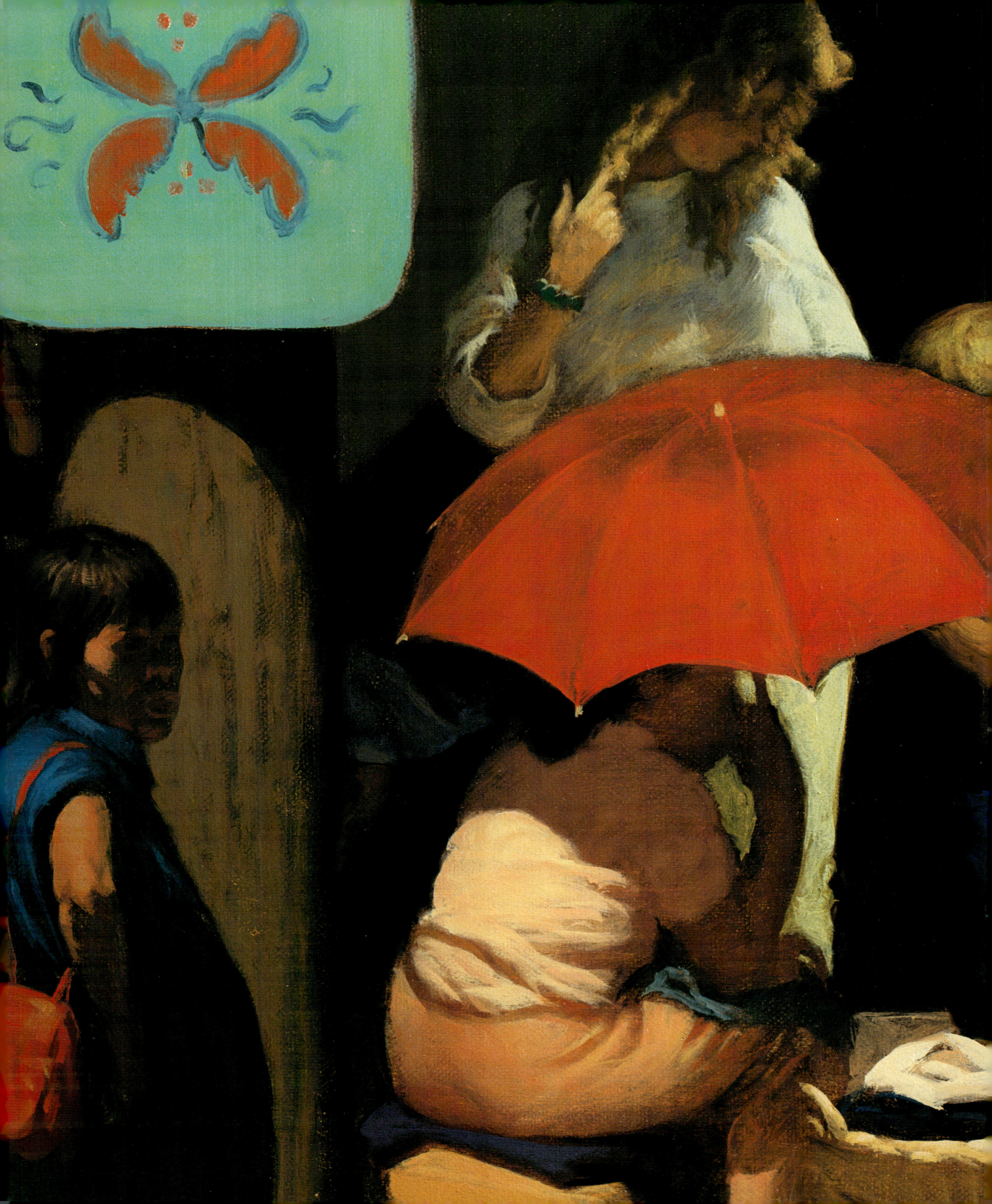

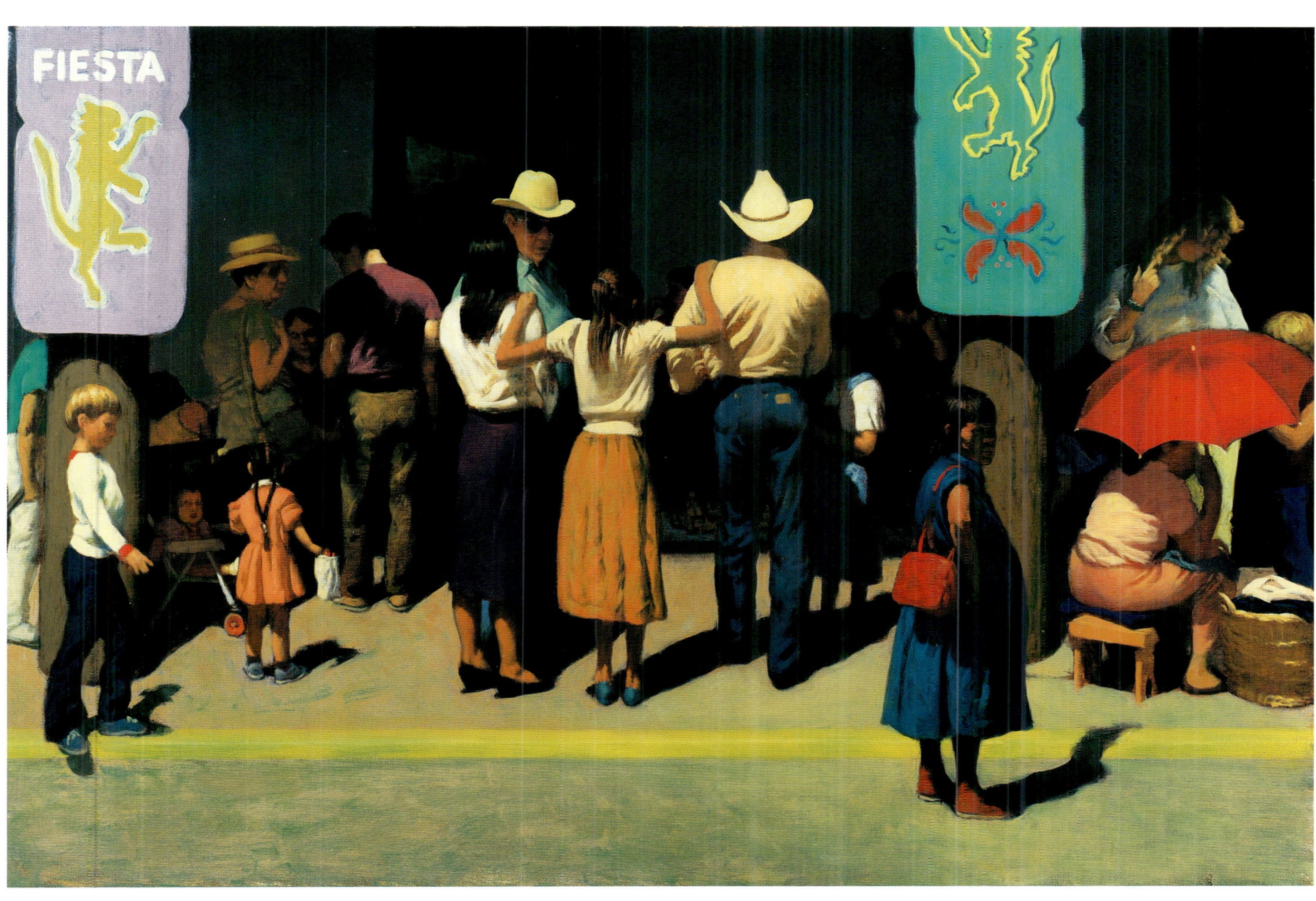

43. FIESTA

1986, oil on canvas, 20 × 30 inches

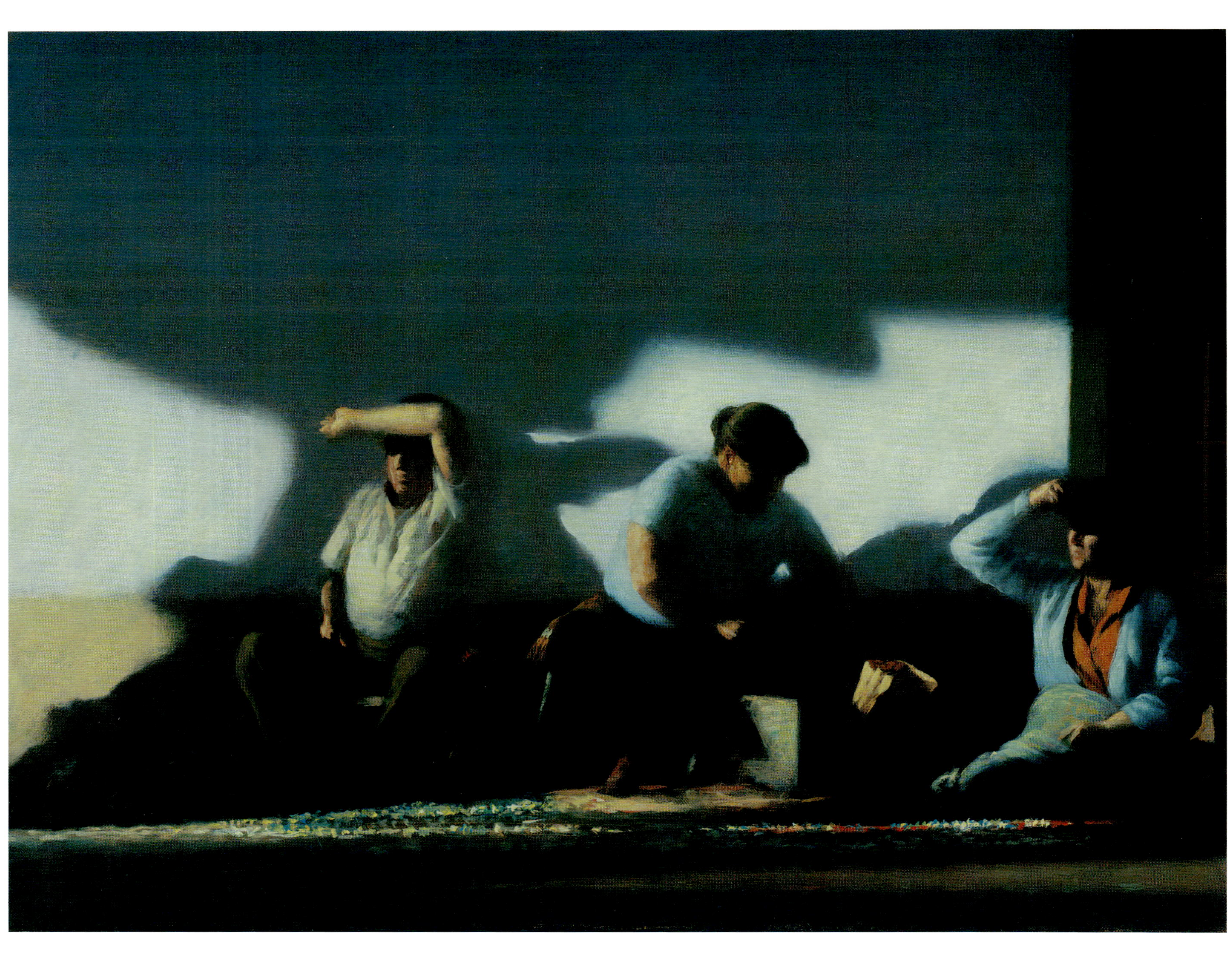

44. UNDER THE PORTAL #1
1986, oil on canvas, 16 × 20 inches

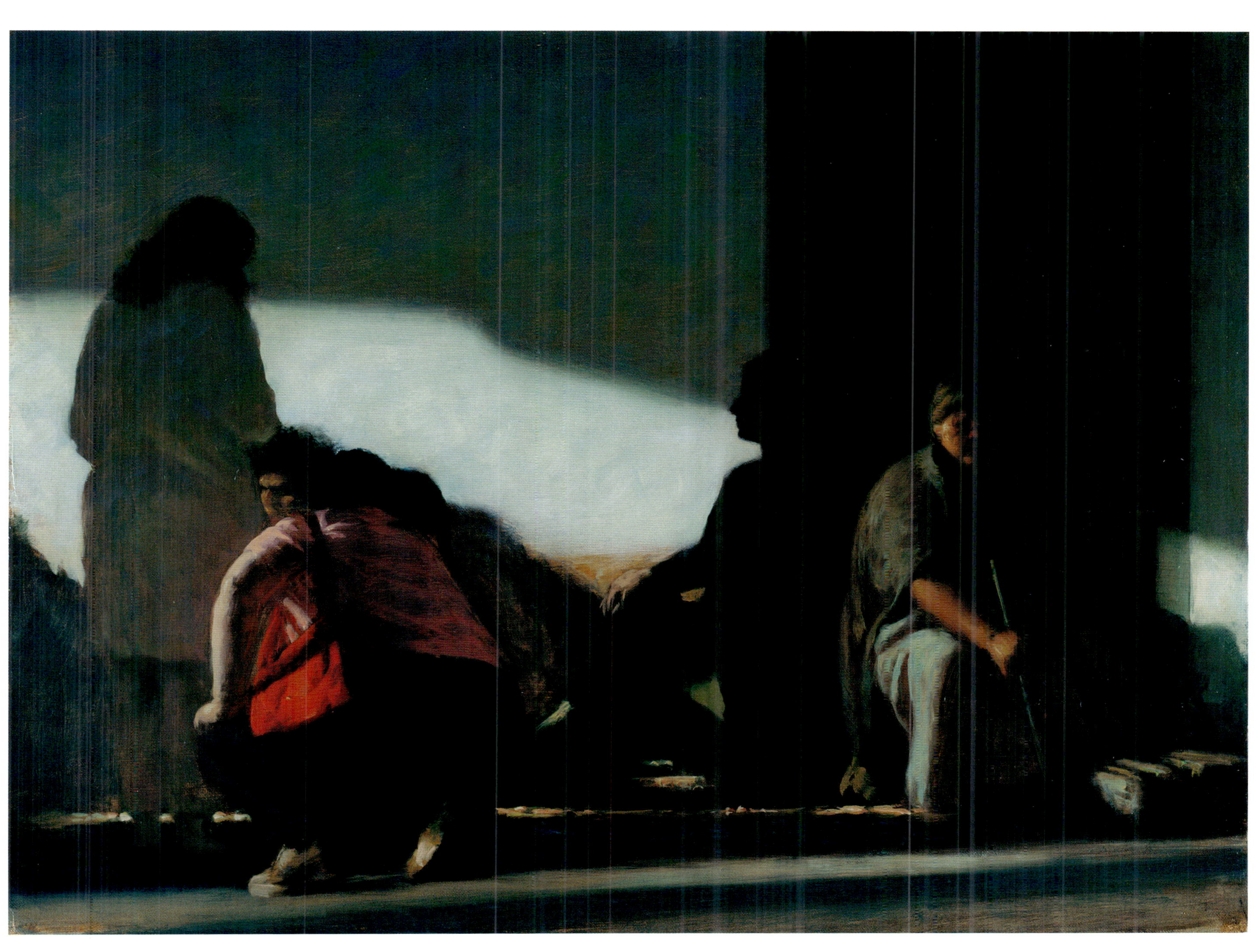

45 UNDER THE PORTAL #2

1986, oil on canvas, 16 × 20 inches

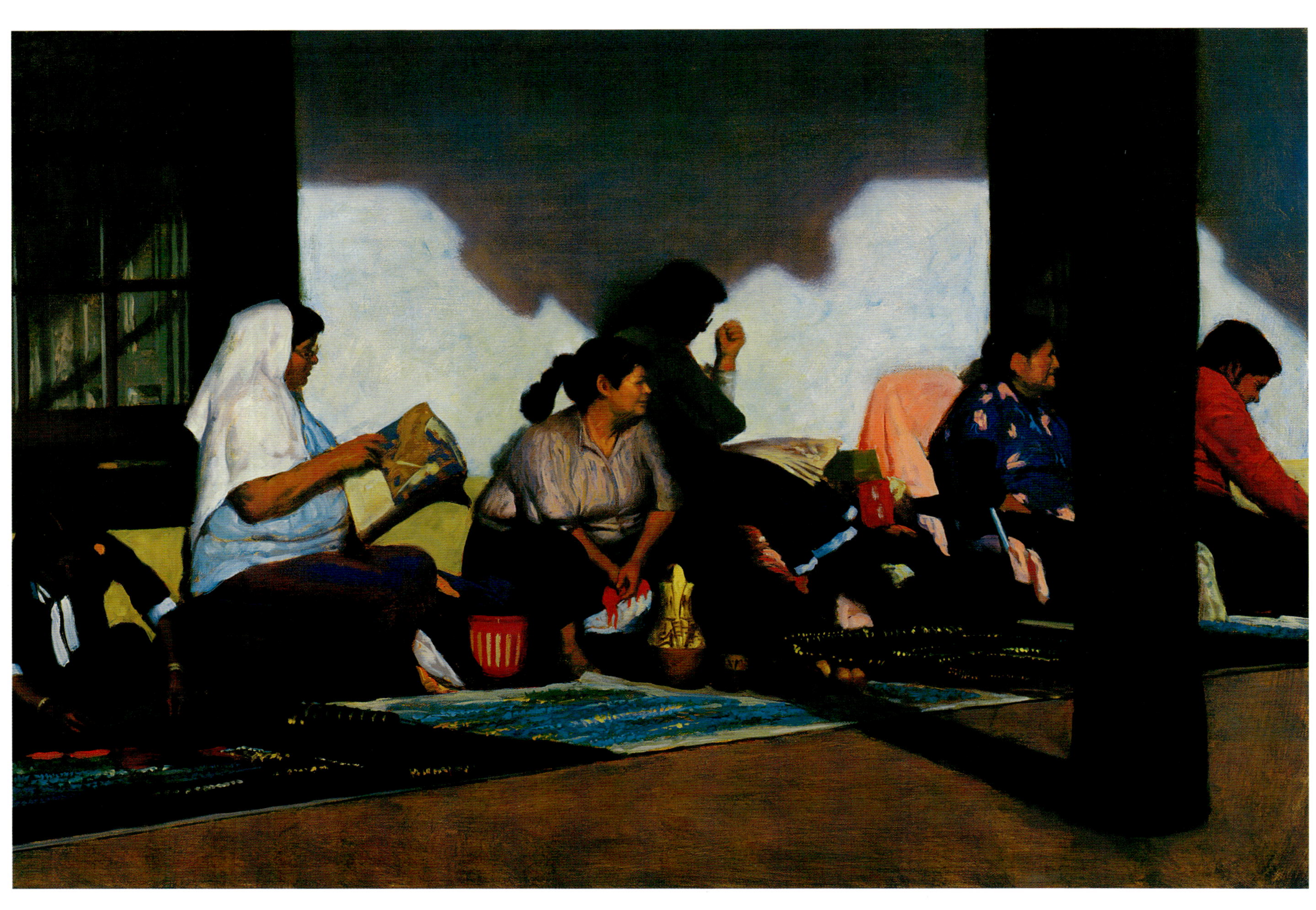

46. UNDER THE PORTAL #4
1986, oil on canvas, 20 × 30 inches

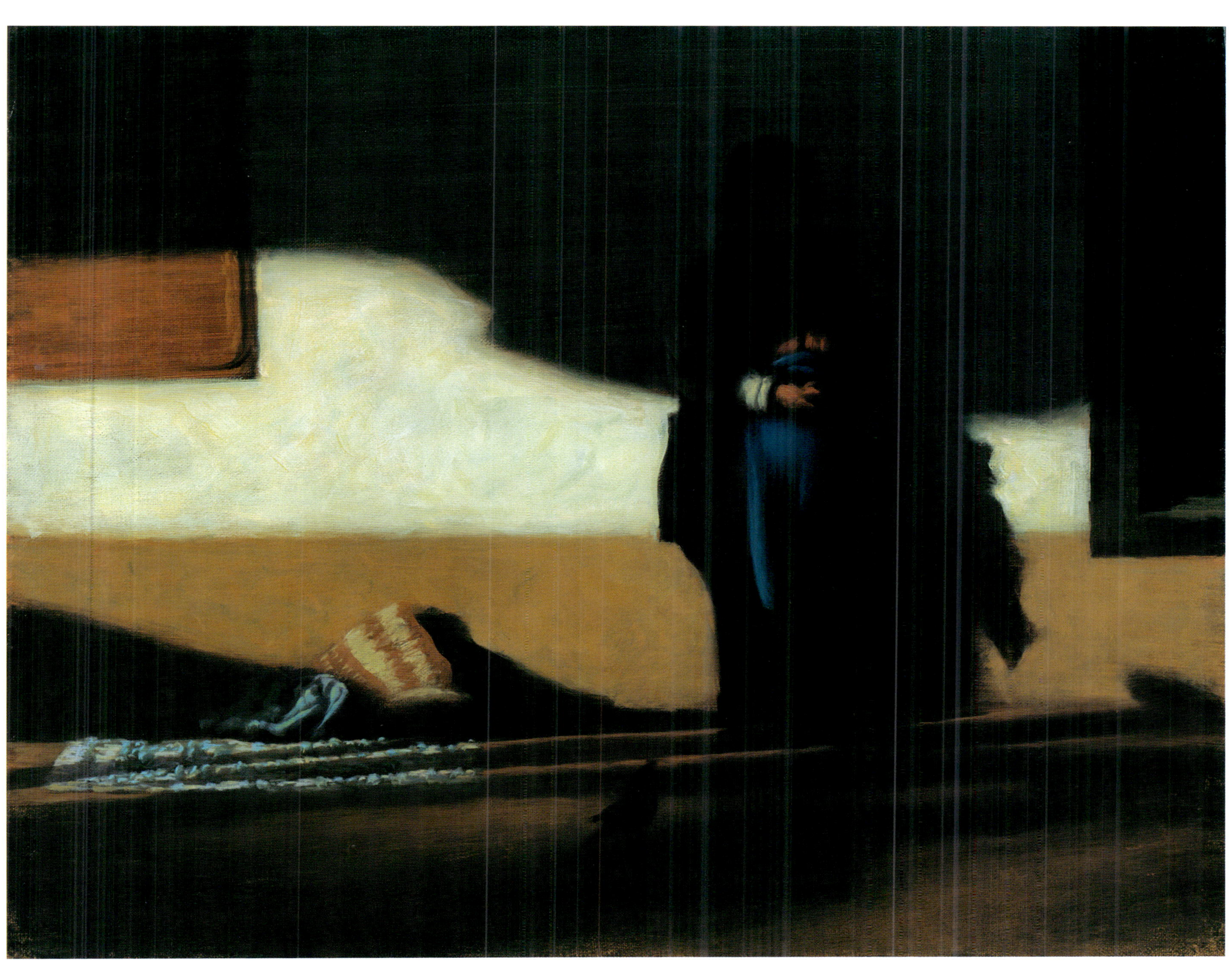

47. UNDER THE PORTAL #5

1986, oil on canvas, 20 × 24 inches

48. UNDER THE PORTAL OF SANTA FE
1988, oil on canvas, 41 × 76 inches
Albuquerque International Sunport Art Collection

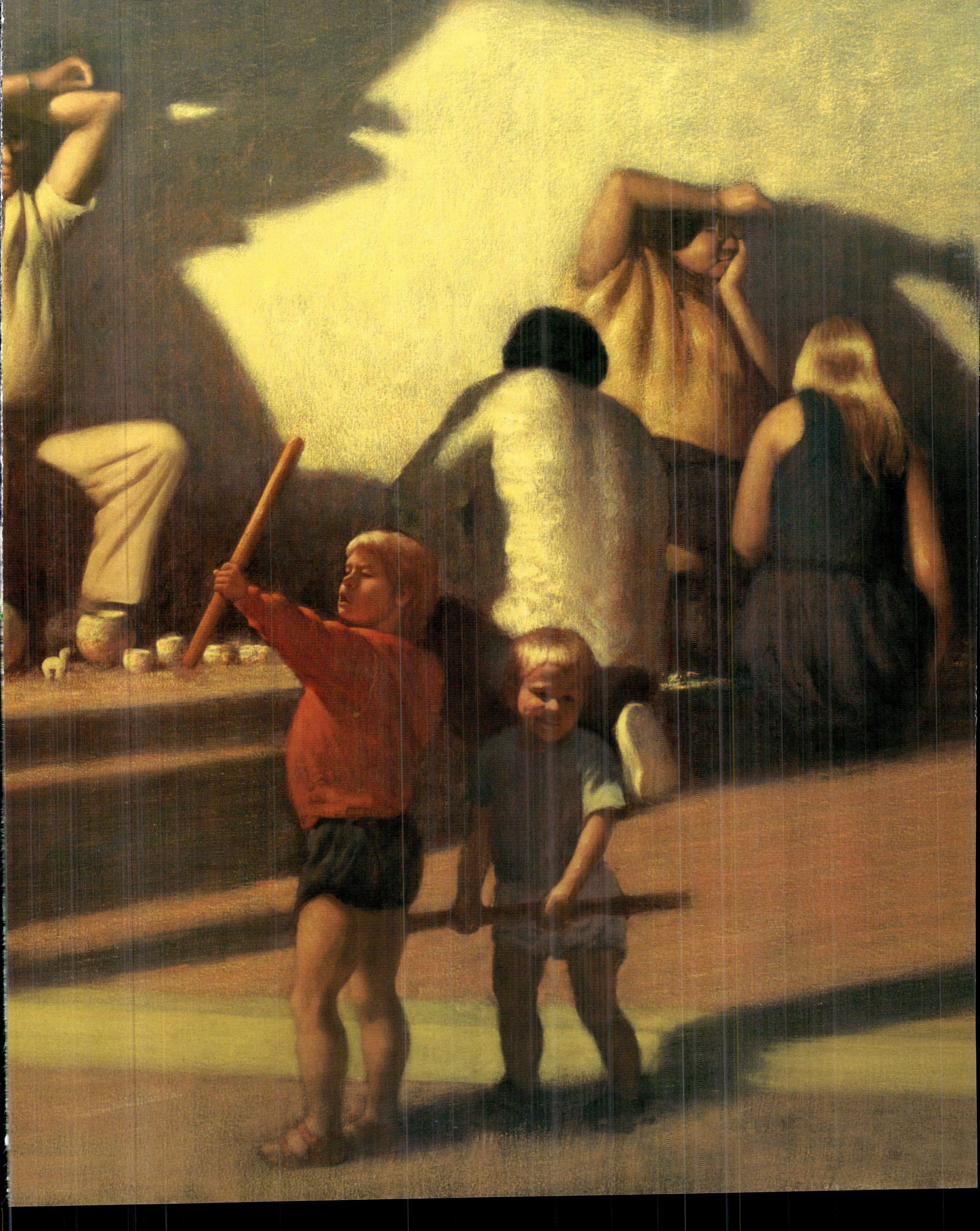

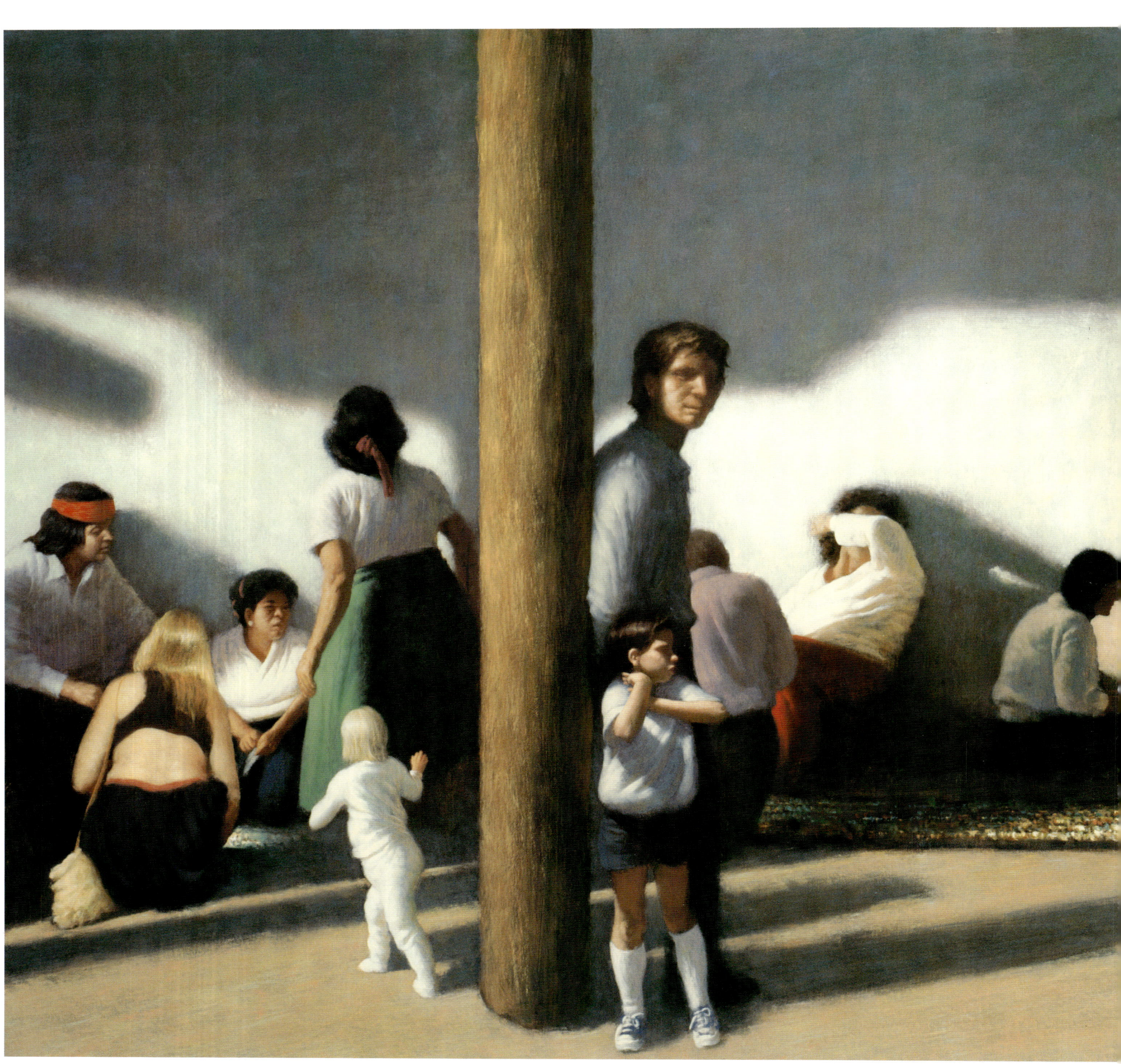

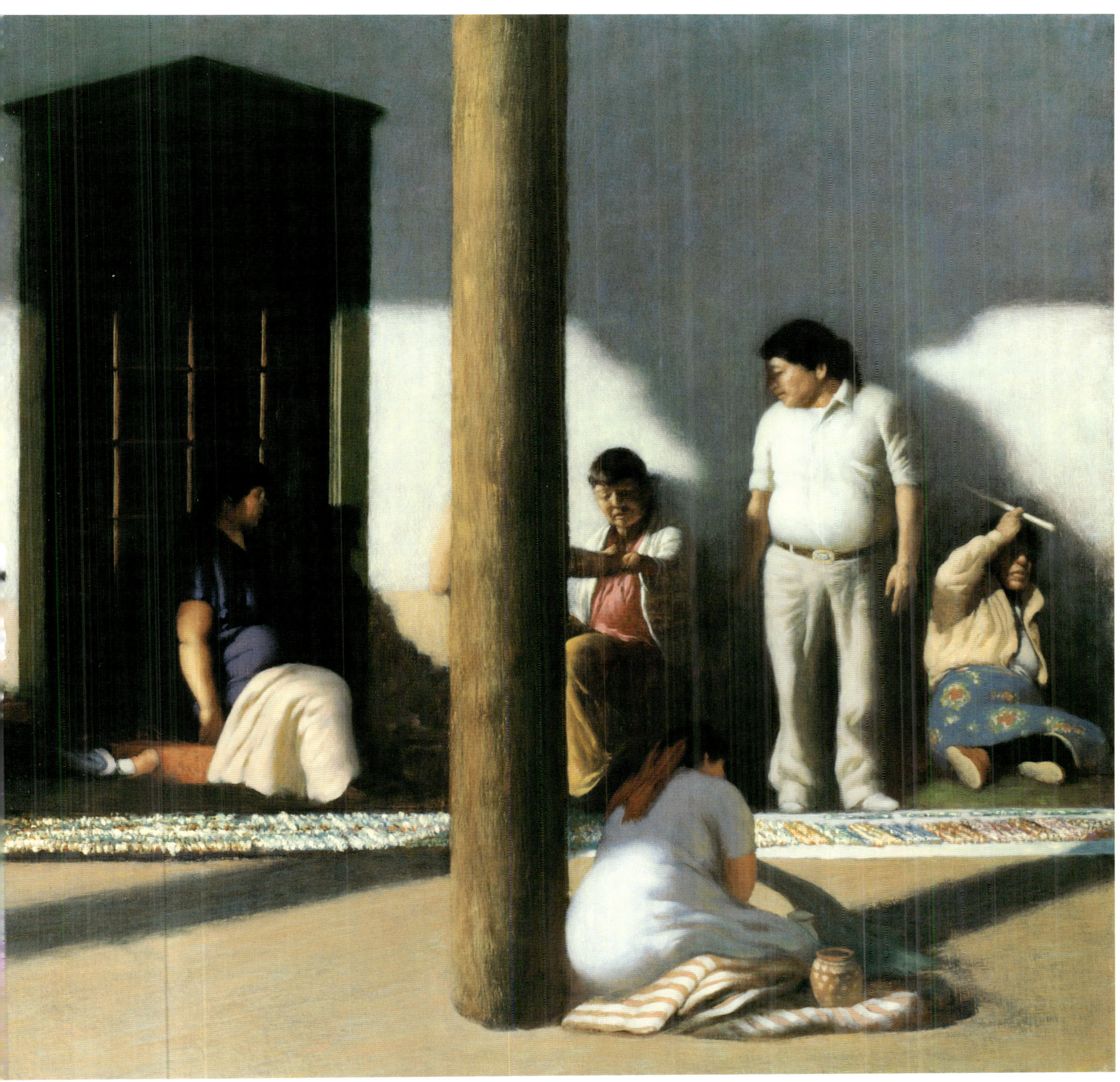

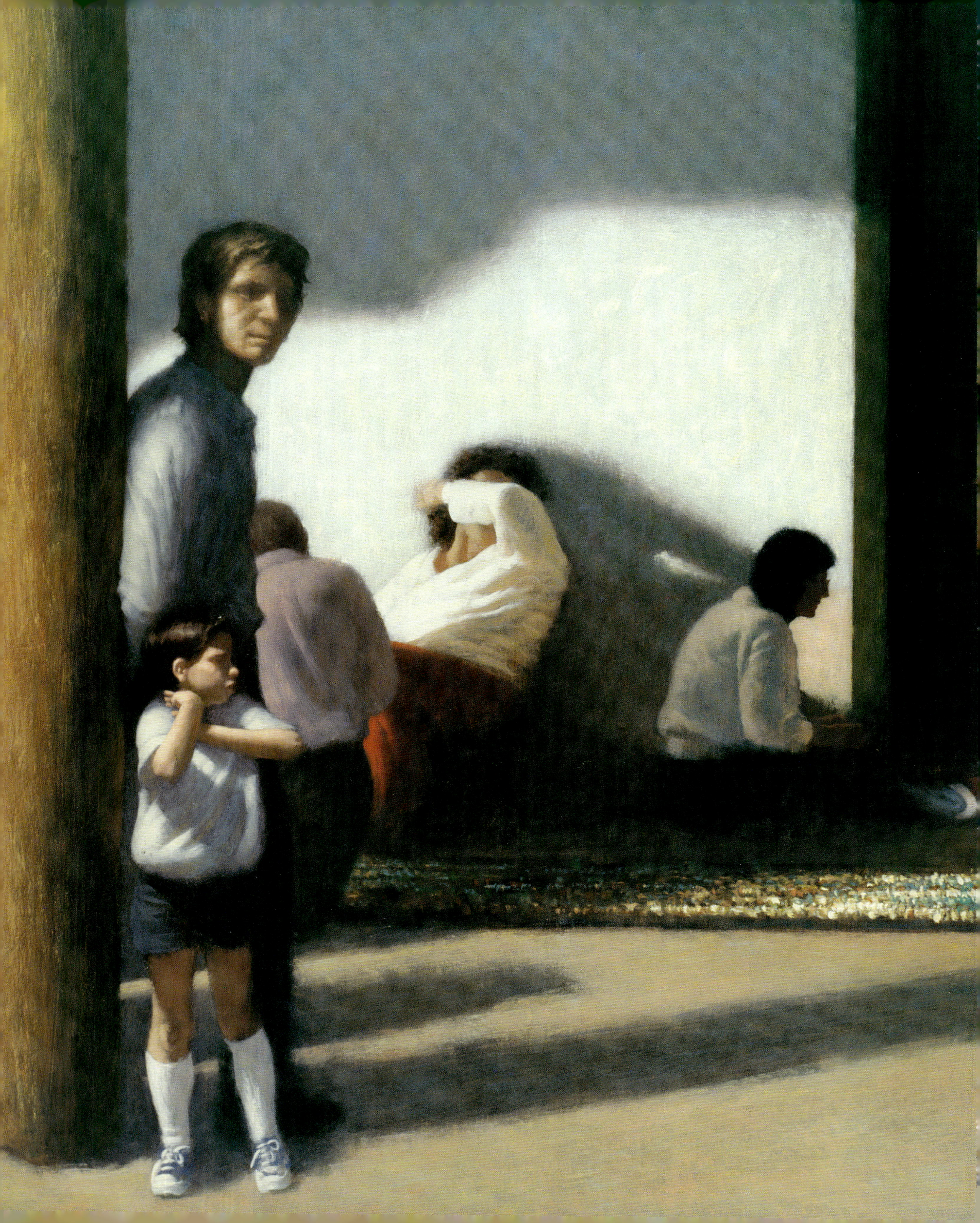

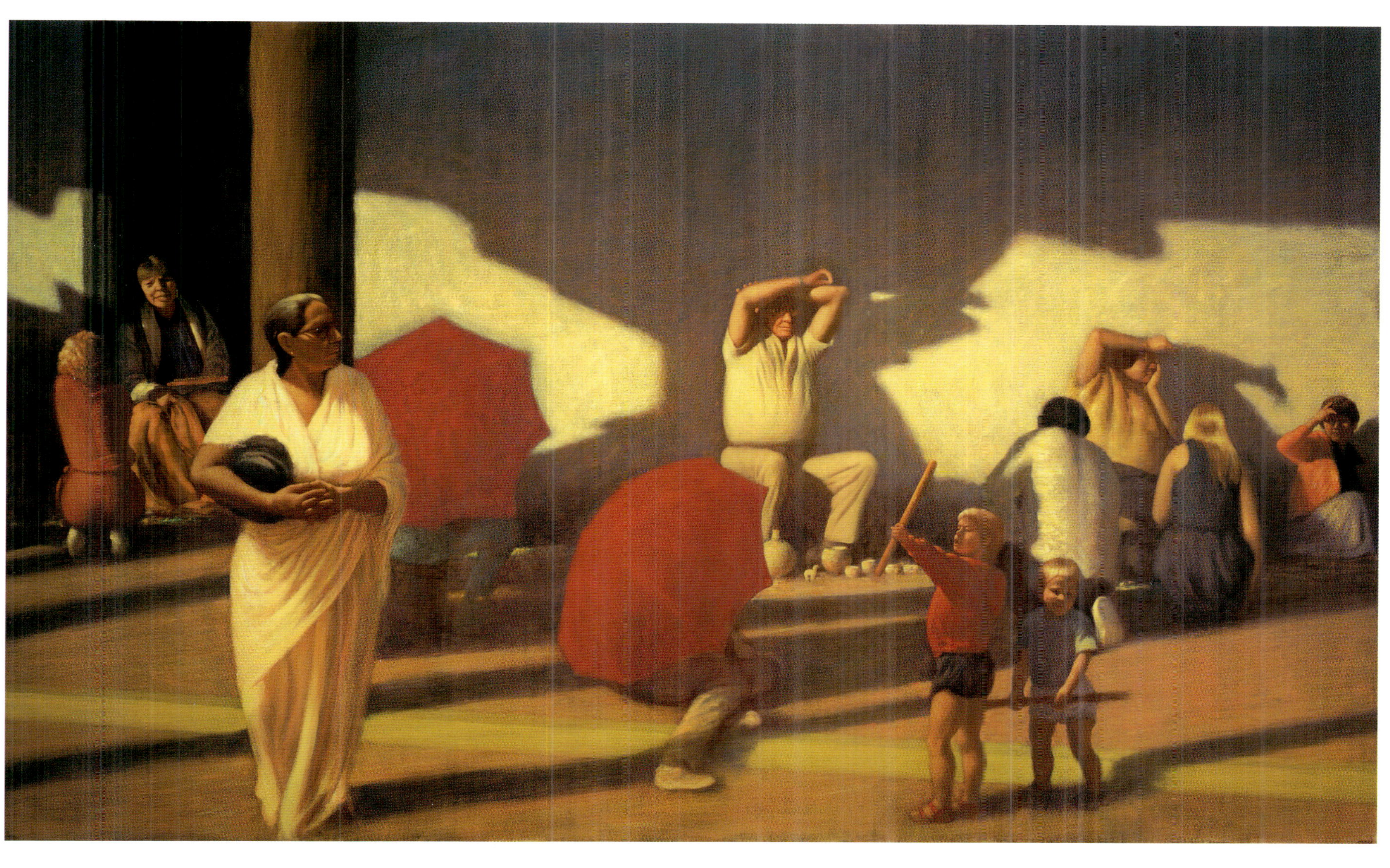

49. UNDER THE PORTAL OF SANTA FE
1992, oil on canvas, 66 × 108 inches
Capitol Art Collection, New Mexico State Capitol

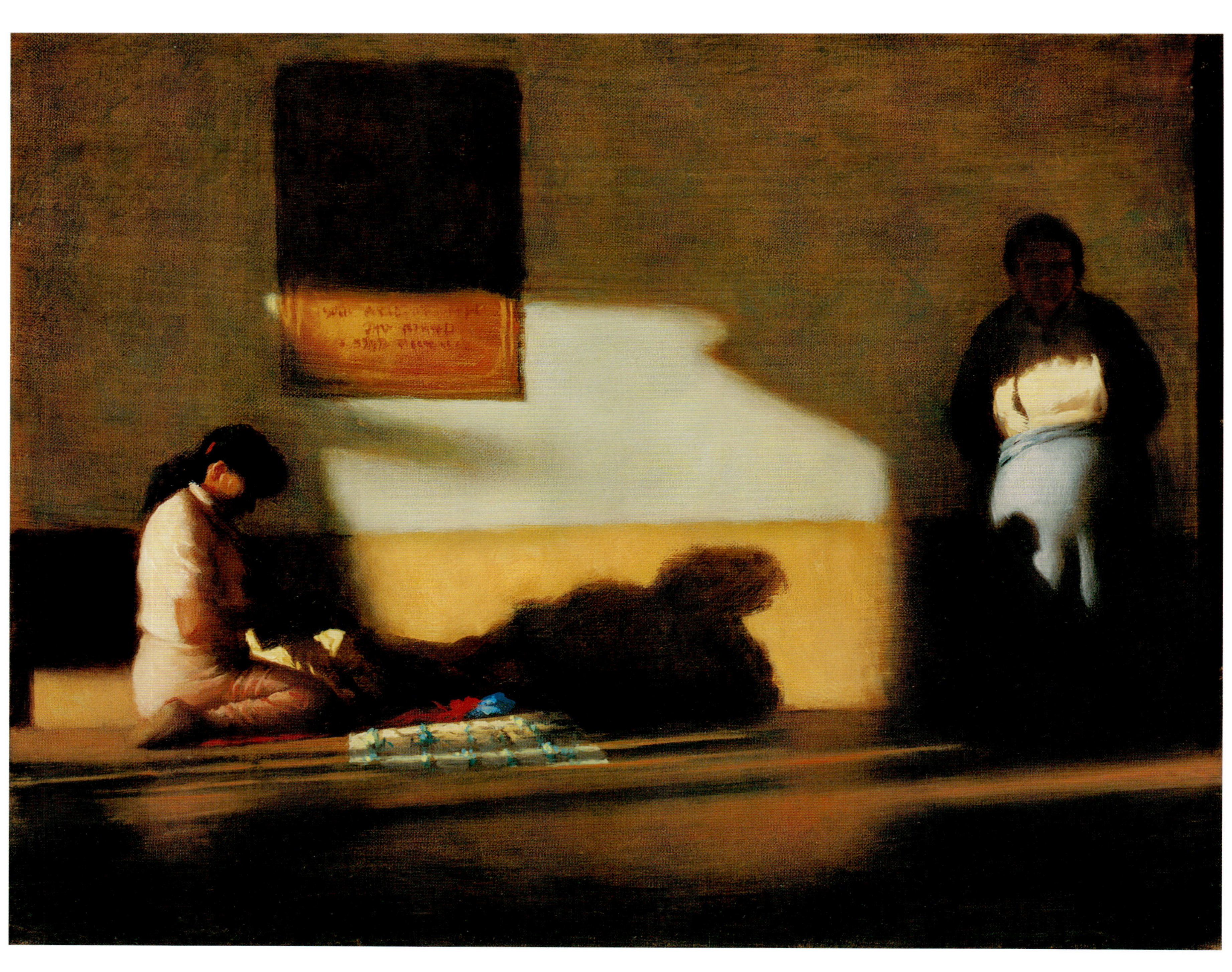

50. UNDER THE PORTAL #9
1986, oil on canvas, 14 × 16 inches

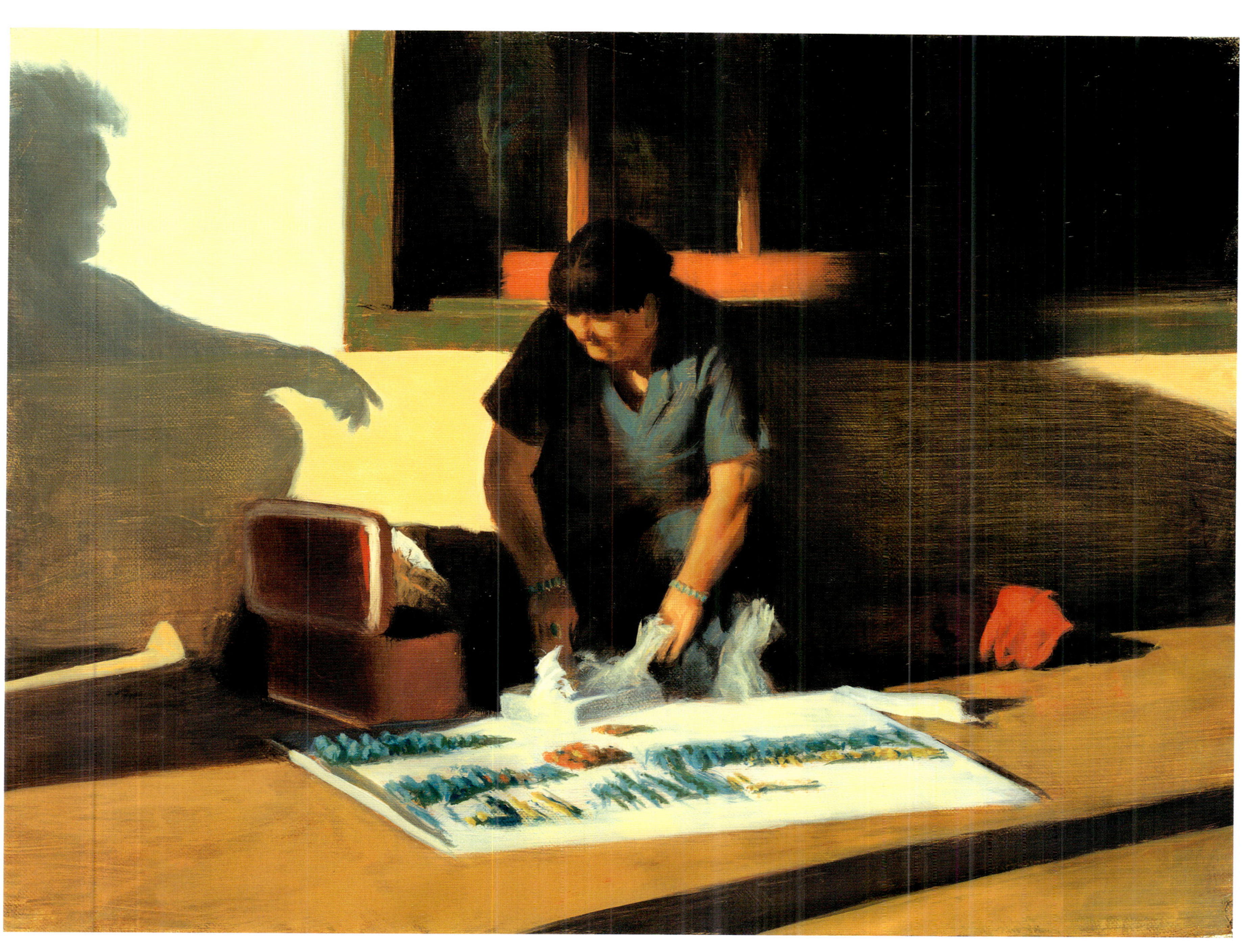

51. UNDER THE PORTAL #12

1986, oil on canvas, 14 × 18 inches

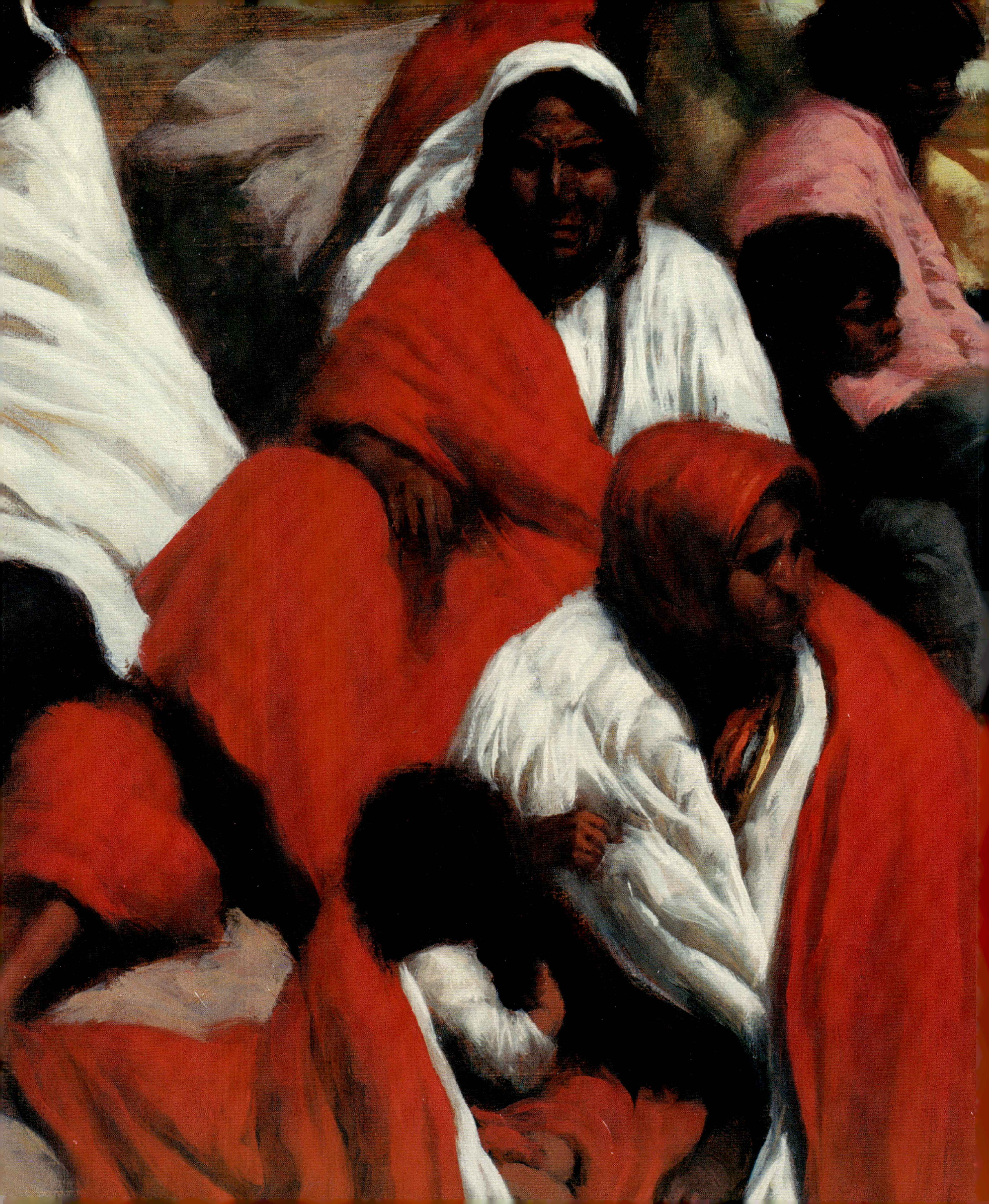

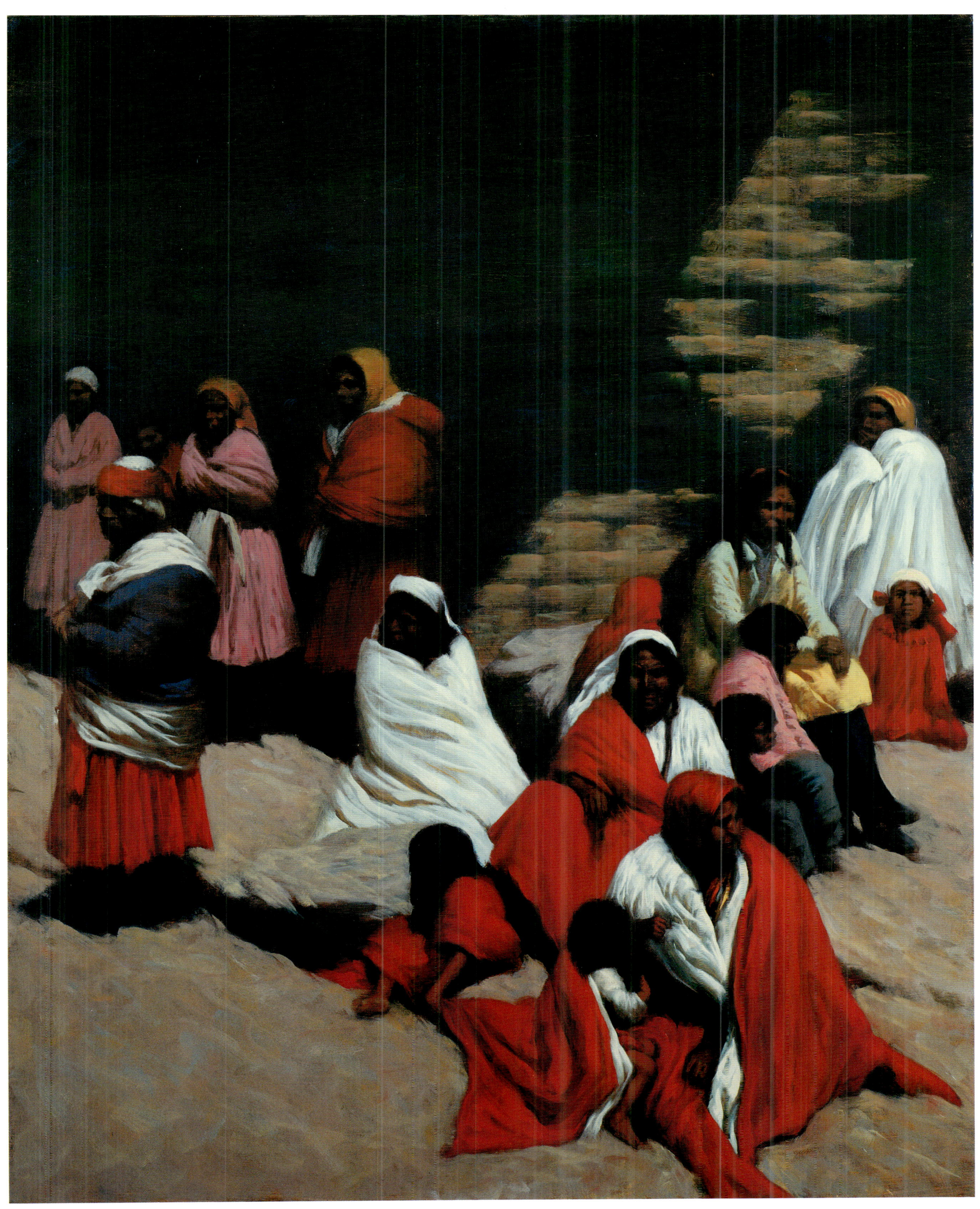

52. TARAHUMARA
1986, oil on canvas, 40 × 30 inches

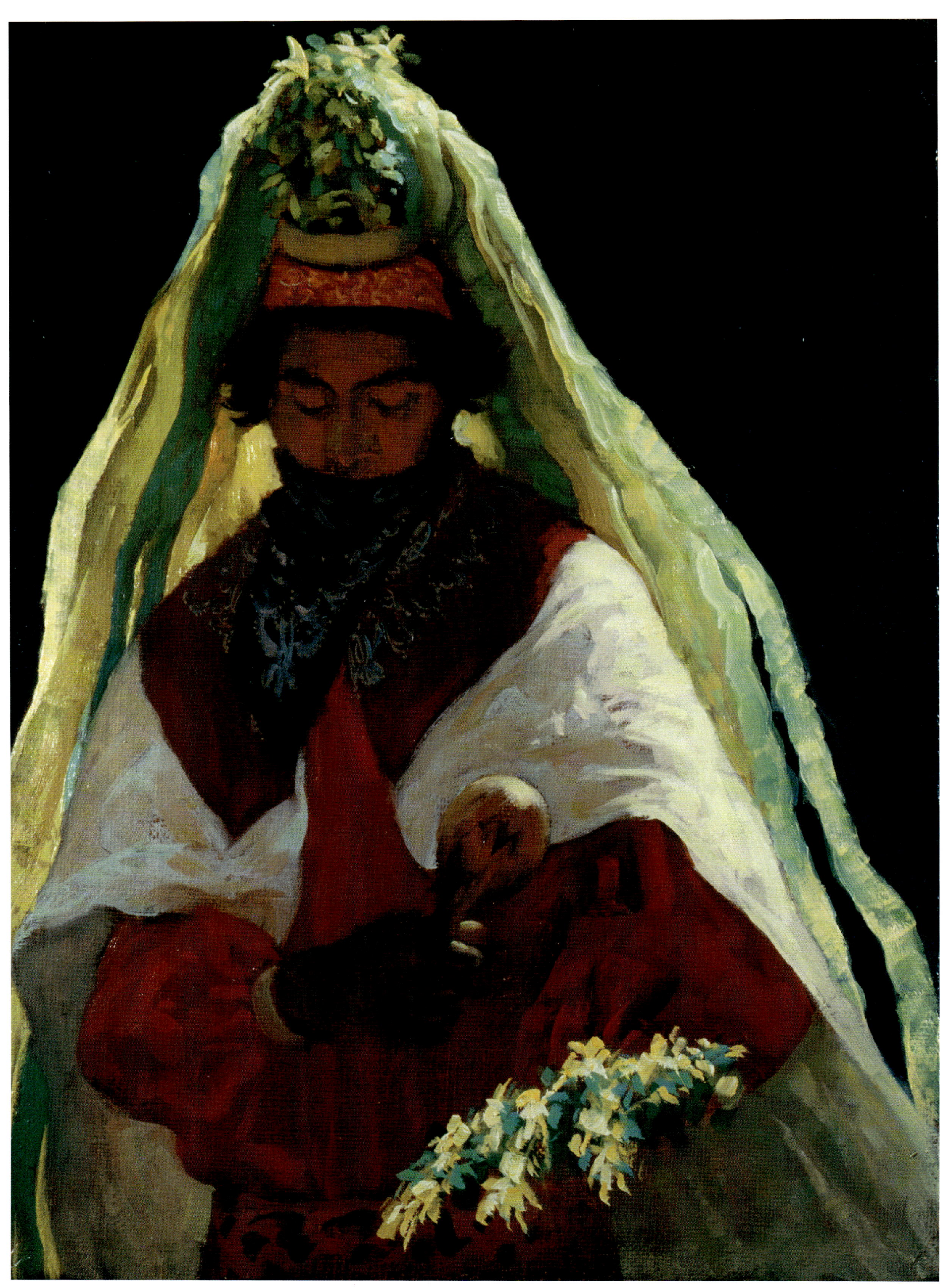

53. TARAHUMARA #1

1986, oil on canvas, 14 × 11 inches

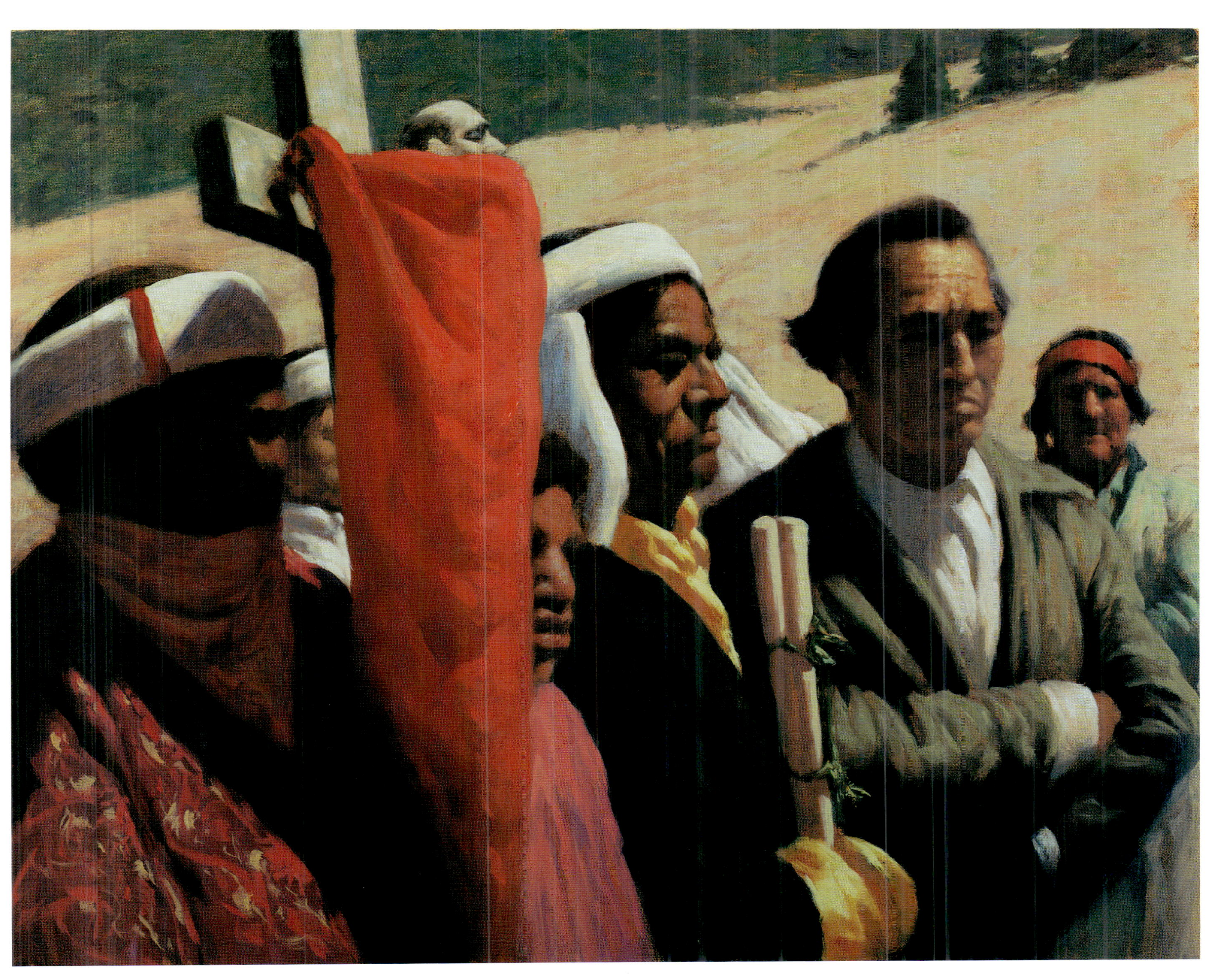

54. TARAHUMARA #2

1986, oil on canvas, 16 × 20 inches

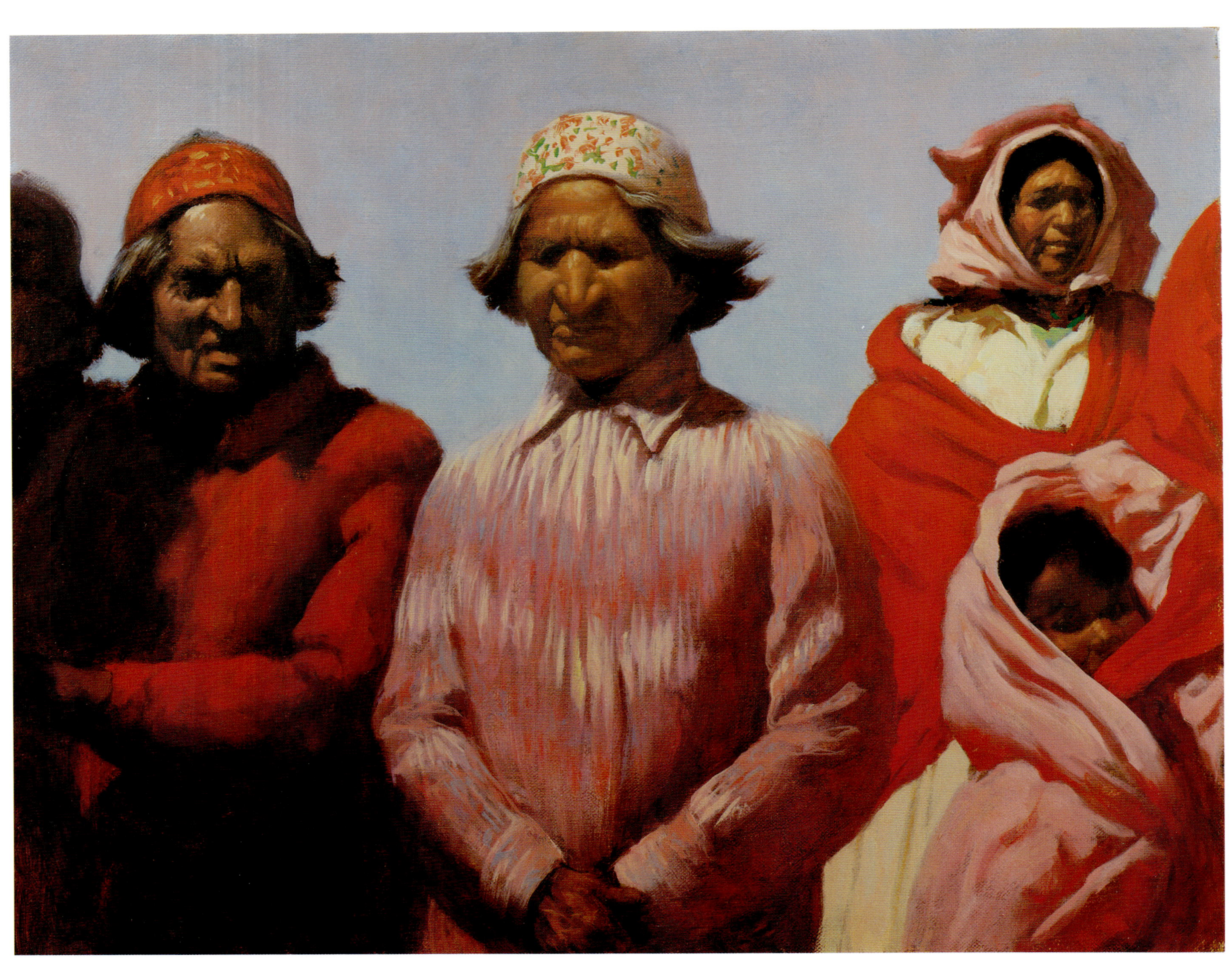

55. TARAHUMARA #4

1986, oil on canvas, 16 × 20 inches

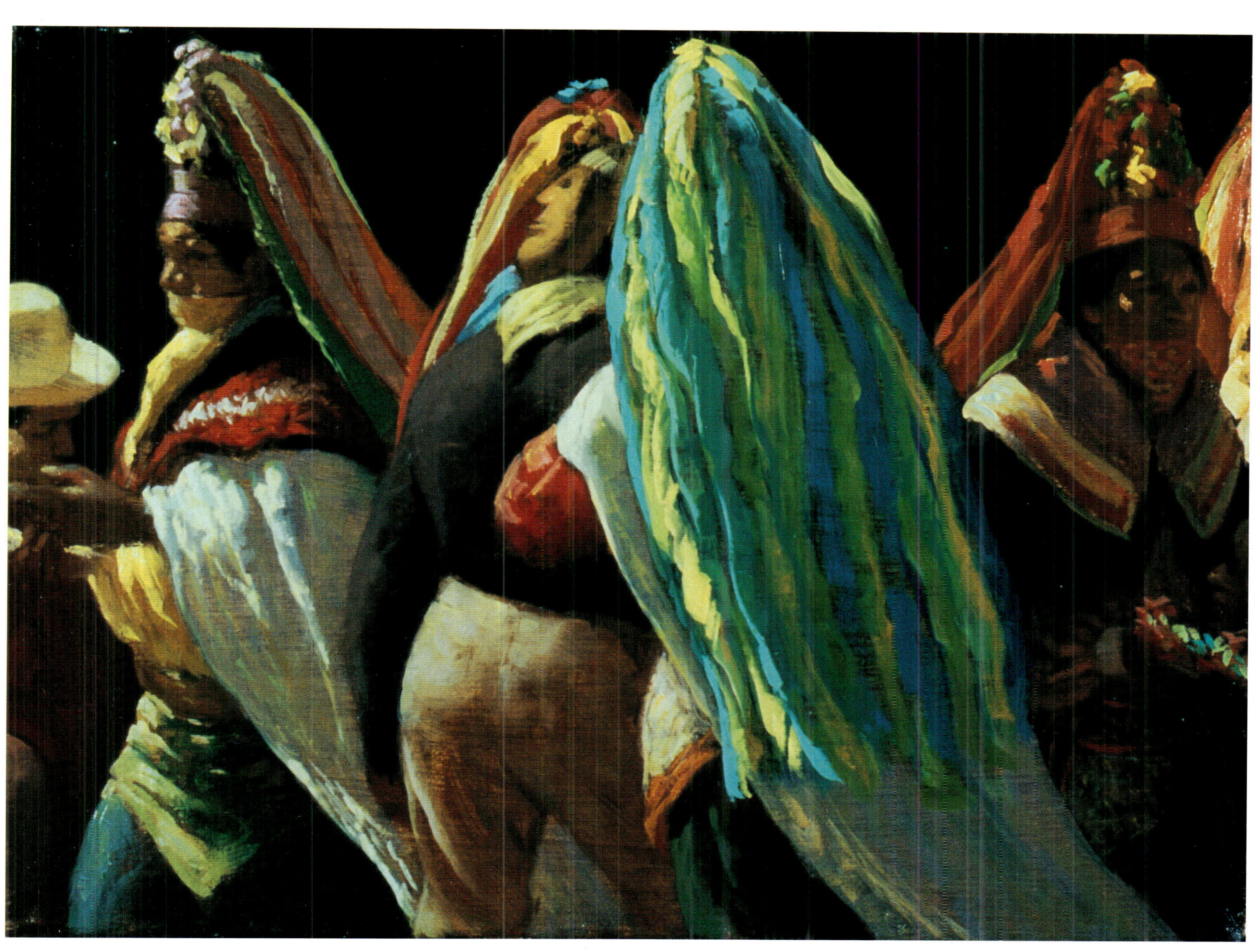

56. TARAHUMARA #5

1986, oil on canvas, 11 × 14 inches

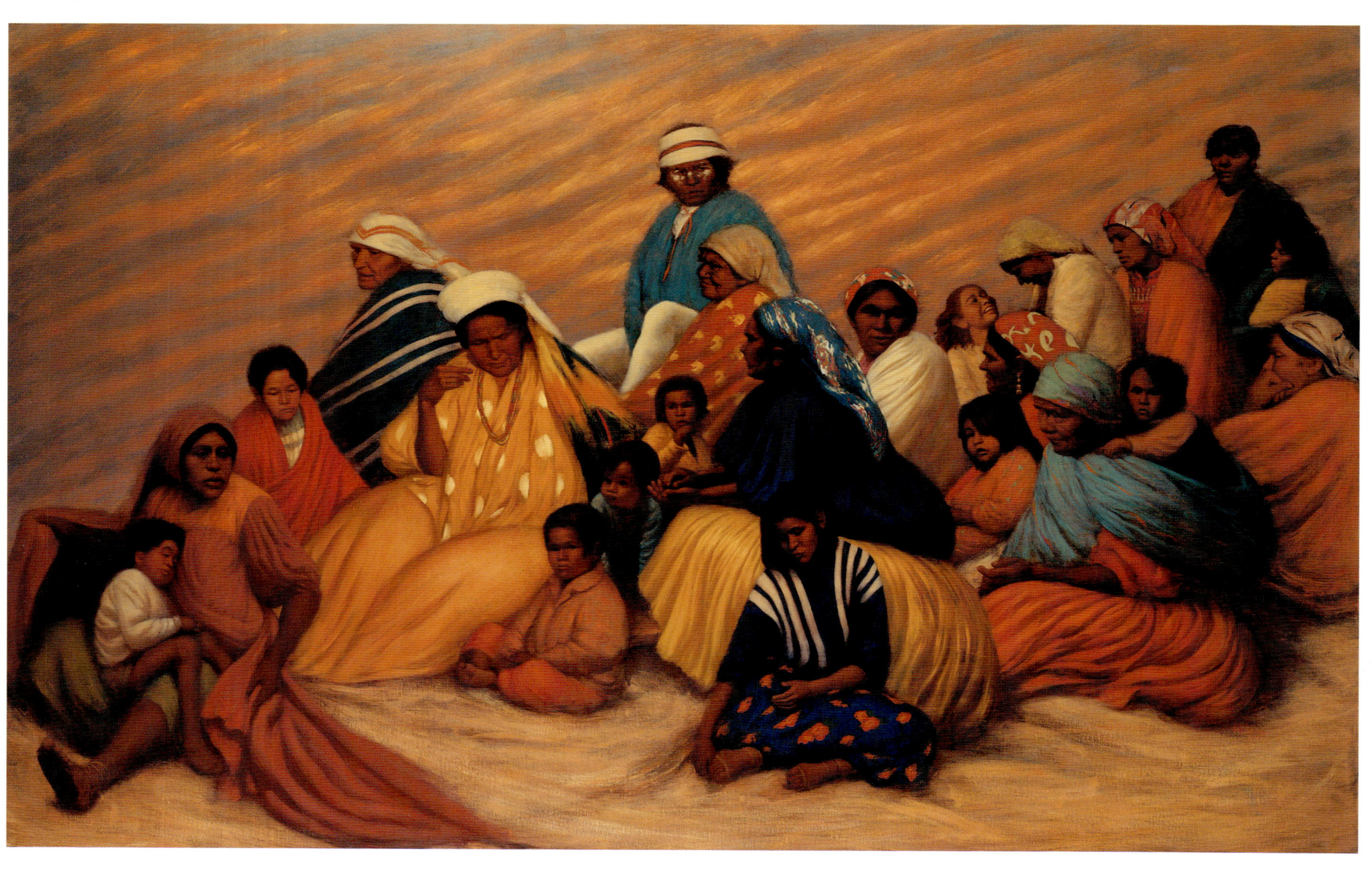

57. TARAHUMARA #7

1986, oil on canvas, 60 × 84 inches

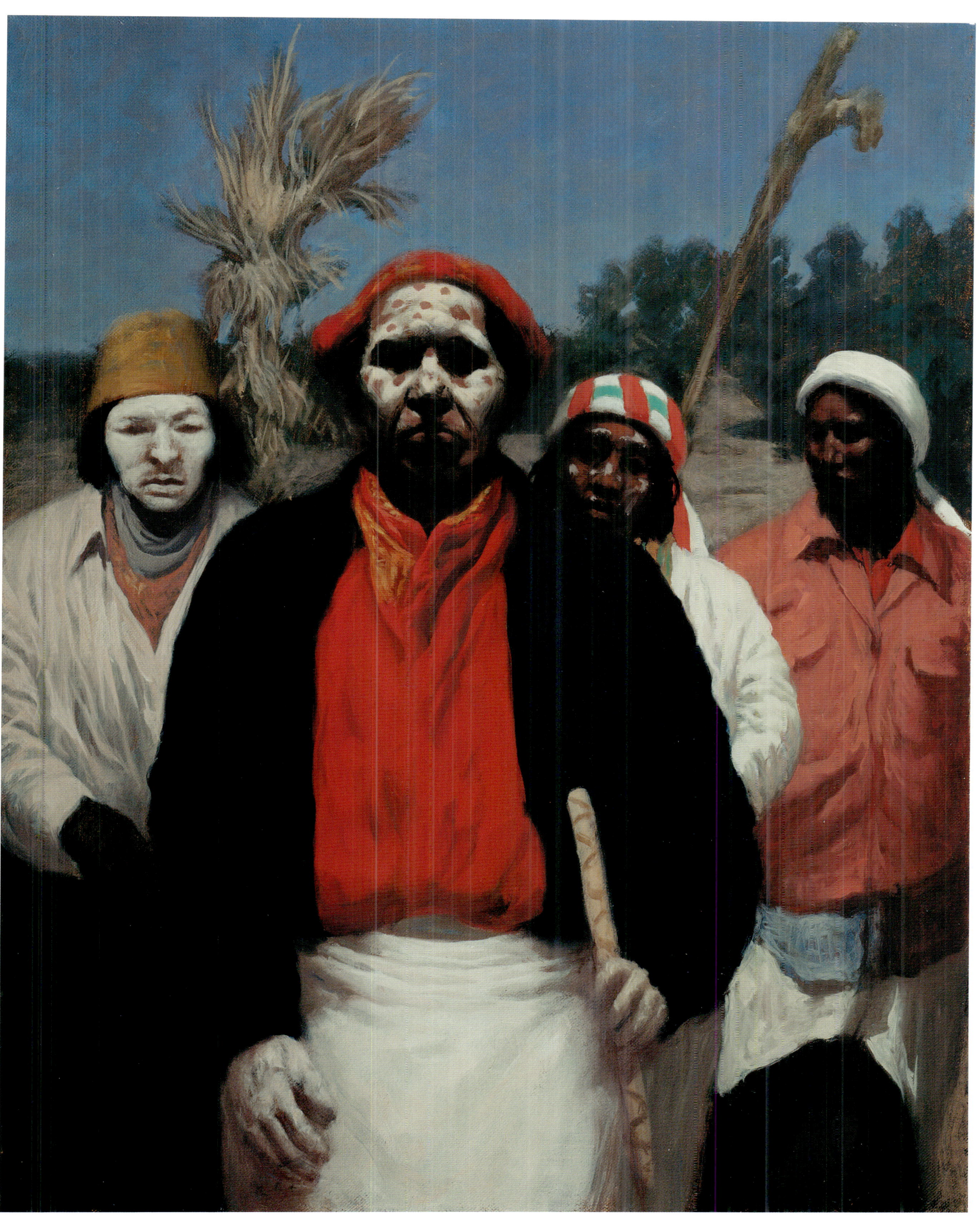

58. TARAHUMARA #8

1987, oil on canvas, 20 × 16 inches

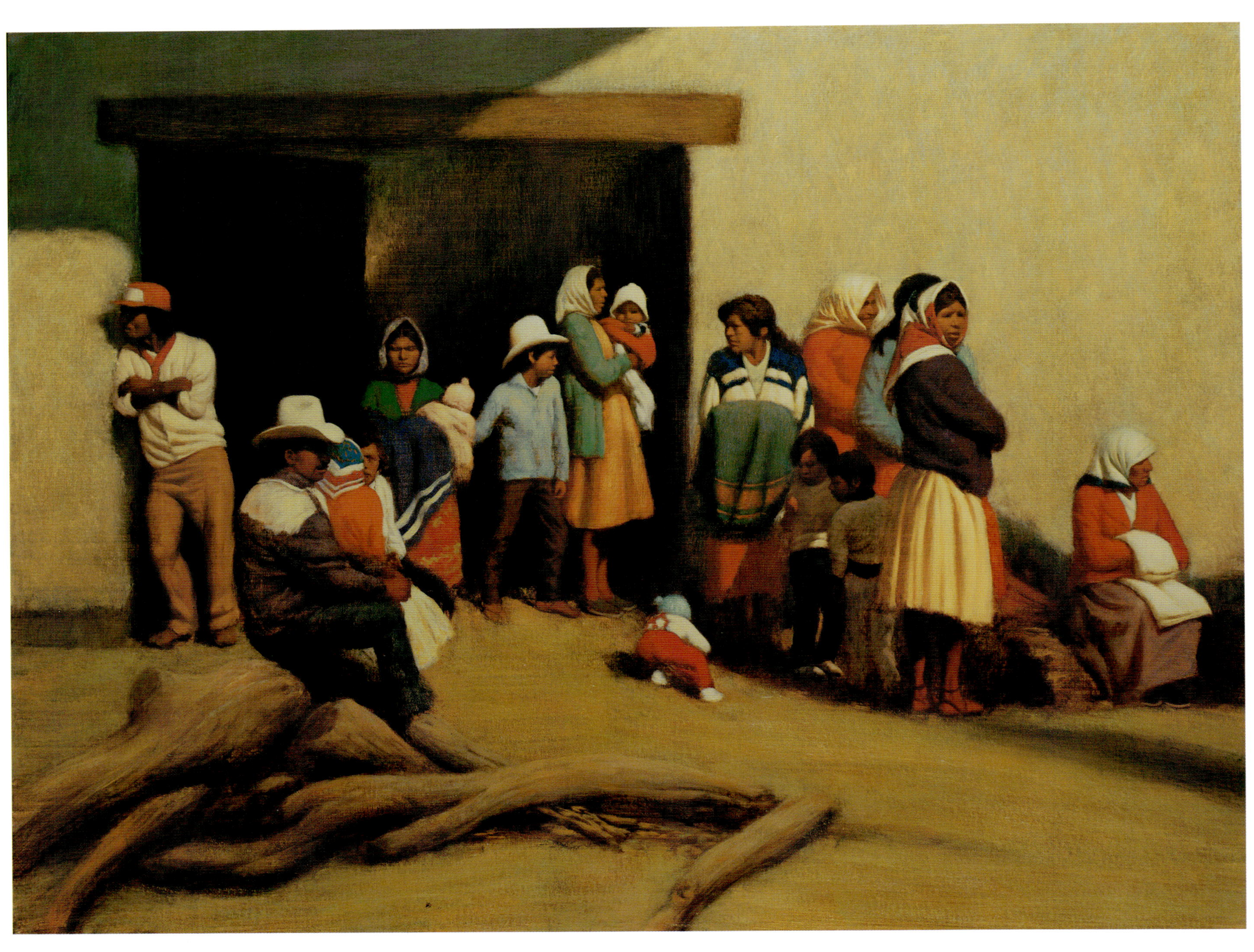

59. EASTER SUNDAY

1987, oil on canvas, 30 × 40 inches

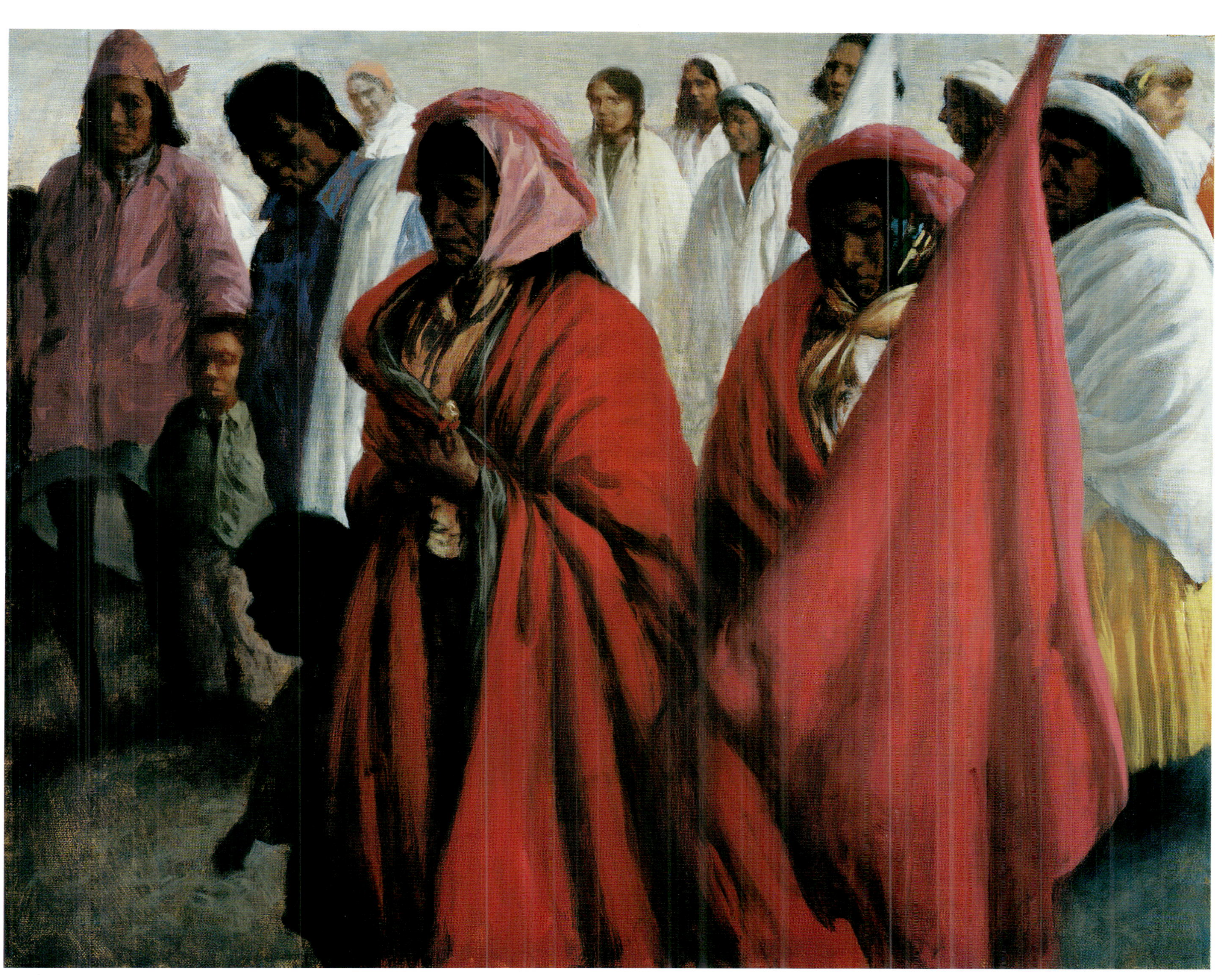

60. PROCESSION
1987, oil on canvas, 16 × 20 inches

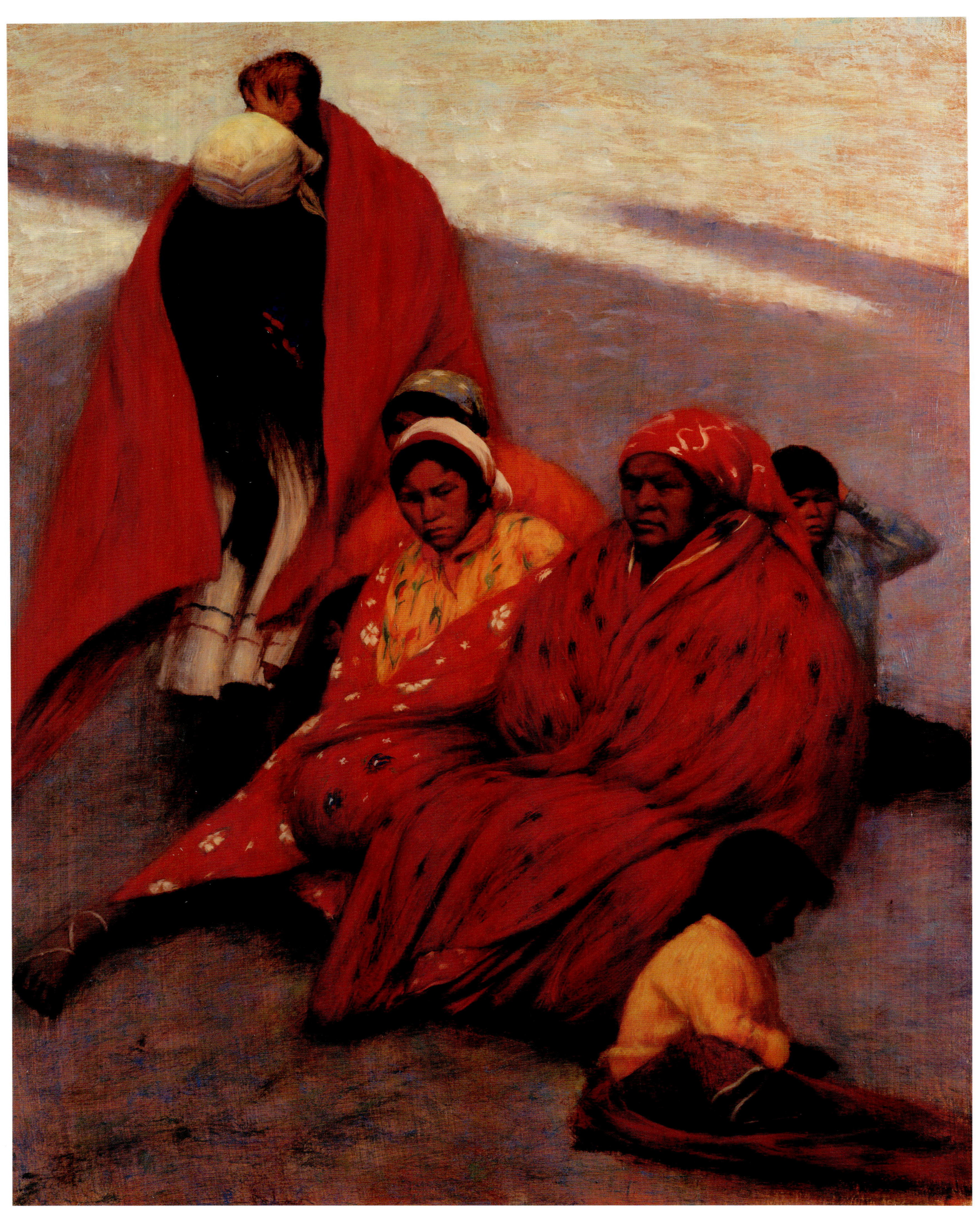

61. TARAHUMARA WOMEN #1

1987, oil on canvas, 24 × 20 inches

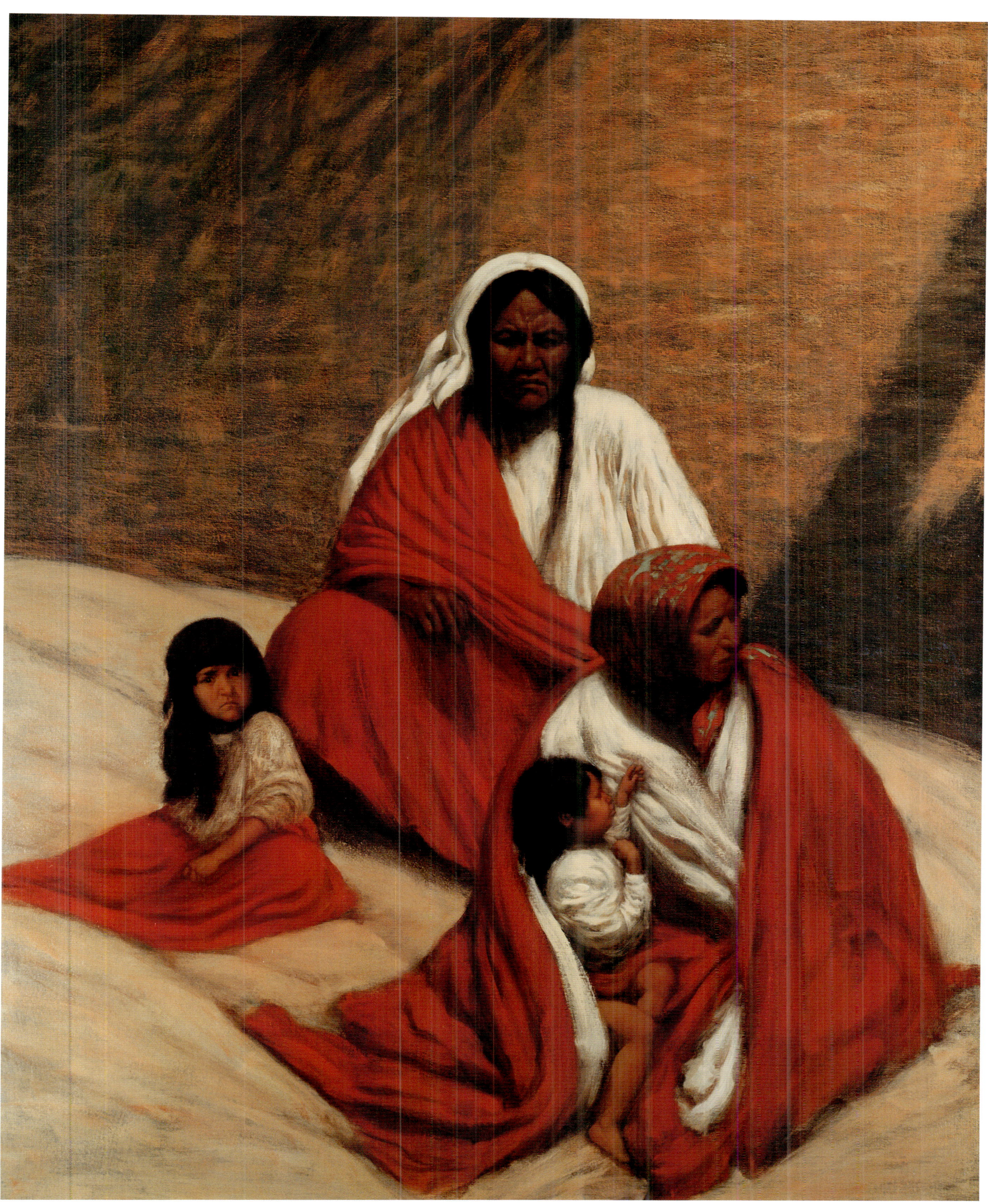

62. TARAHUMARA WOMEN #2

1987, oil on canvas, 60 × 48 inches

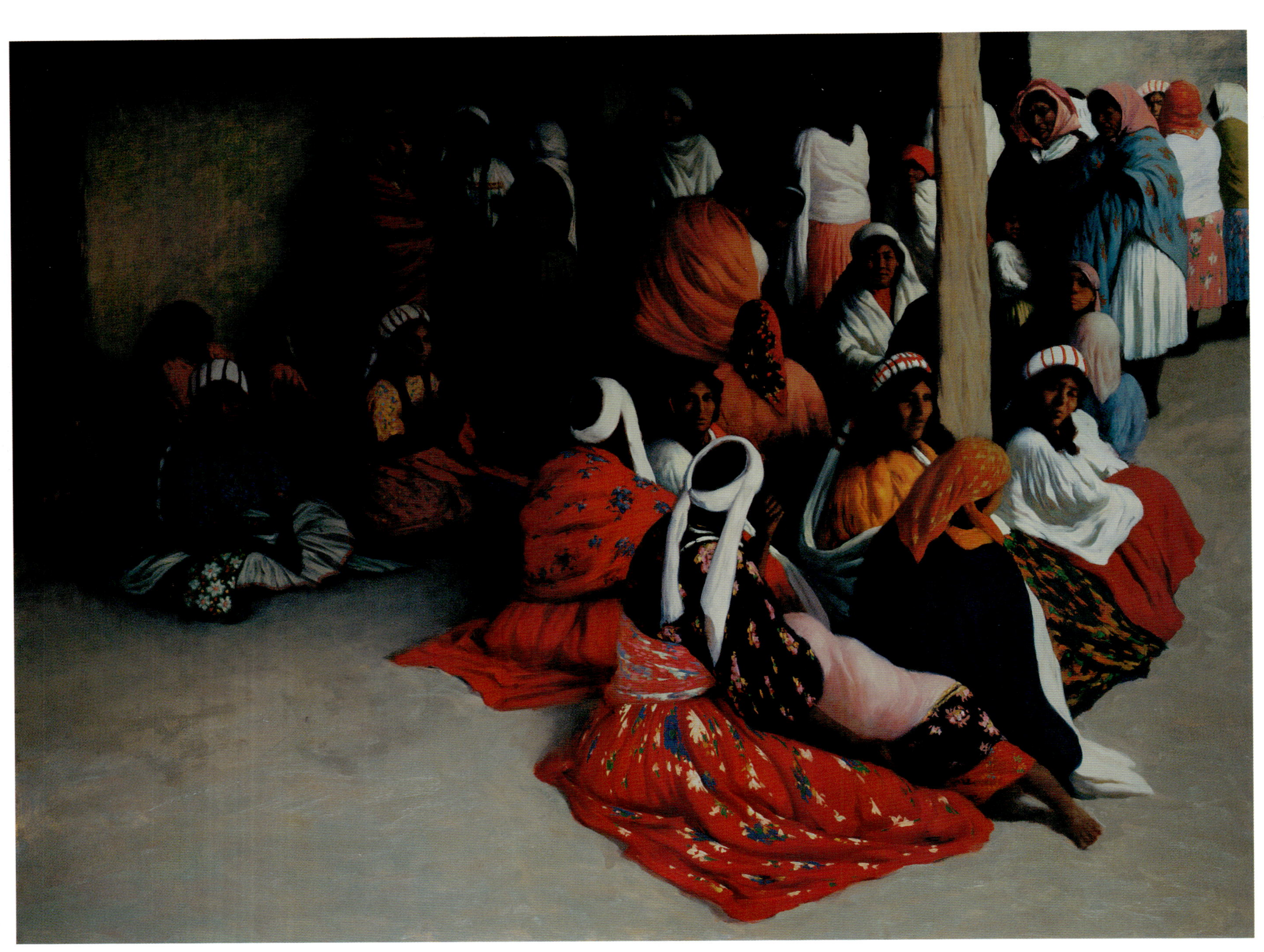

63. TARAHUMARA WOMEN #3
1987, oil on canvas, 36 × 48 inches

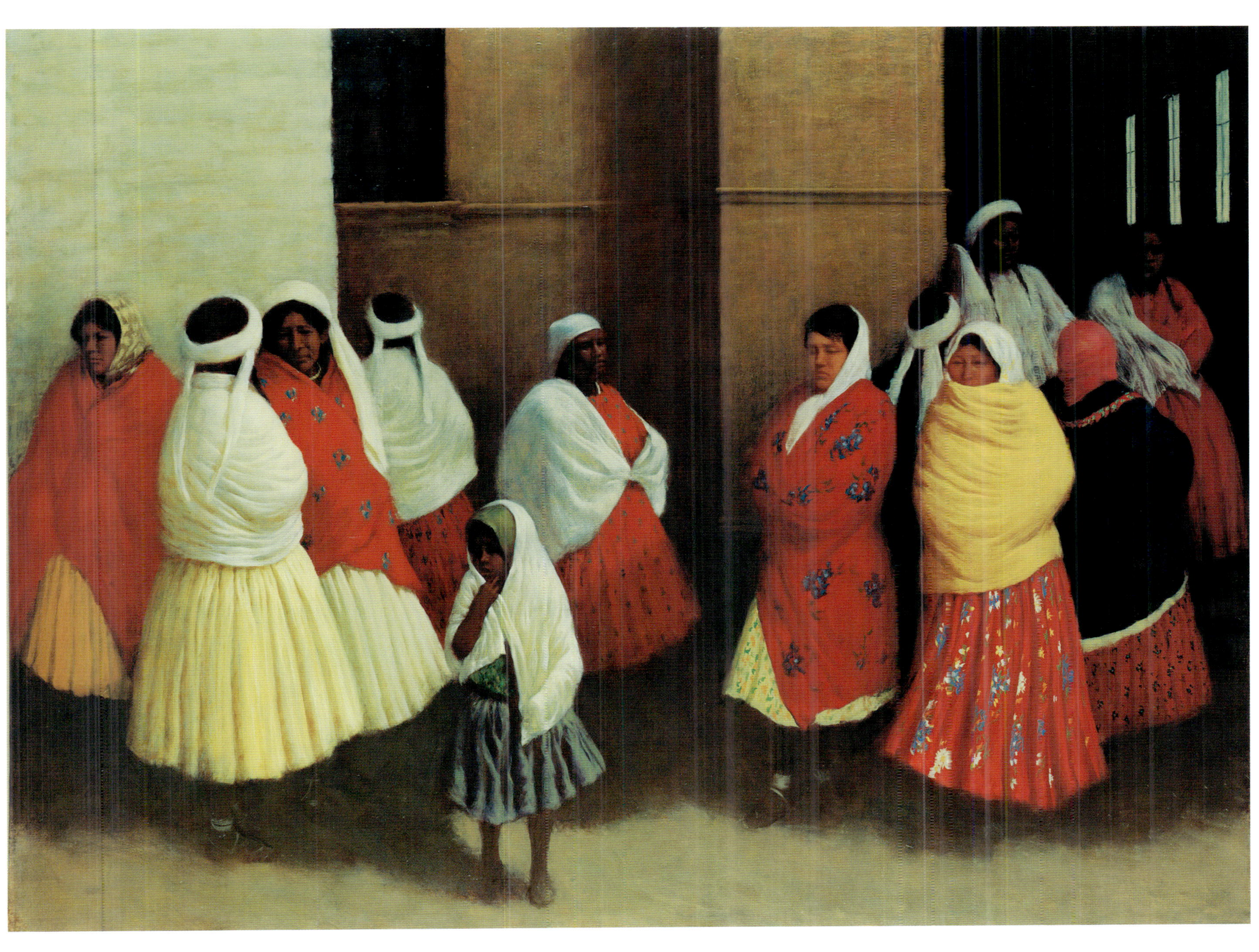

64. TARAHUMARA WOMEN #7
1987, oil on canvas, 30 × 40 inches

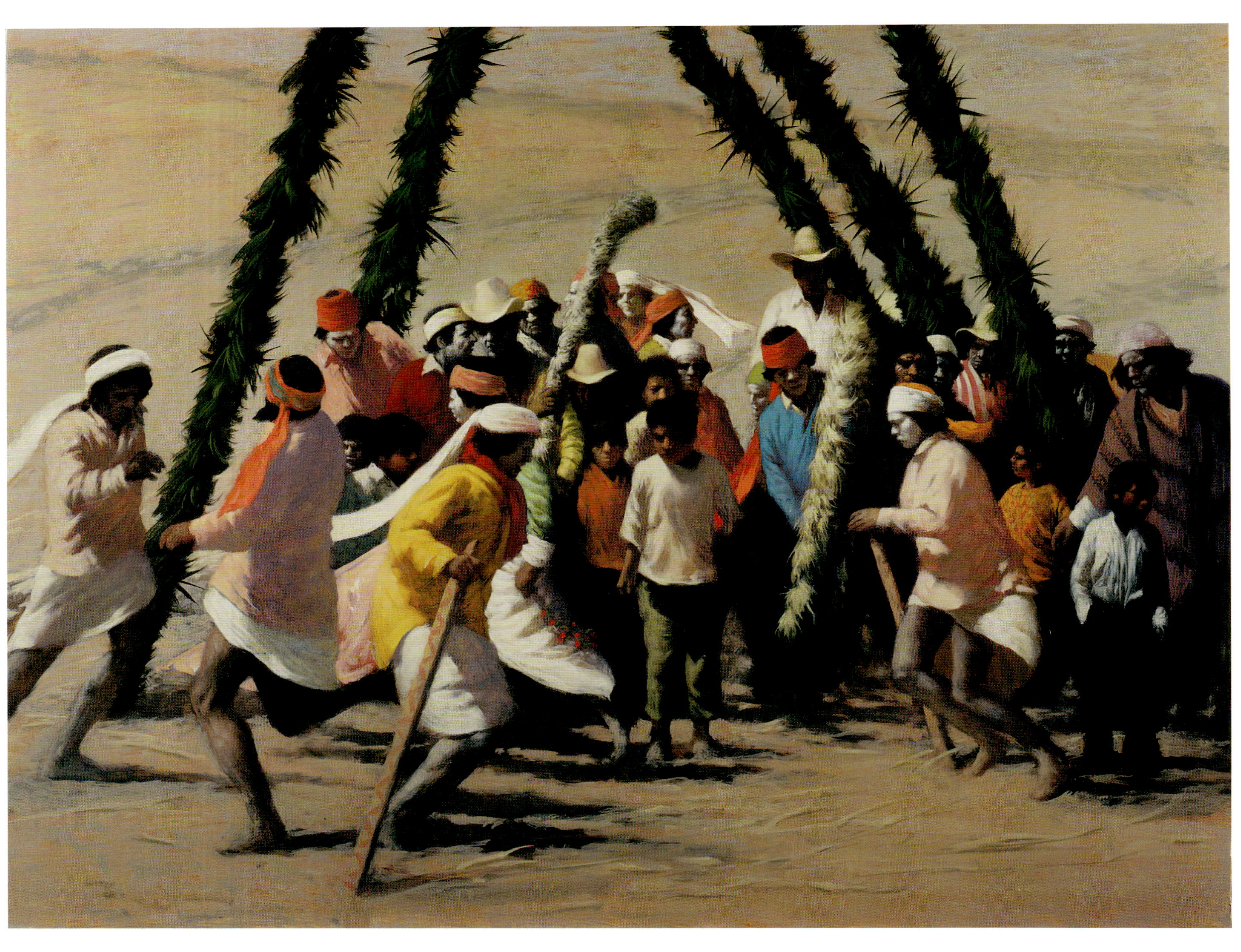

65. CEREMONIAL DANCE #1

1987, oil on canvas, 30 × 40 inches

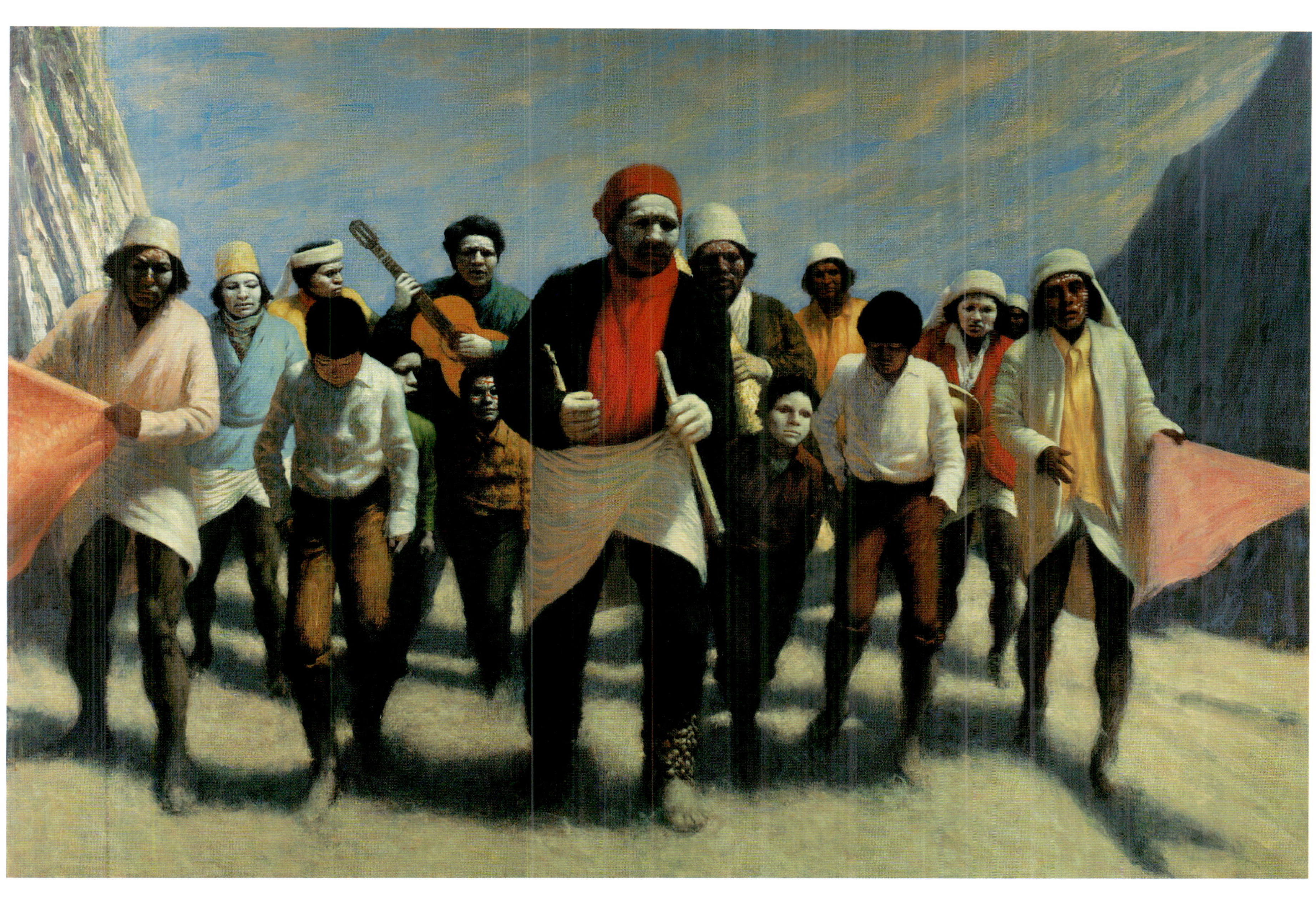

66. CEREMONIAL DANCE #2

1987, oil on canvas, 48 × 72 inches

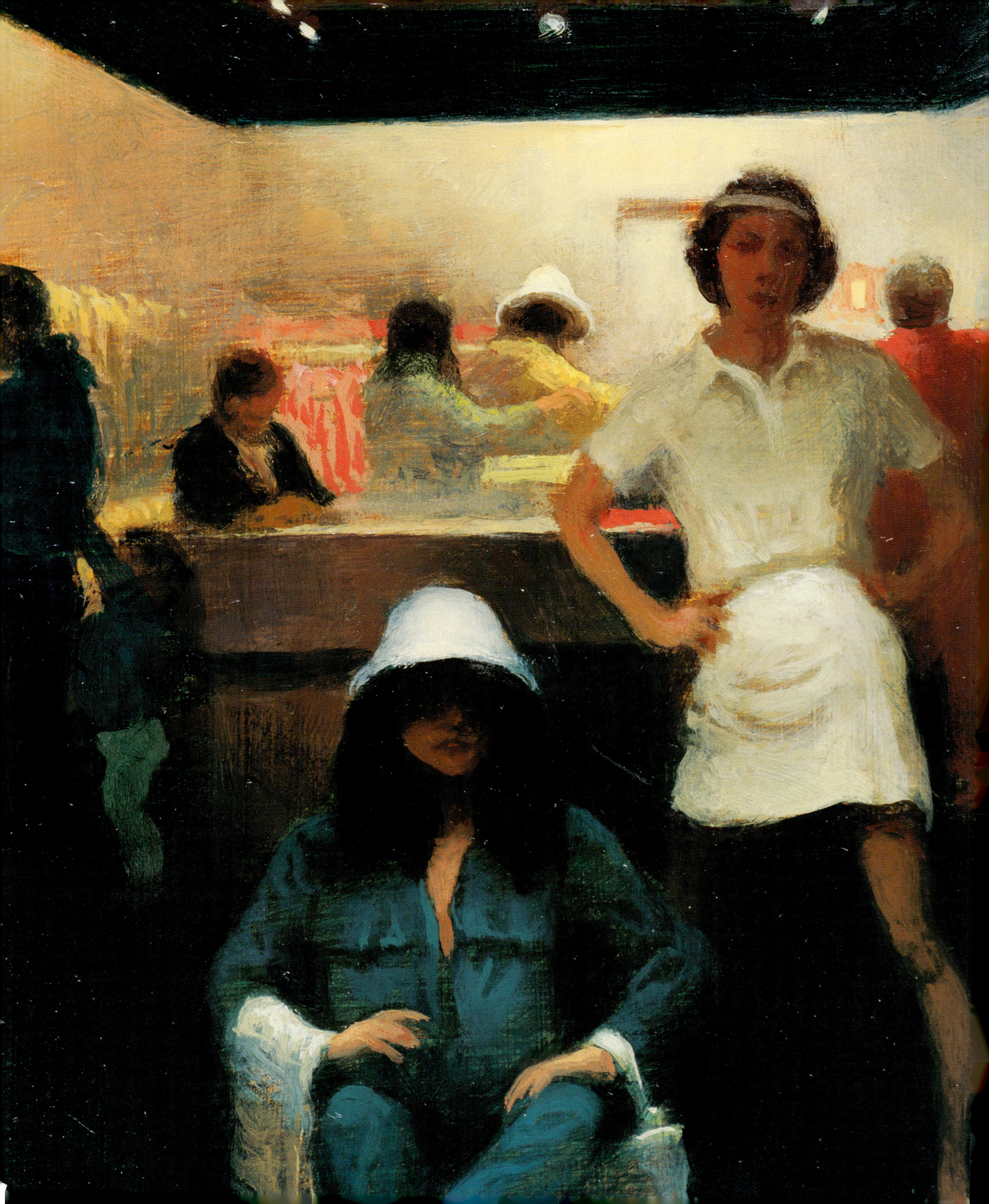

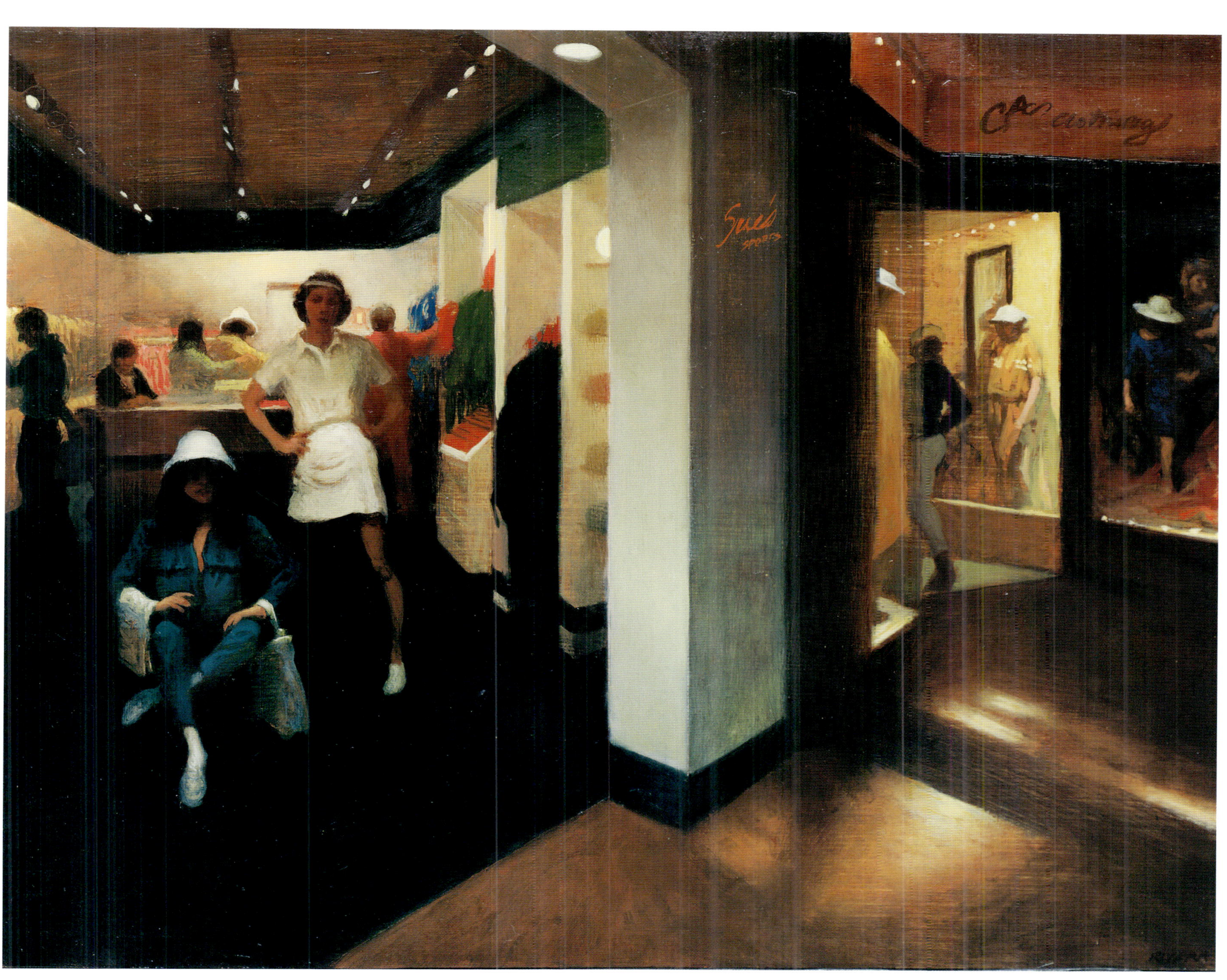

67. GEORGETOWN MALL

1988, oil on canvas, 11 × 14 inches

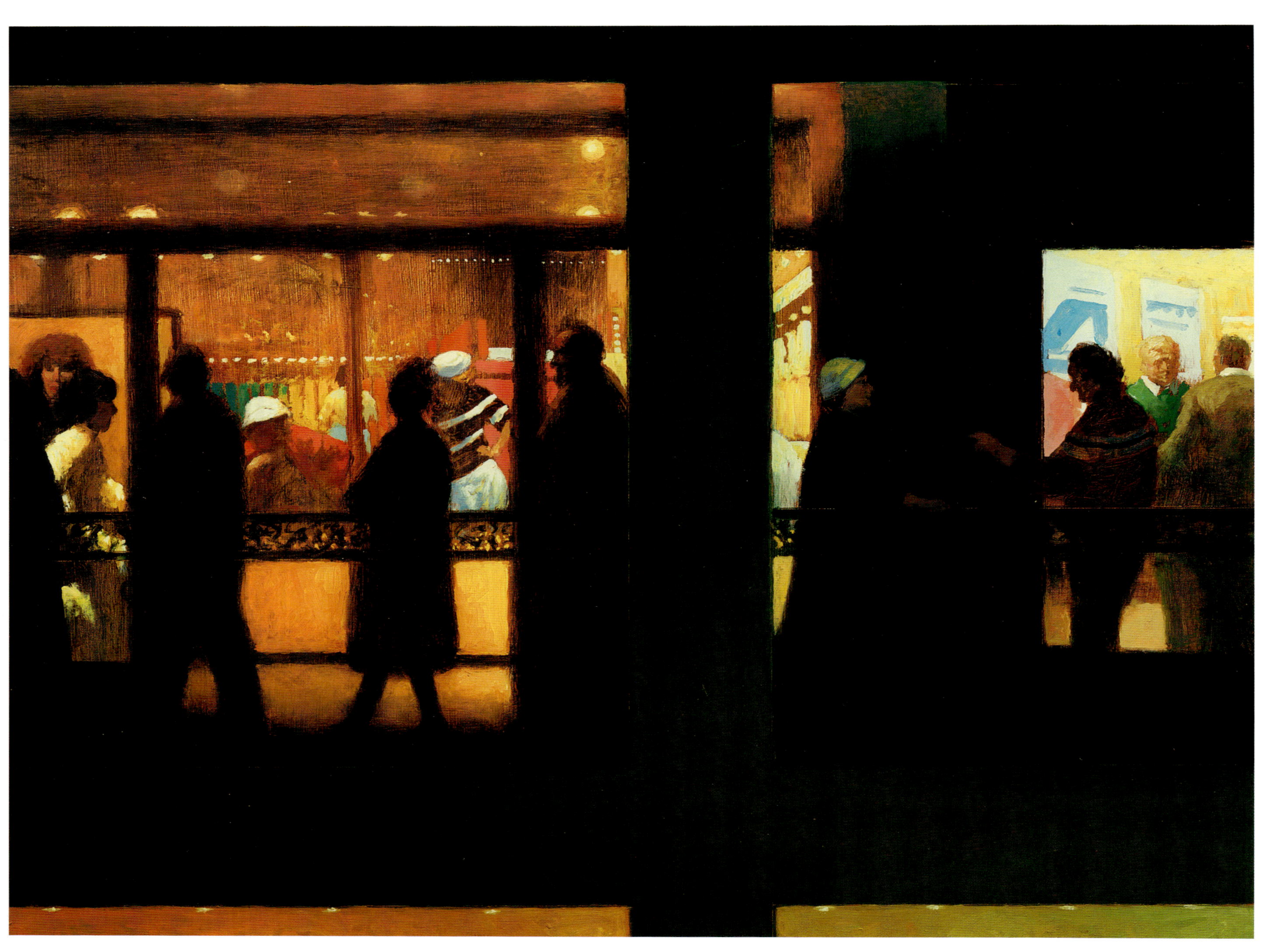

68. GEORGETOWN MALL #2

1988, oil on canvas, 11 × 14 inches

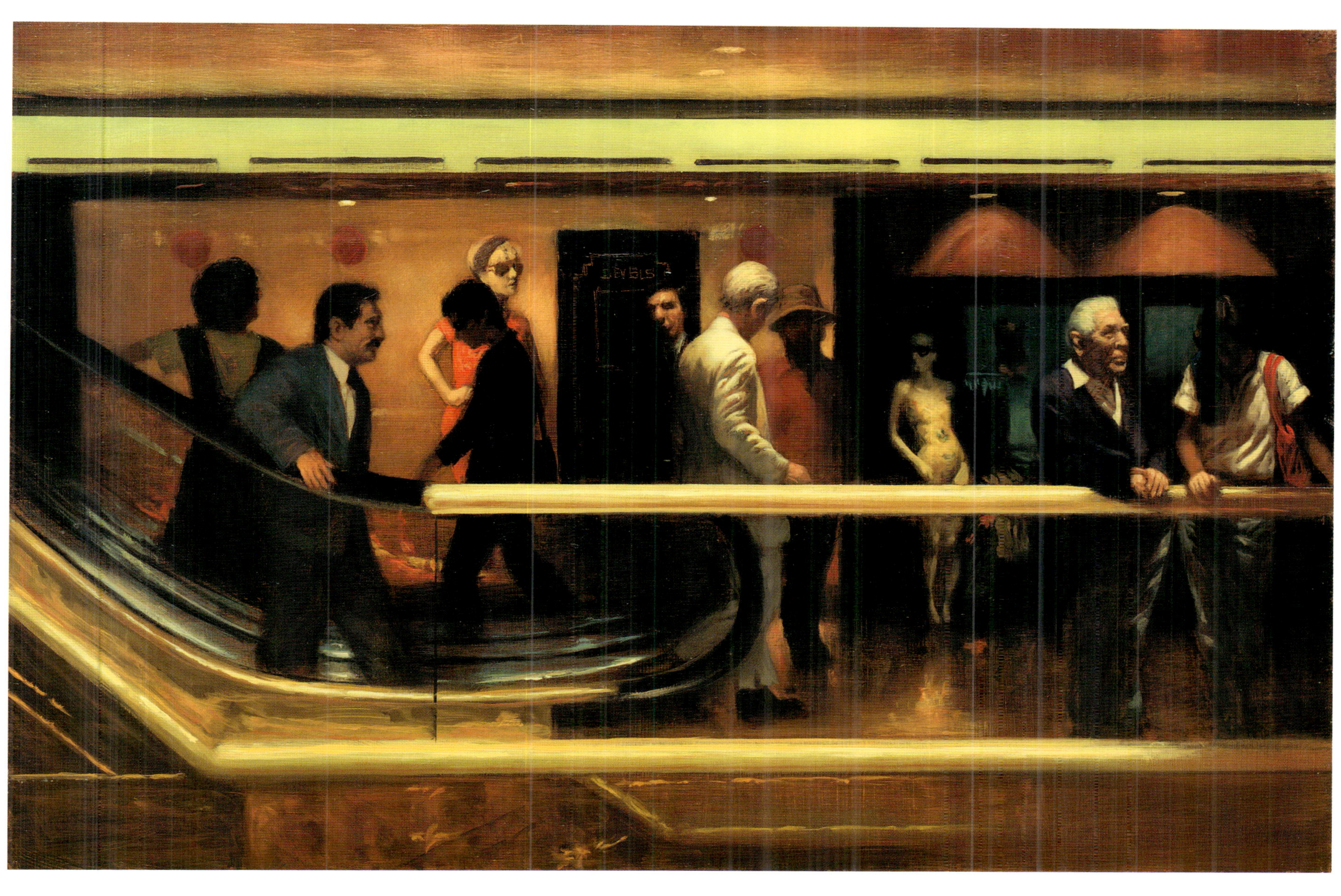

69. TRUMP TOWER #1

1988, oil on canvas, 18 × 24 inches

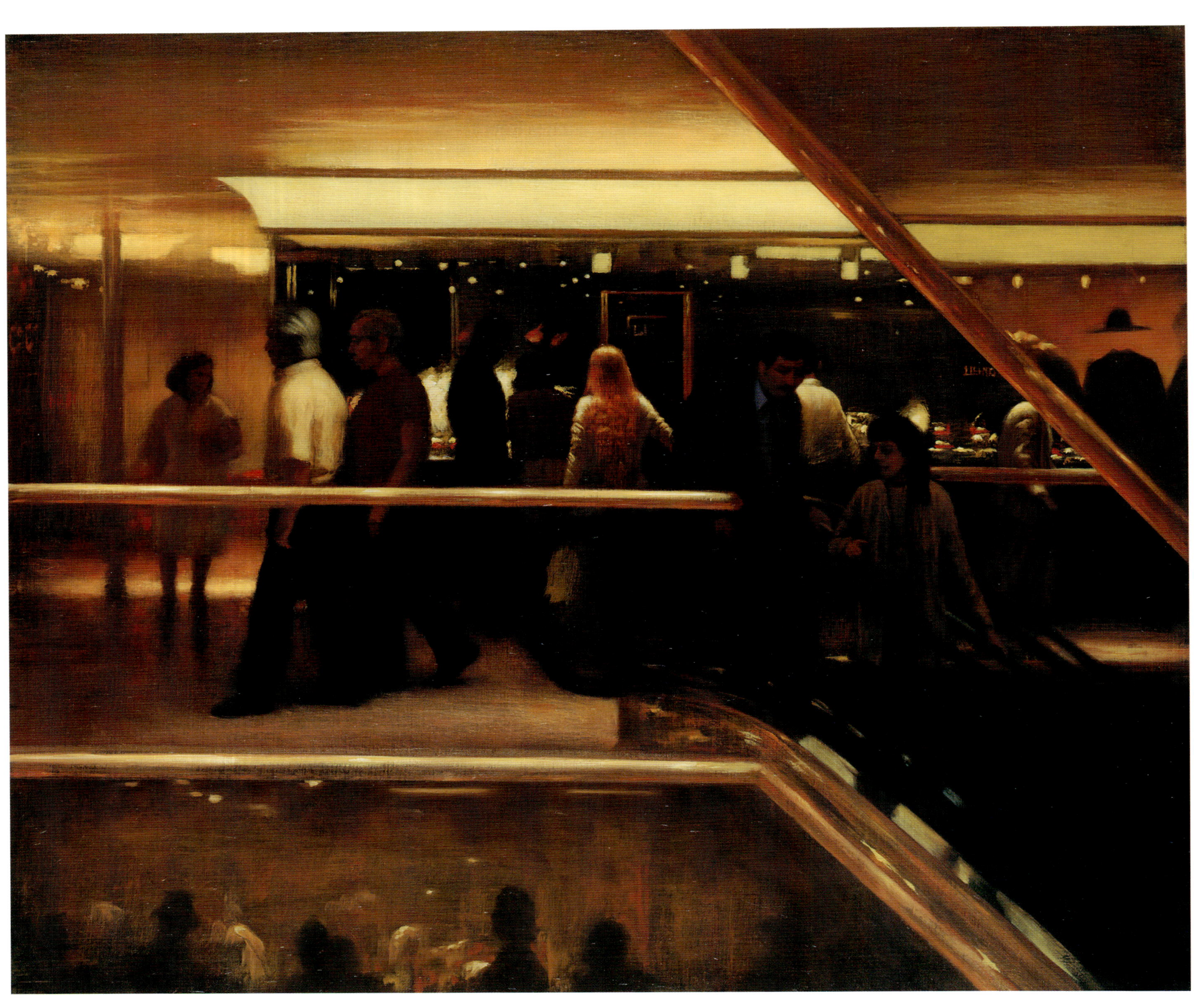

70. TRUMP TOWER #2

1988, oil on canvas, 16 × 20 inches

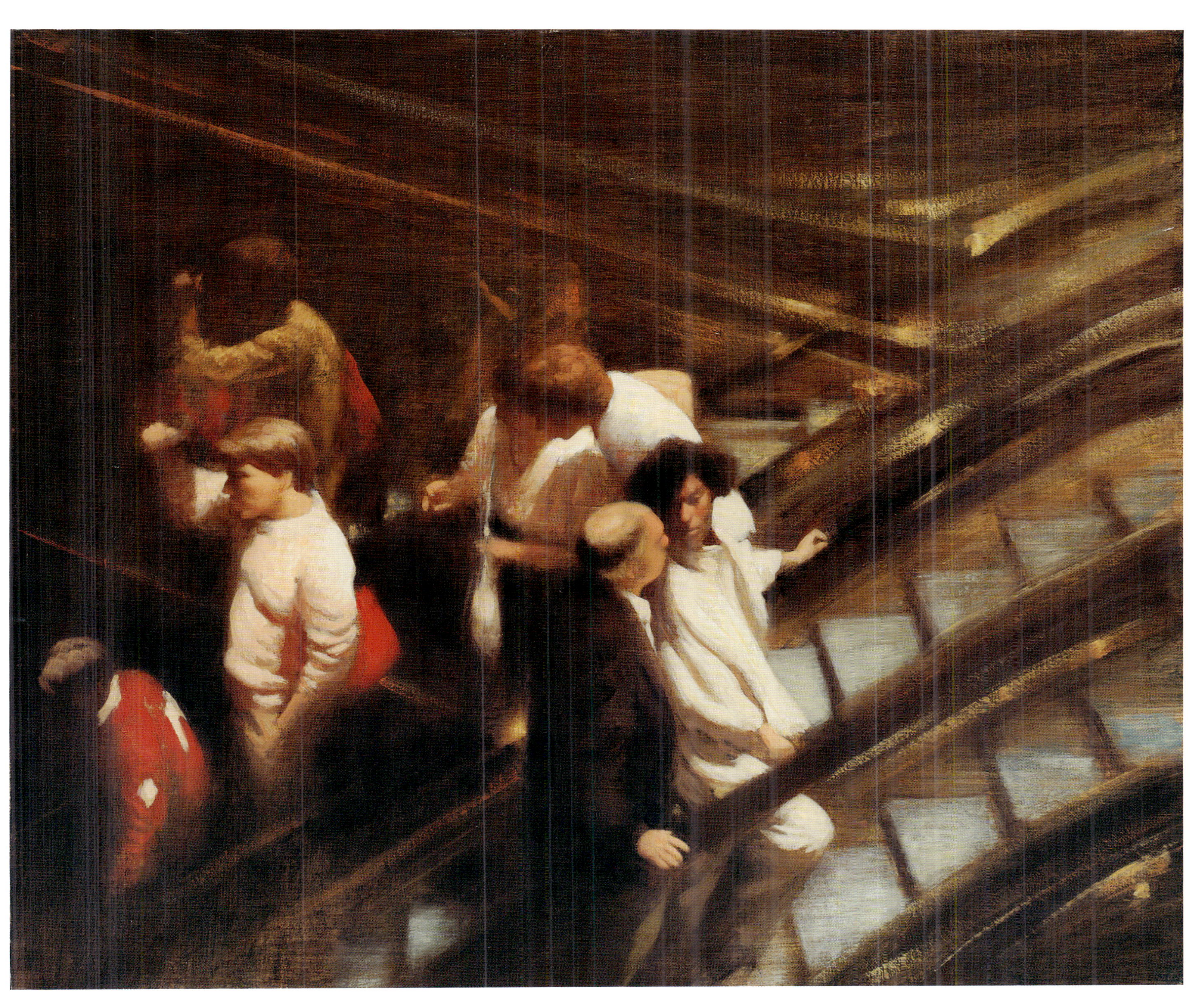

71. TRUMP TOWER #7

1988, oil on canvas, 16 × 20 inches

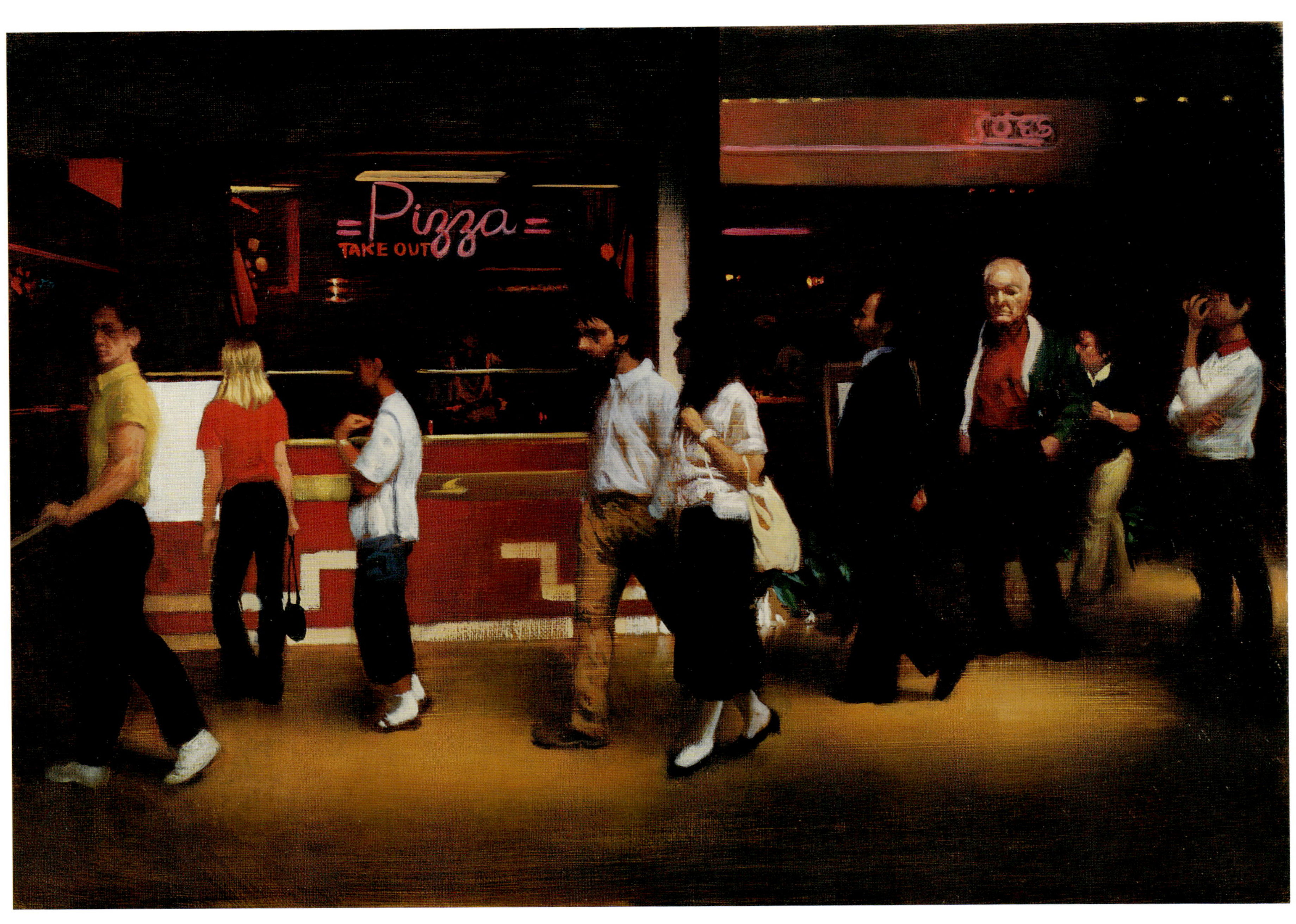

72. BEVERLY CENTER

1989, oil on canvas, 24 × 30 inches

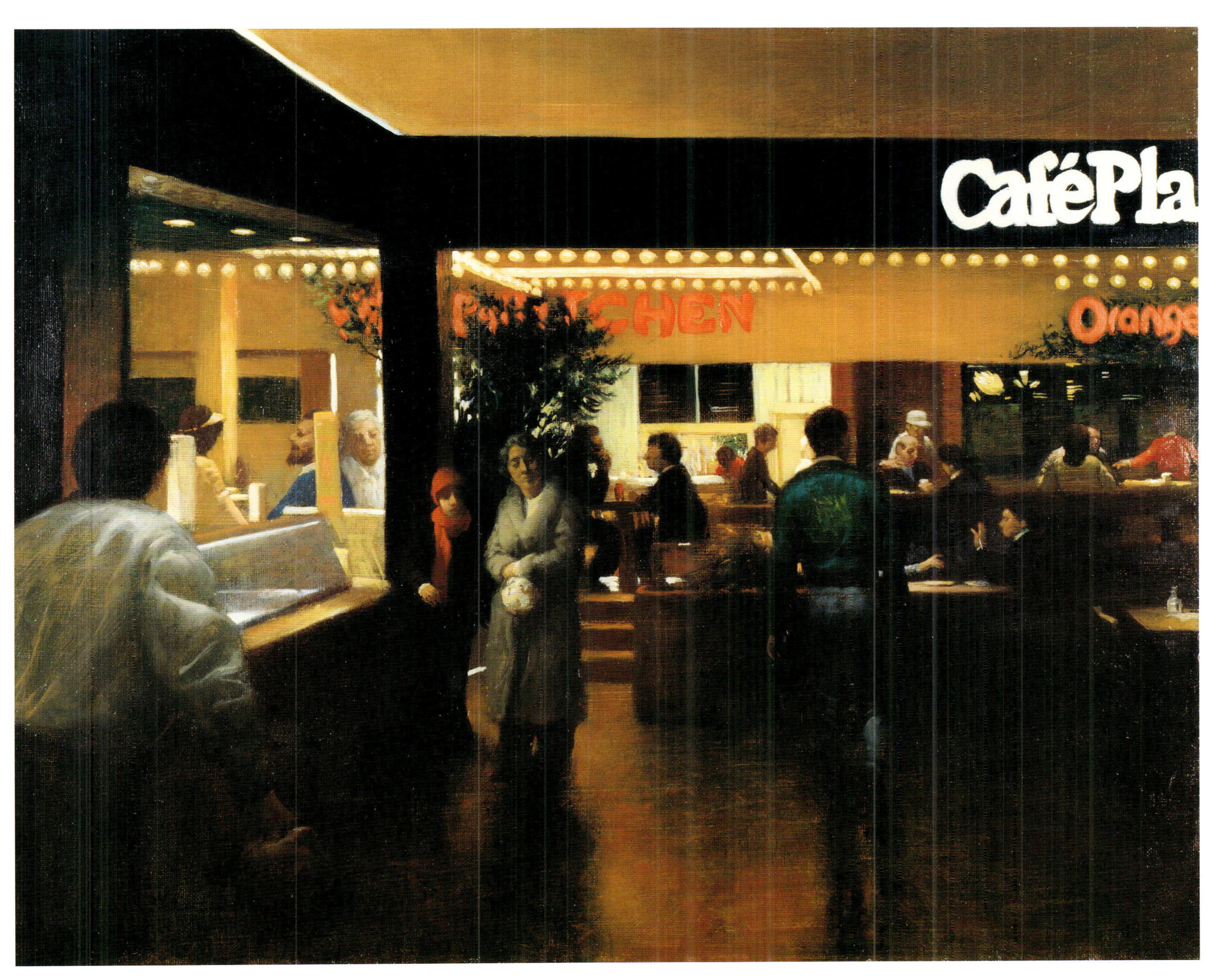

73. CAFE PLA

1939, oil on canvas, 16 × 20 inches

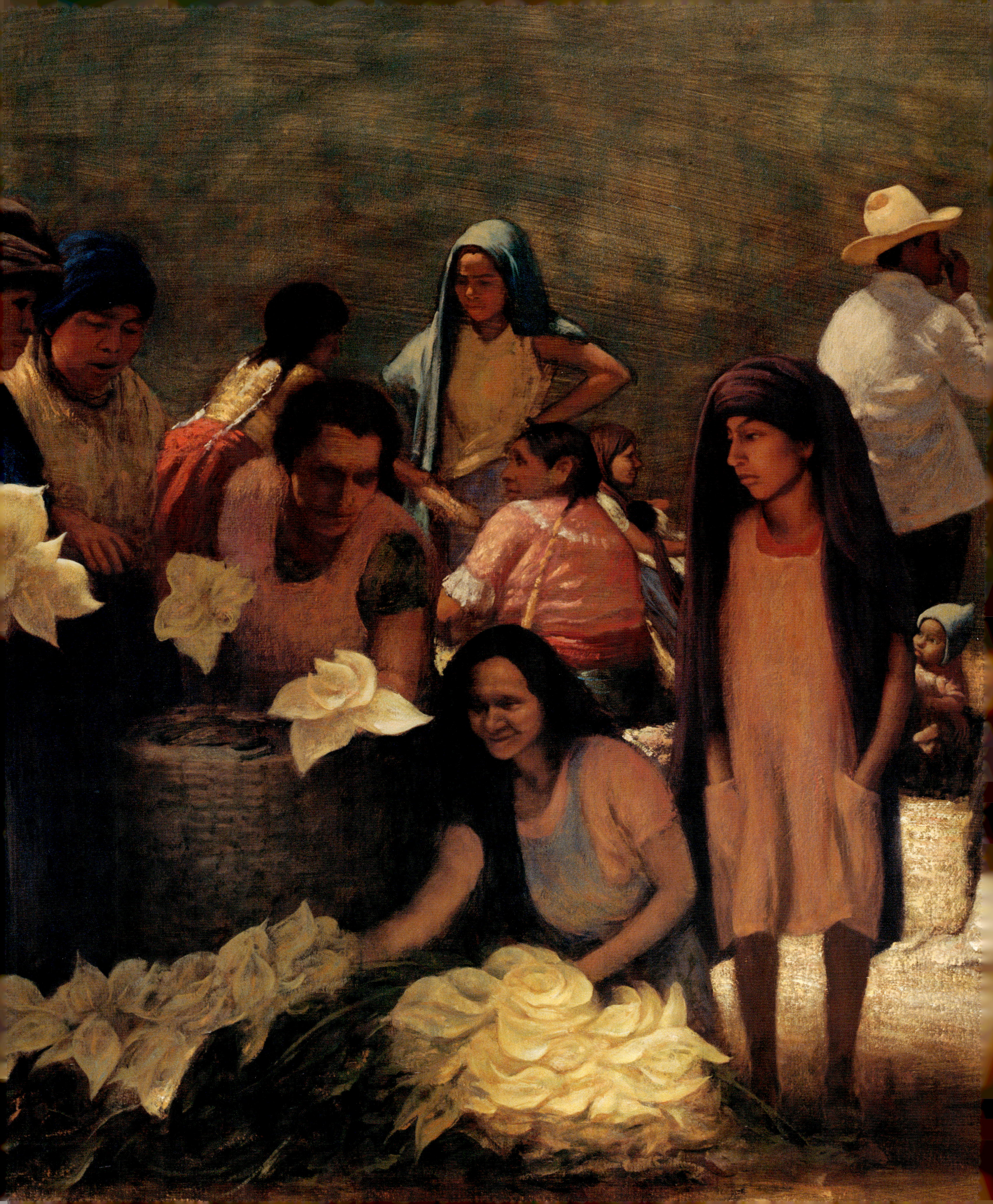

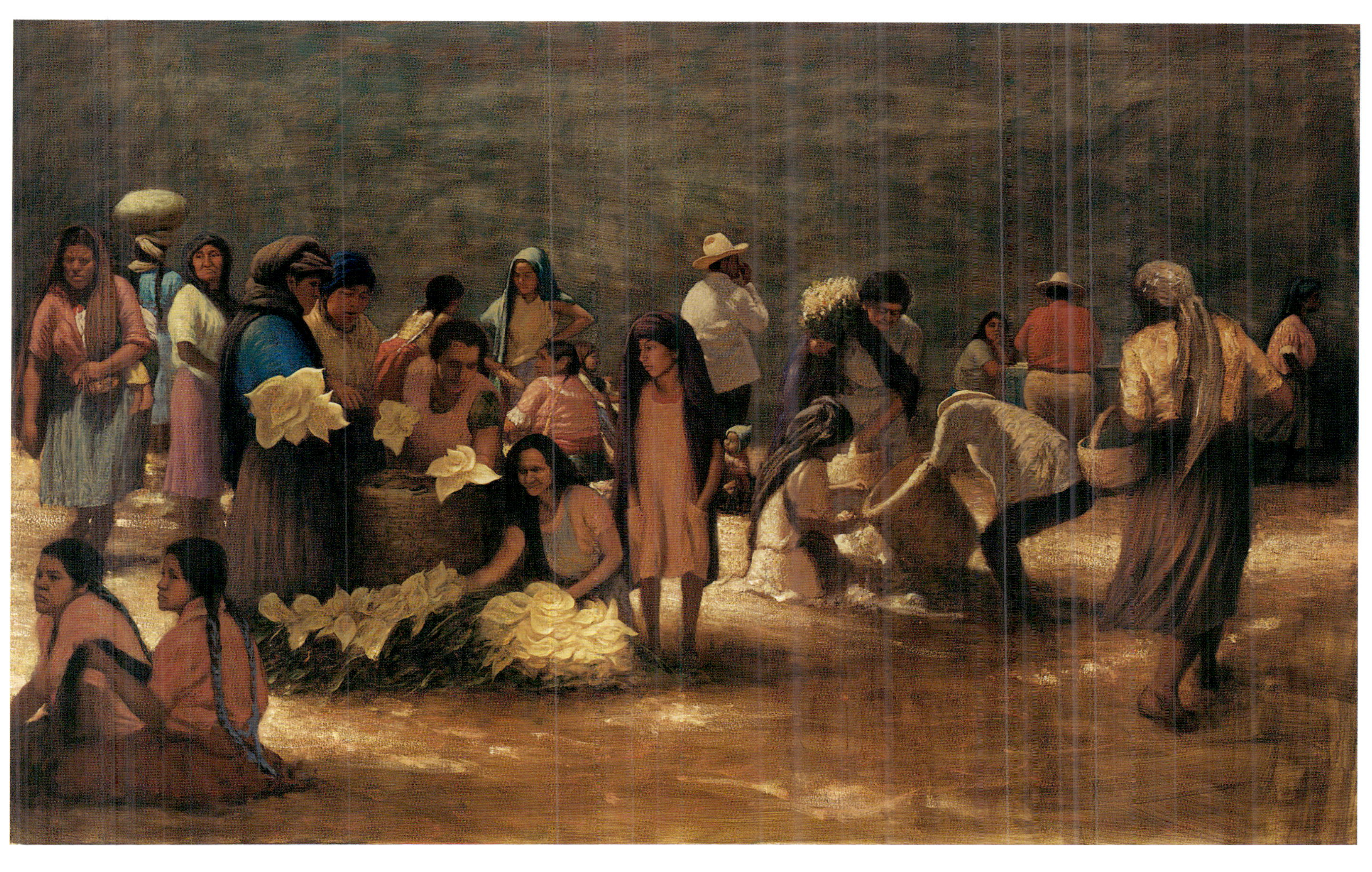

74. EASTER LILIES

1990, oil on canvas, 60 × 96 inches

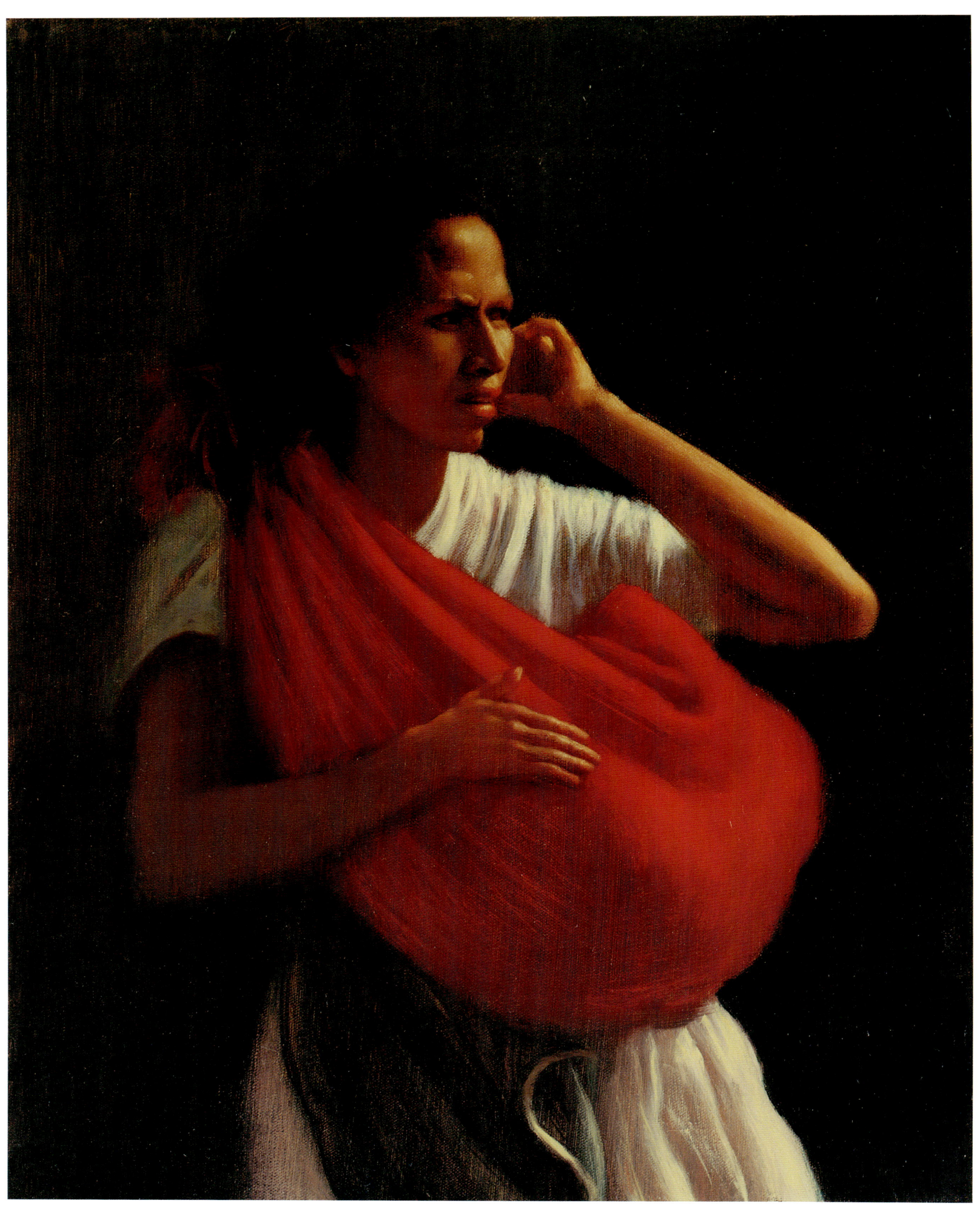

75. ANTIGUA WOMAN

1993, oil on canvas, 20 × 16 inches

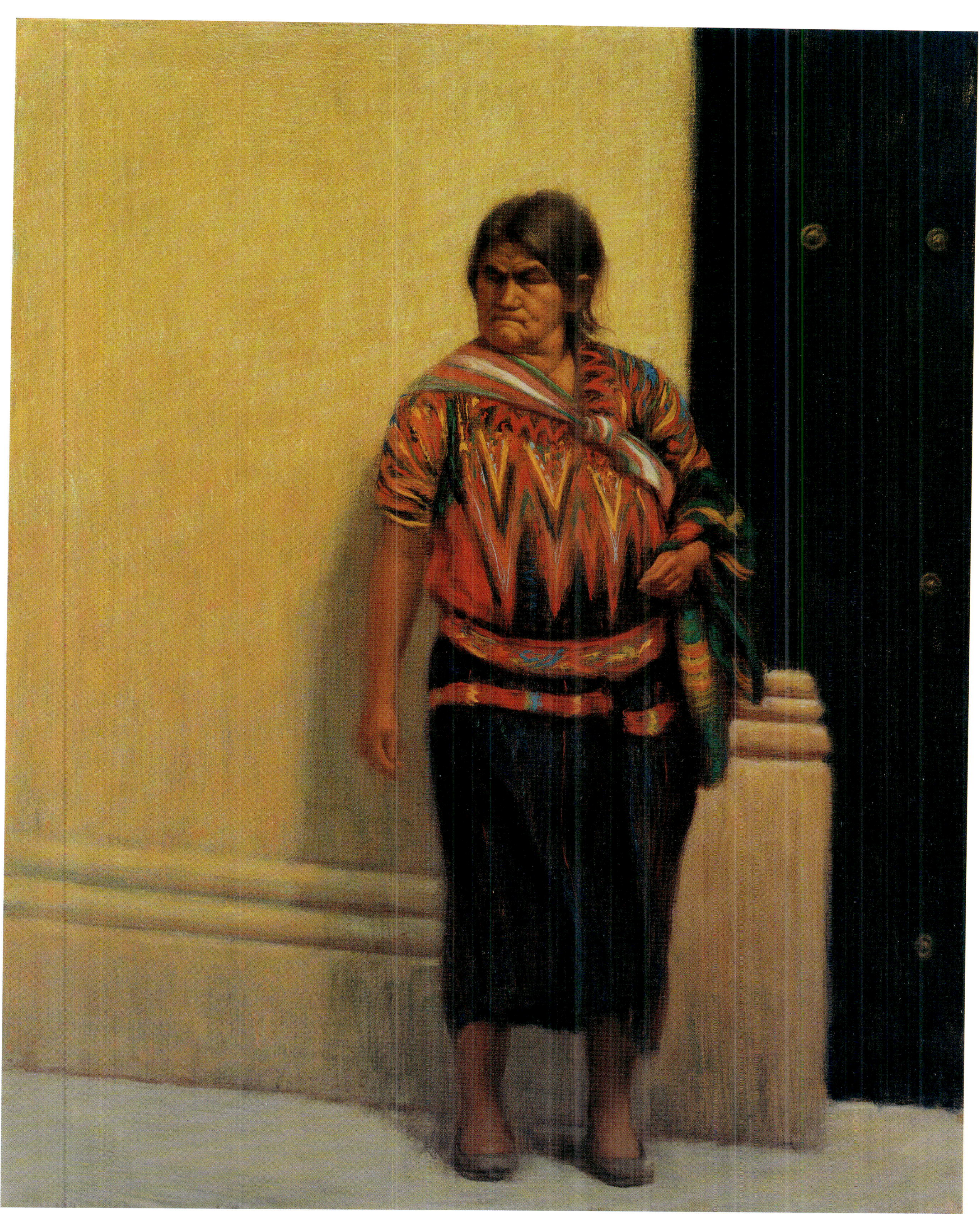

76. ANTIGUA WOMAN #2
1993, oil on canvas, 30 × 24 inches

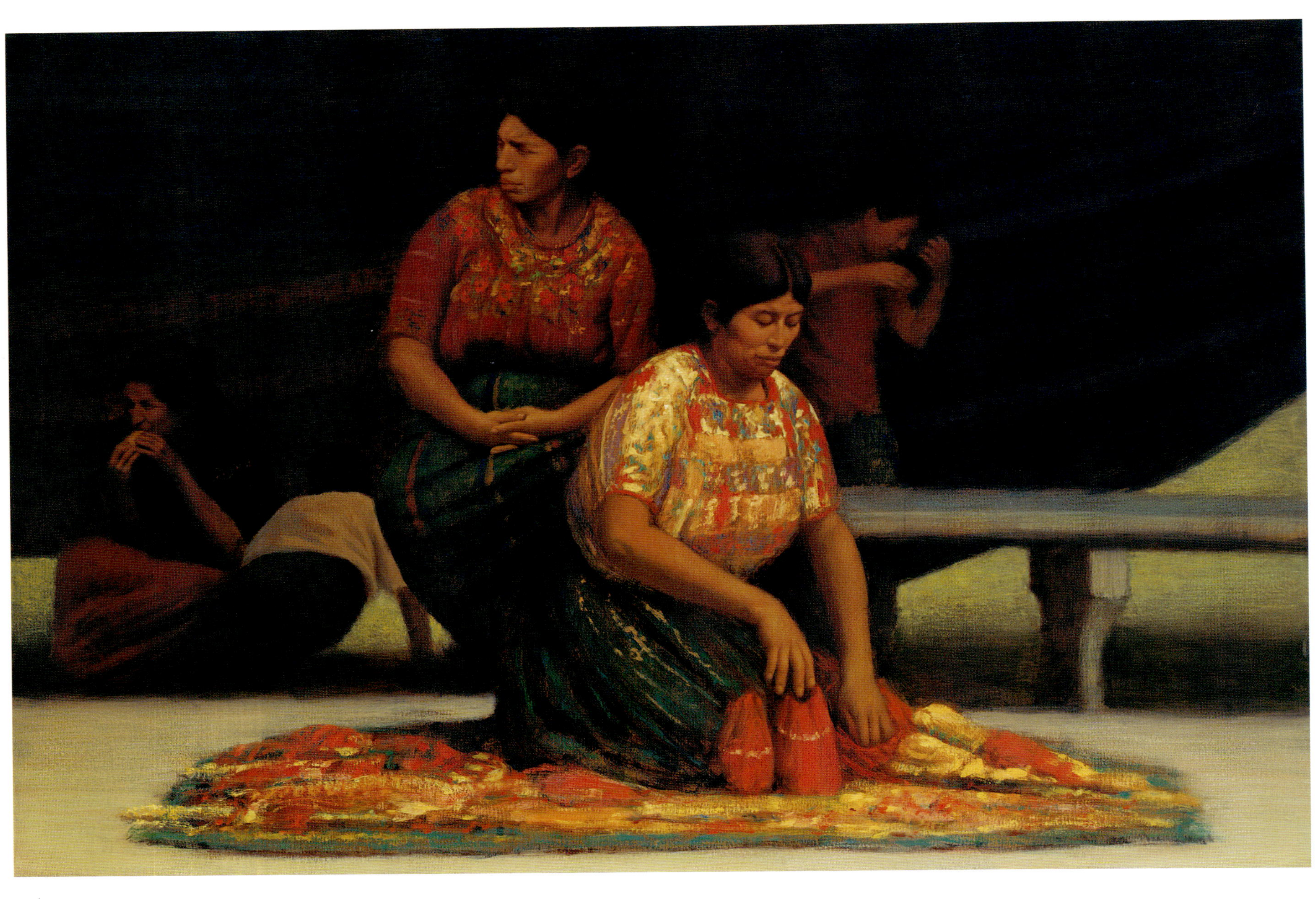

77. CHI CHI CASTENANGO
1993, oil on canvas, 40 × 60 inches

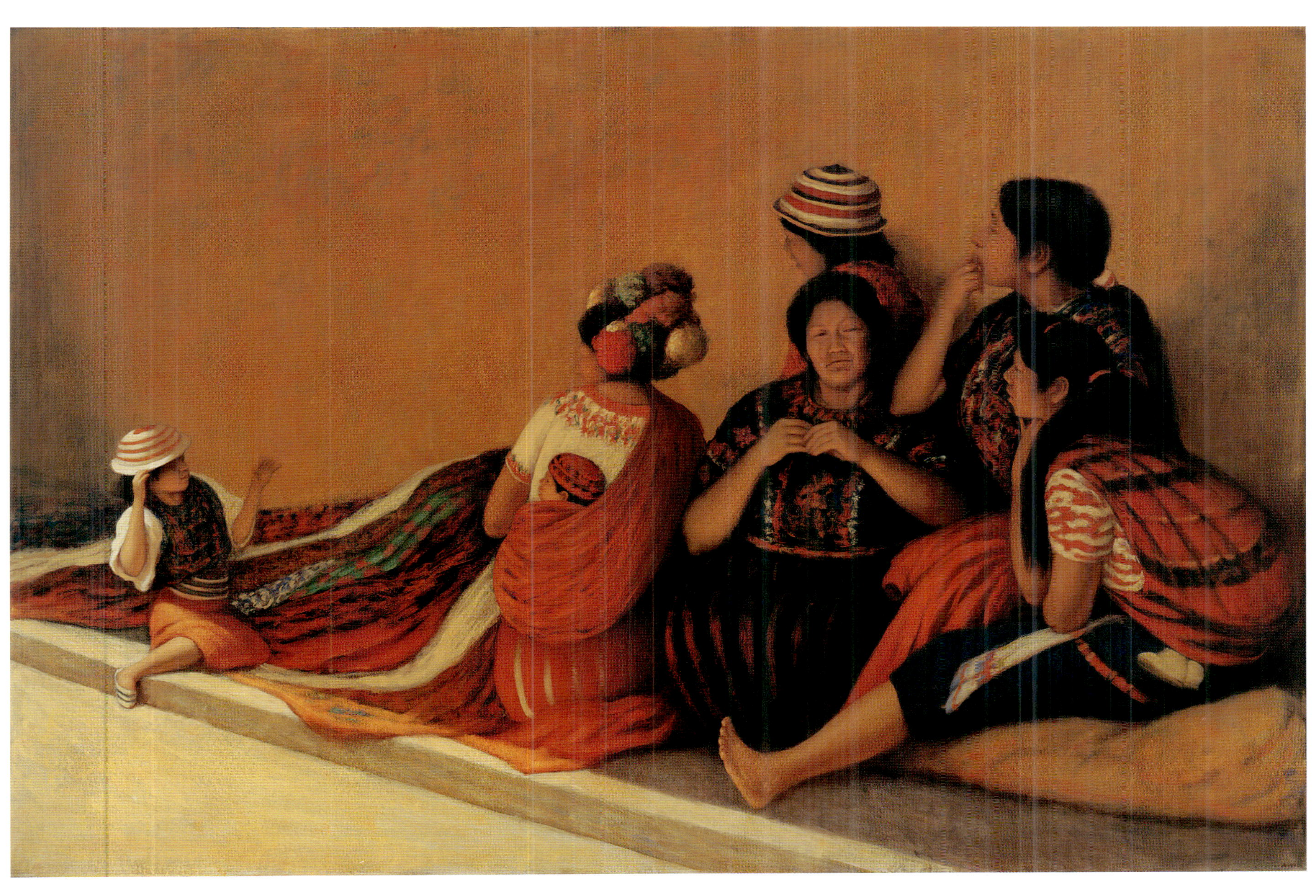

78. ANTIGUA: IN THE SHADE

1993, oil on canvas, 40 × 60 inches

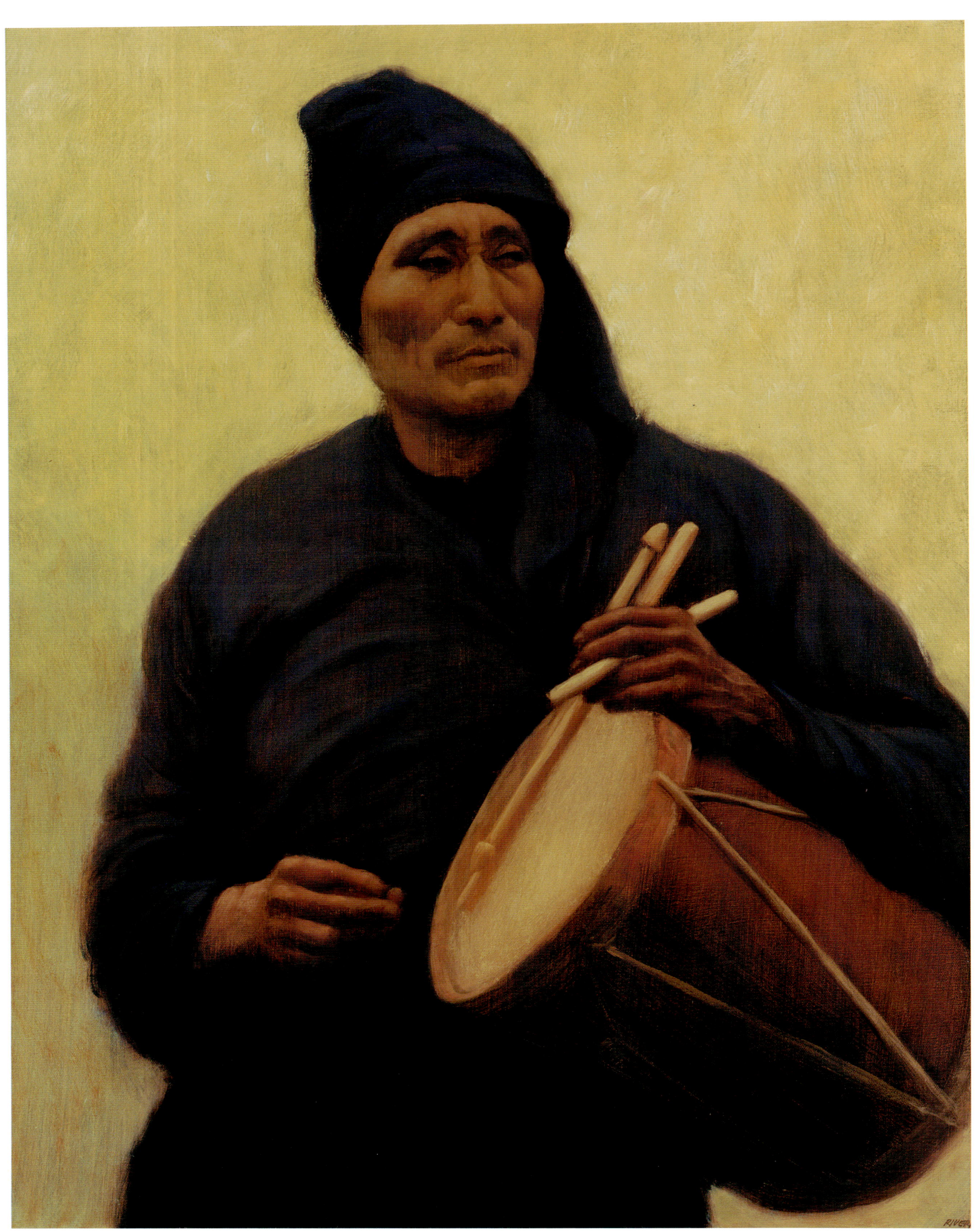

79. A PAUSE IN THE PROCESSION II

1993, oil on canvas, 30 × 24 inches

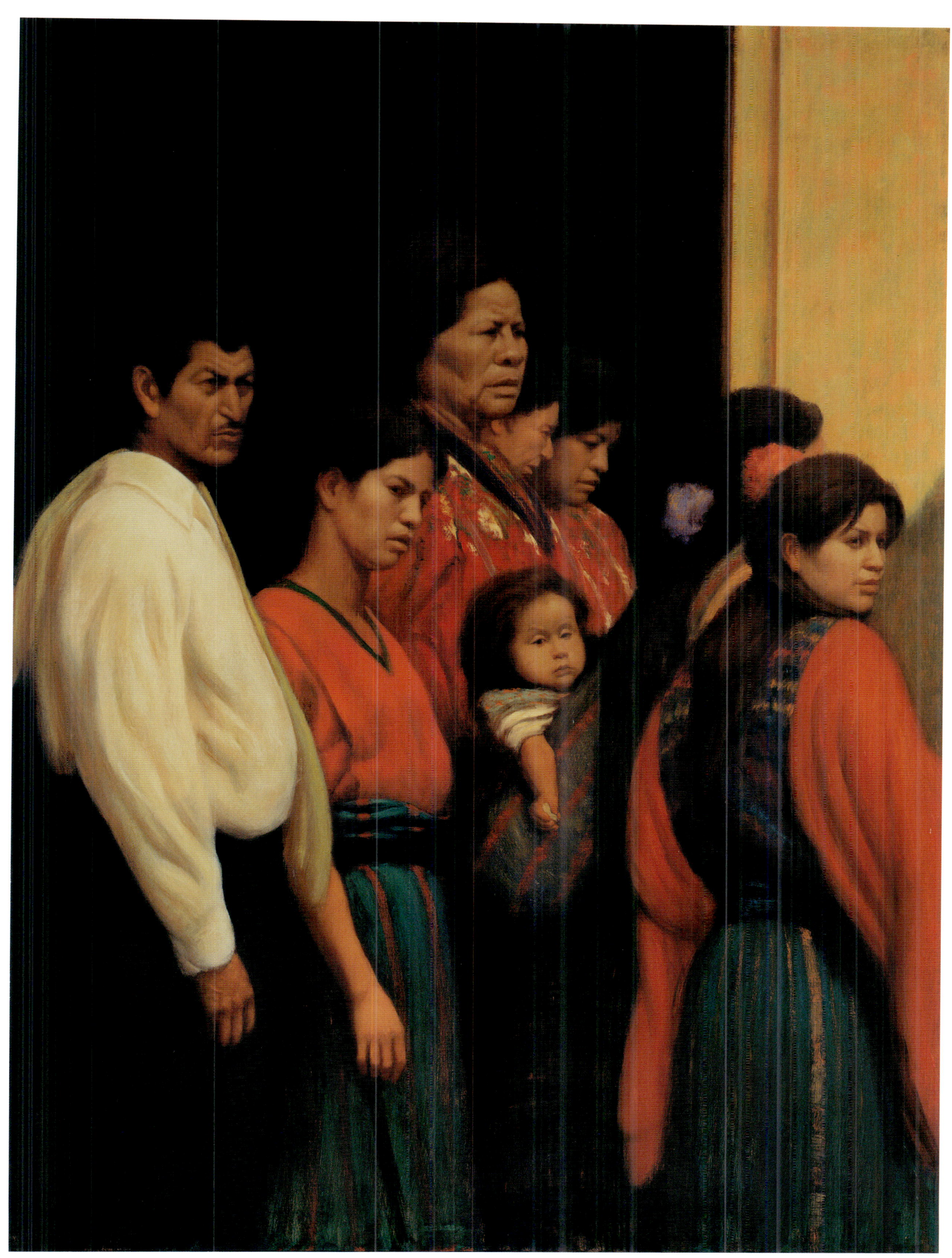

80. WATCHING THE PROCESSION

1993, oil on canvas, 48 × 36 inches

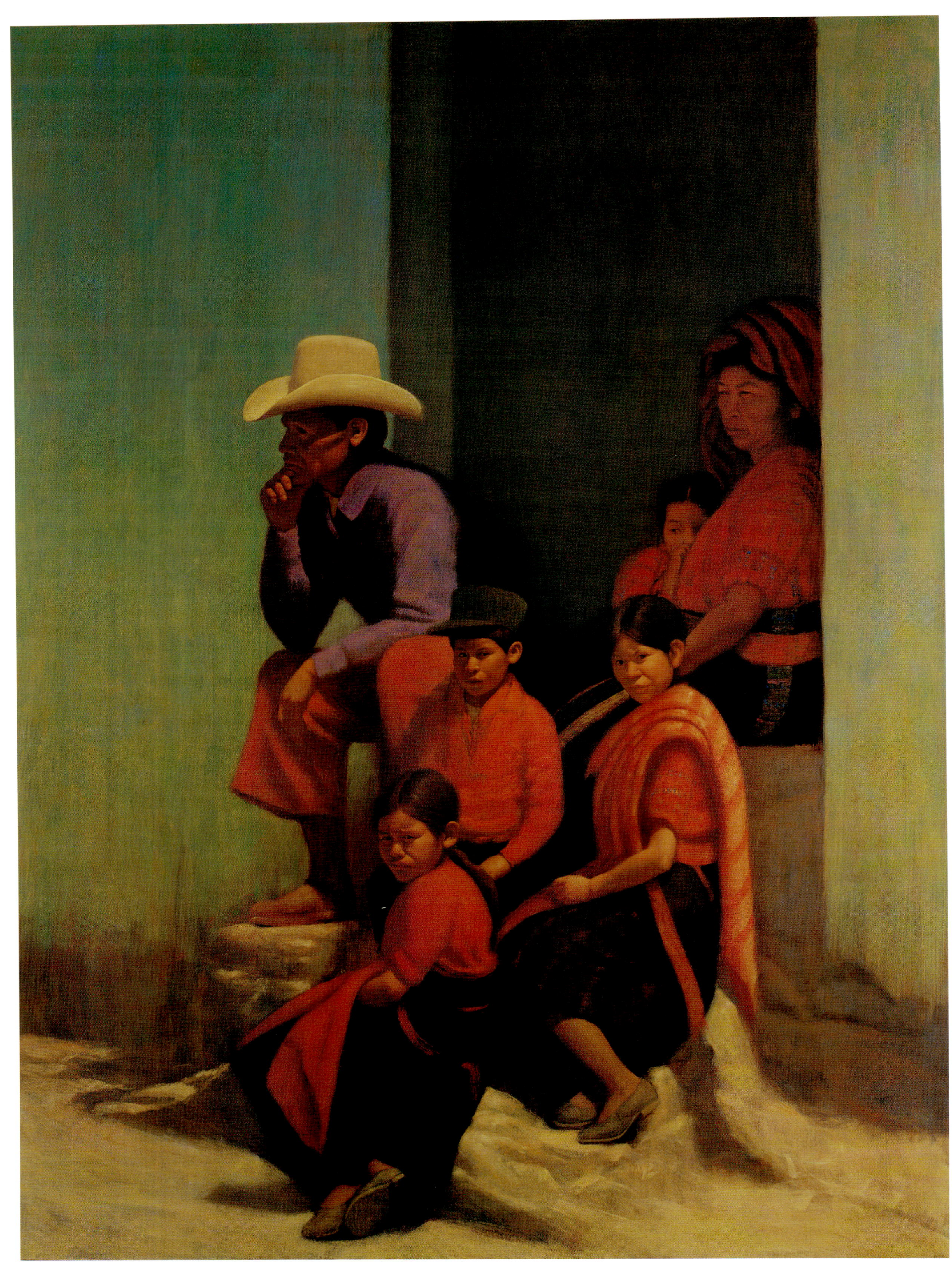

81. SOLOLA FAMILY

1994, oil on canvas, 108 × 80 inches

Collection of the Museum of Fine Arts, MNM, Department of Cultural Affairs

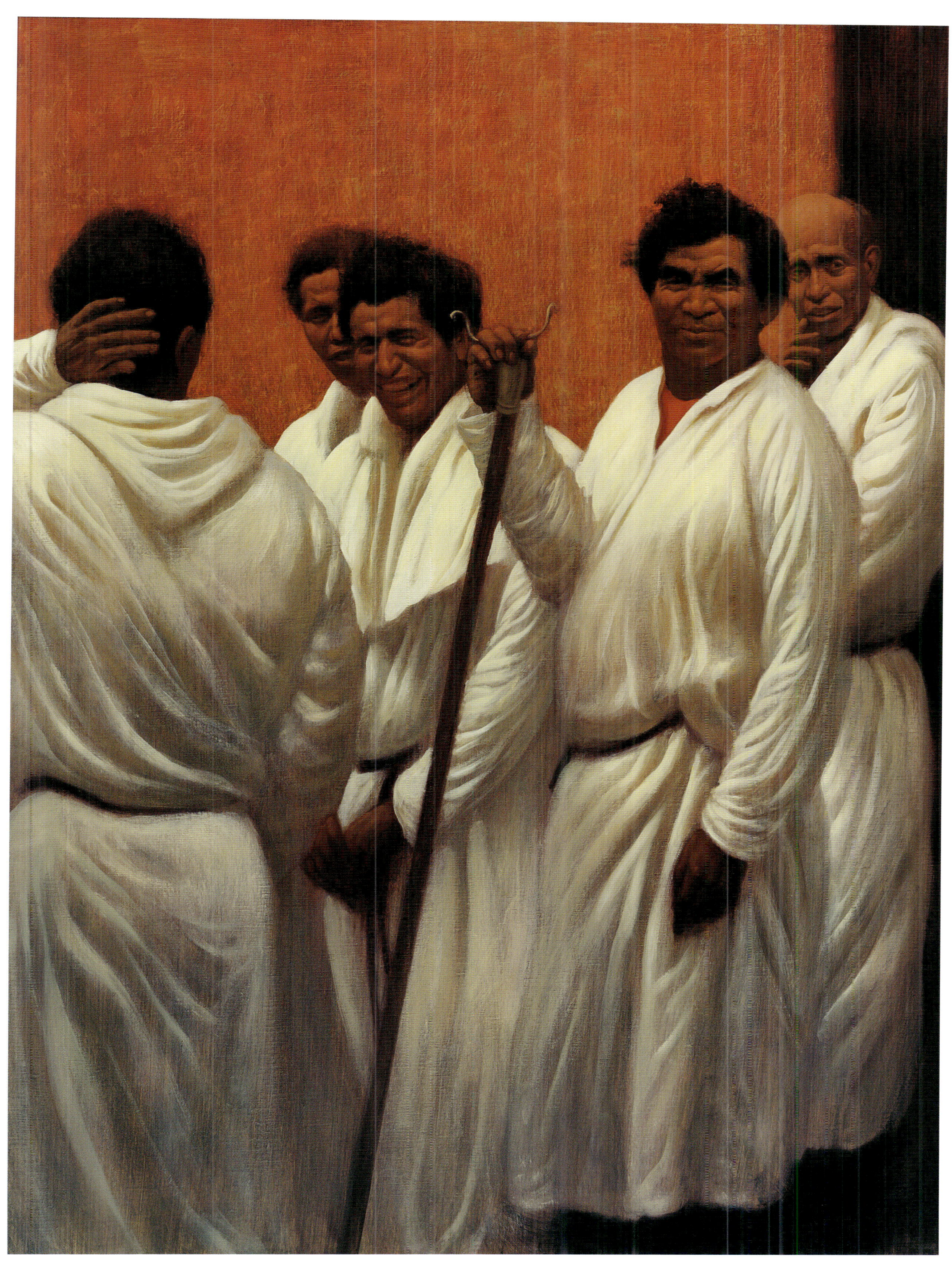

82. A WHIMSICAL MOMENT
1994, oil on canvas, 48 × 36 inches

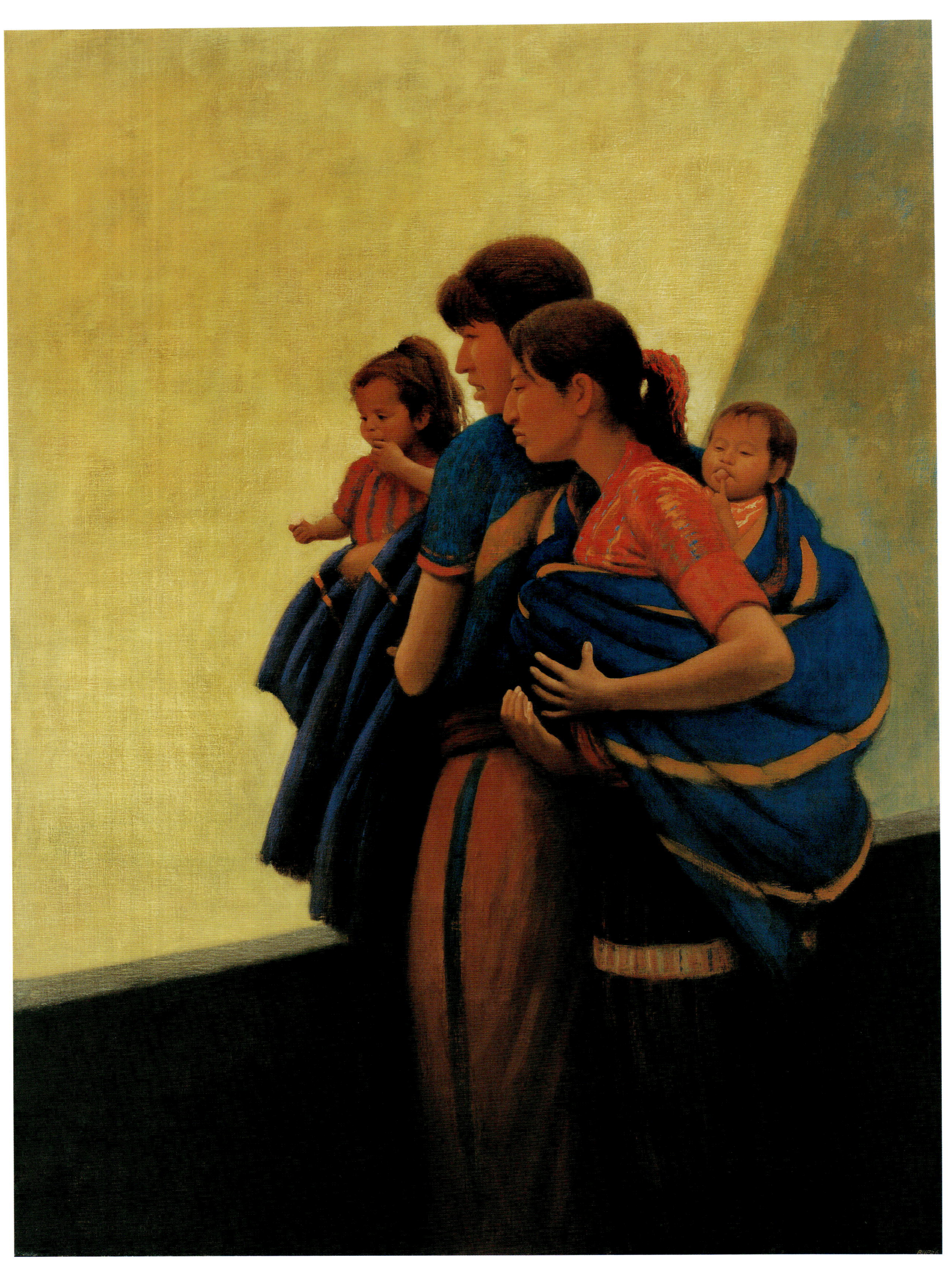

83. BLUE BLANKET
1994, oil on canvas, 70 × 52 inches

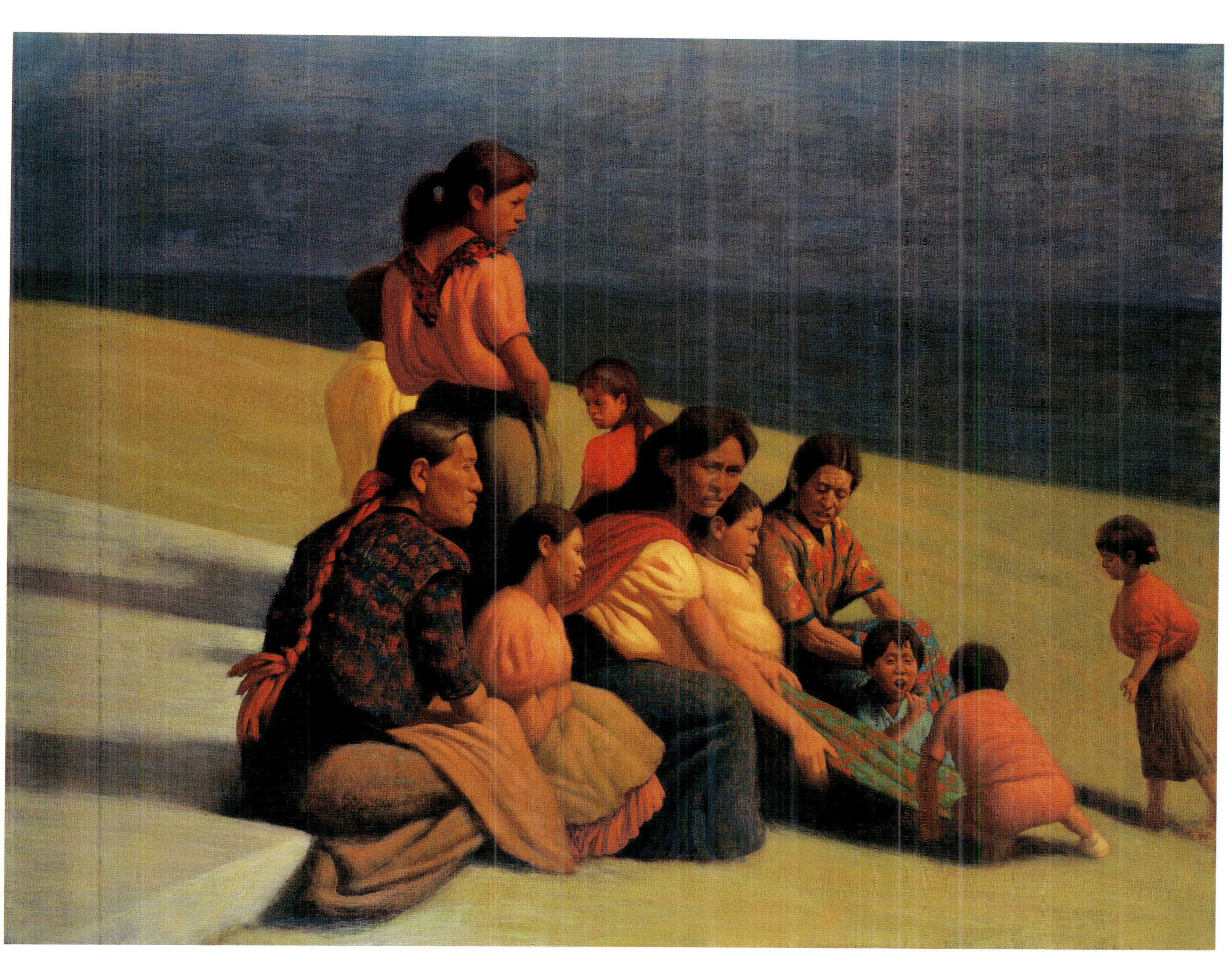

84. SOLOLA: WHISPERS BY THE LAKE

1994, oil on canvas, 60 × 78 inches

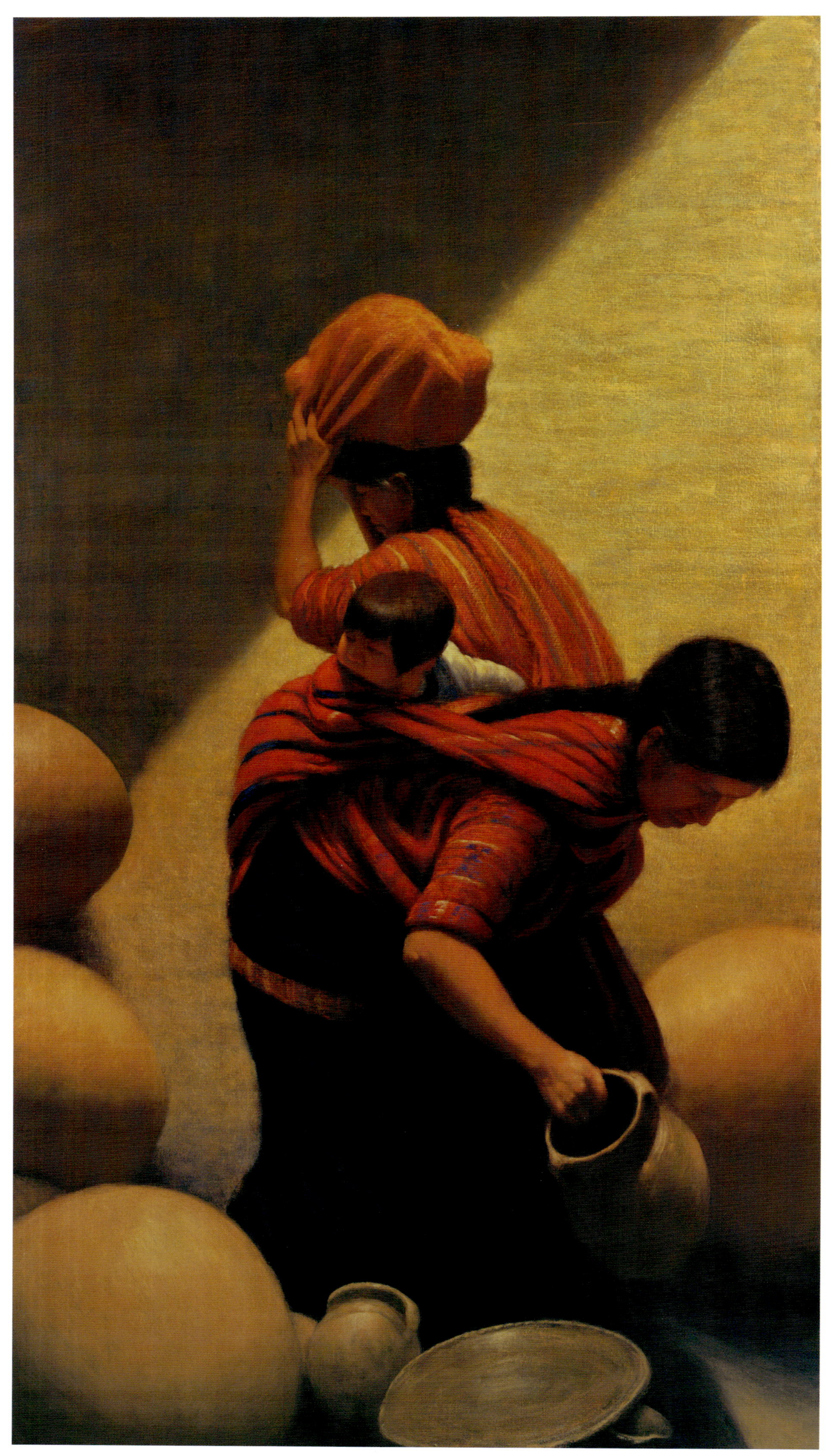

85. VISIONS OF CLAY

1994, oil on canvas, 72 × 40 inches

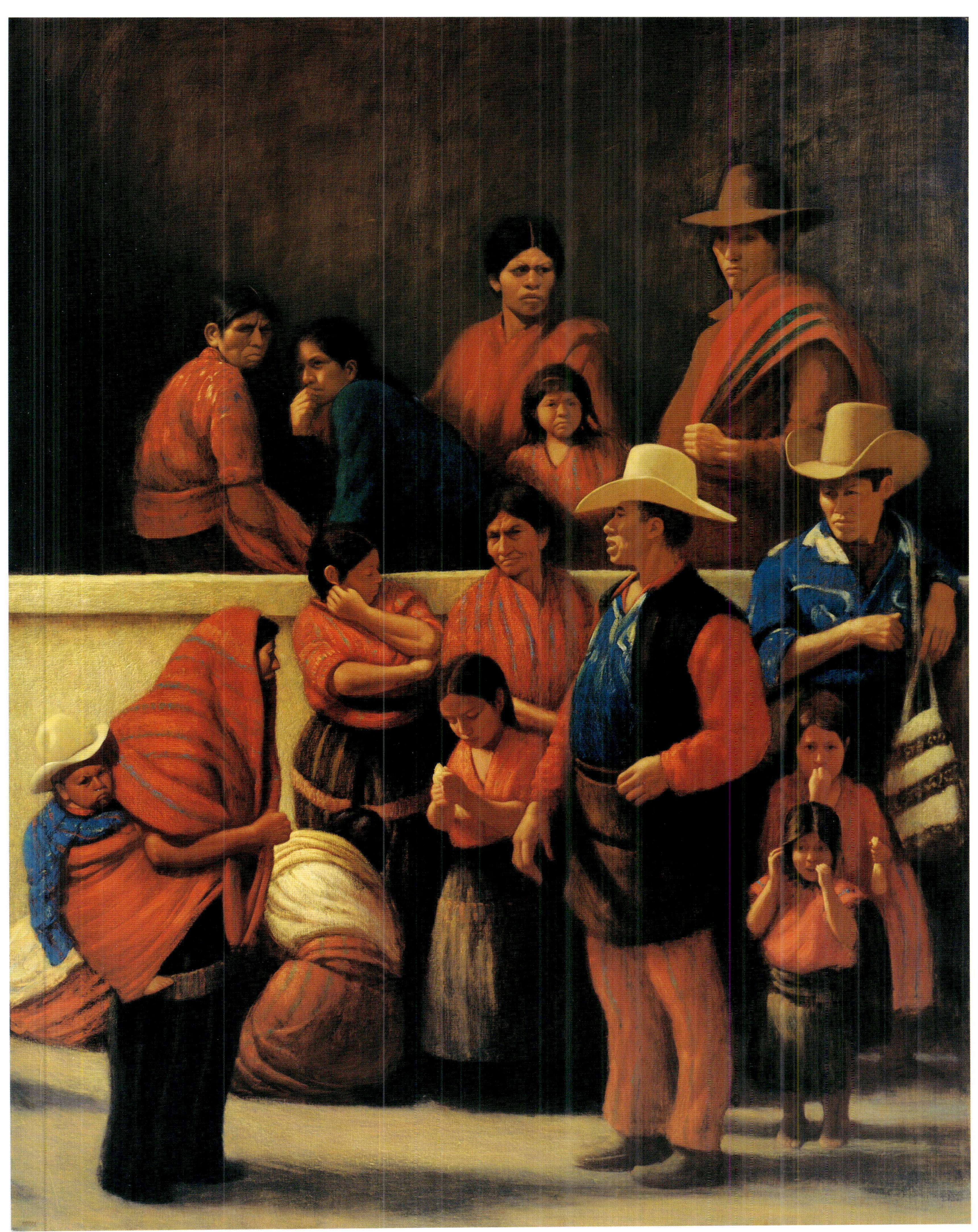

86. SOLOLA MARKETPLACE

1994, oil on canvas, 100 × 78 inches

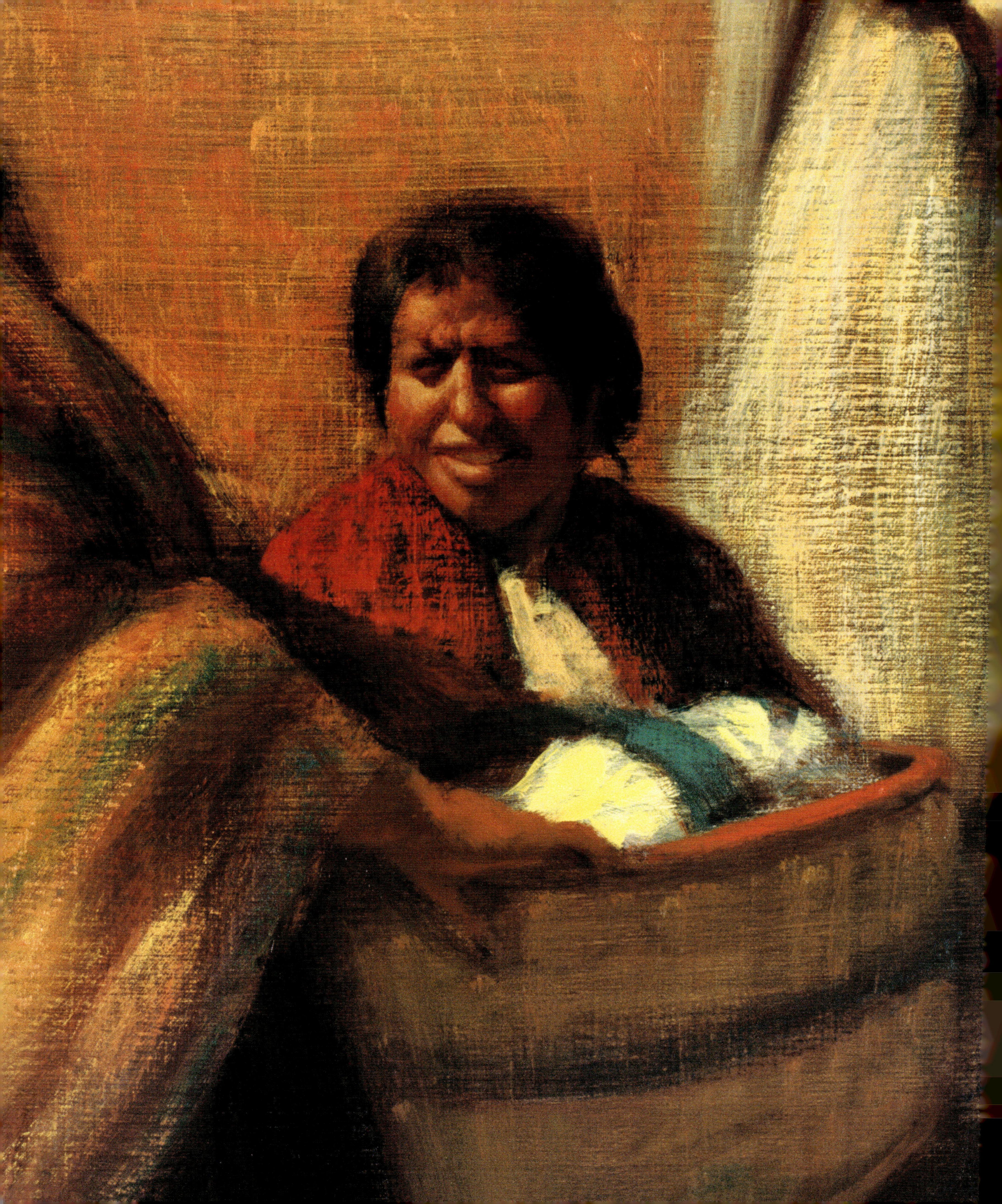

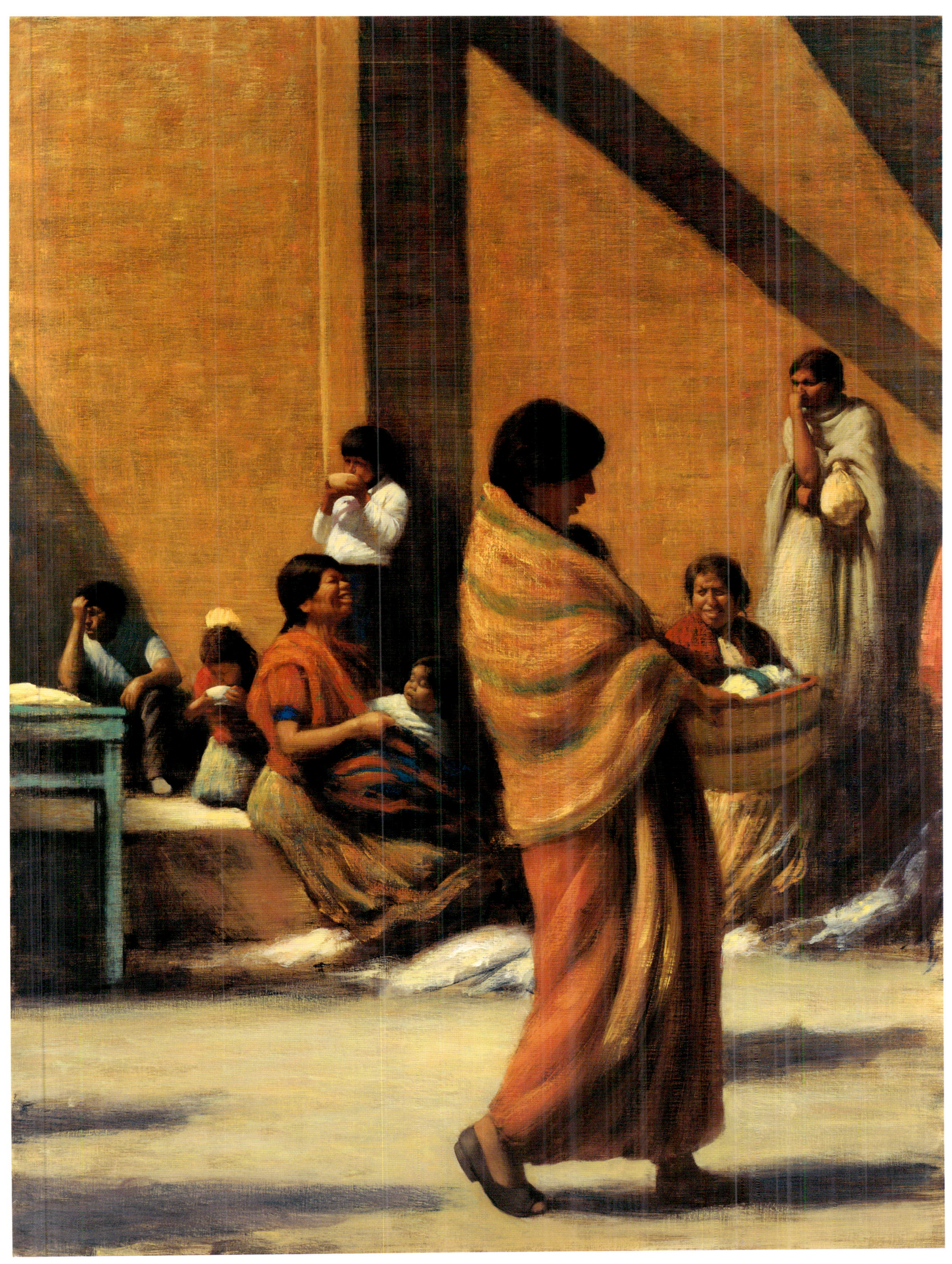

87. PATZUN #1

1994, oil on canvas, 72 × 48 inches

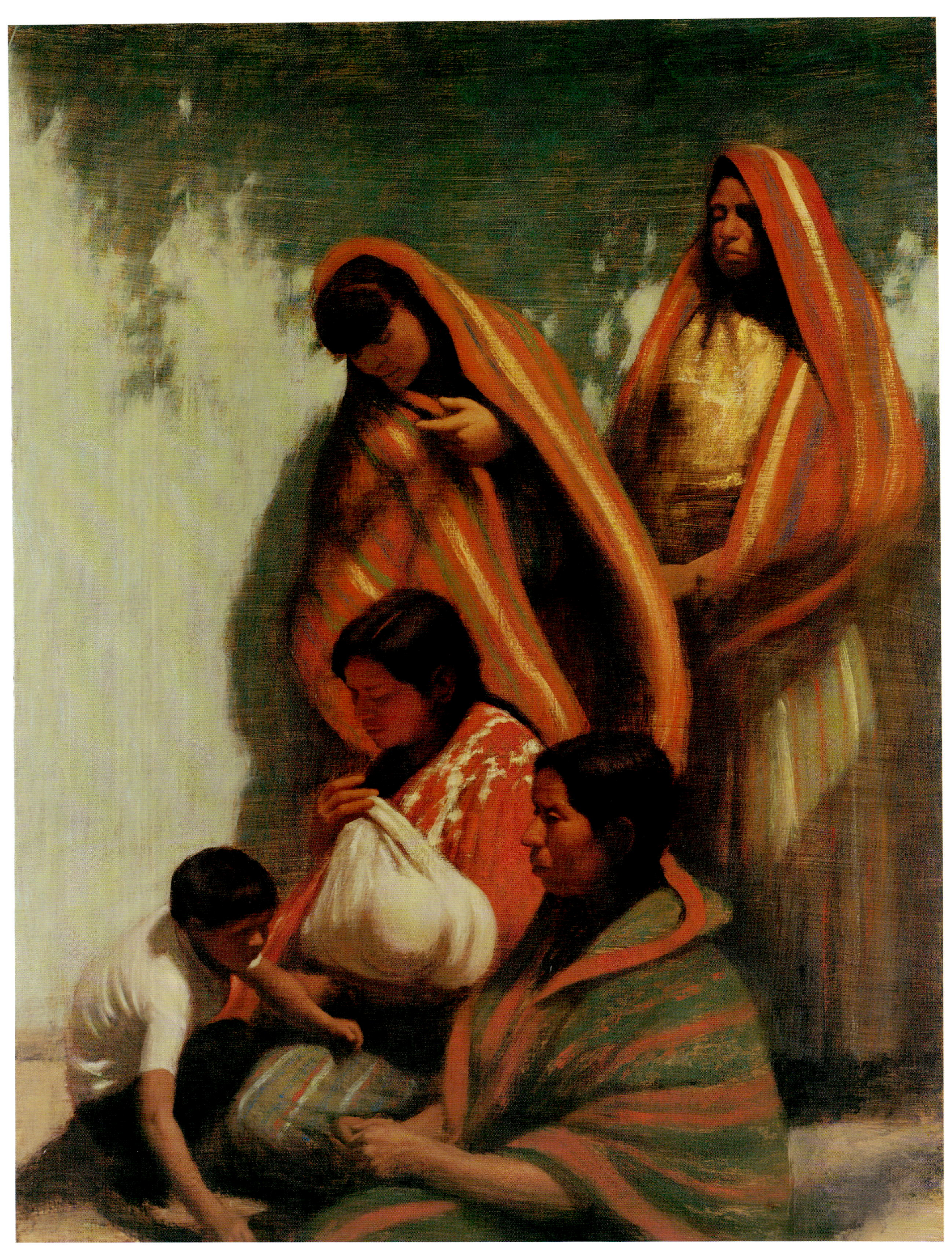

88. PATZUN #2

1994, oil on canvas, 24 × 20 inches

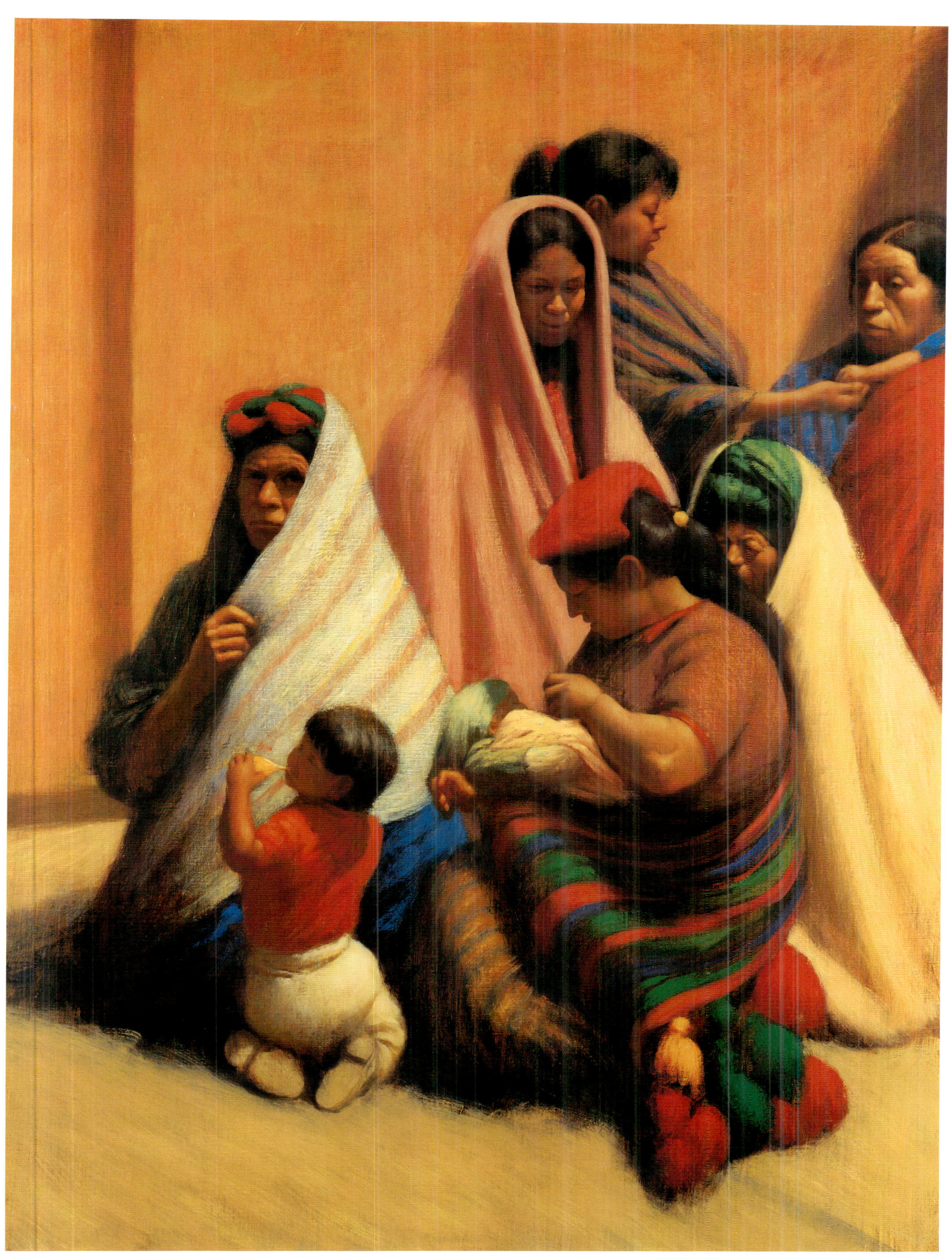

89. PATZUN #3

1994, oil on canvas, 24 × 20 inches

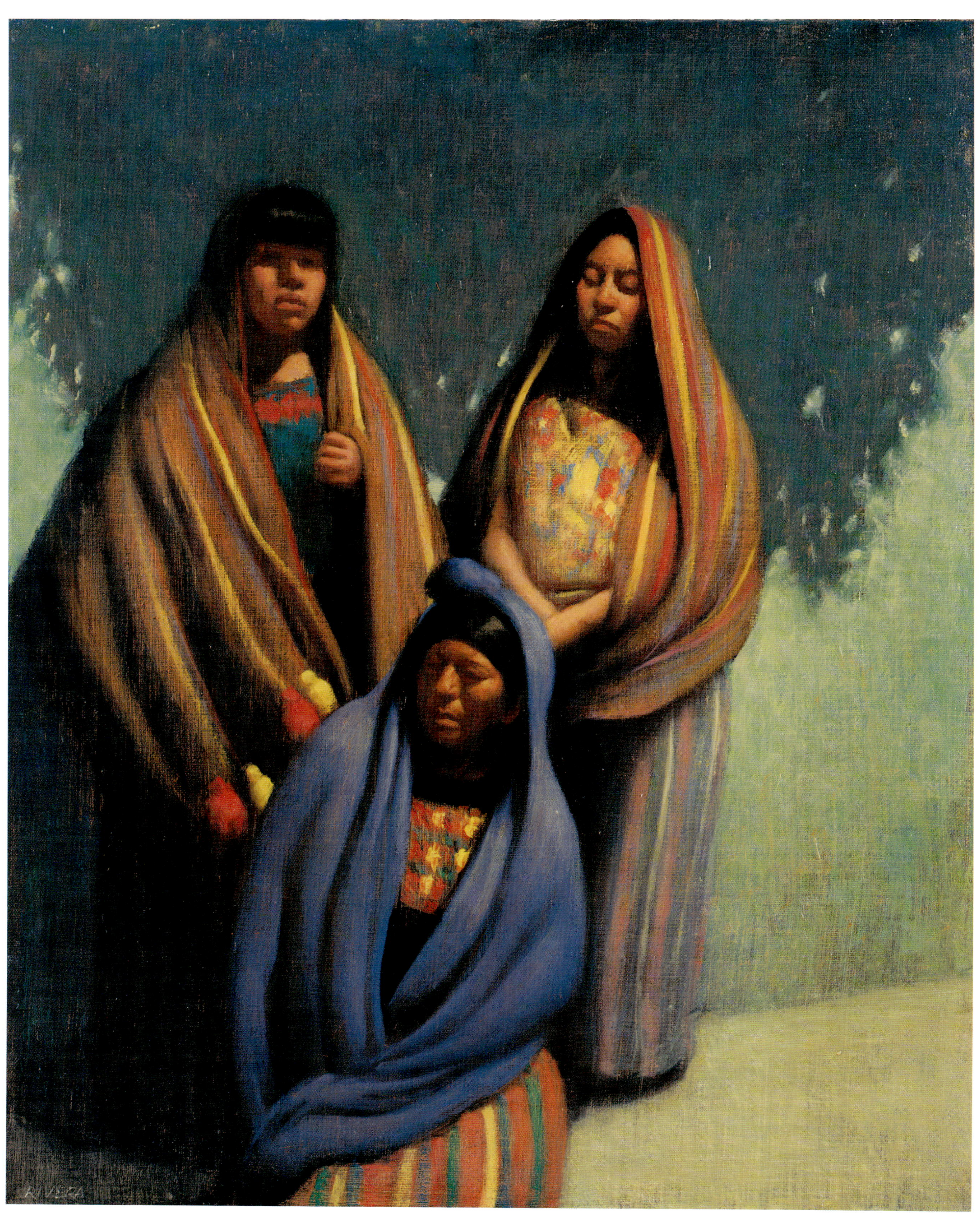

90. PATZUN #4

1994, oil on canvas, 24 × 20 inches

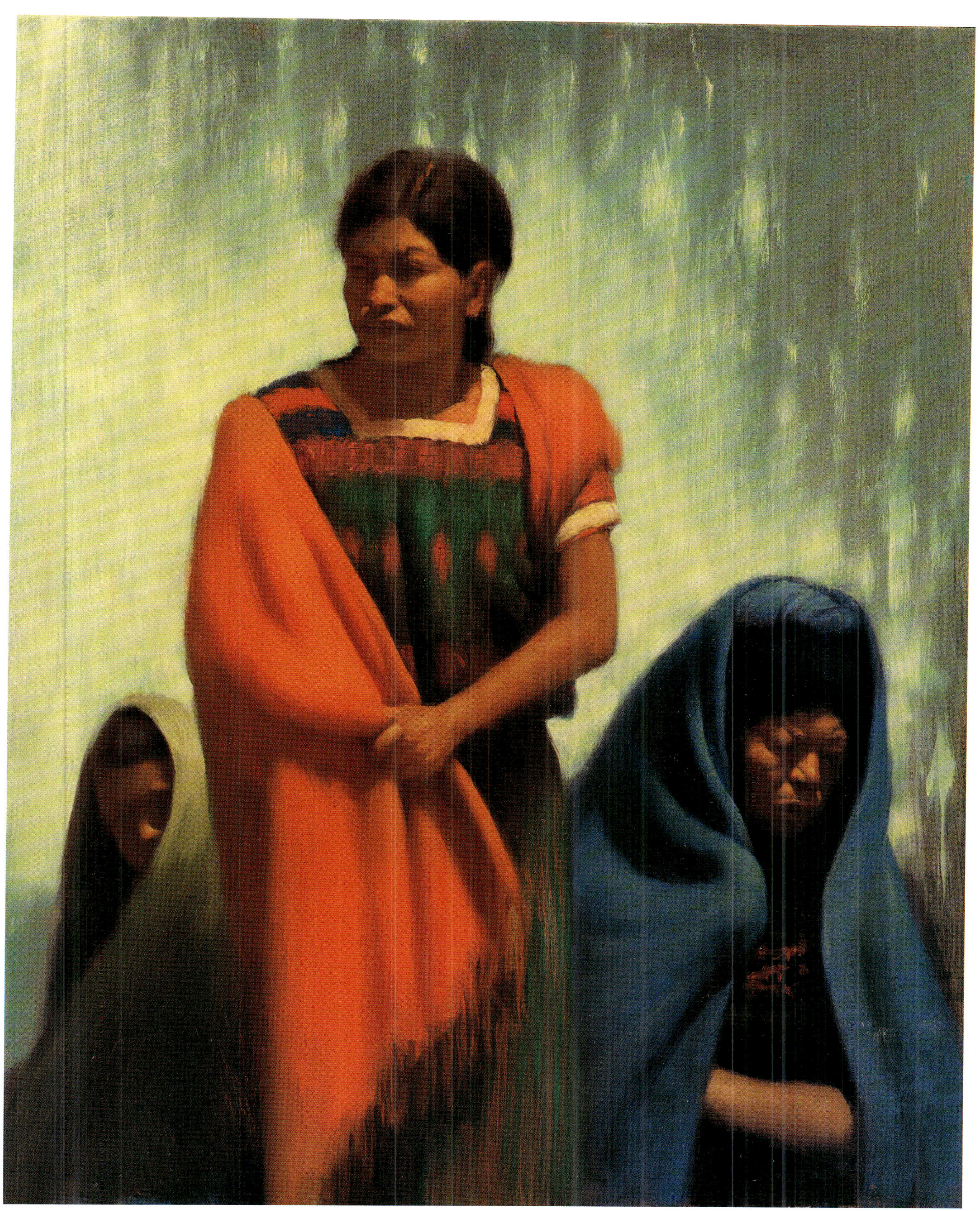

91 PATZUN #5

1994, oil on canvas, 24 × 20 inches

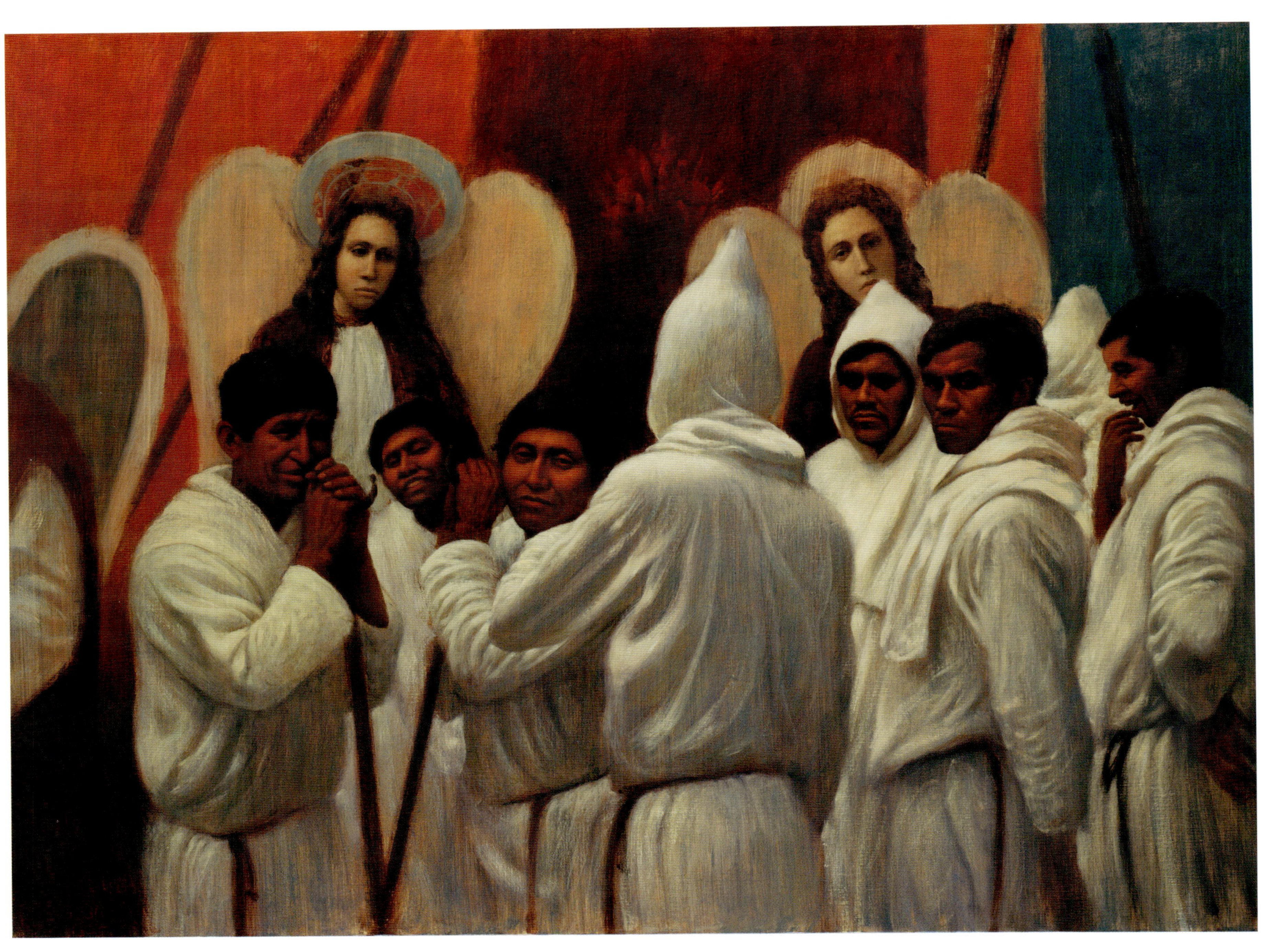

92. A PAUSE IN THE PROCESSION III

1994, oil on canvas, 52 × 70 inches

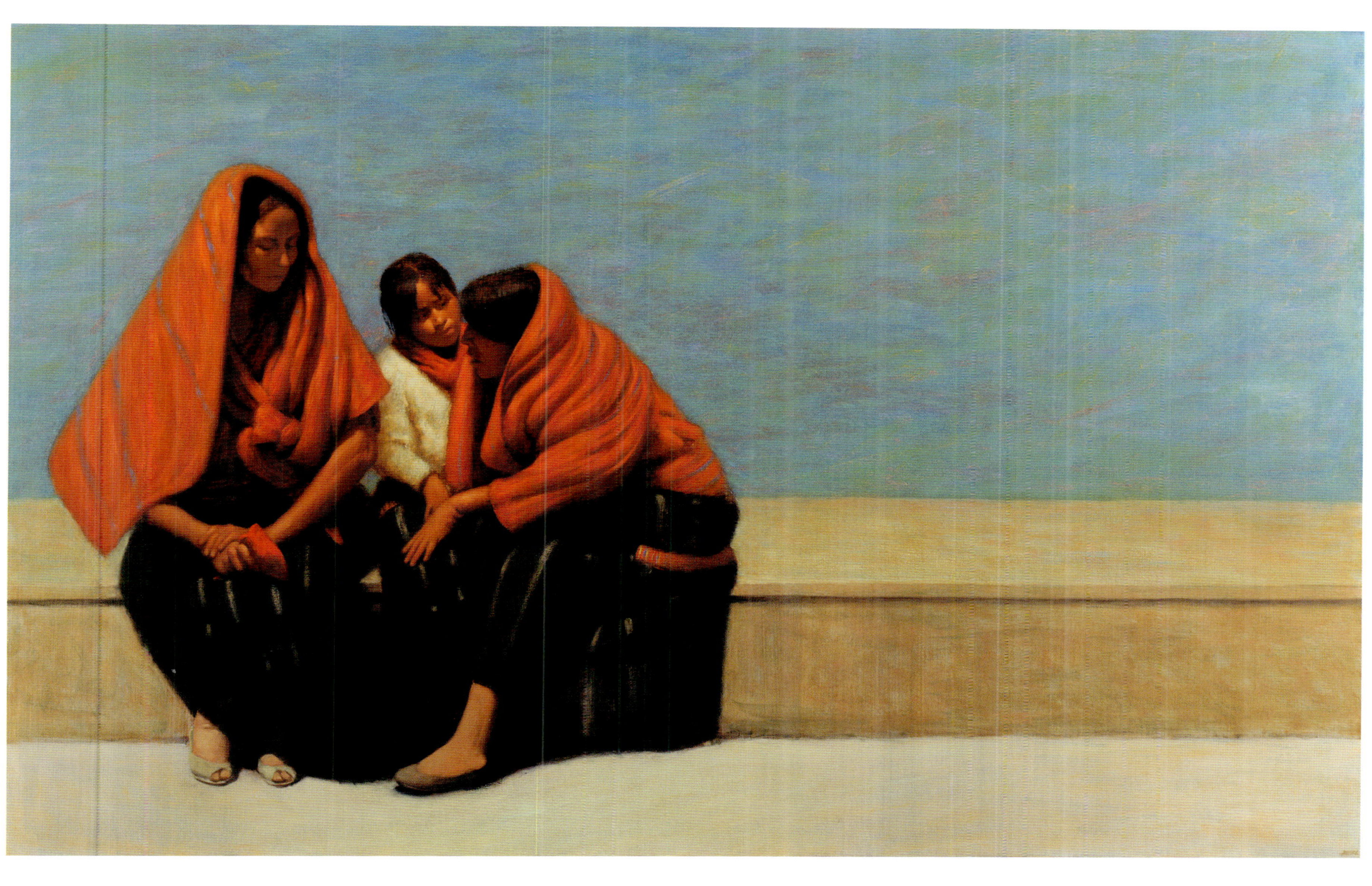

93. SIMPLE SECRETS
1955, oil on canvas, 60 × 96 inches

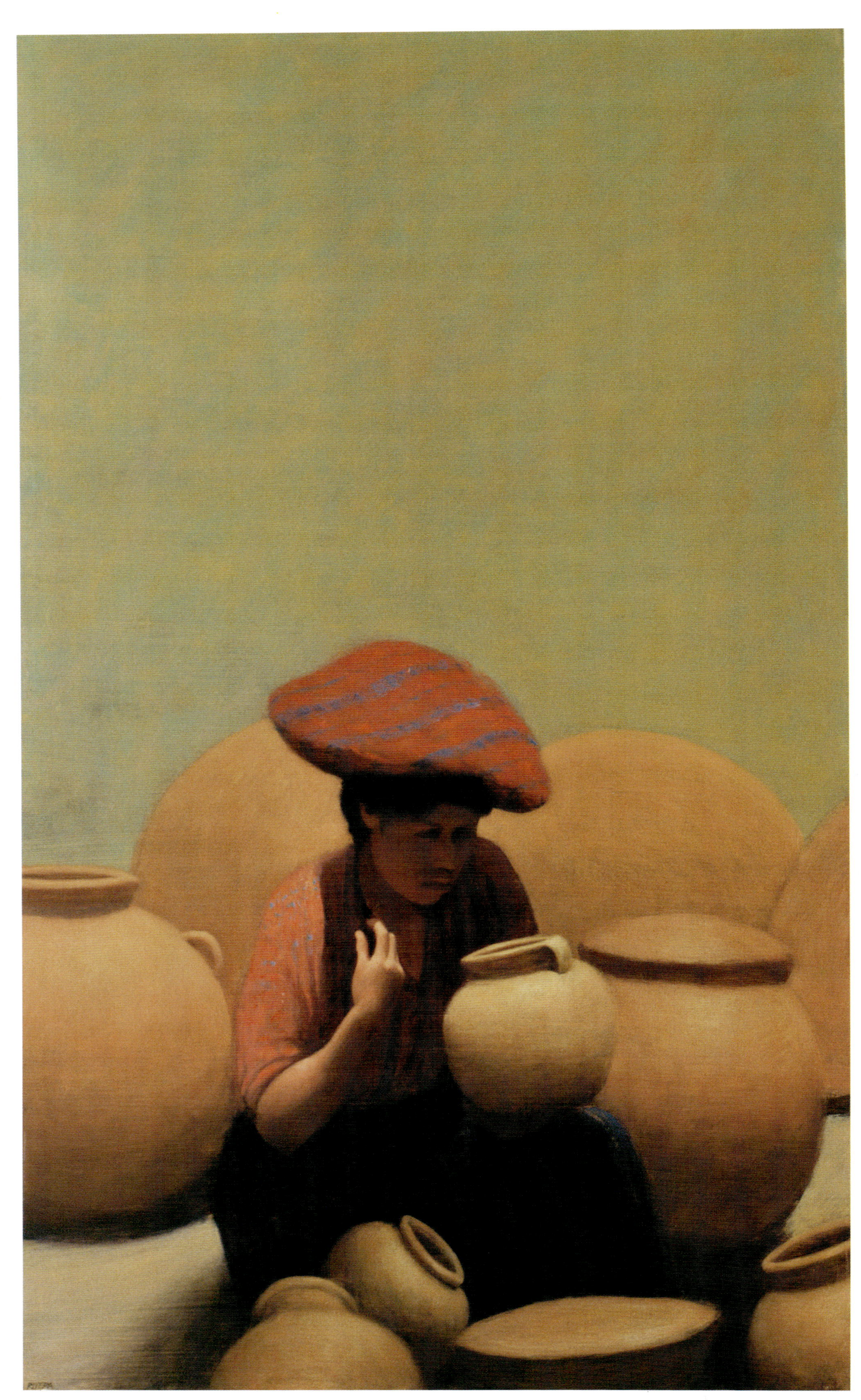

94. THE LONE POTTER (diptych)
1995, oil on canvas, 60 × 132 inches

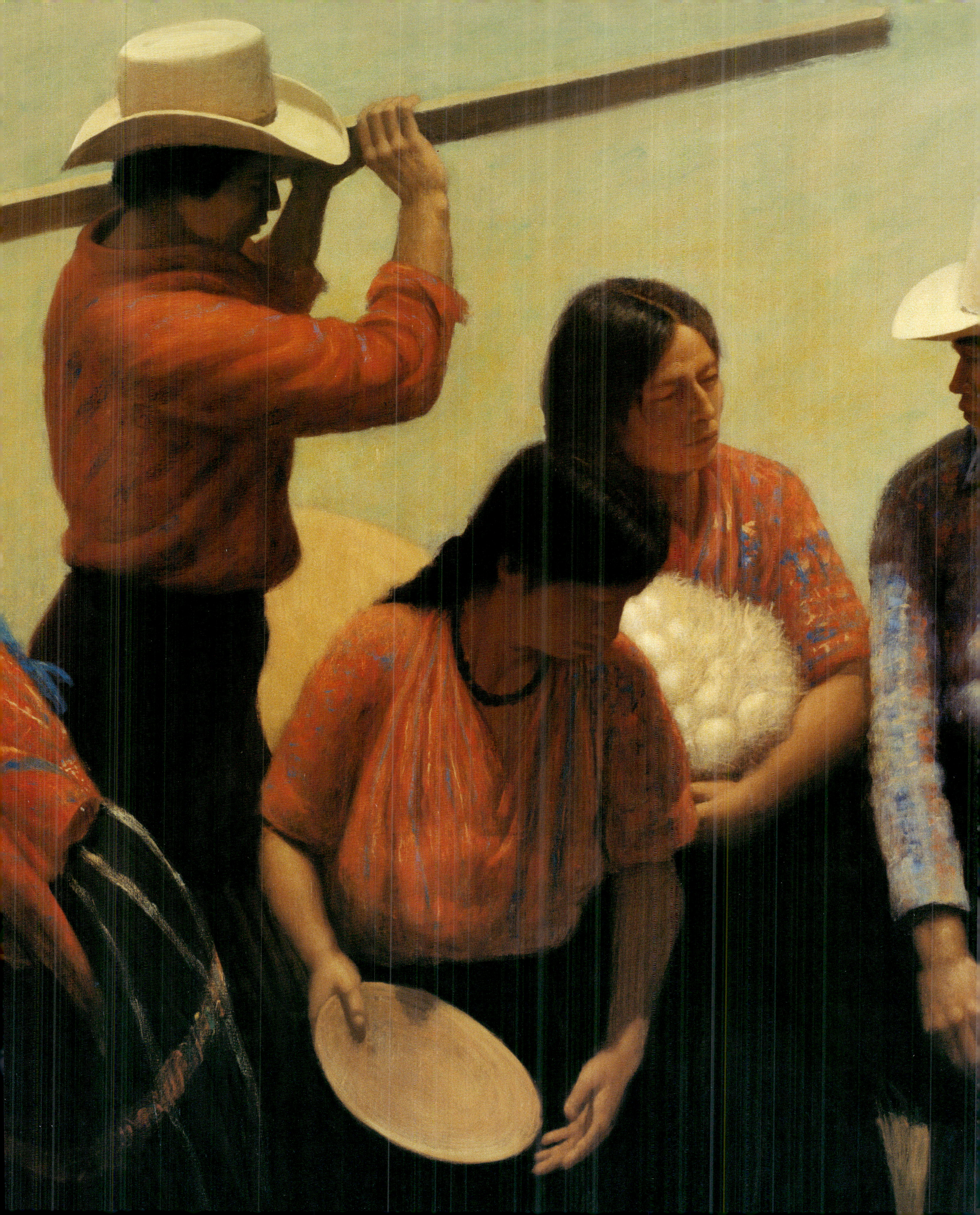

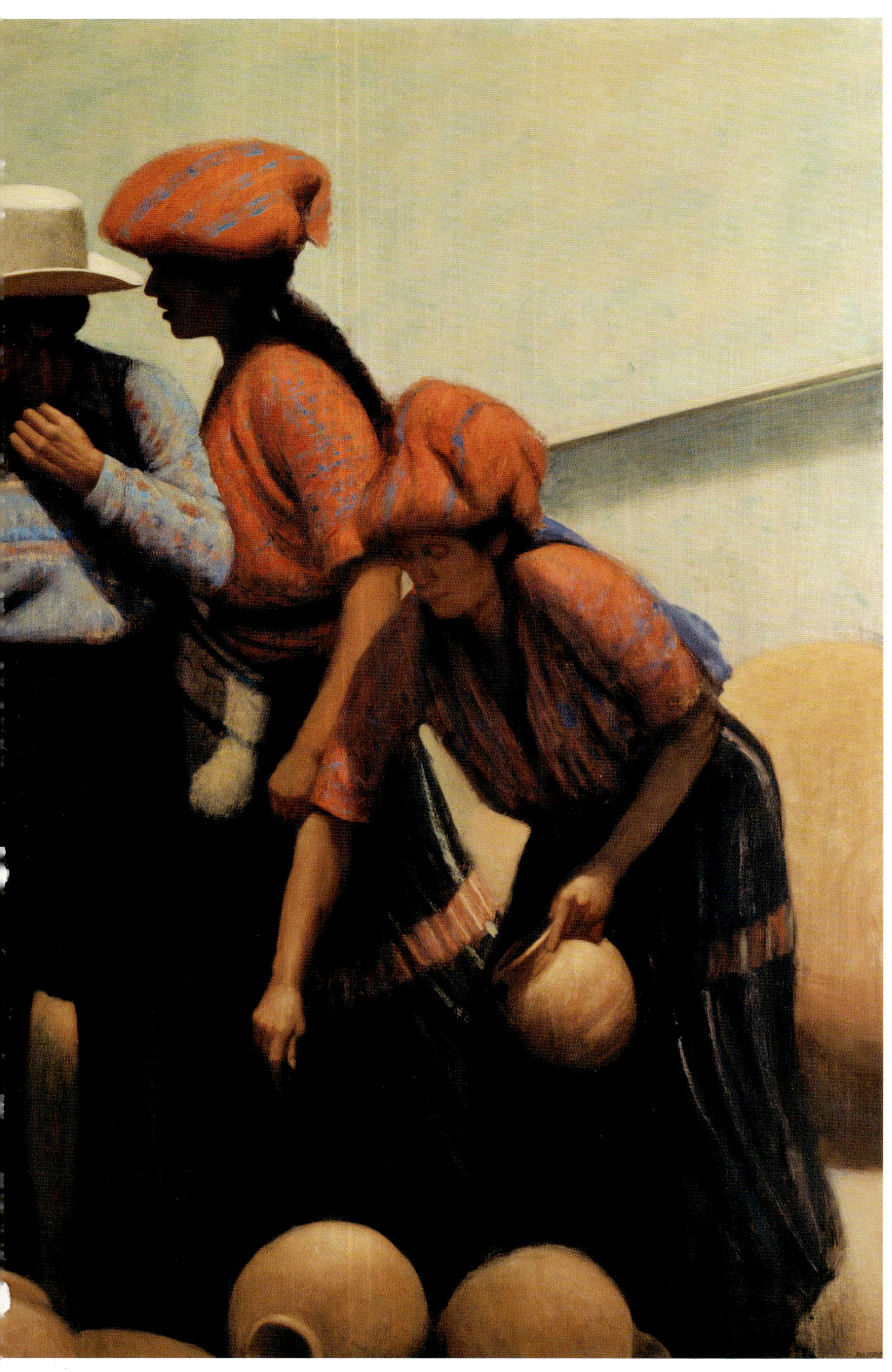

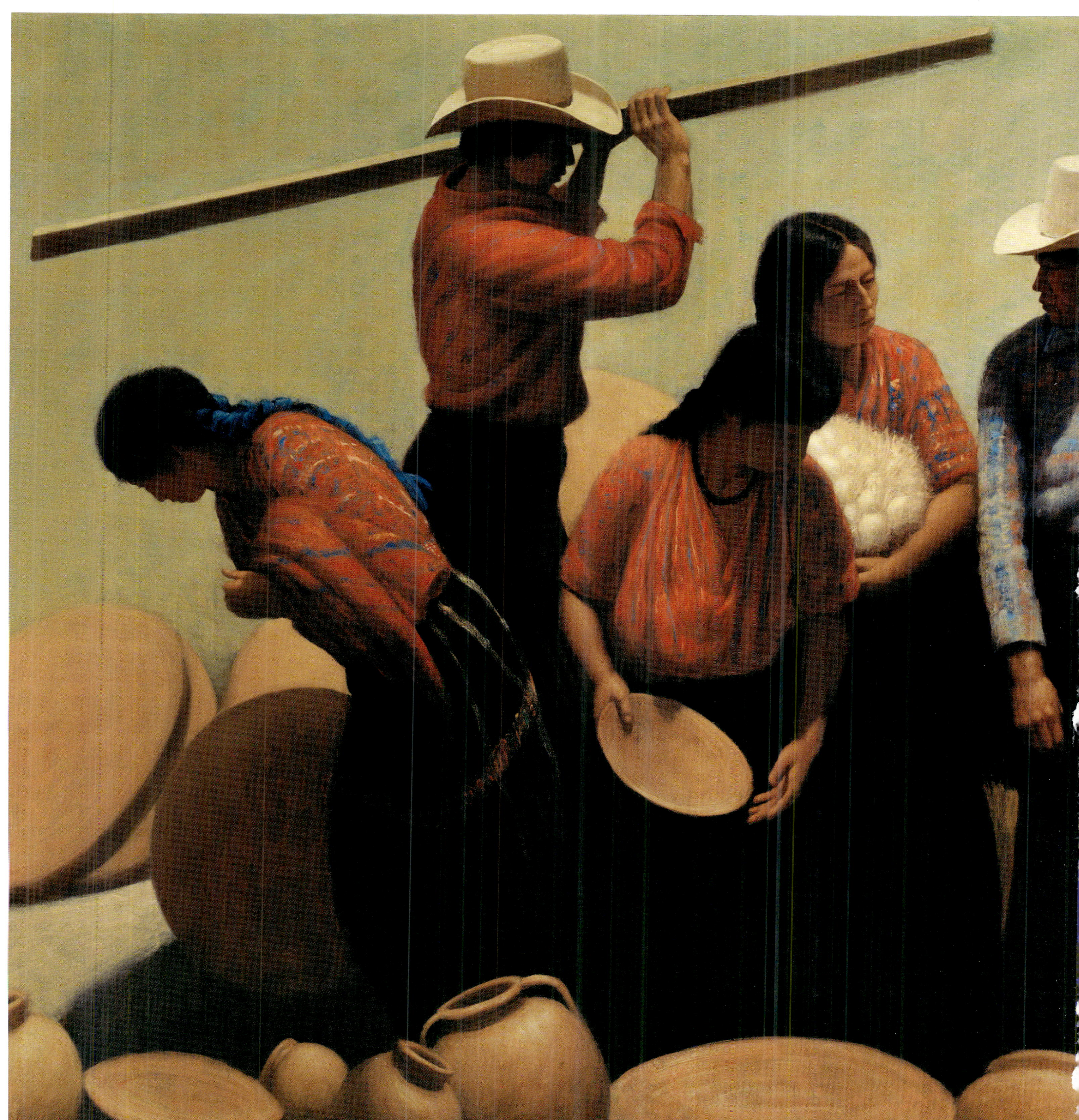

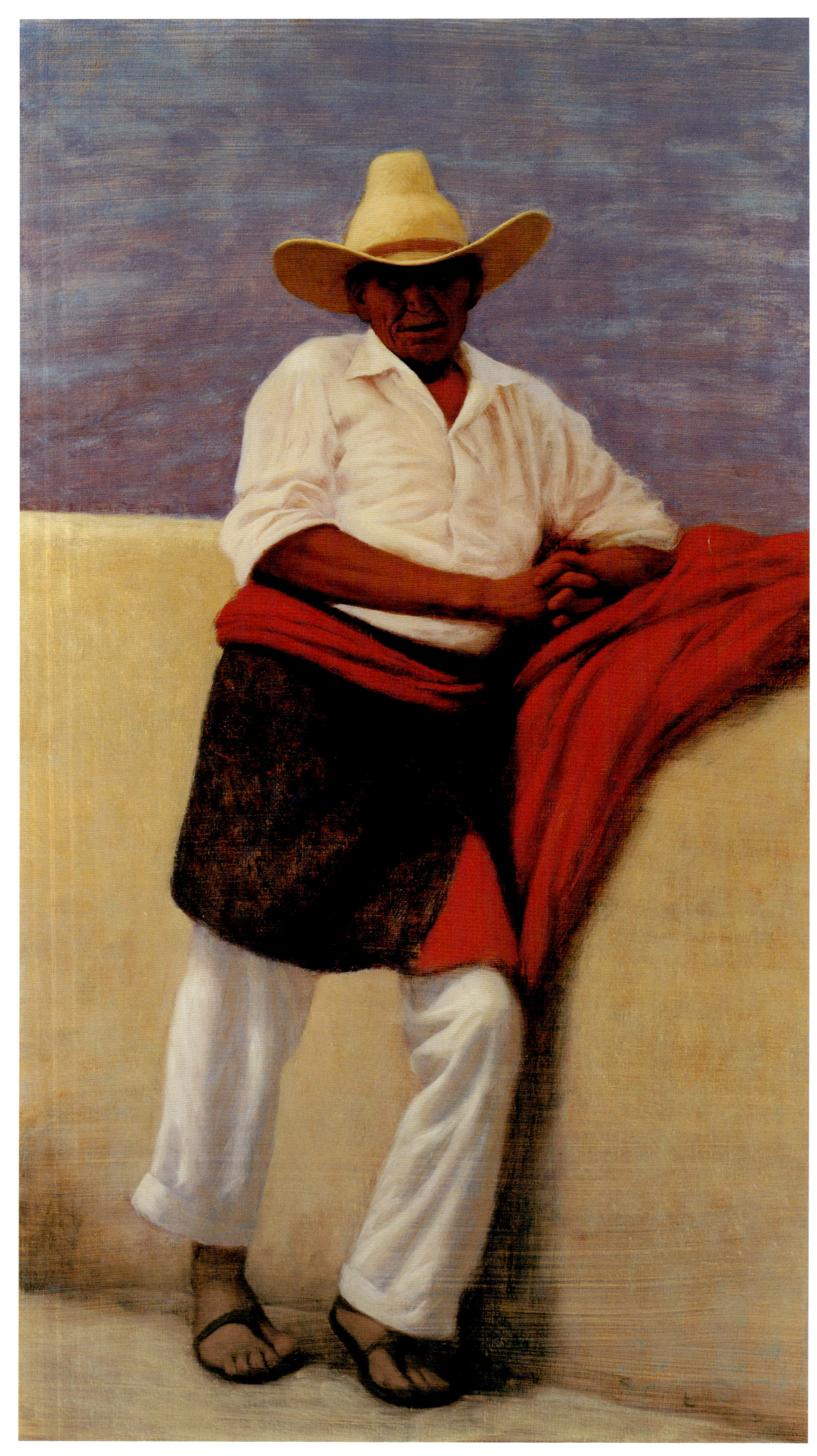

95. VILLAGER
1995, oil on canvas, 72 × 40 inches

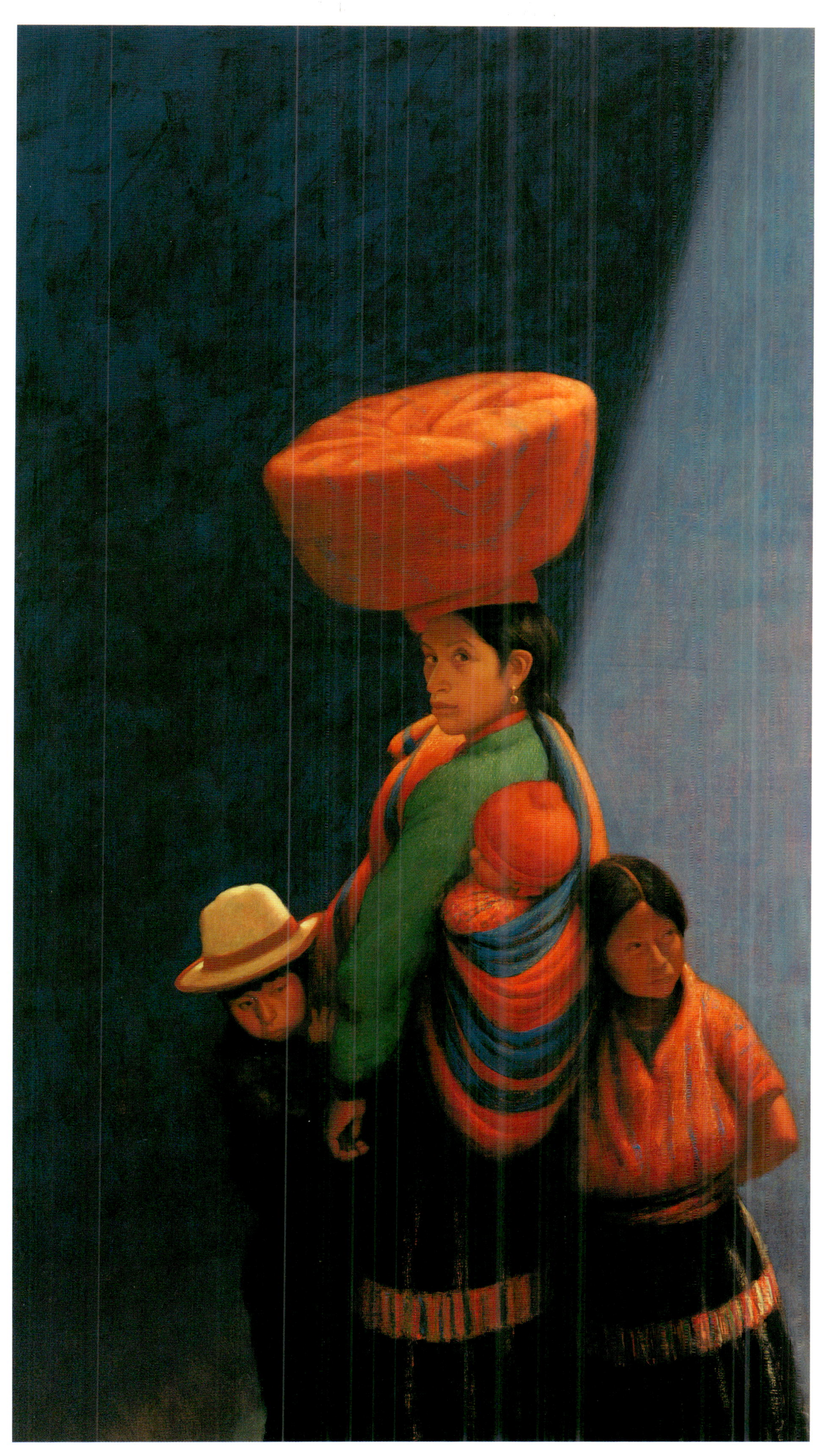

96. BALANCE OF FOUR

1995, oil on canvas, 72 × 40 inches

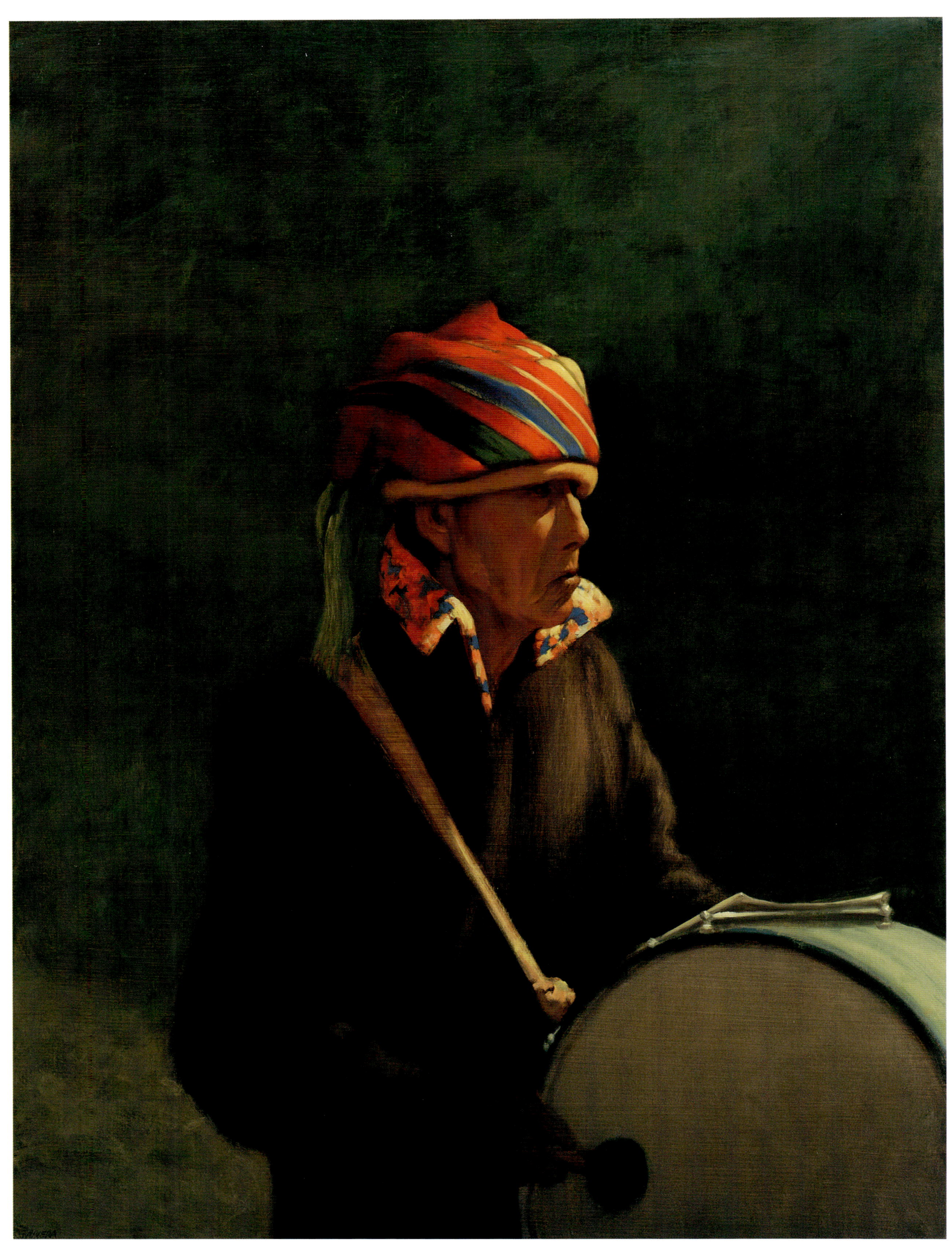

97. THE SILENT DRUM

1995, oil on canvas, 48 × 36 inches

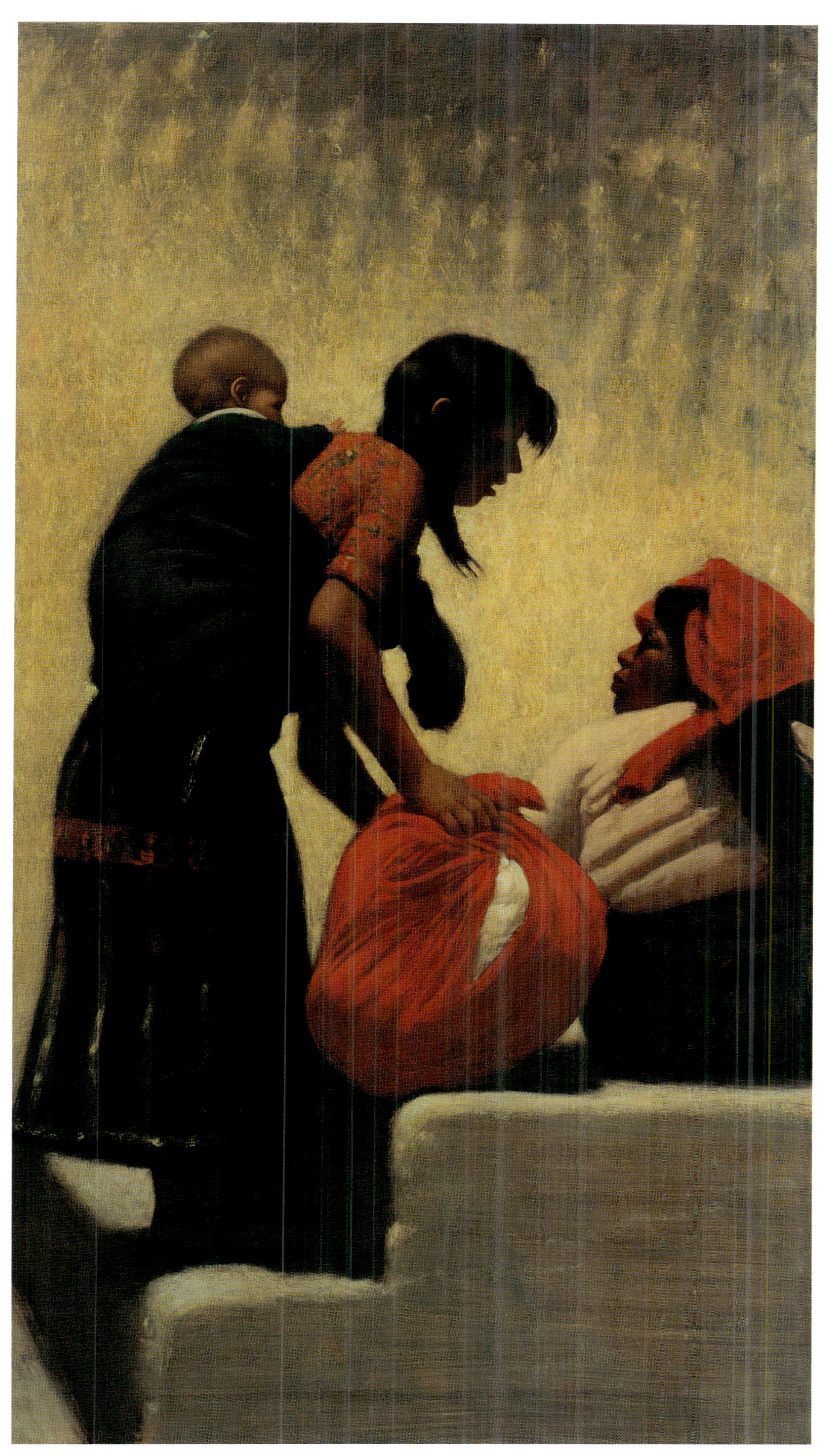

93. THE STEPS OF LABOR

1995, oil on canvas, 72 × 40 inches

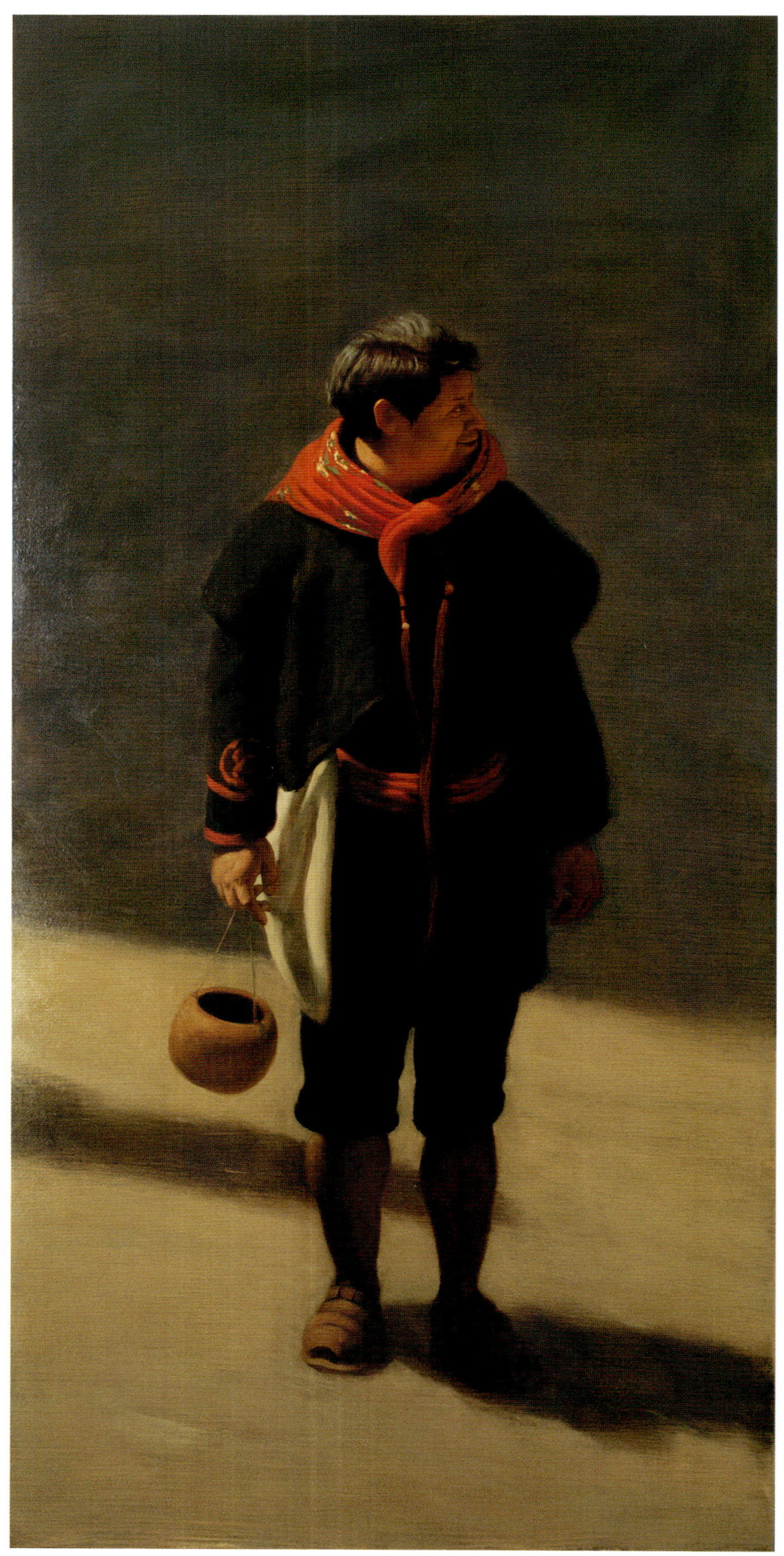
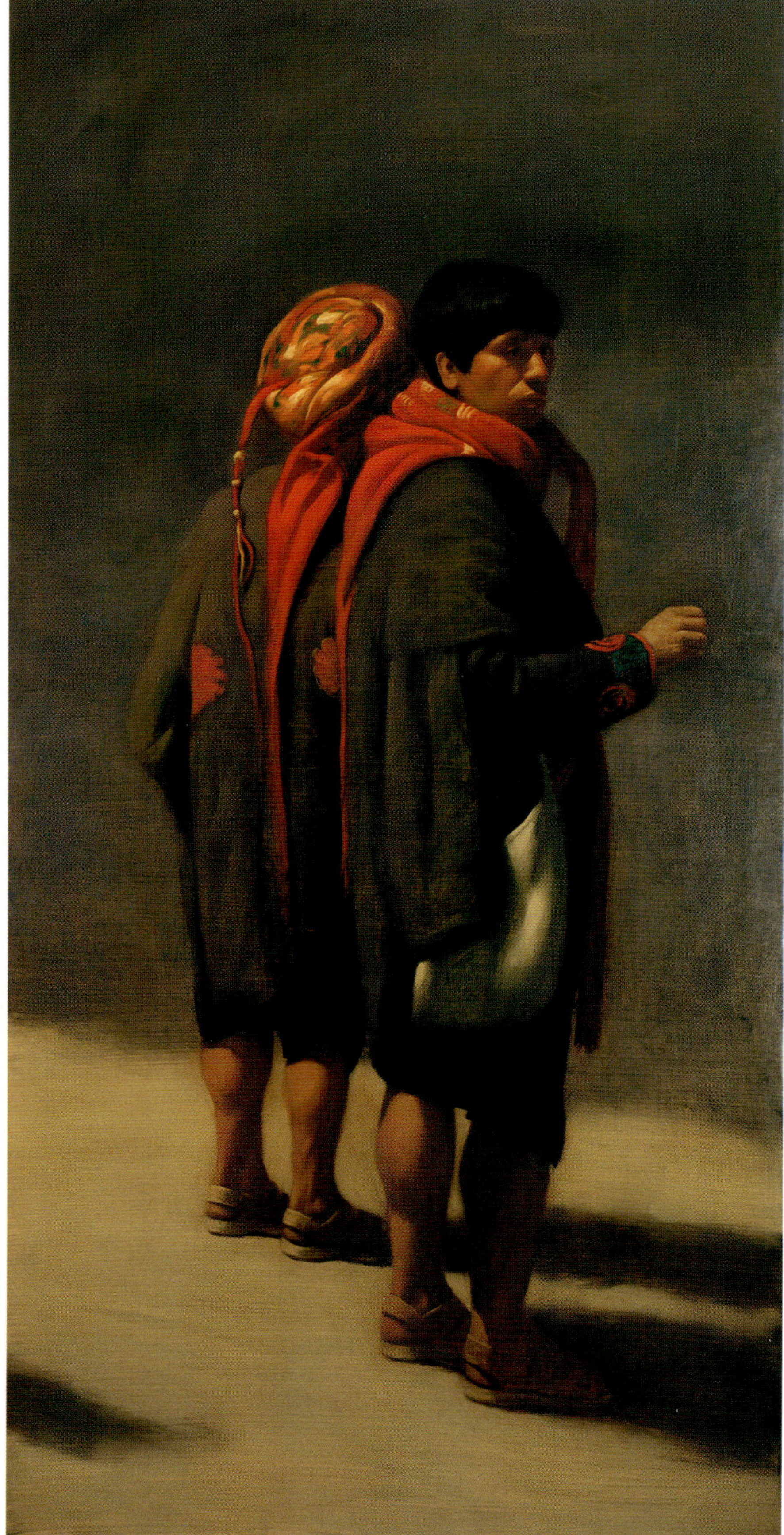

99. FEAST OF FOOLS (diptych)
1995, oil on canvas, 84 × 82 inches

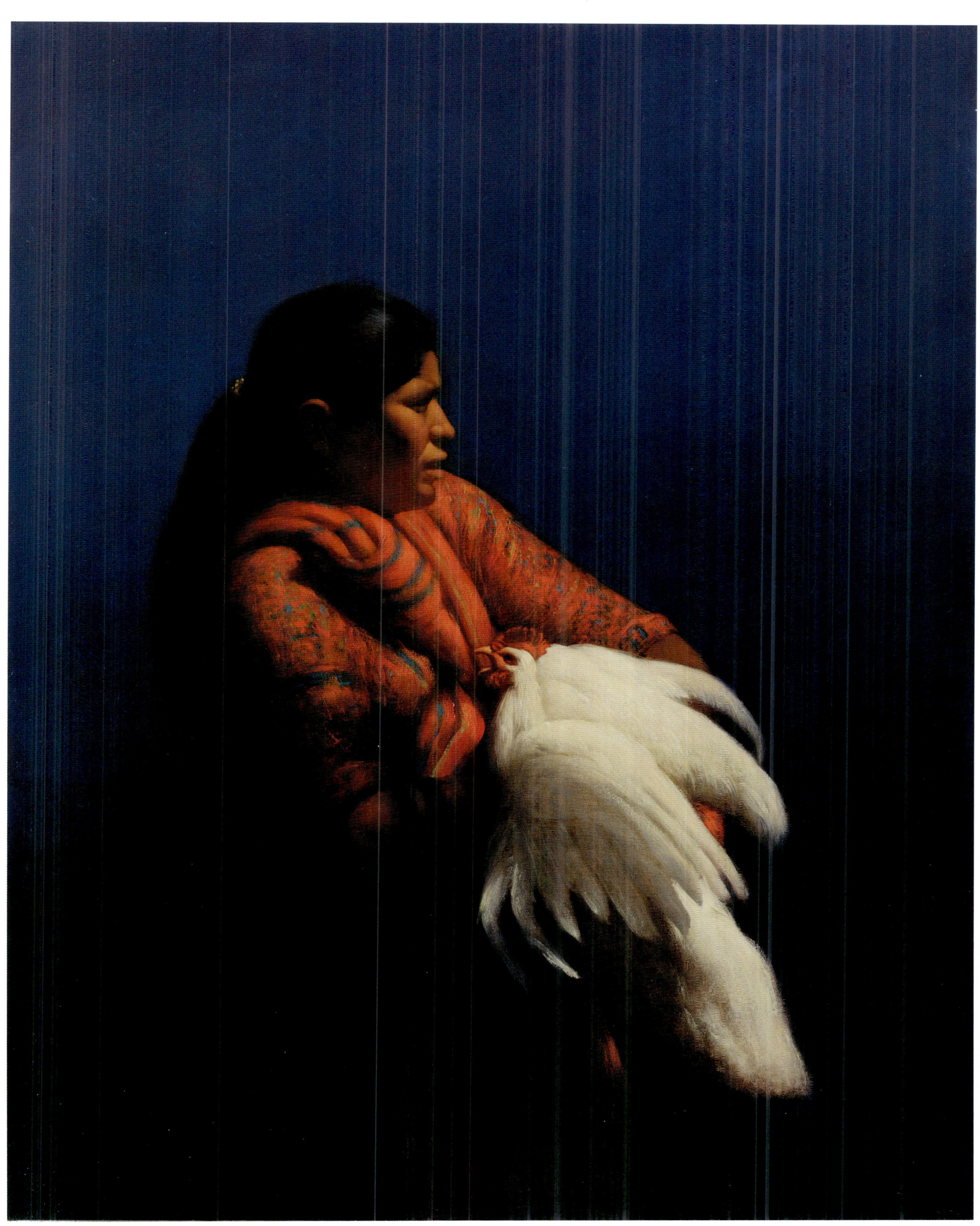

100. THE WHITE ROOSTER

1995, oil on canvas, 48 × 36 inches

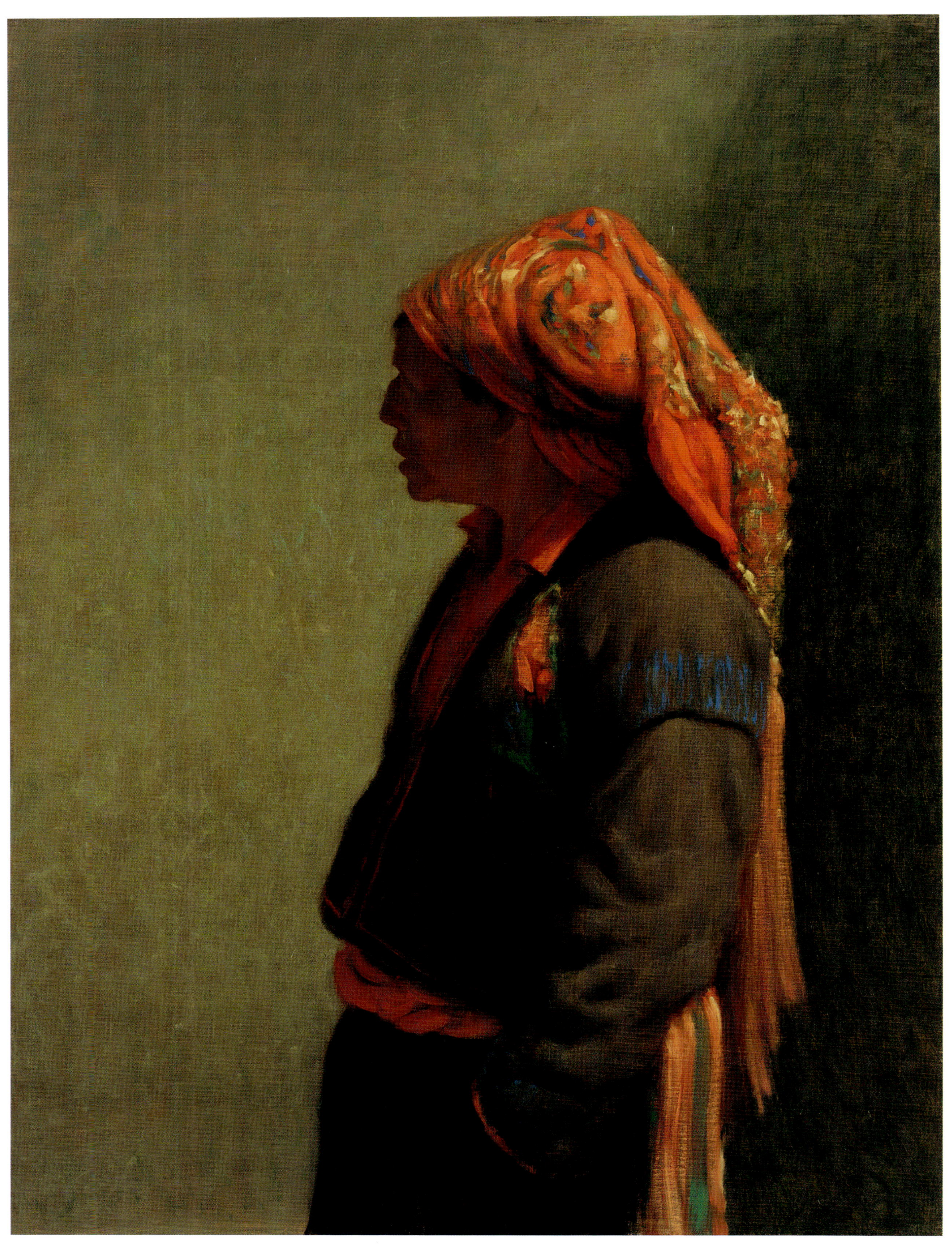

101. SOLOLA SOLEDAD

1995, oil on canvas, 48 × 36 inches

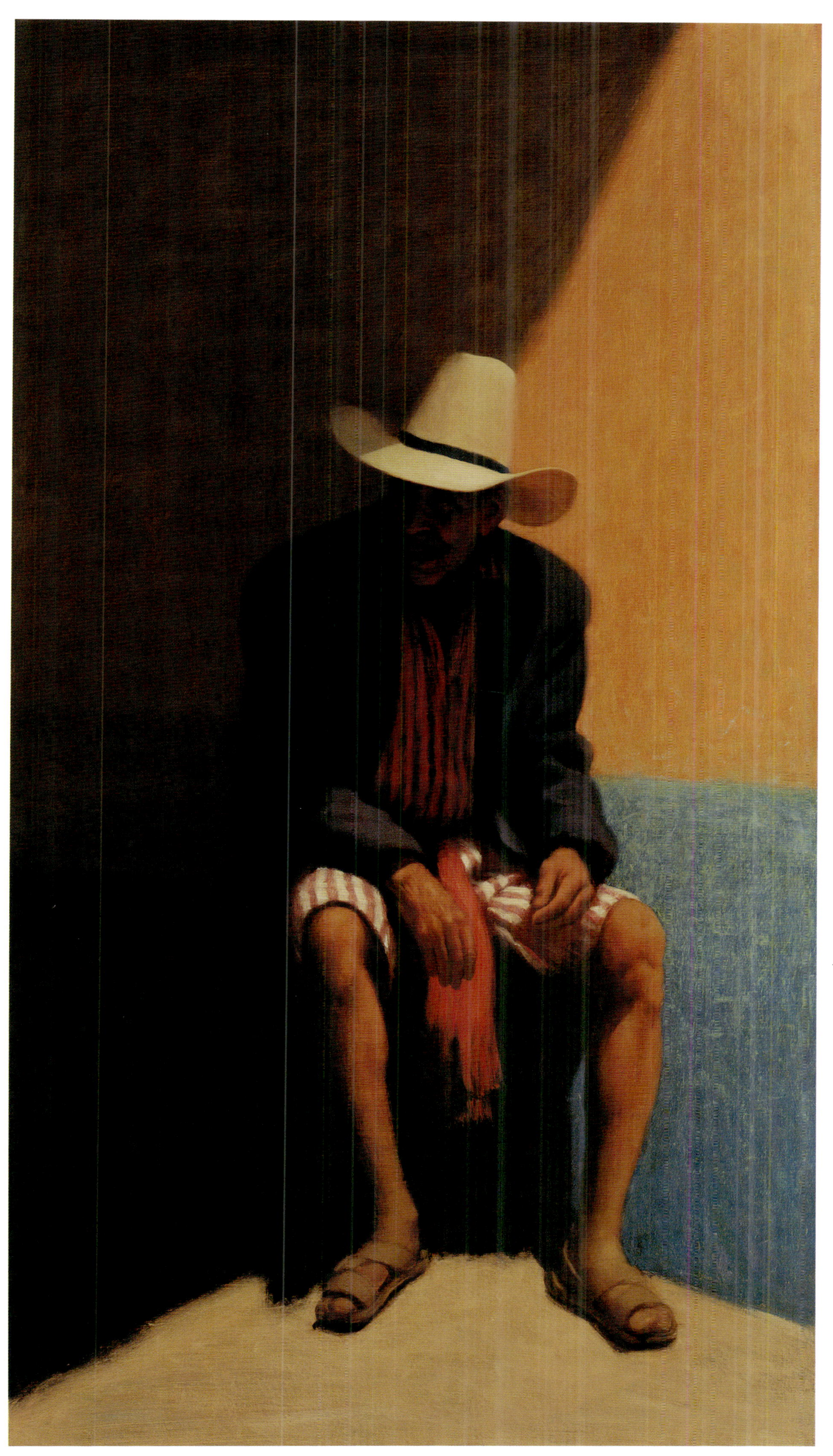

102. PENSANDO
1995, oil on canvas, 72 × 40 inches

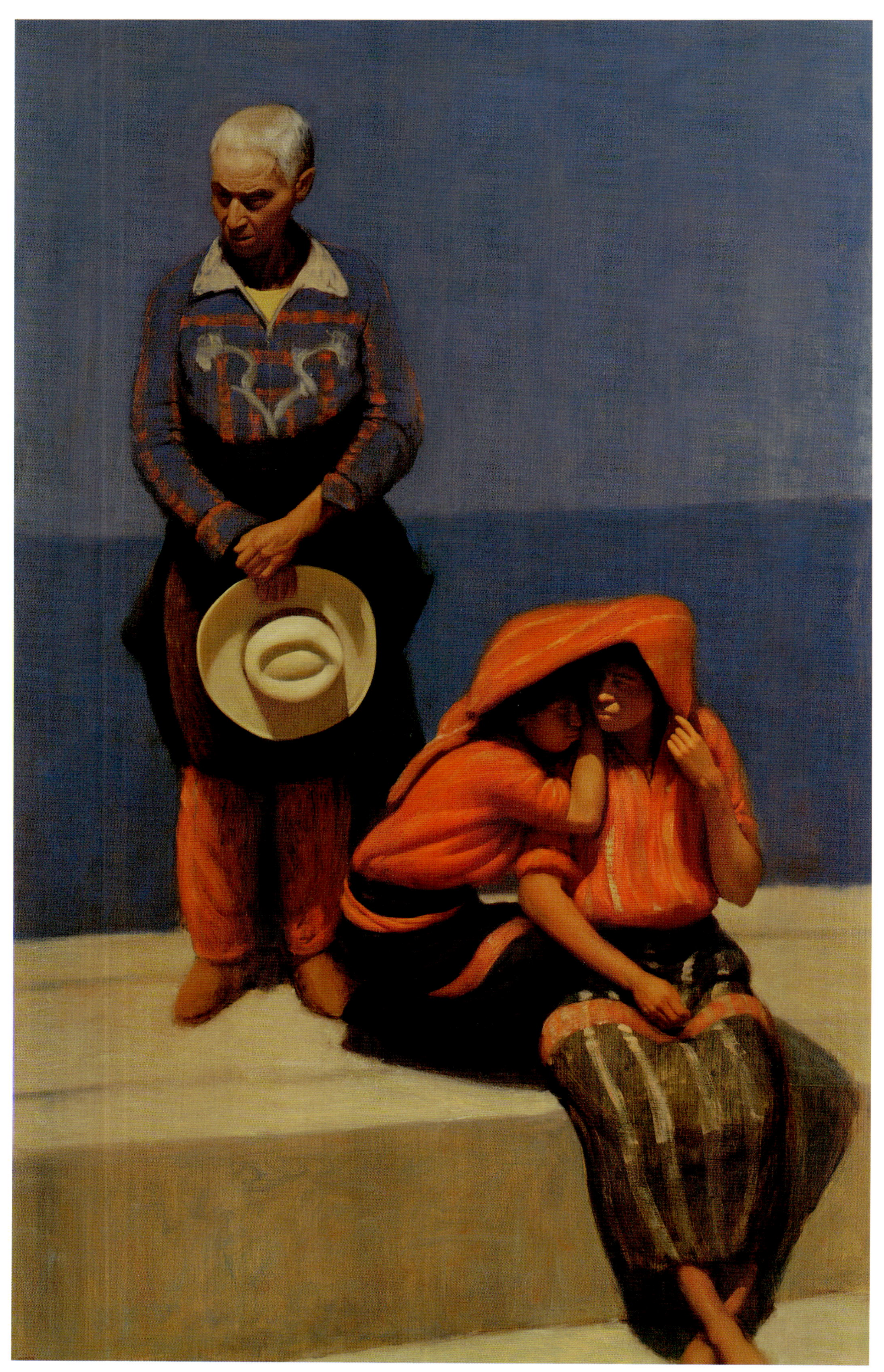

103. SHADOWS OF WISDOM

1995, oil on canvas, 96 × 60 inches

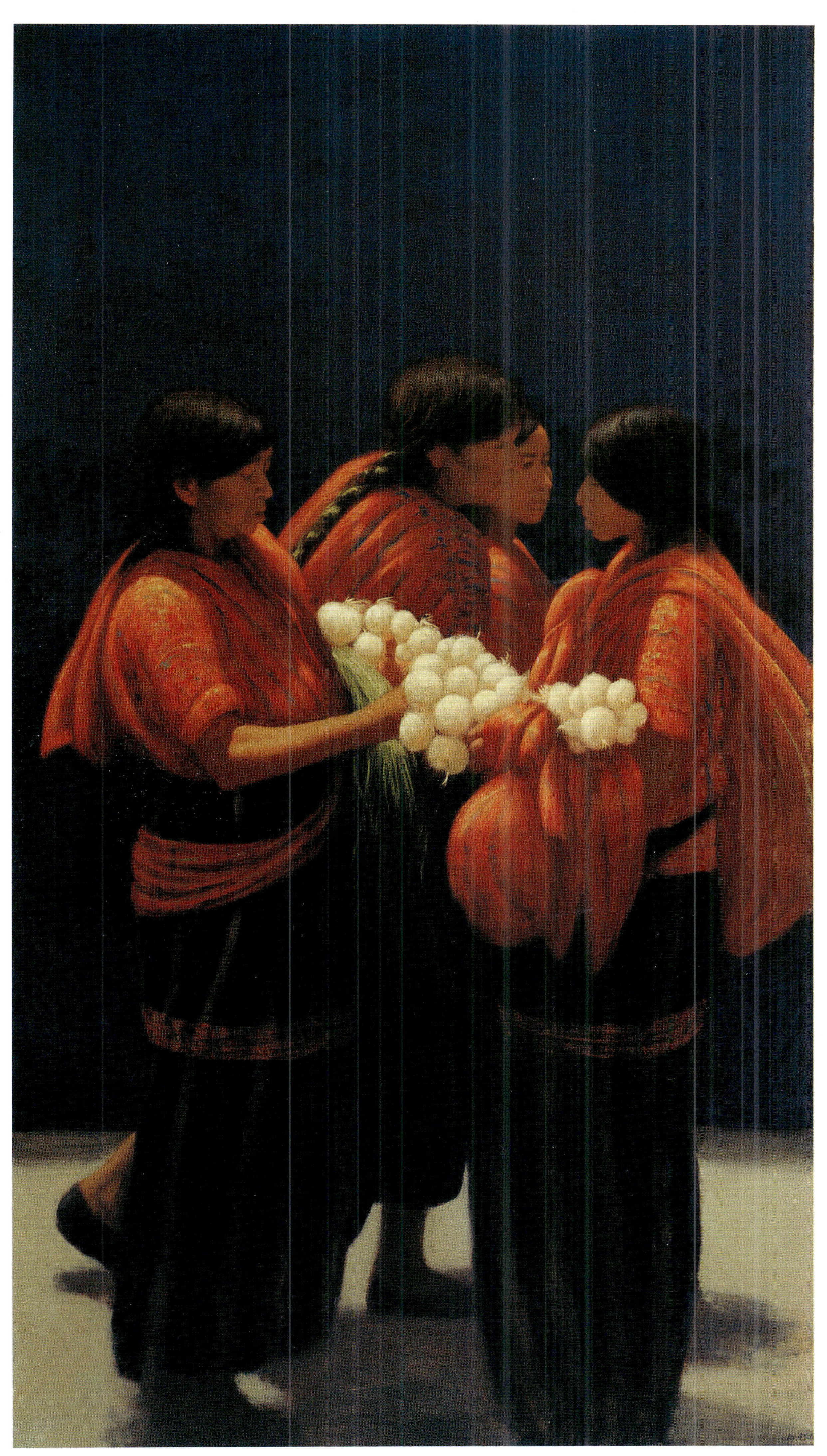

104. WHITE ONIONS
1995, oil on canvas, 72 × 40 inches

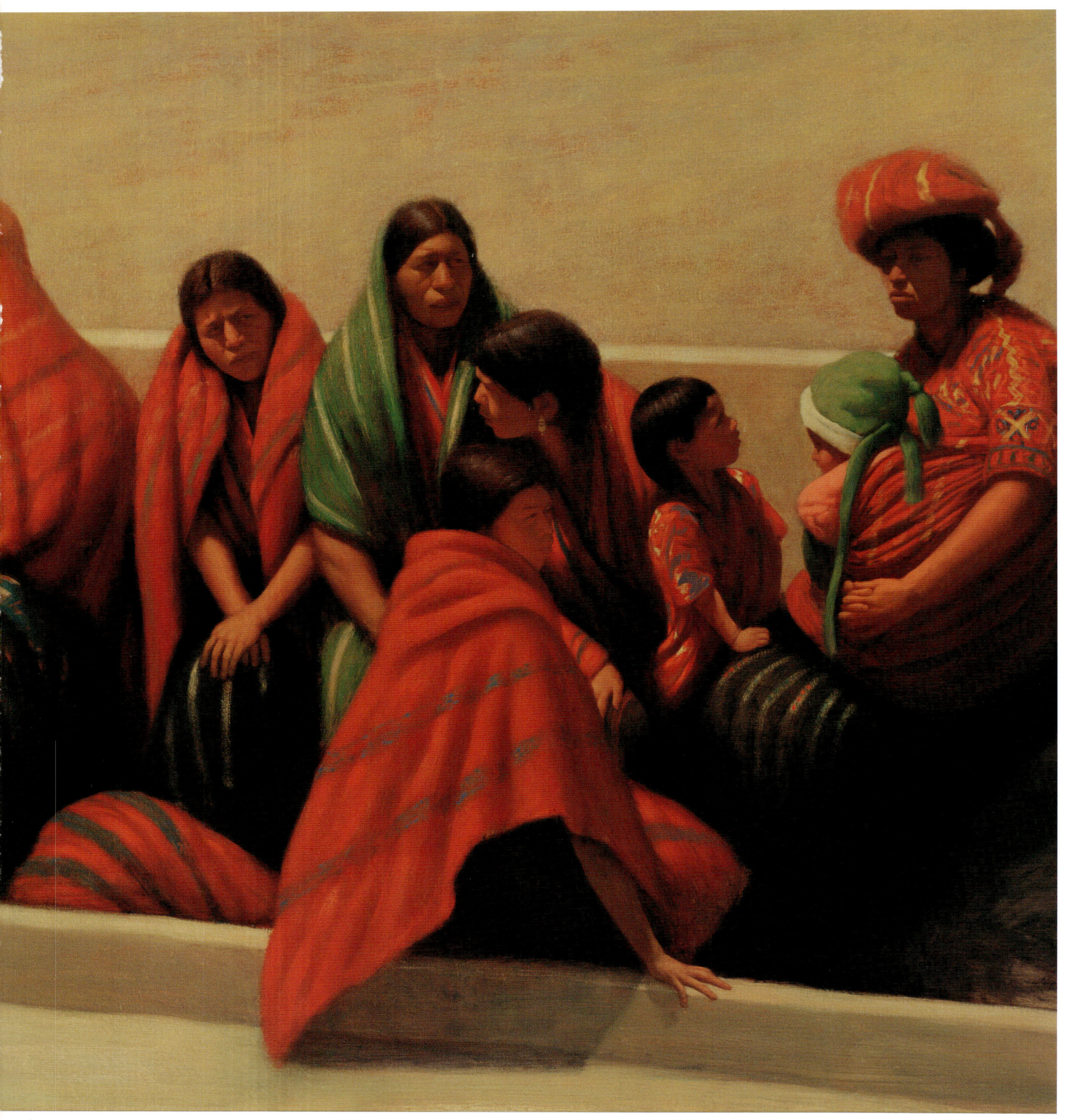

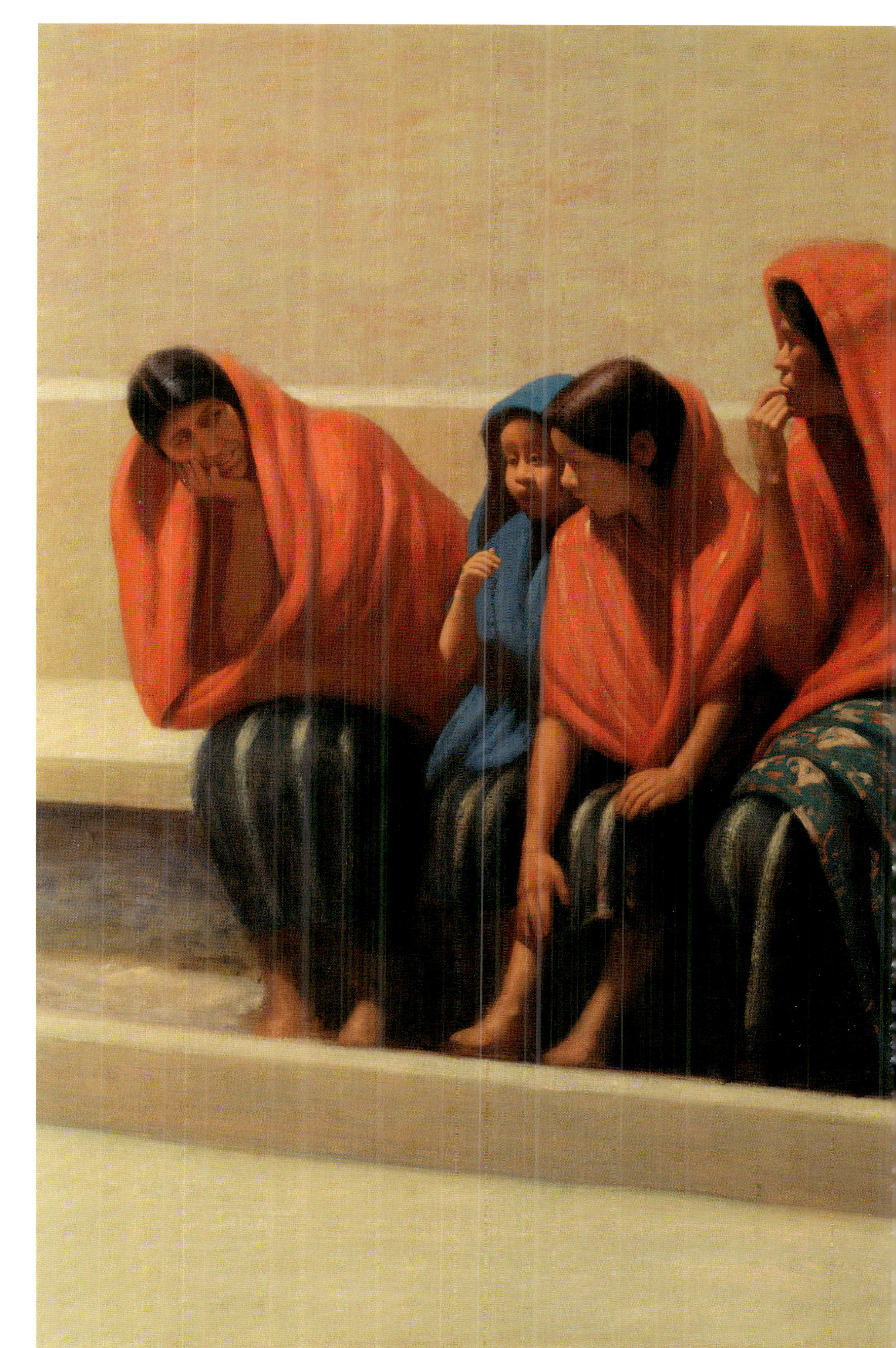

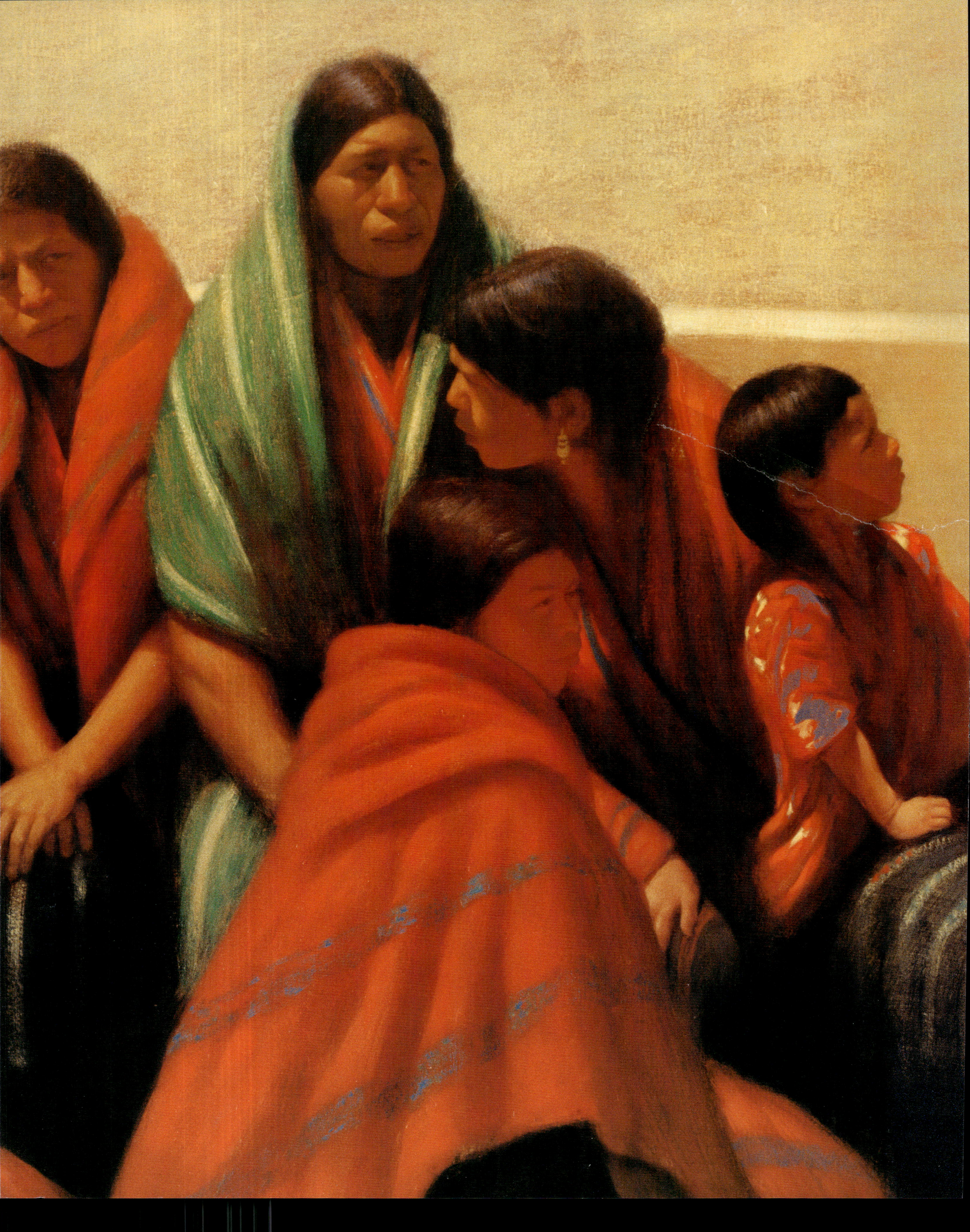

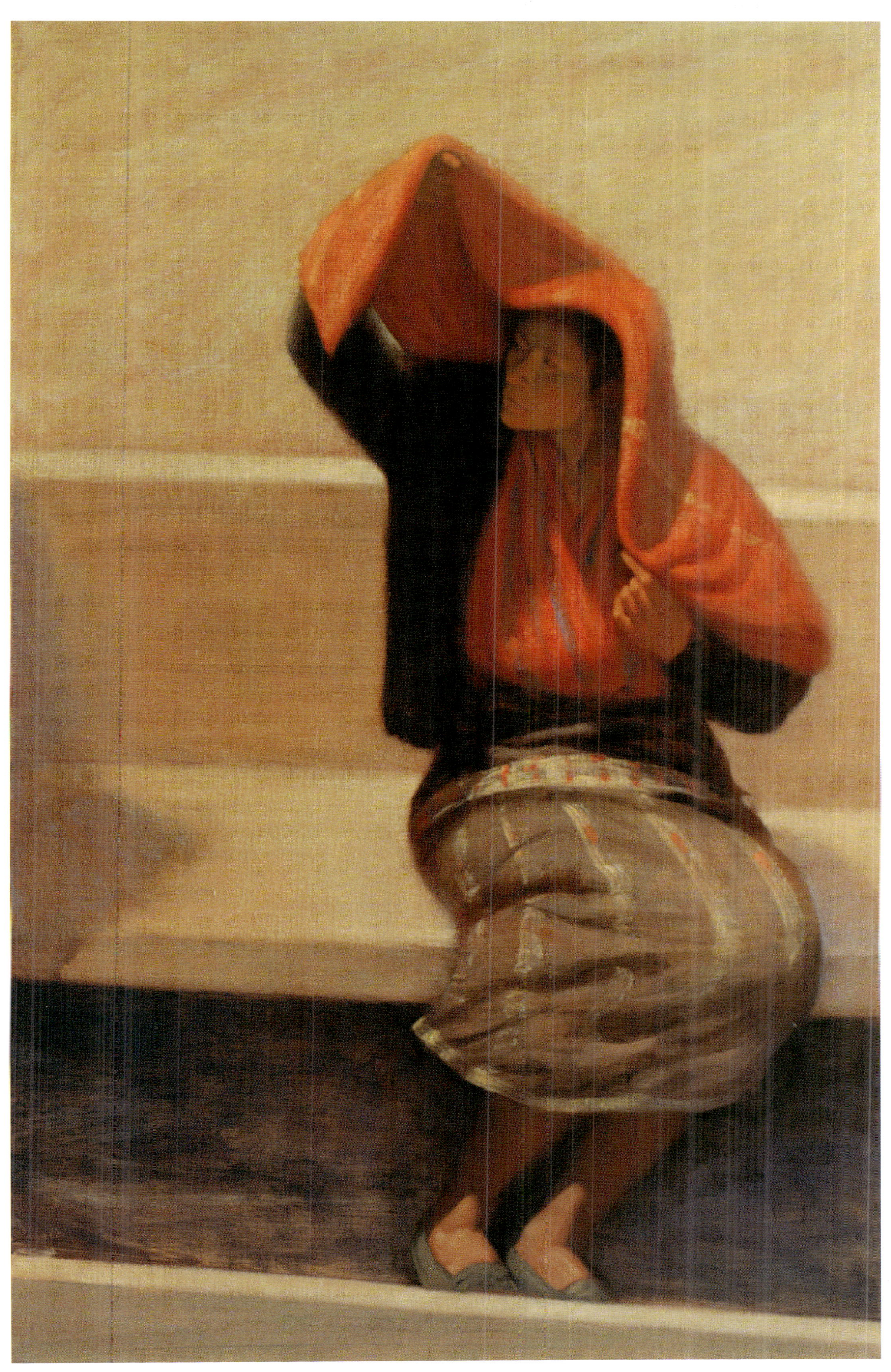

105. THE LONGEST BENCH (diptych)
1995, oil on canvas, 60 × 132 inches

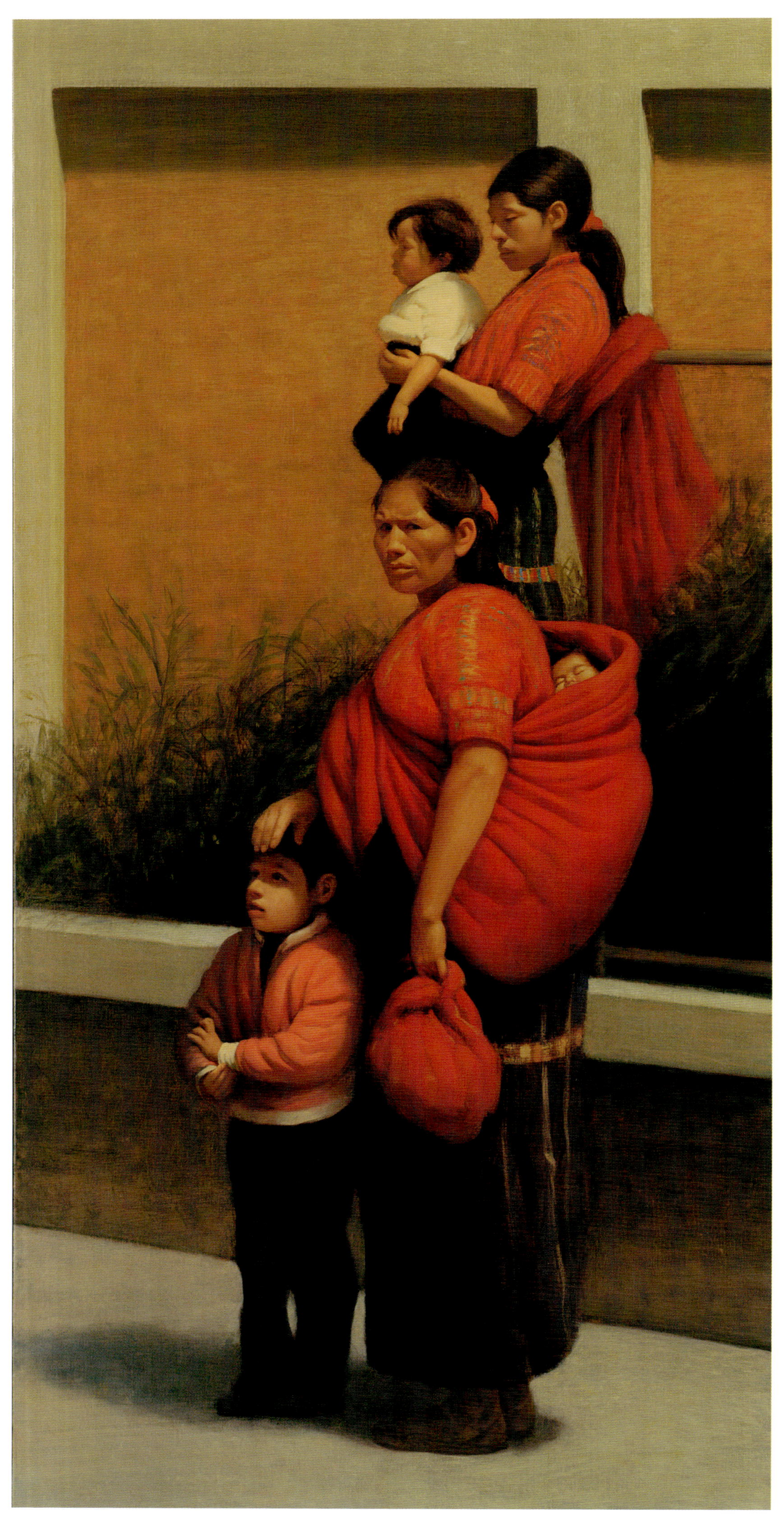

106. A TIME APART
1995, oil on canvas, 84 × 41 inches

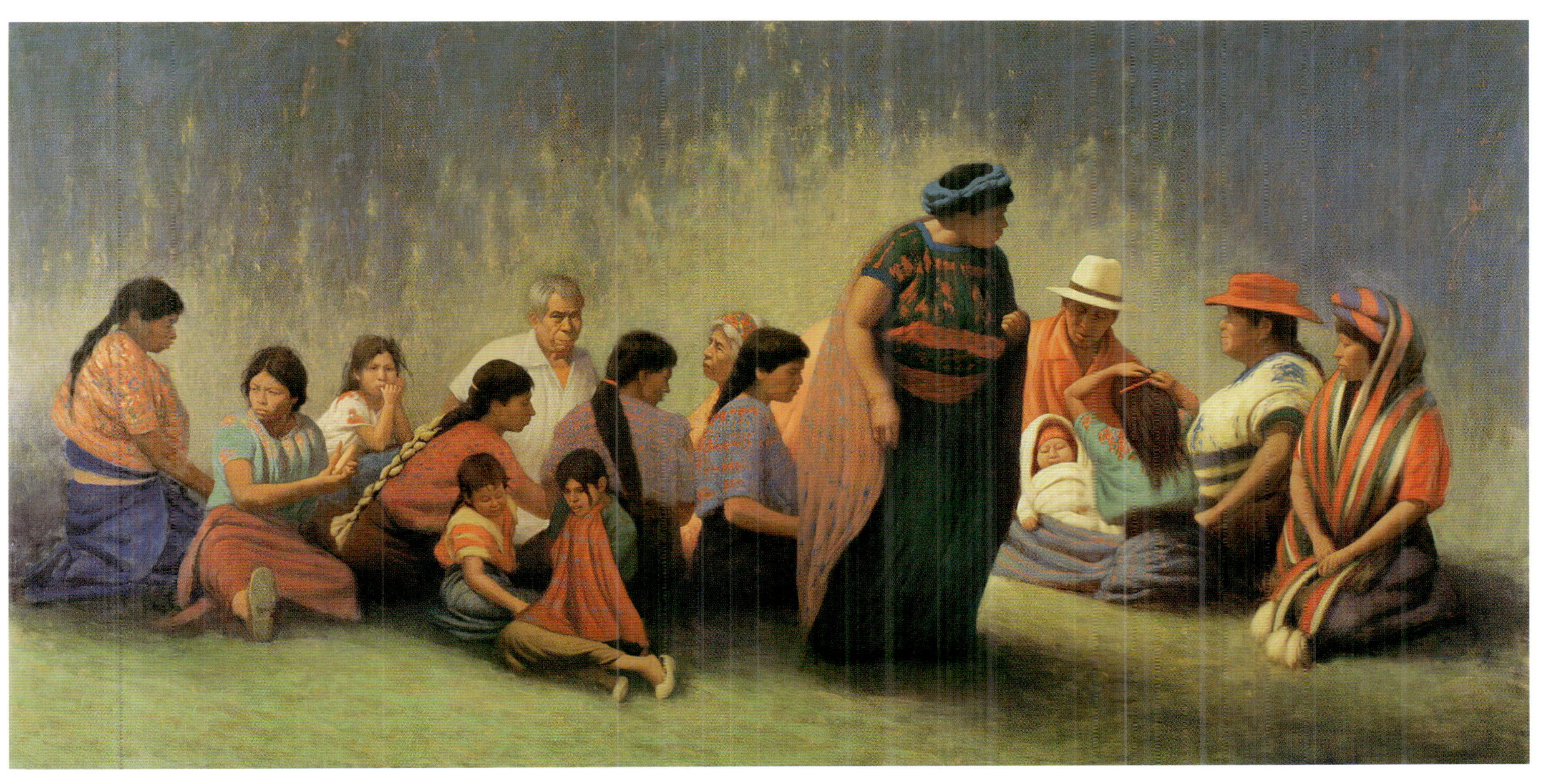

107. VISIONS OF SOLOLA
1995, oil on canvas, 84 × 168 inches

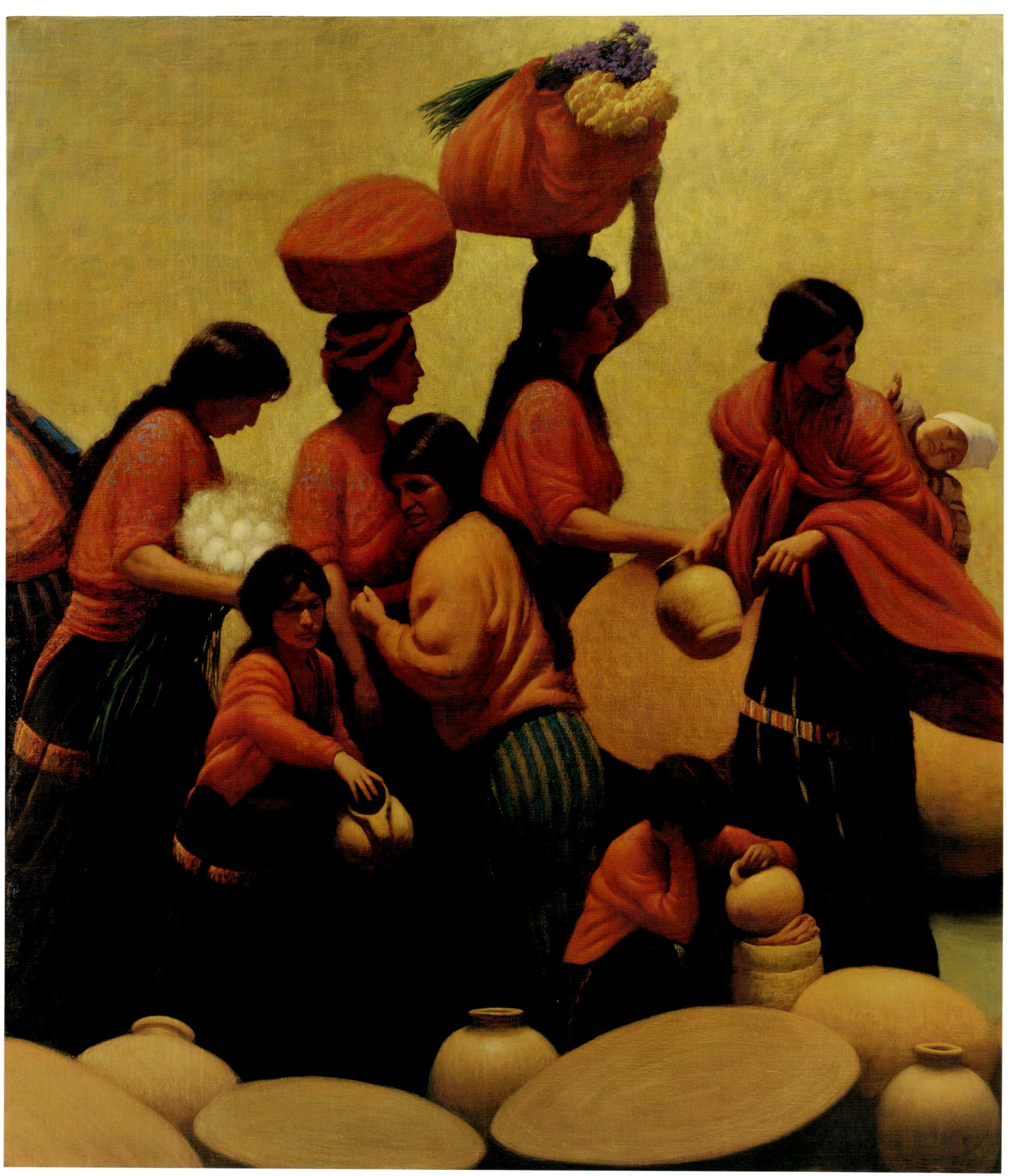

108. UNTITLED
1996, oil on canvas, 80 × 68 inches

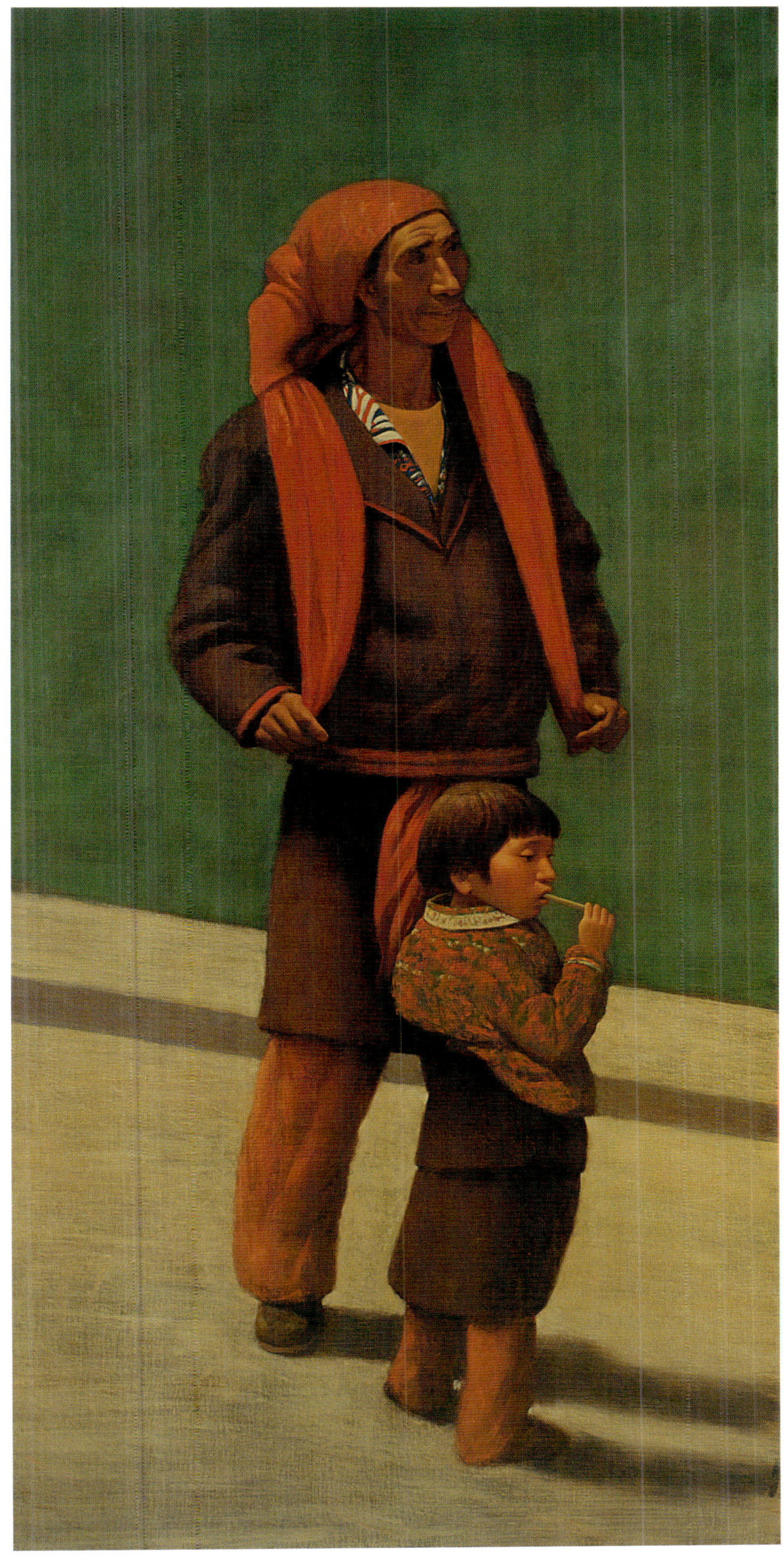

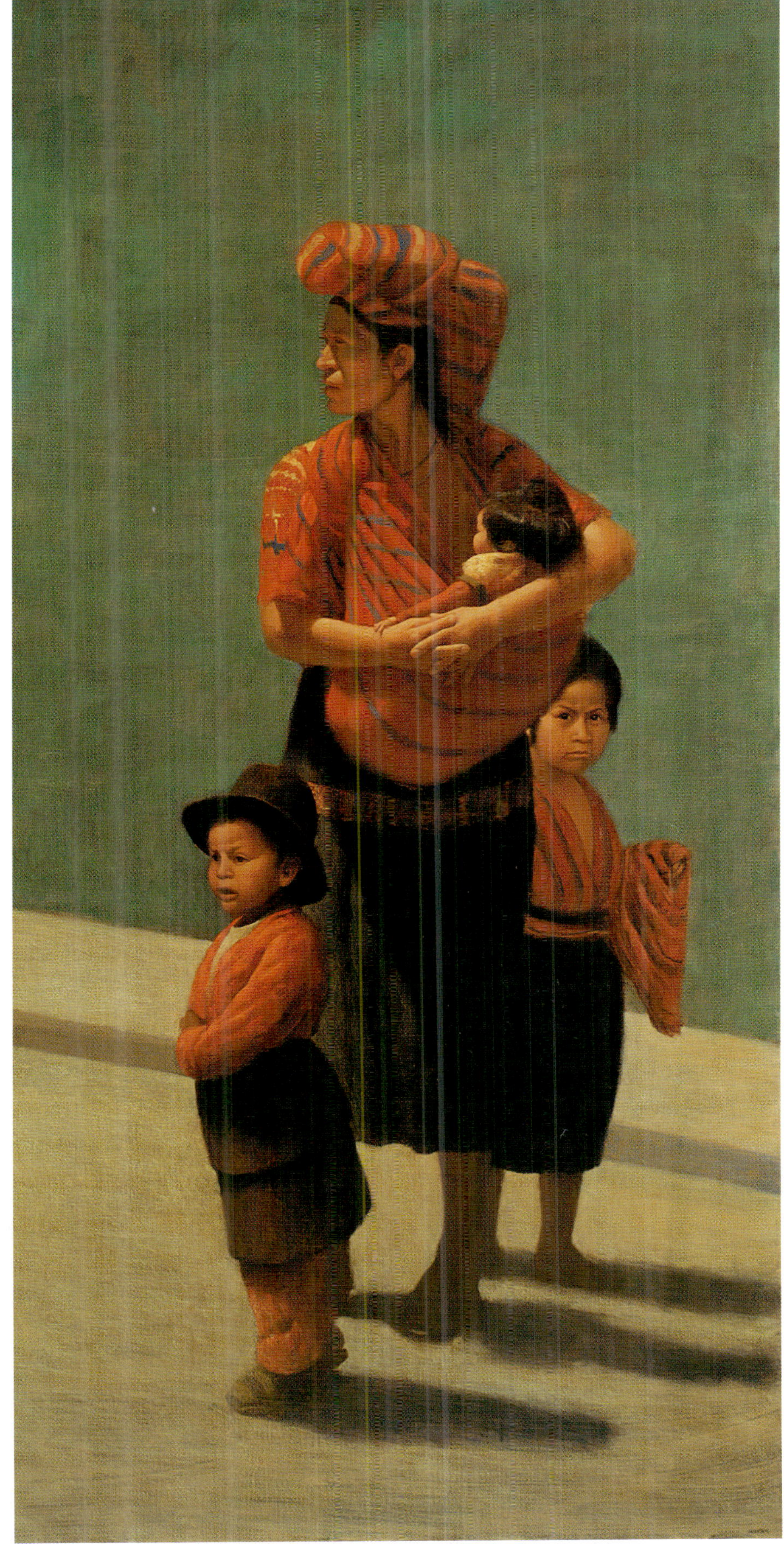

109. CHI CHI RESPITE (diptych)
1996, oil on canvas, 84 × 82 inches

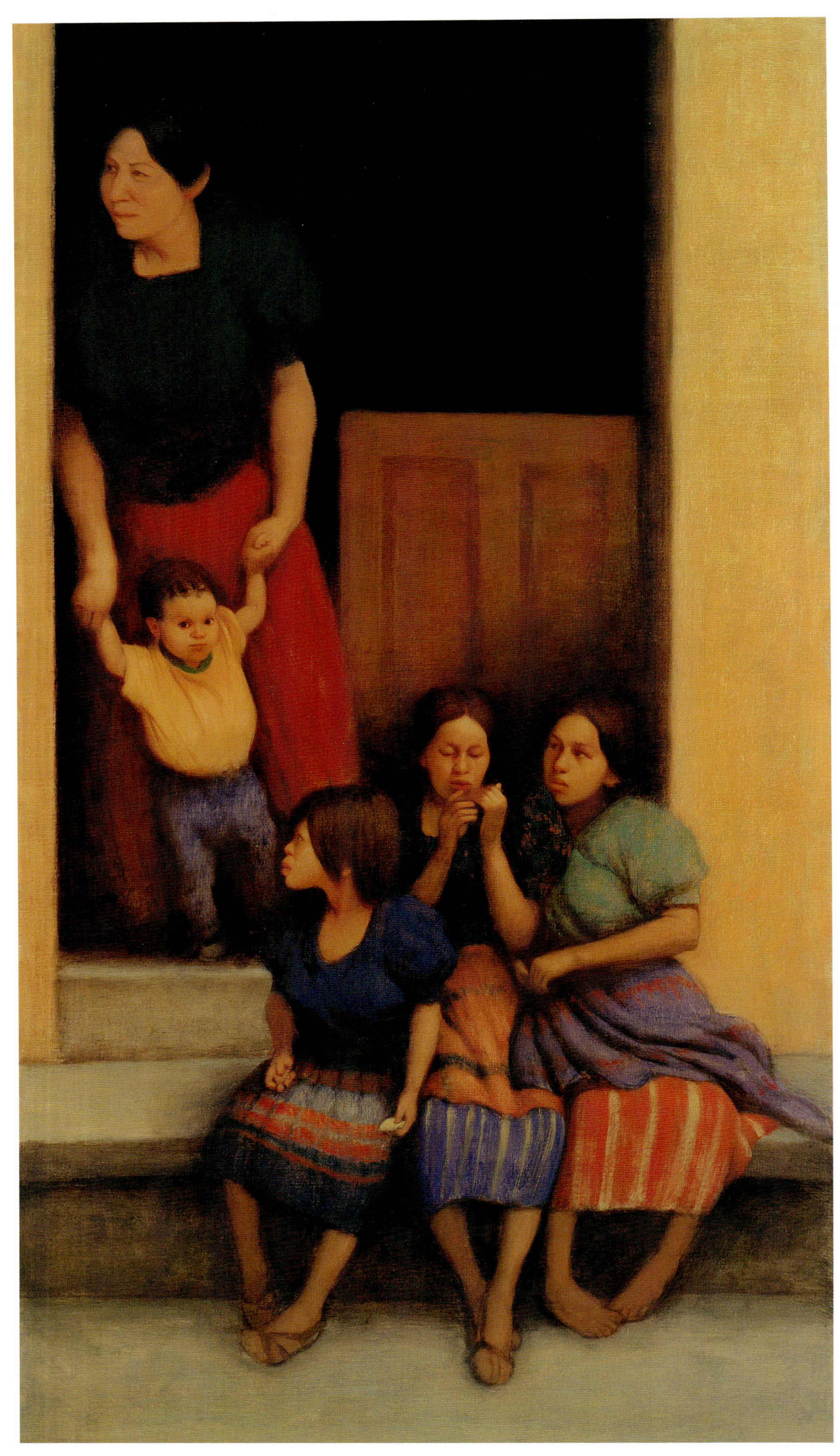

110. WAITING FOR THE BUS
1996, oil on canvas, 72 × 40 inches

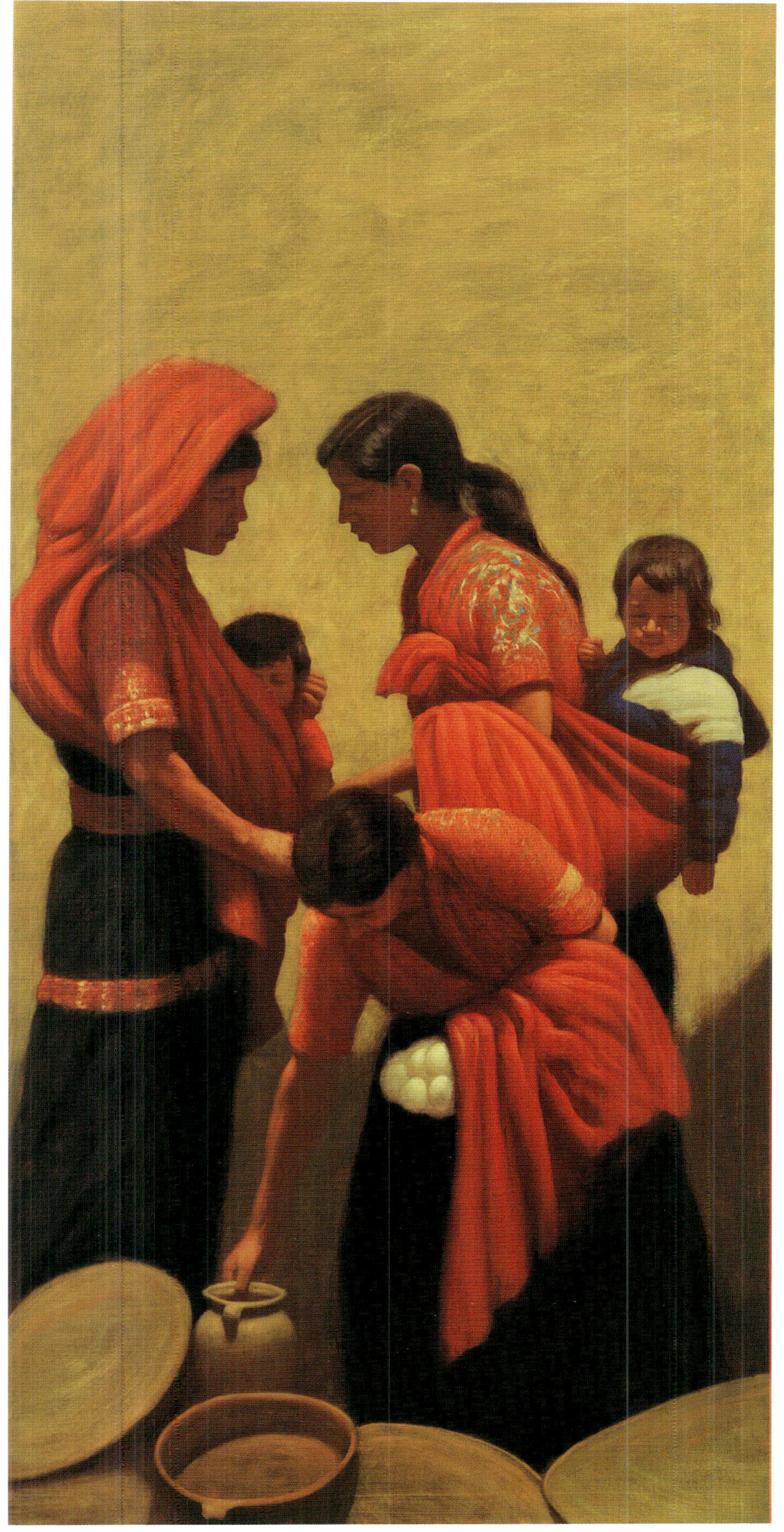

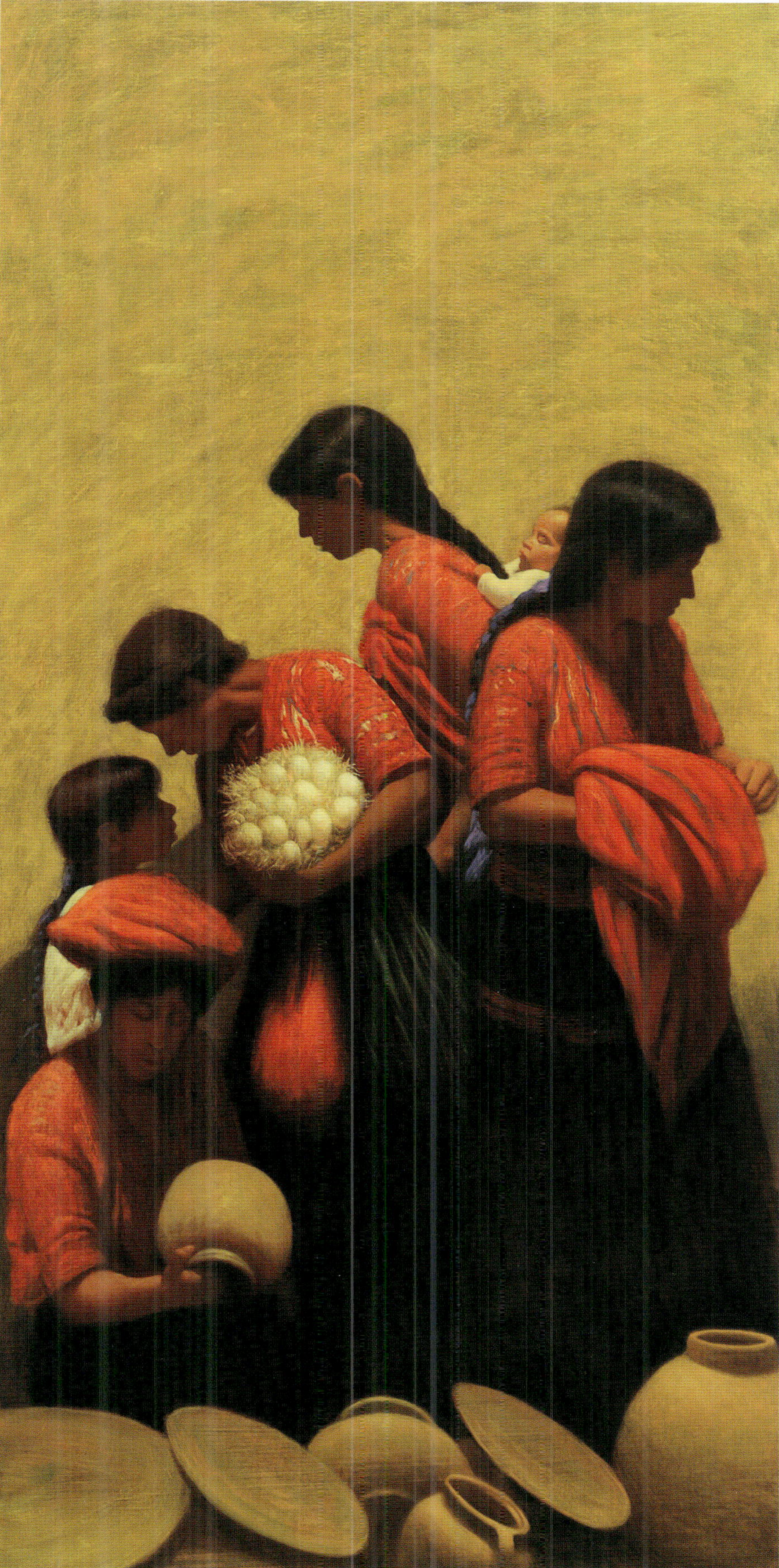

111. THE POTTERY
1996, oil on canvas, 84 × 82 inches

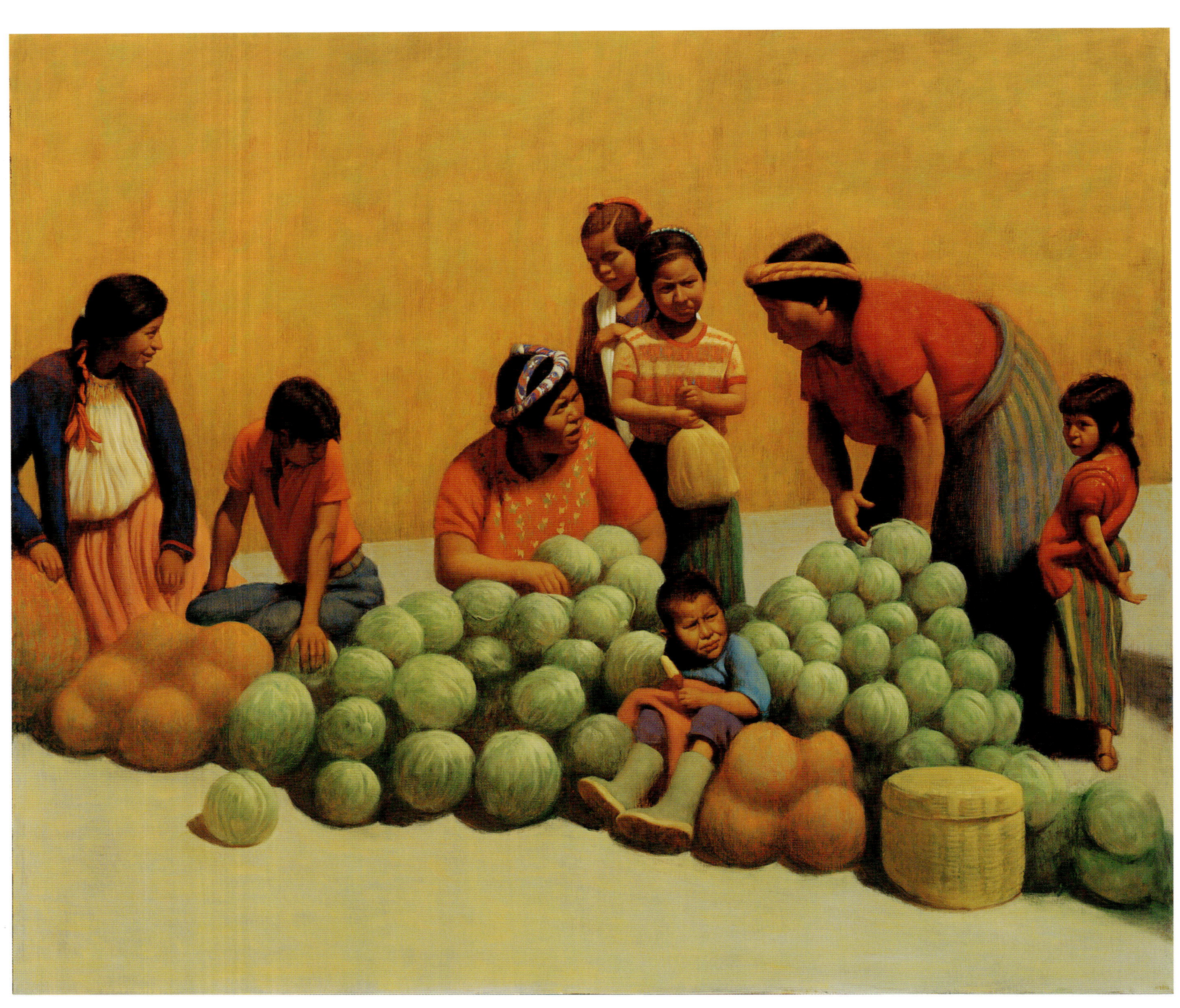

112. FRUITS OF THE HARVEST
1997, oil on canvas, 68 × 80 inches

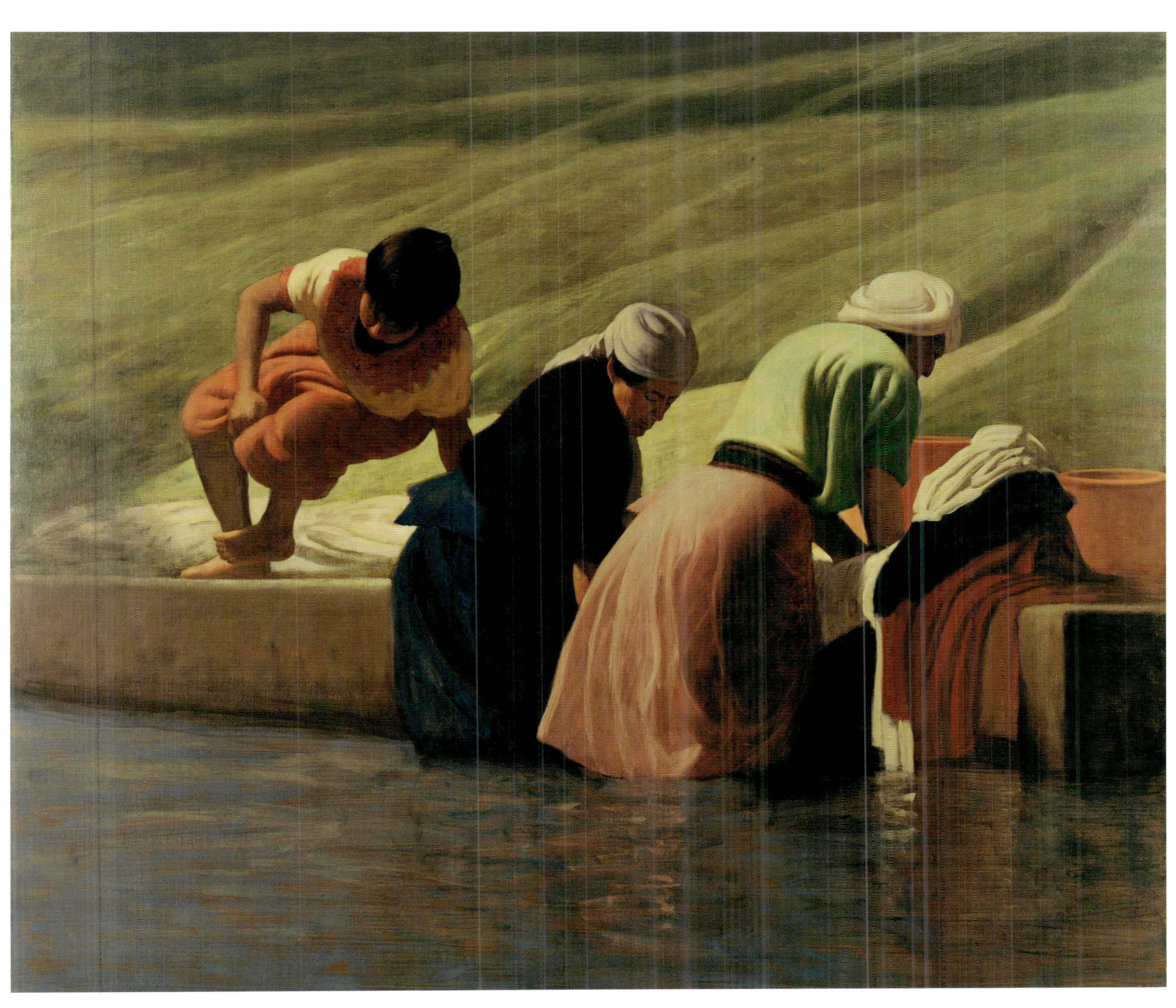

113. OUTDOOR LAUNDRY
1997, oil on canvas, 68 × 80 inches

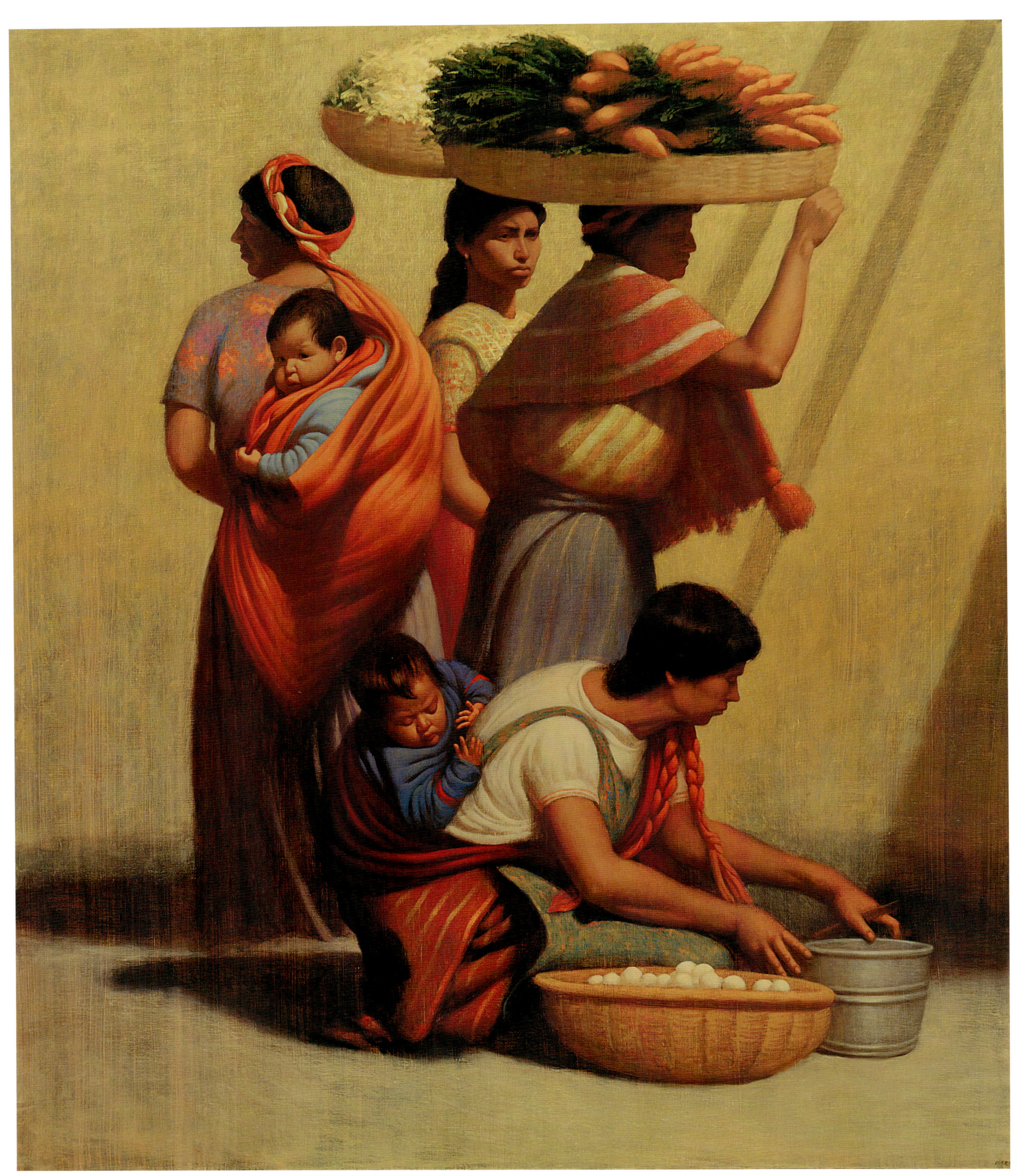

114. THROUGH A MOVING WINDOW
1997, oil on canvas, 80 × 68 inches

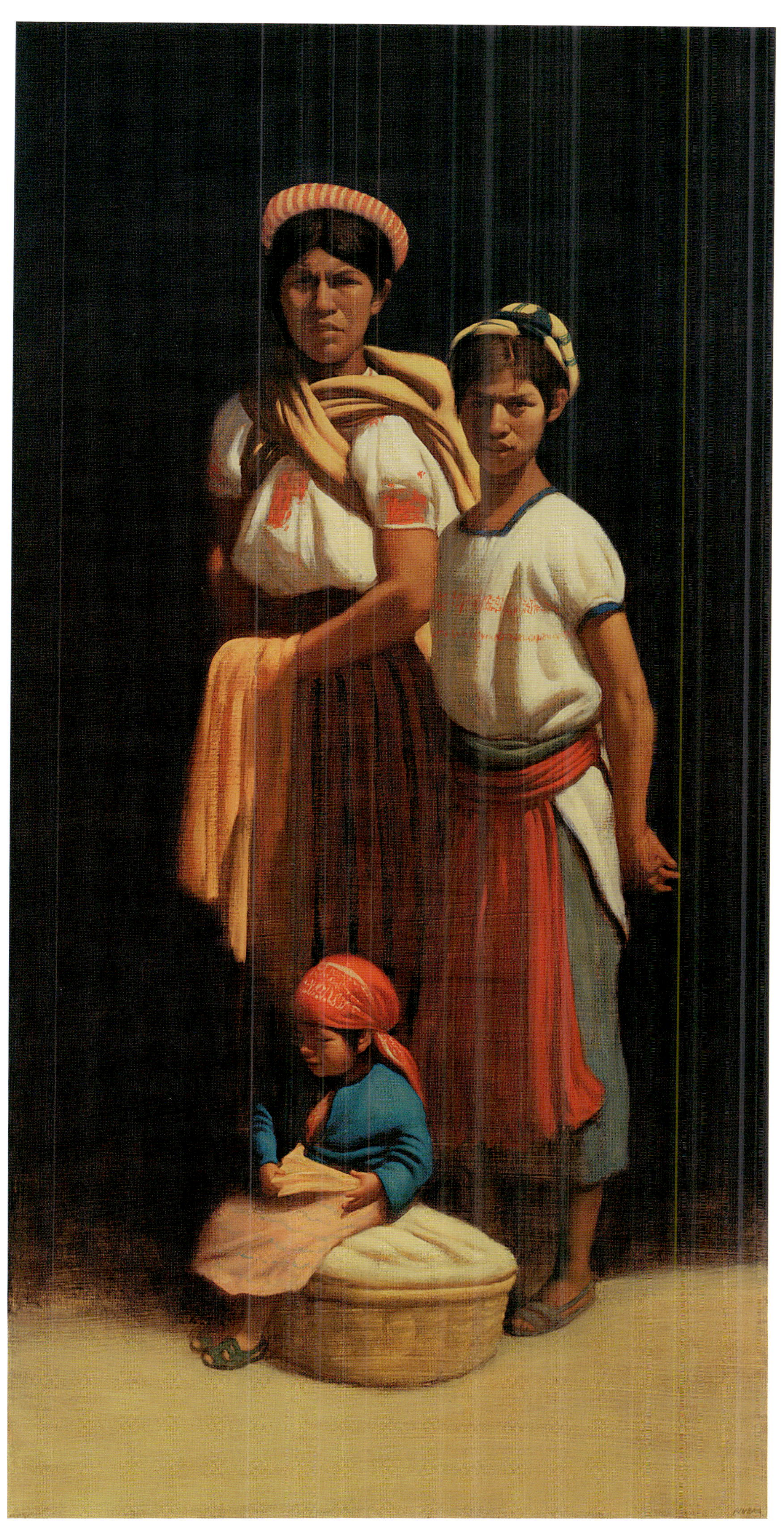

115. GOLDEN INNOCENCE
1997, oil on canvas, 72 × 40 inches

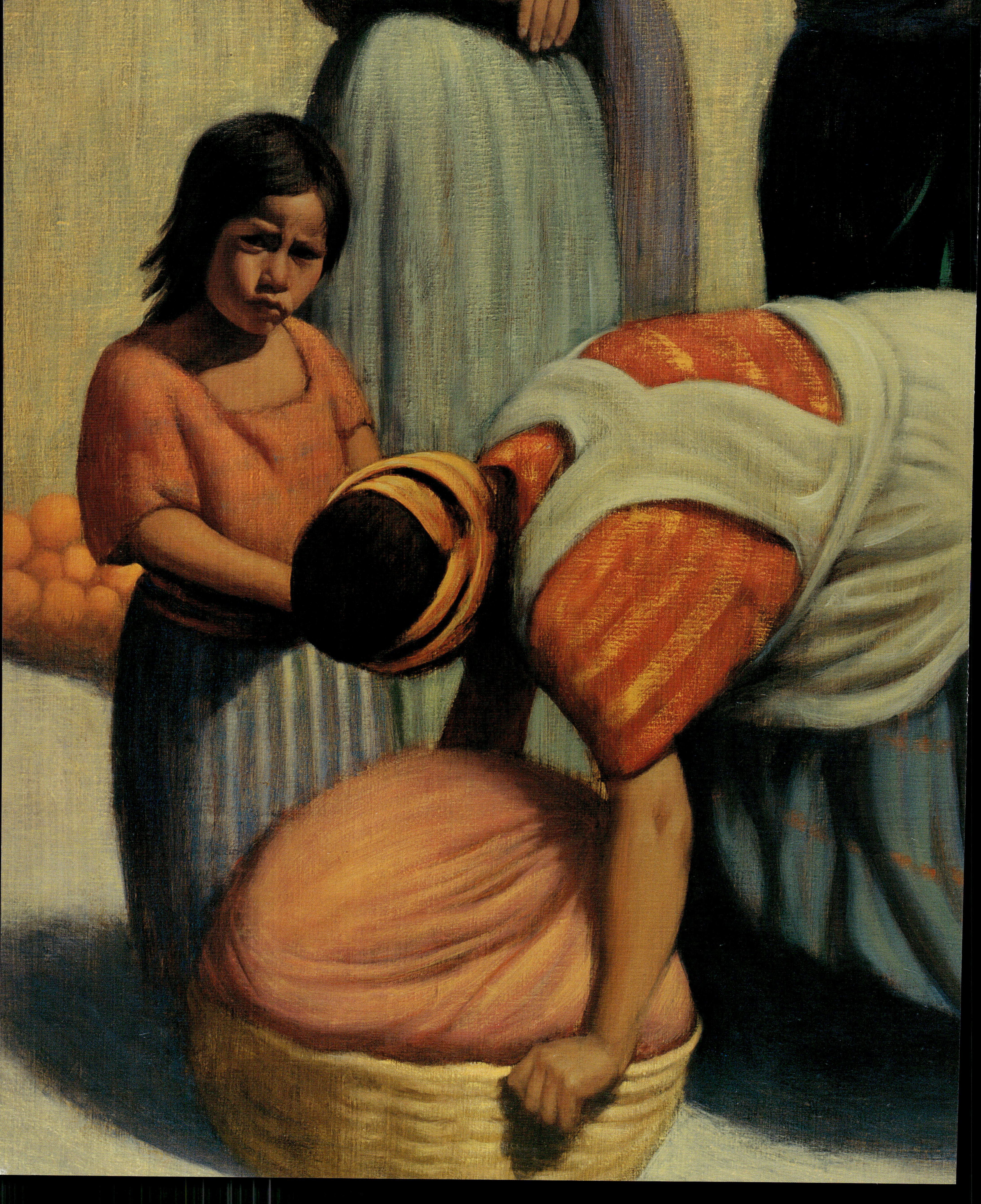

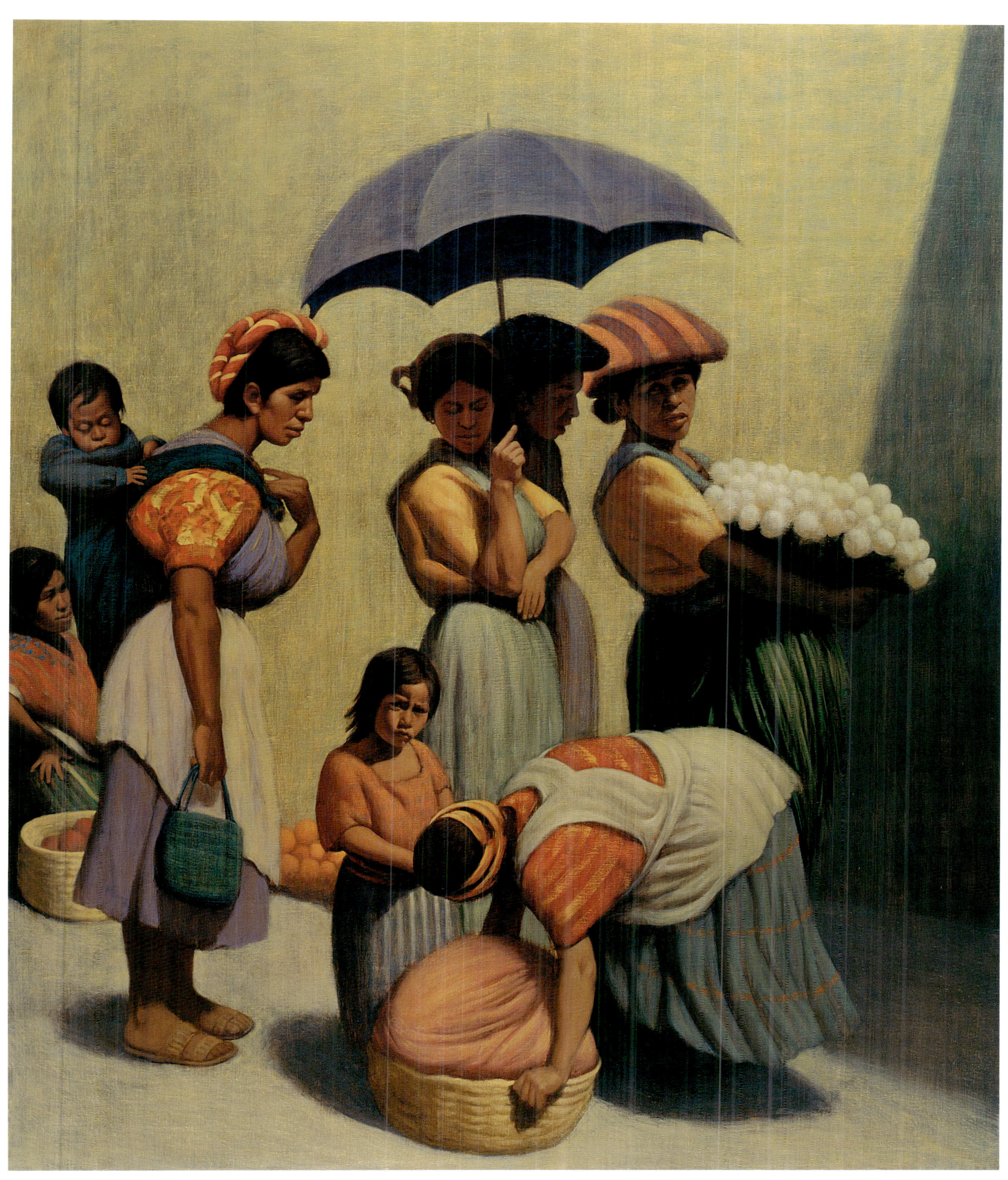

116. UNDER THE UMBRELLA
1997, oil on canvas, 80 × 68 inches

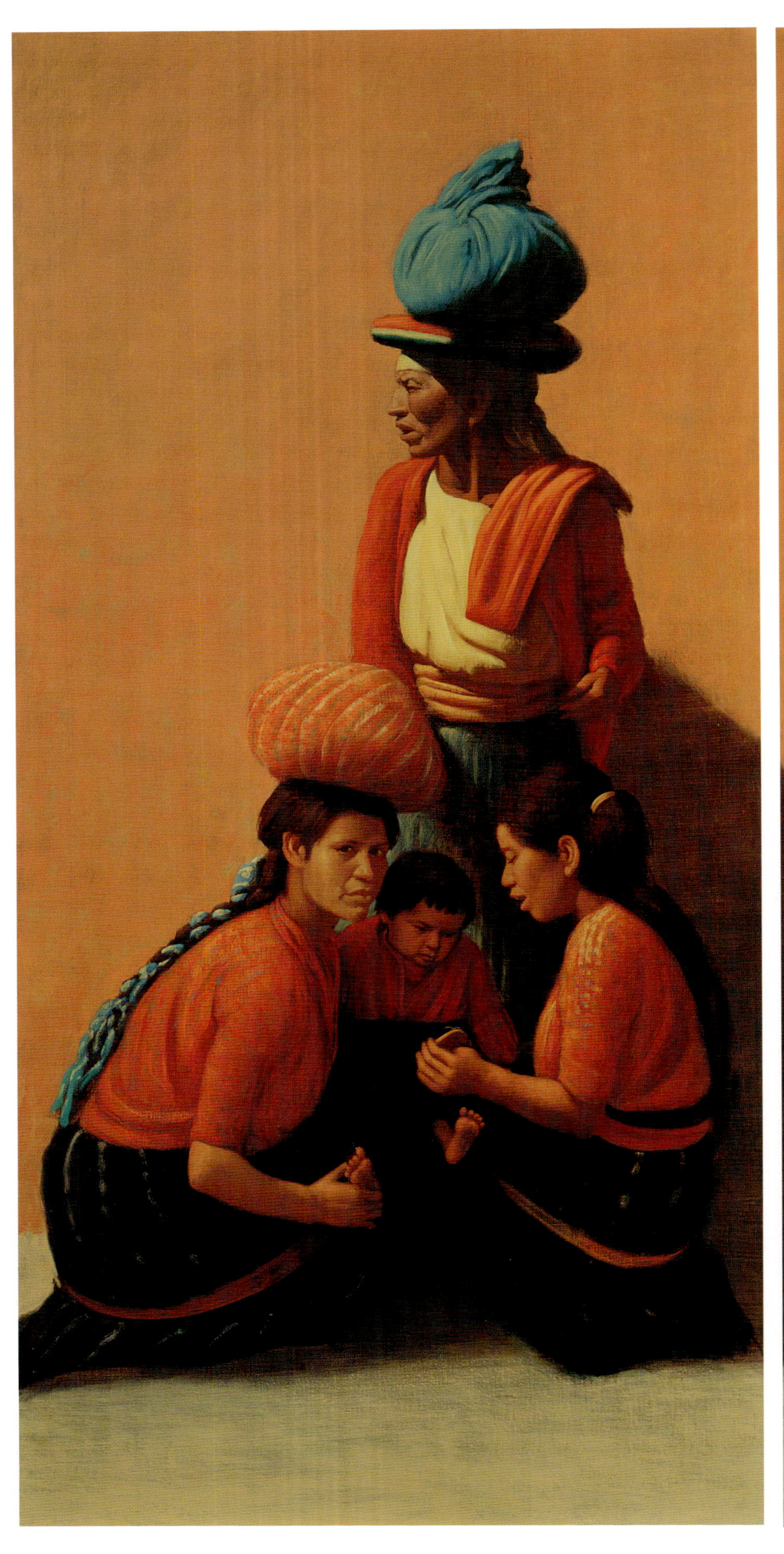

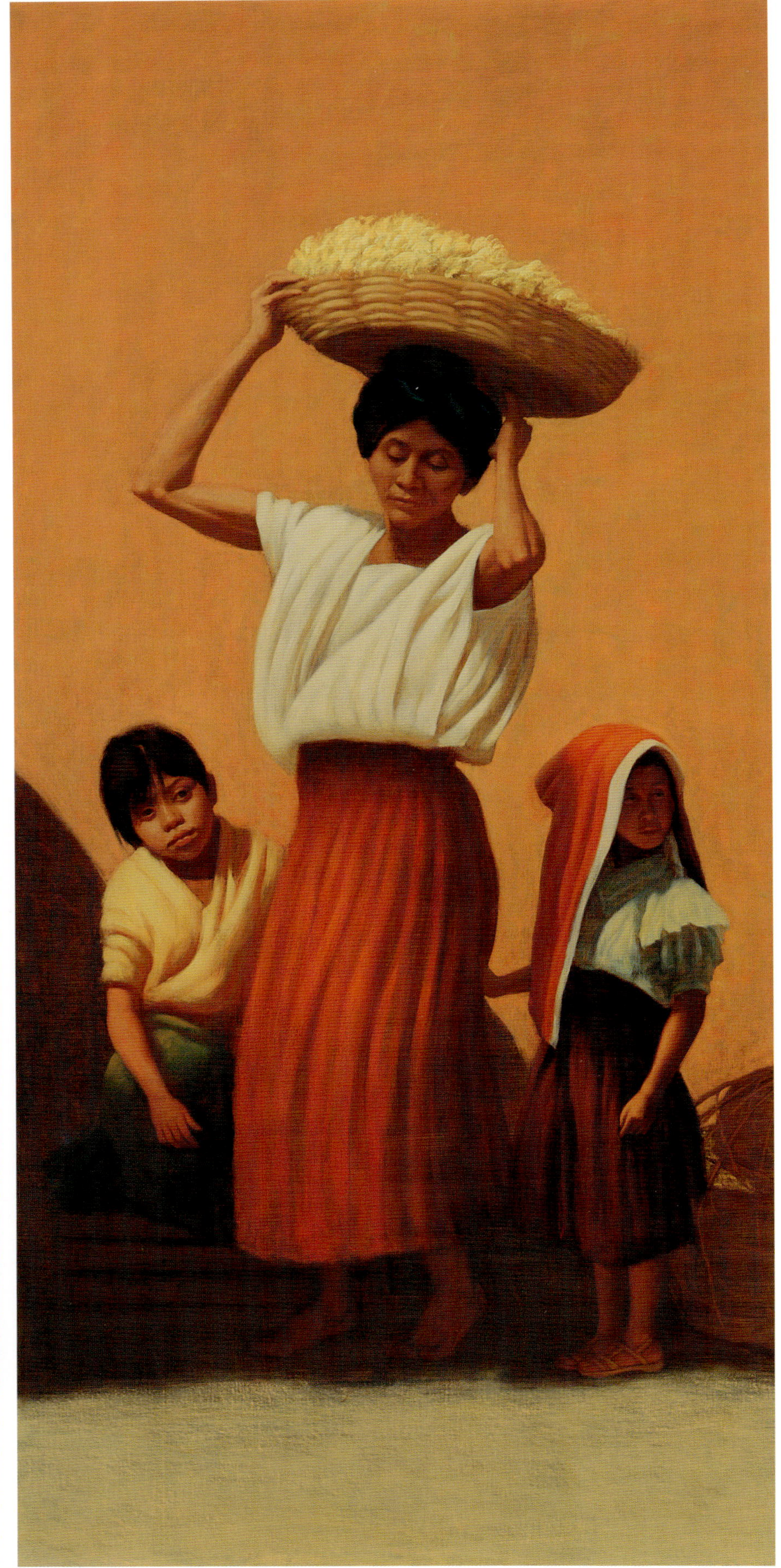

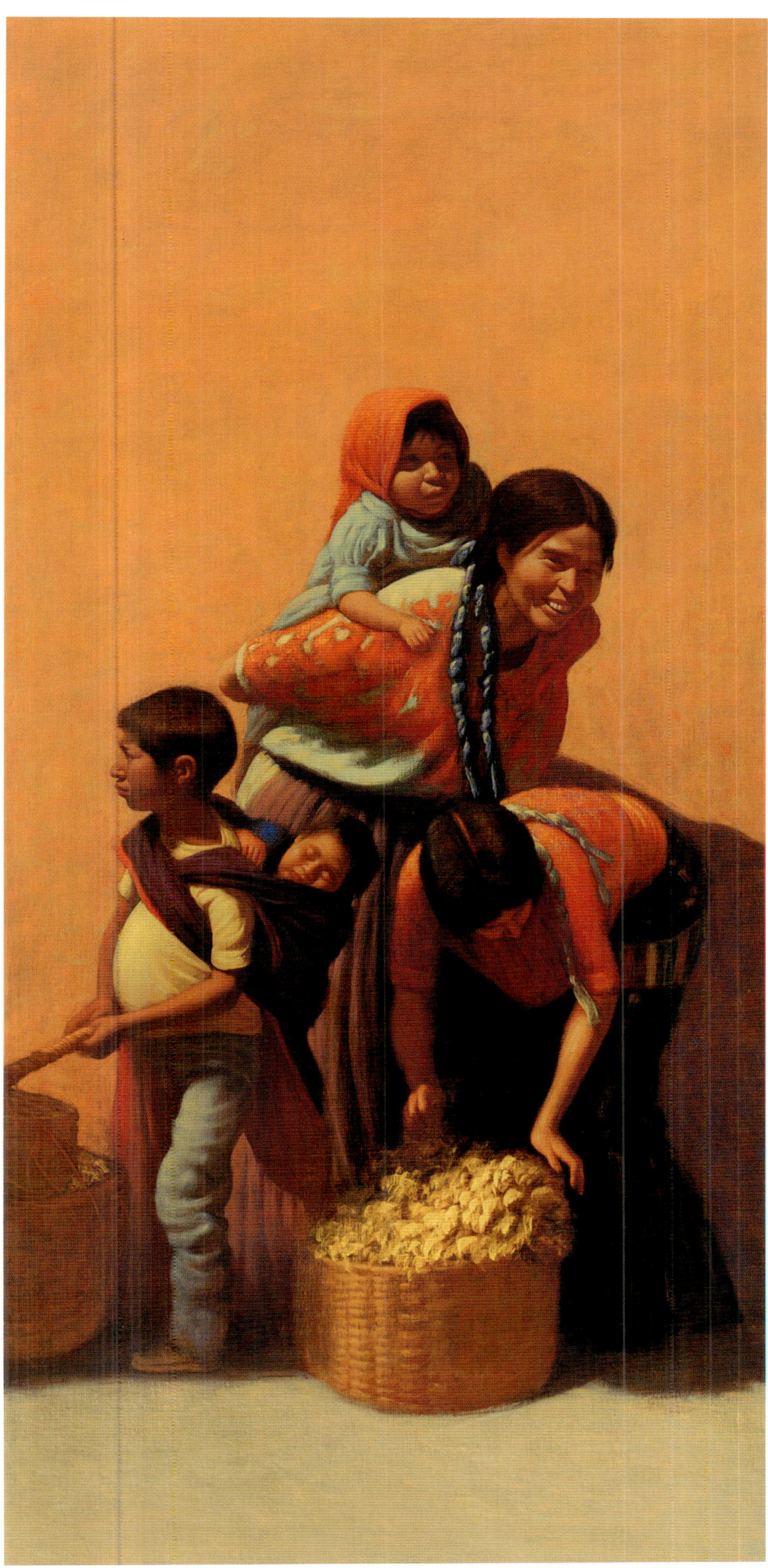
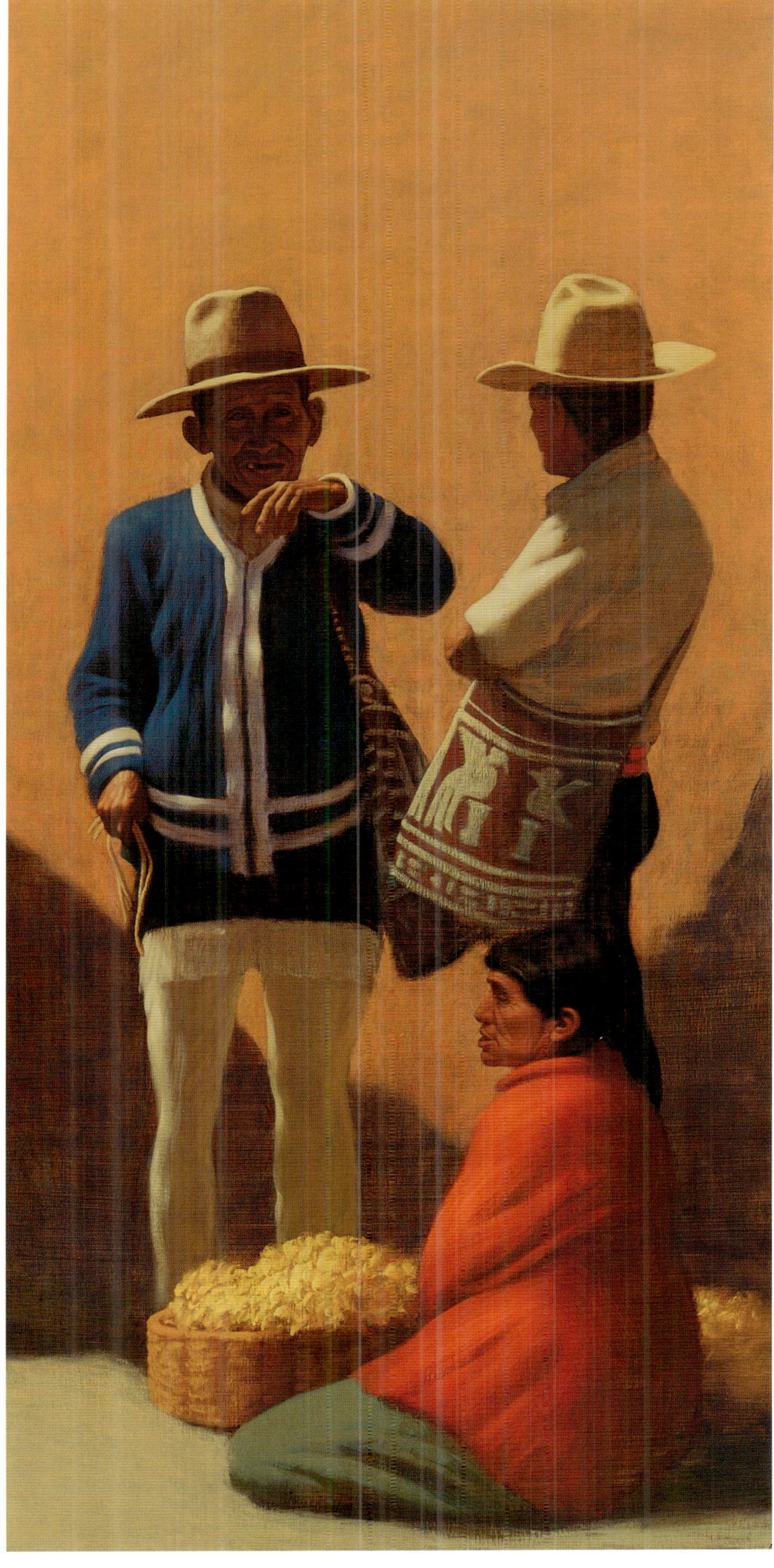

117. SAN FRANCISCO EL ALTO (polyptych)
1997, oil on canvas, 84 × 164 inches

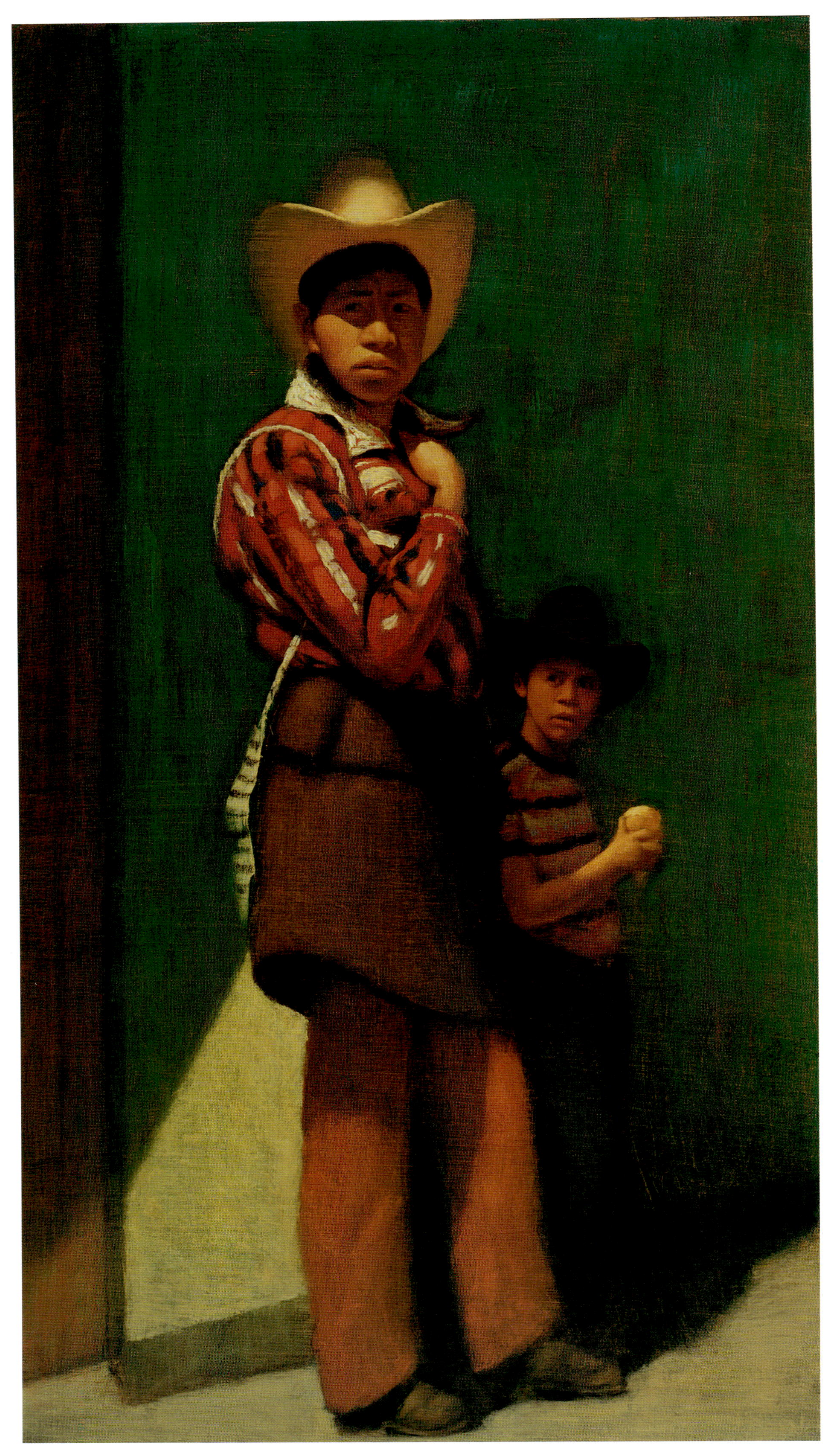

118. BROTHERS

1997, oil on canvas, 30 × 18 inches

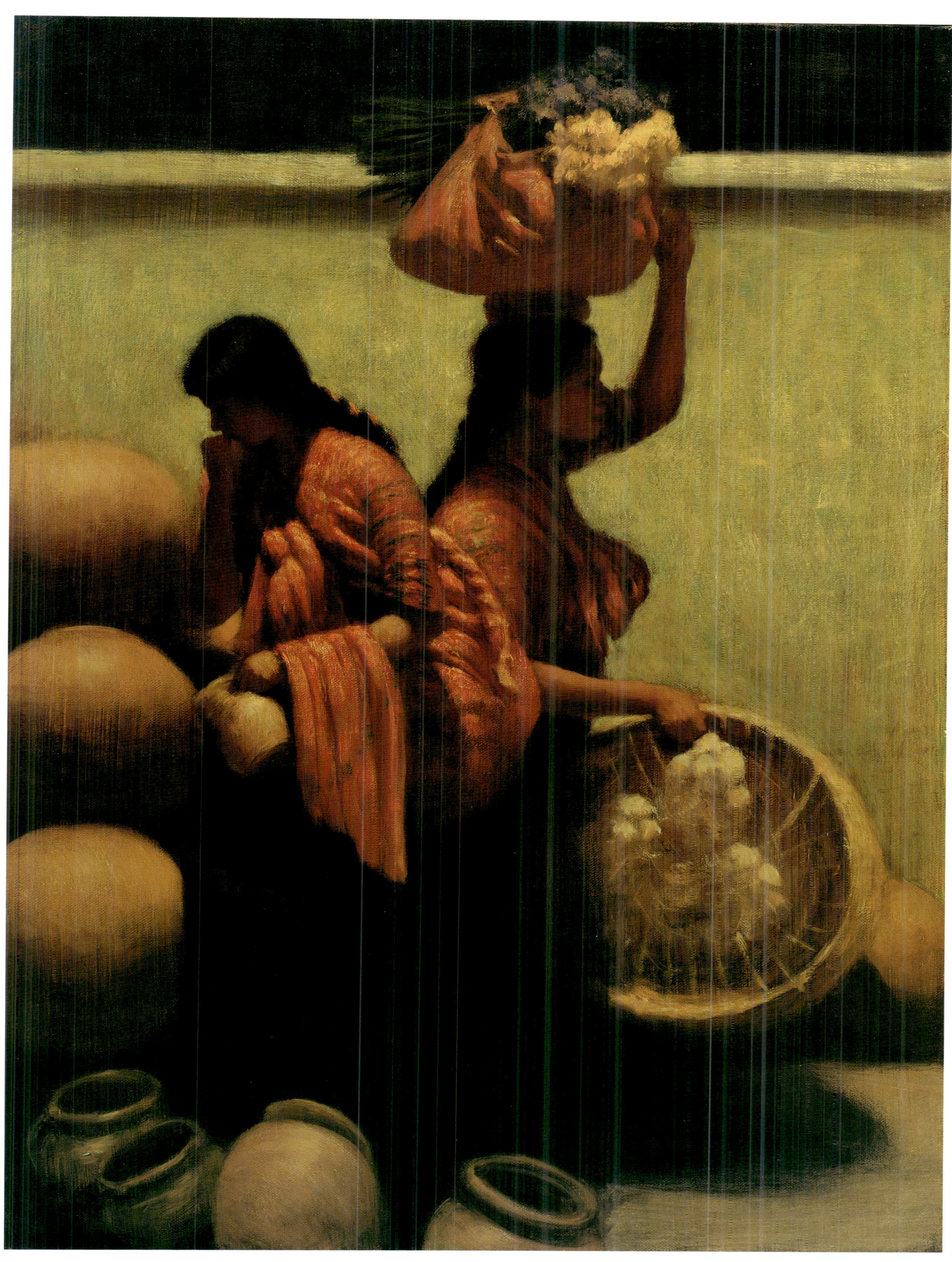

119. SOLOLA WOMEN
1997, oil on canvas, 20 × 16 inches

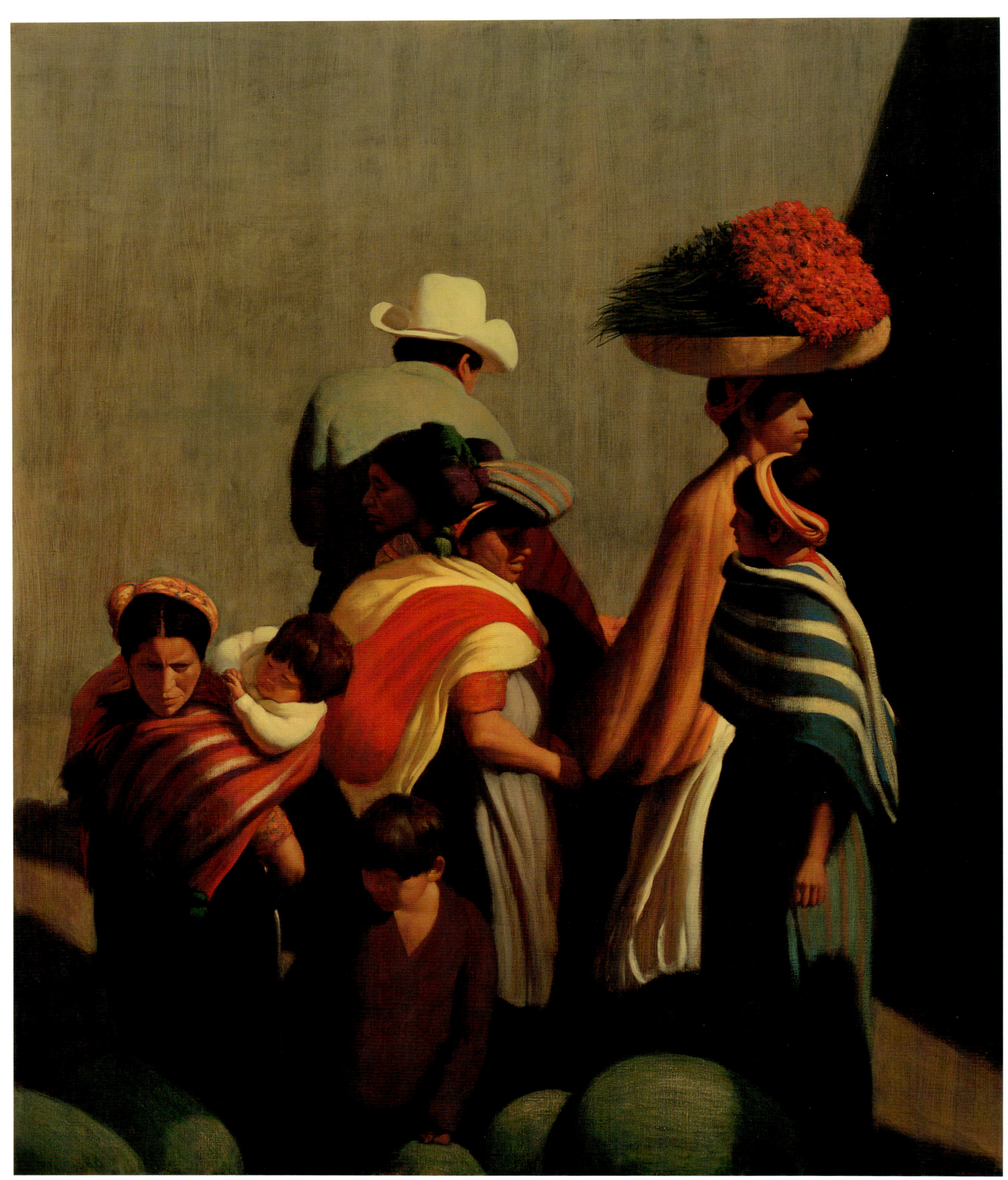

120. EXPRESSIONS OF THE SUN

1997, oil on canvas, 80 × 68 inches

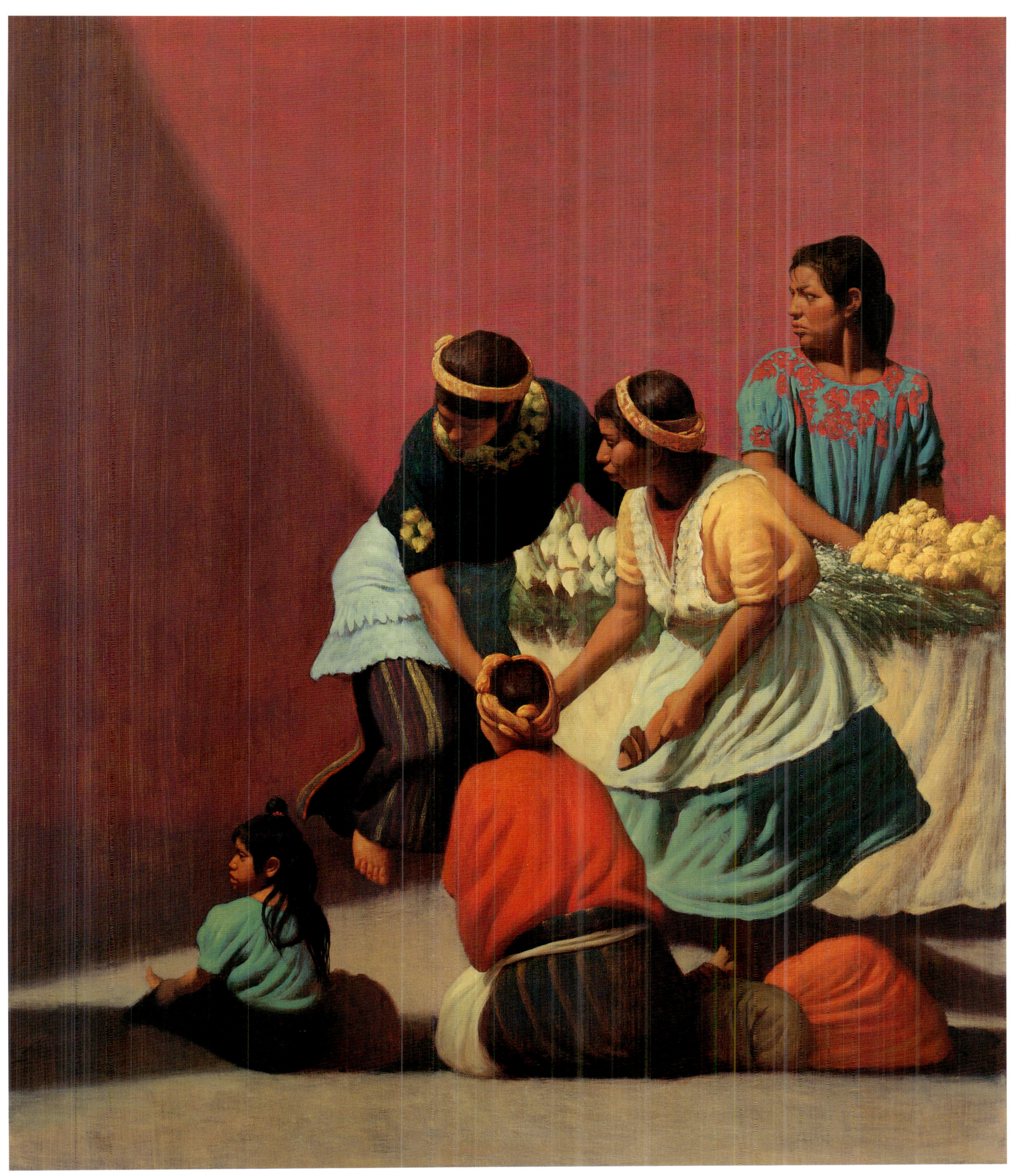

121. WALL OF PASSION
1997, oil on canvas, 80 × 68 inches

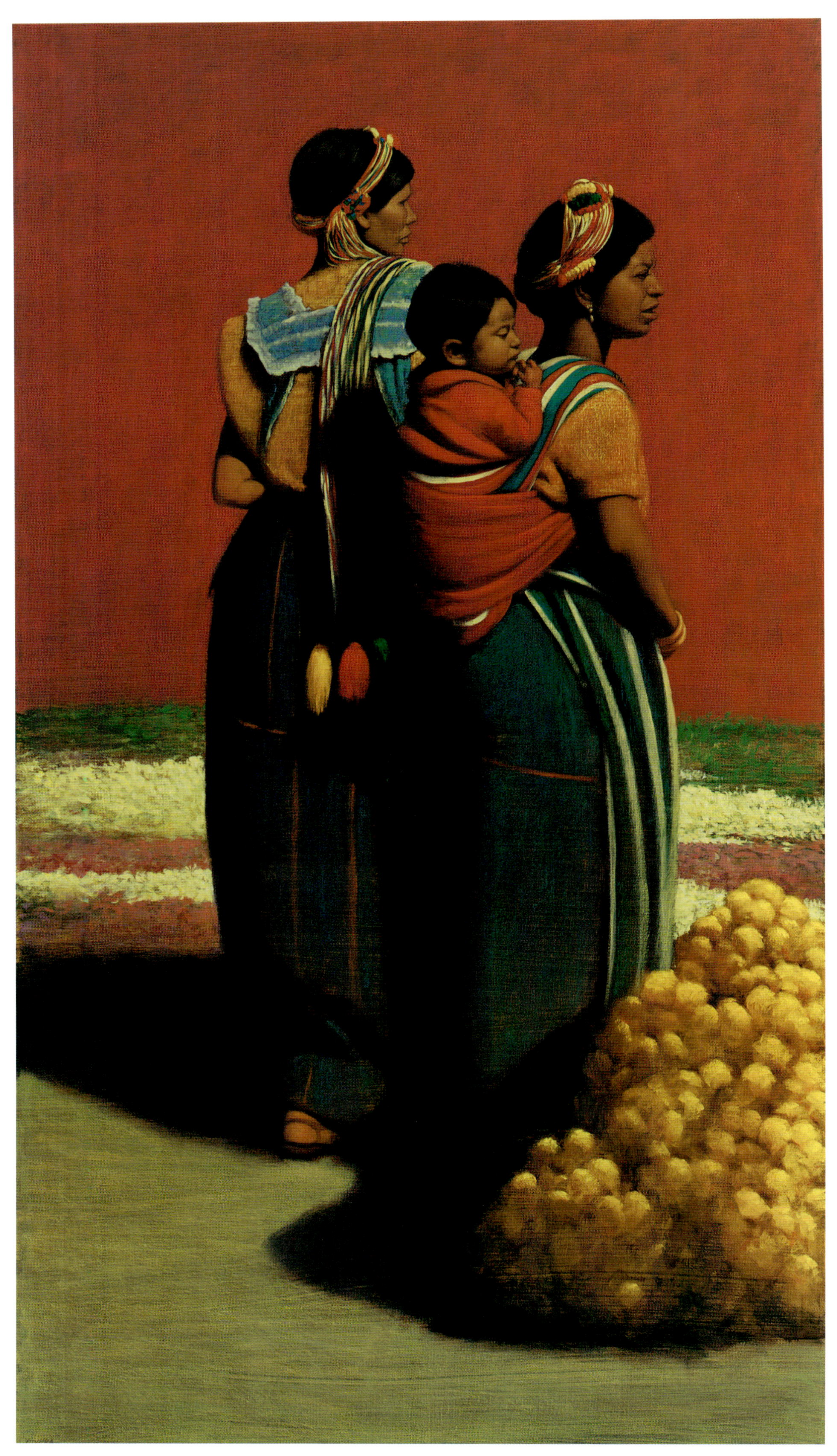

122. COLOR FIELDS

1998, oil on canvas, 72 × 40 inches

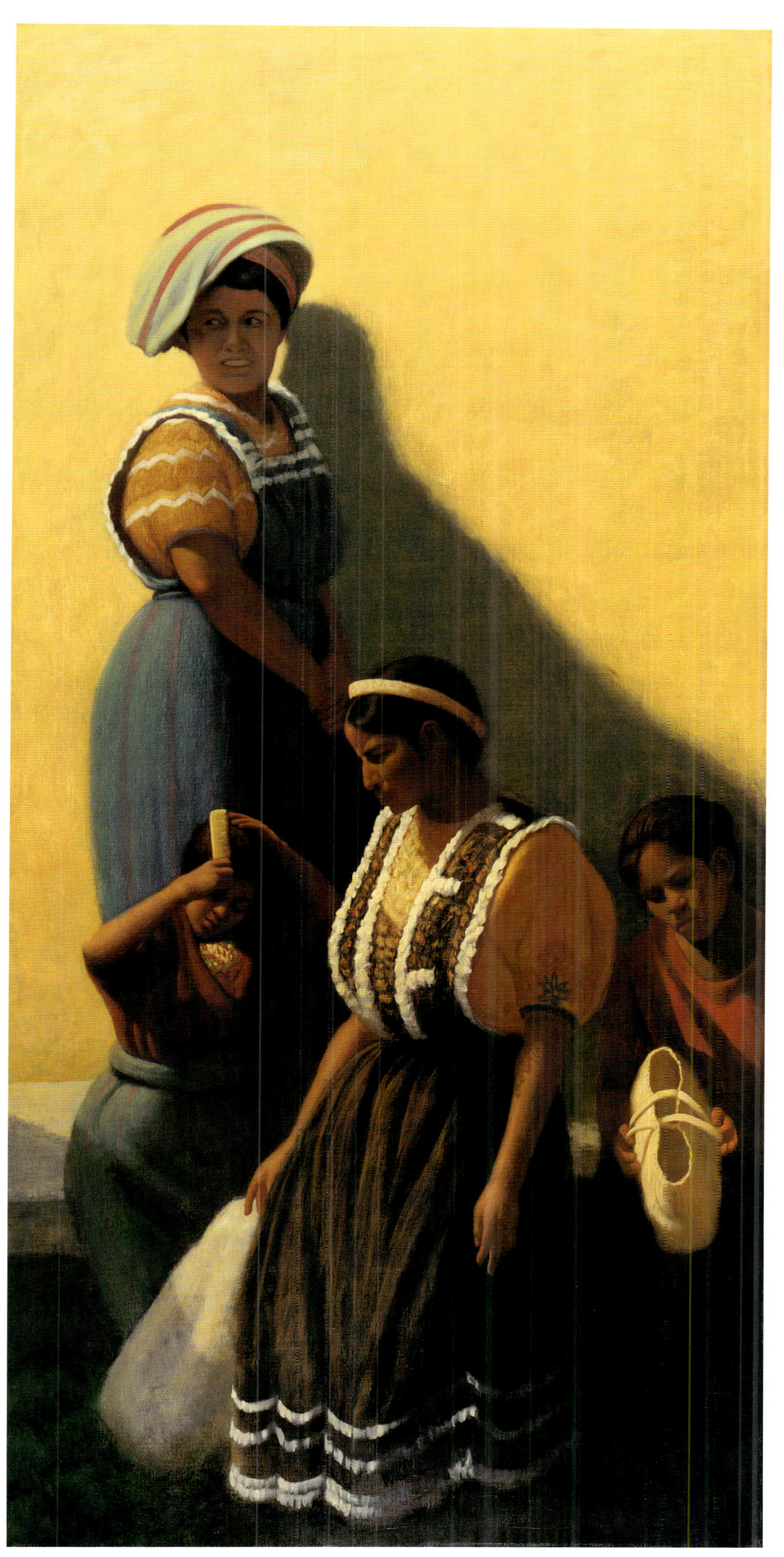

123. PASSING TIME

1993, oil on canvas, 84 × 41 inches

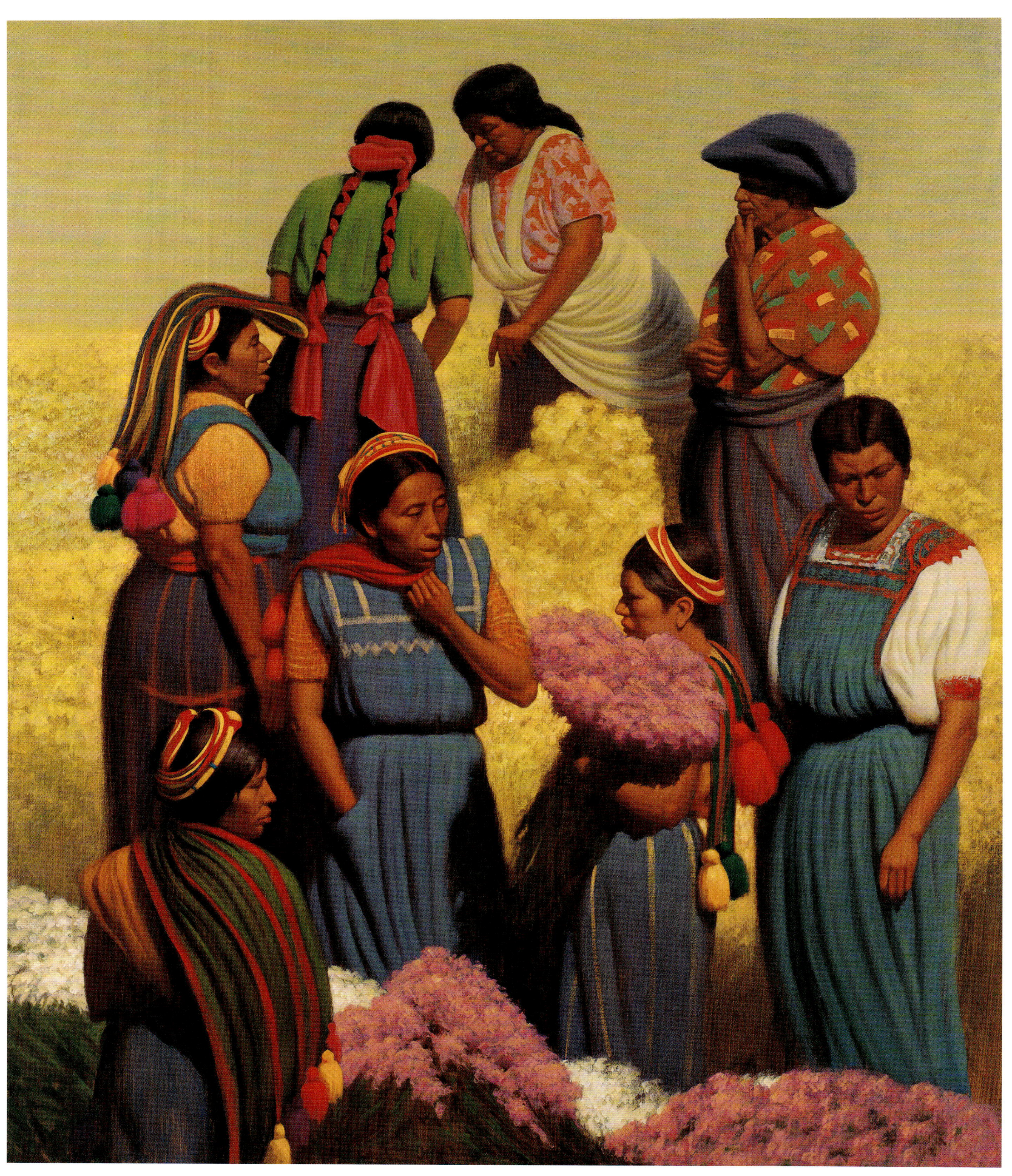

124. FLOWERS OF THE EARTH

1998, oil on canvas, 80 × 68 inches

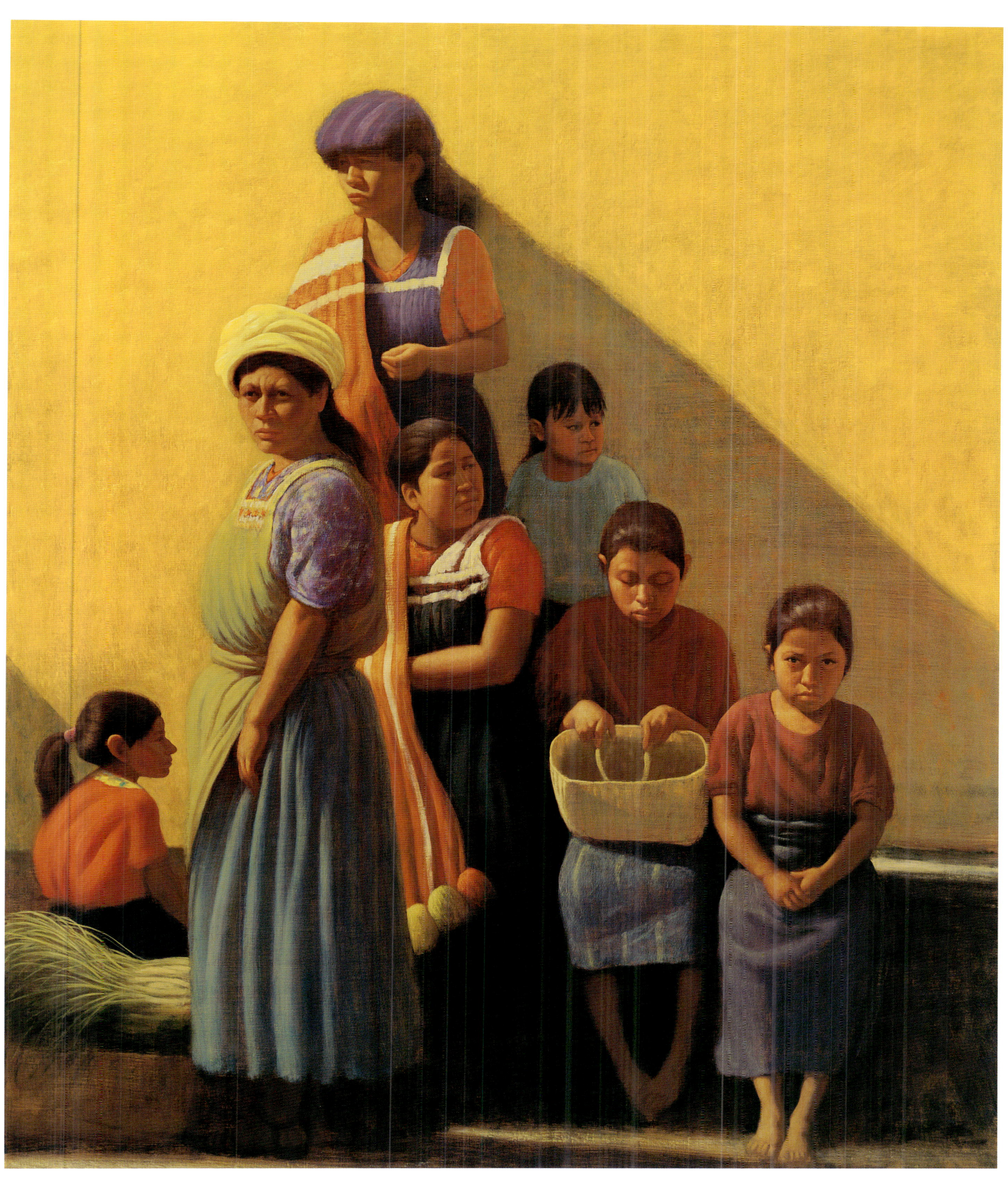

125. THE EMPTY BASKET

1998, oil on canvas, 80 × 68 inches

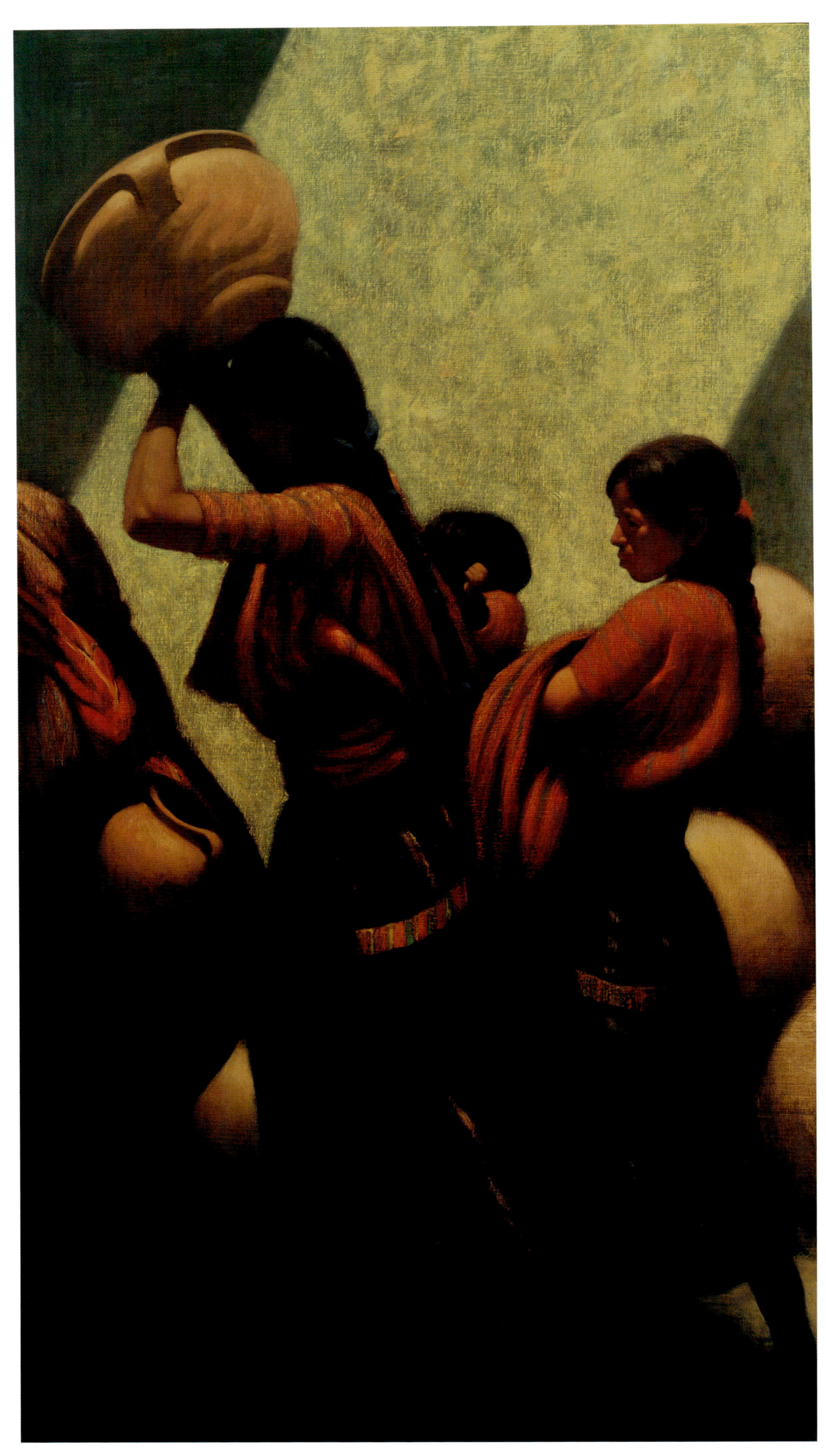

126. LIVING WITH CLAY
1998, oil on canvas, 72 × 40 inches

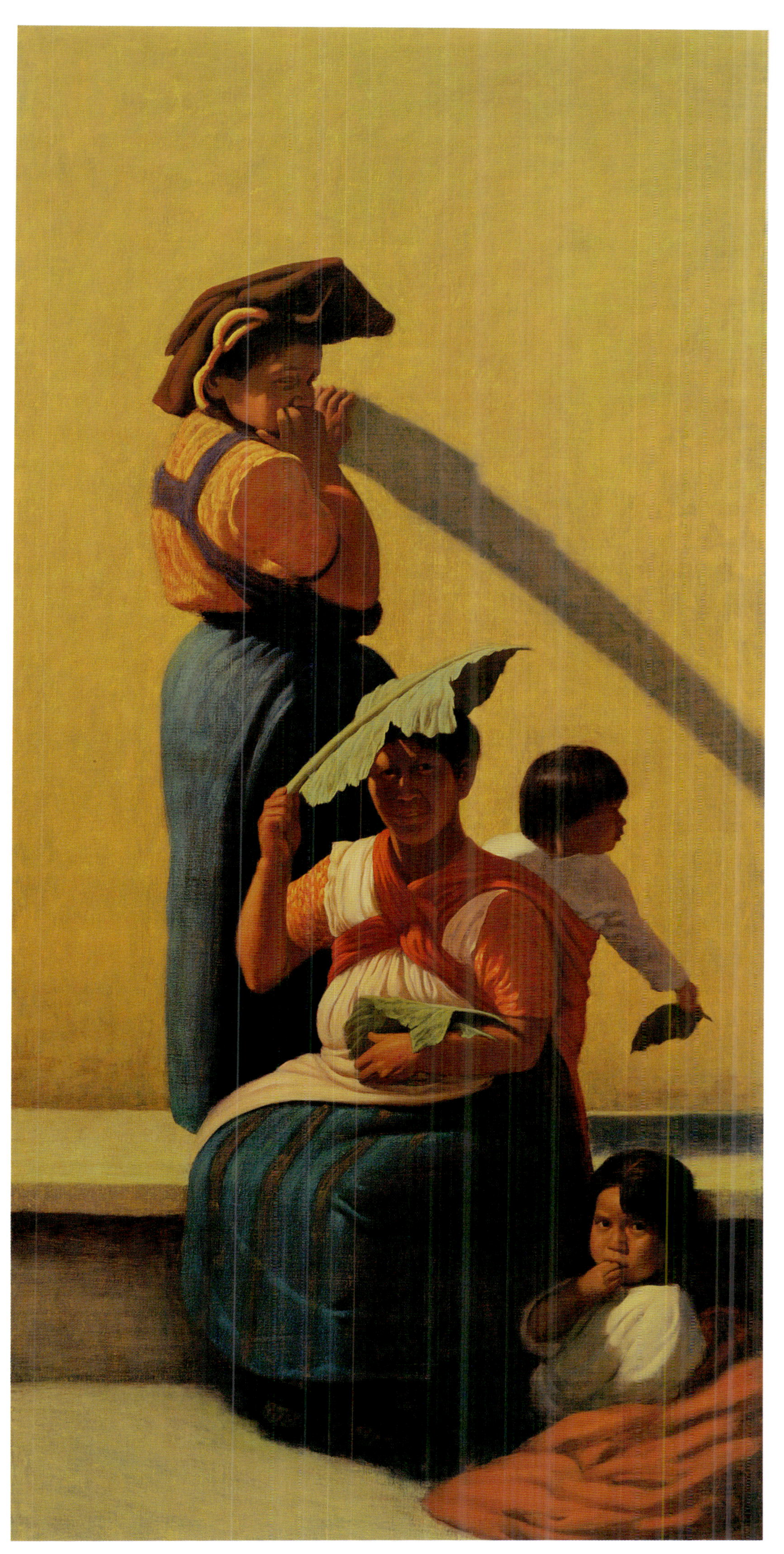

127. BREAKING THE LIGHT

1998. oil on canvas, 84 × 41 inches

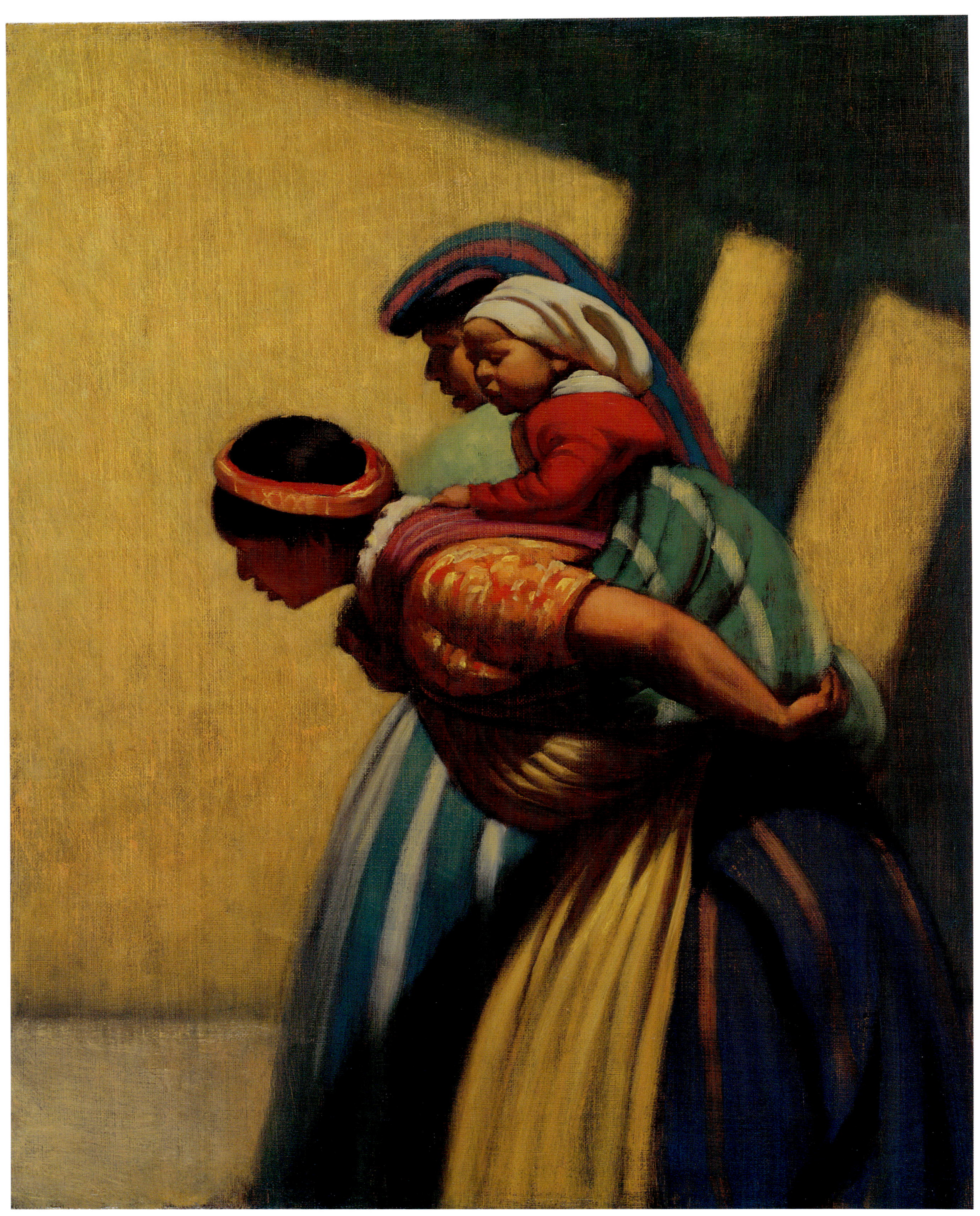

128. INTO THE LIGHT

1999, oil on board, 20 × 16 inches

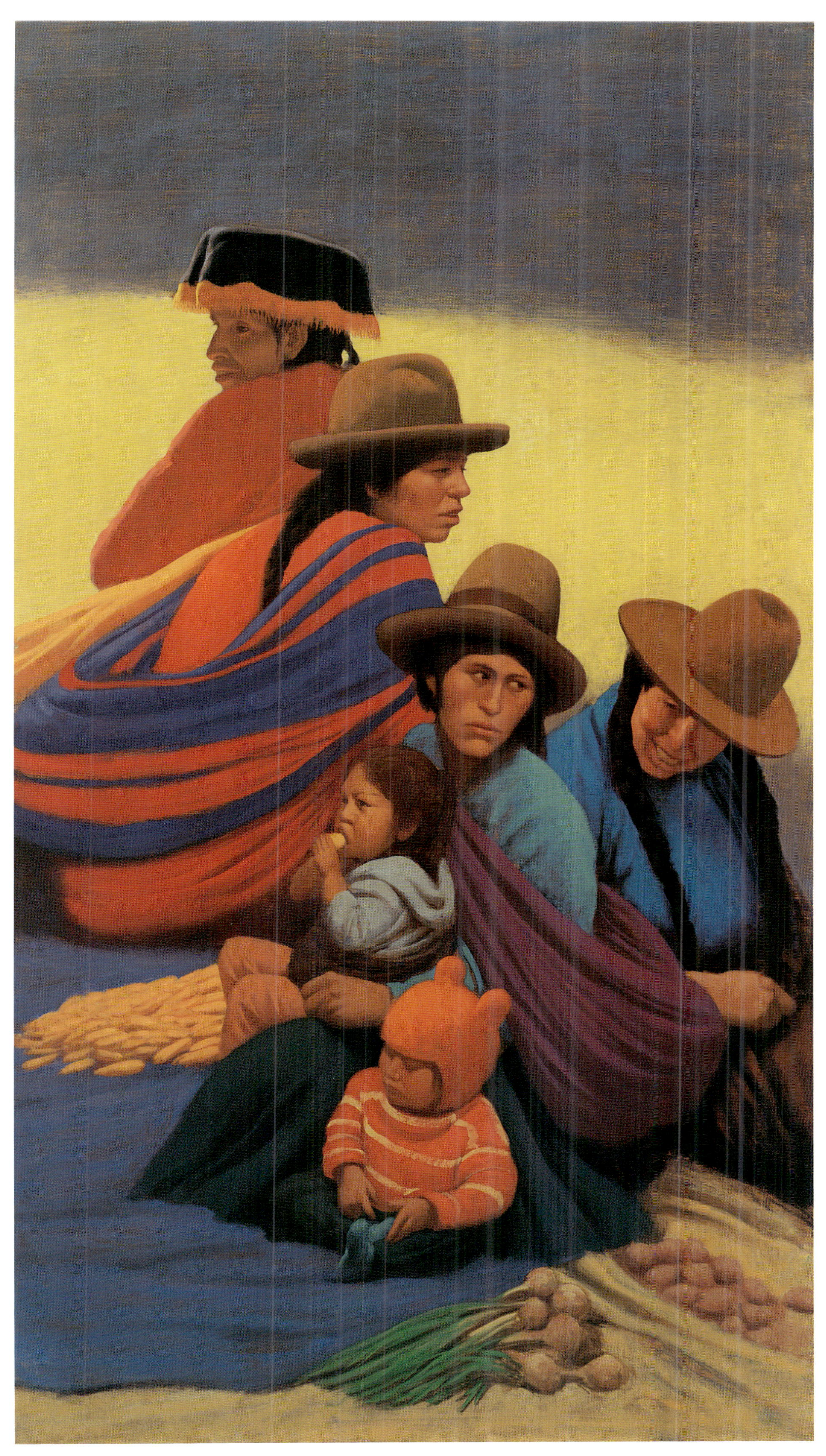

129. FIRST GLIMPSE OF PERU

1999. oil on canvas, 72 × 40 inches

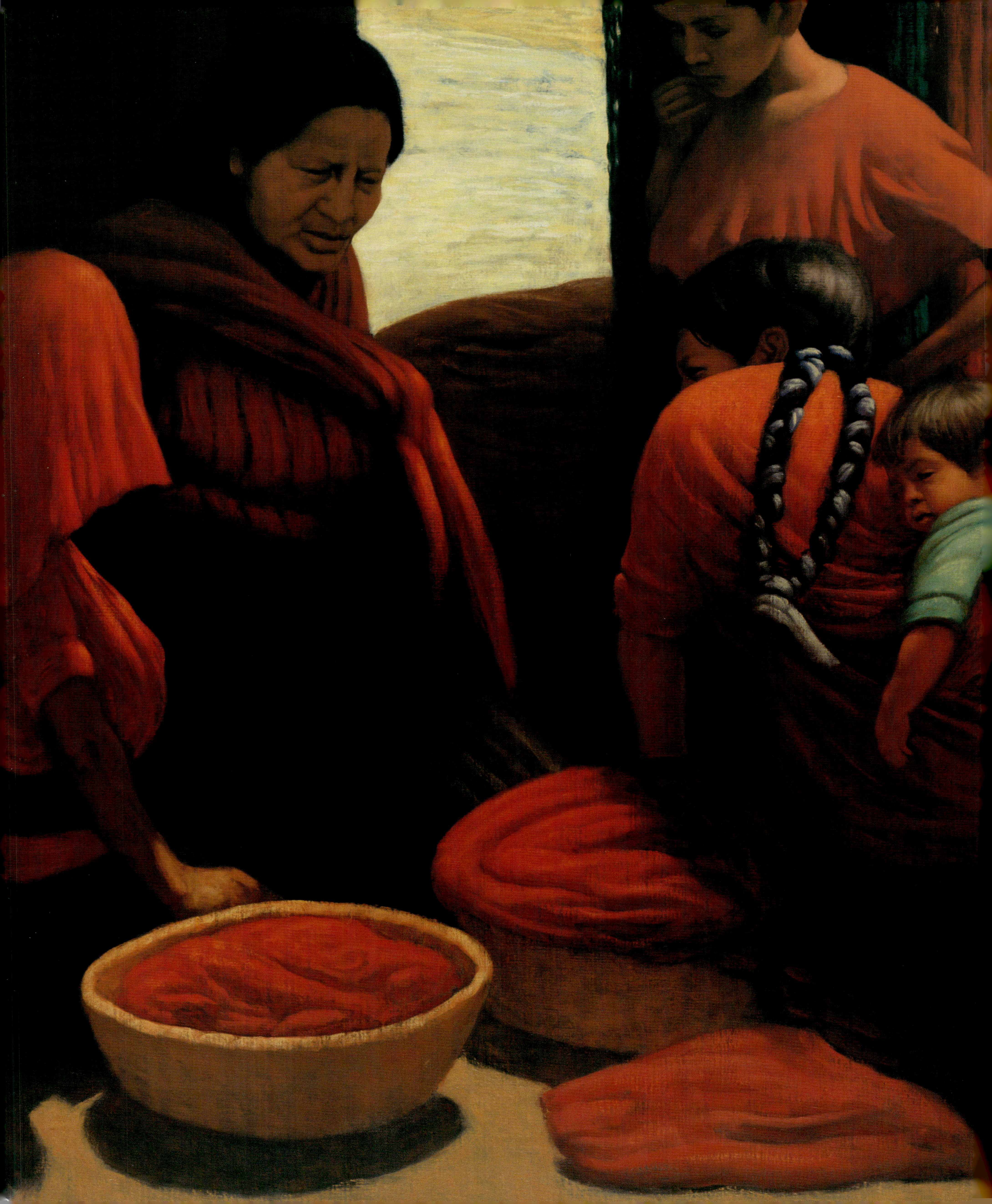

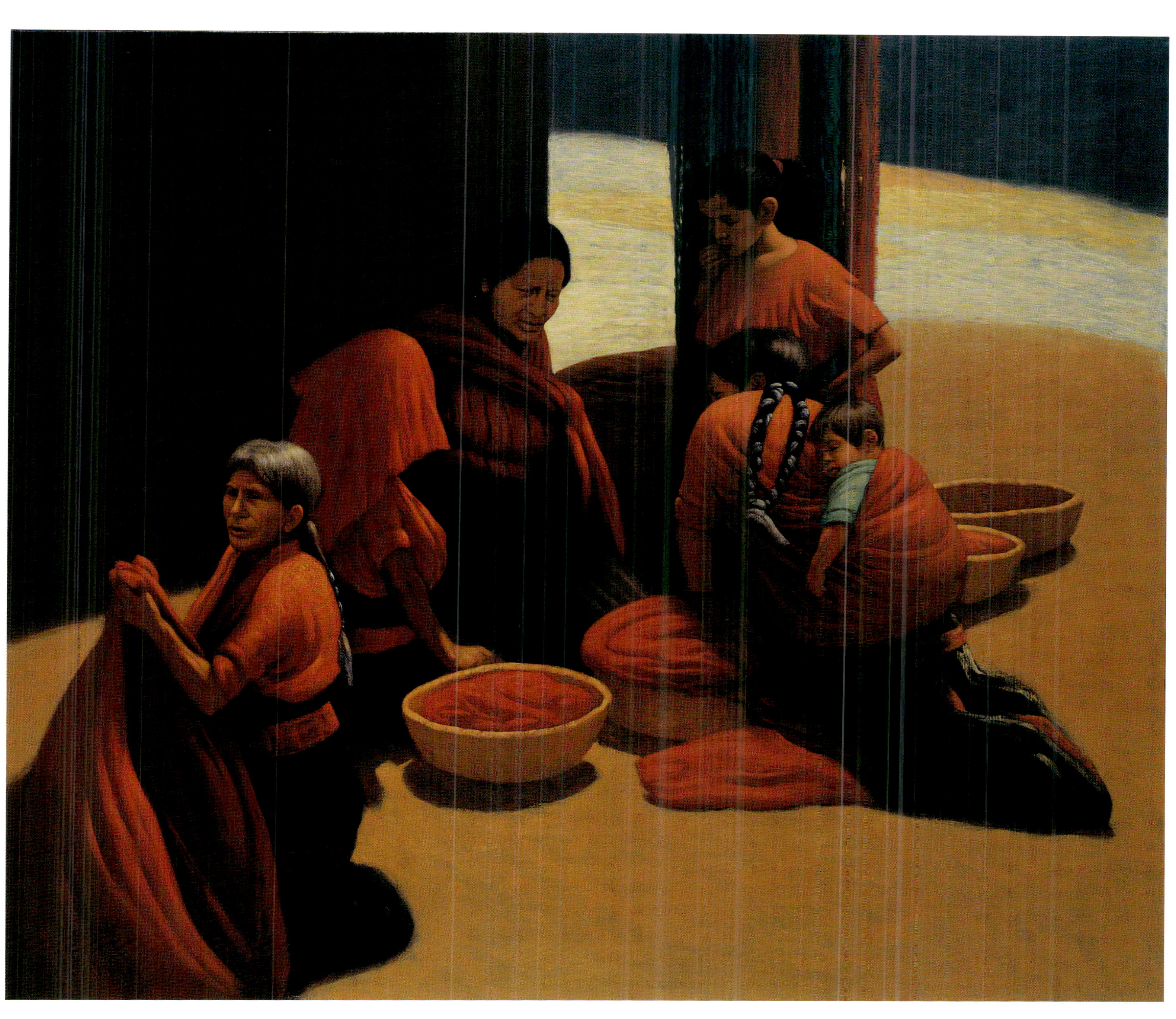

130. WOMEN IN RED
2000, oil on canvas, 68 × 80 inches

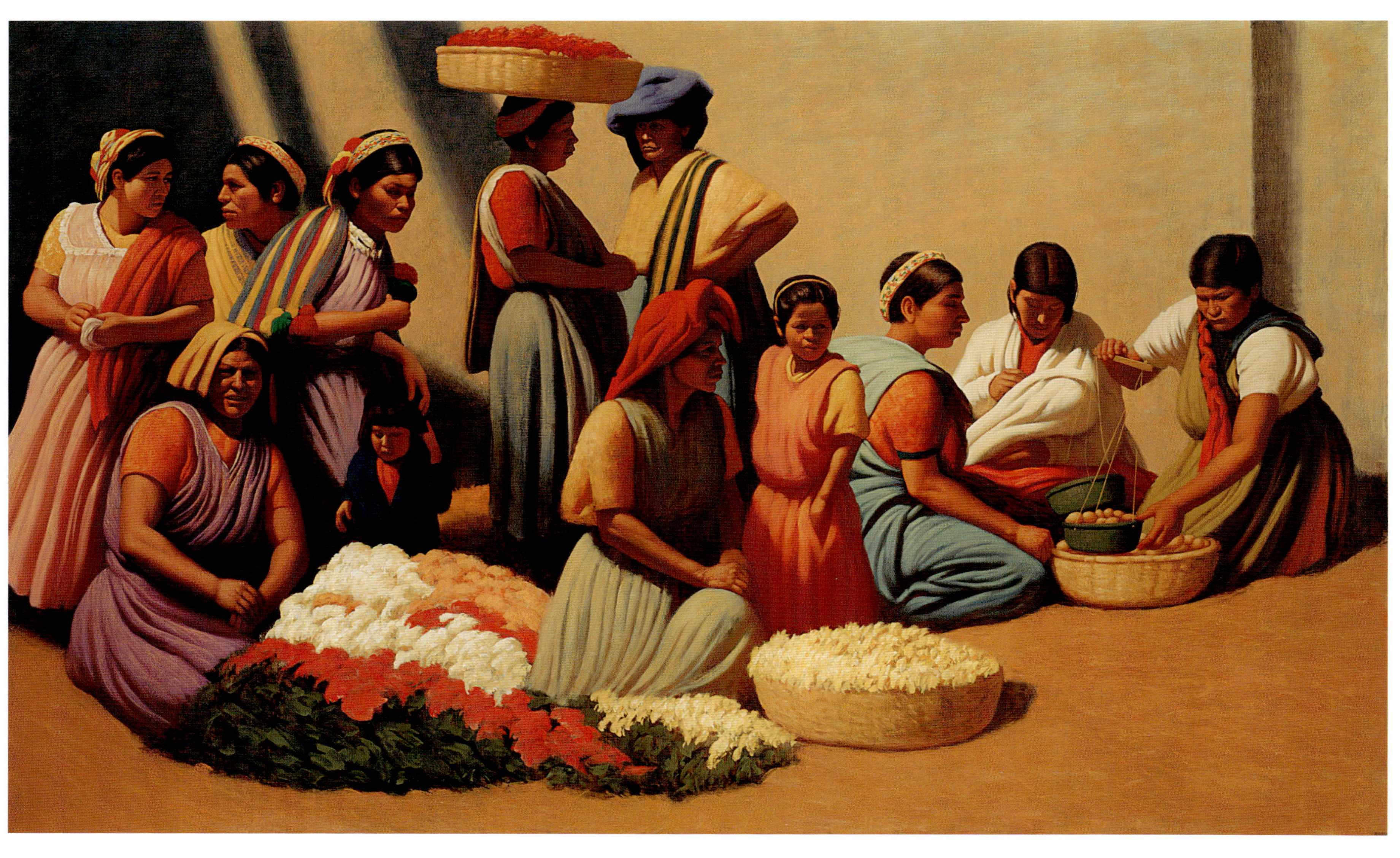

131. SPONTANEOUS GATHERING
2000, oil on canvas, 72 × 120 inches

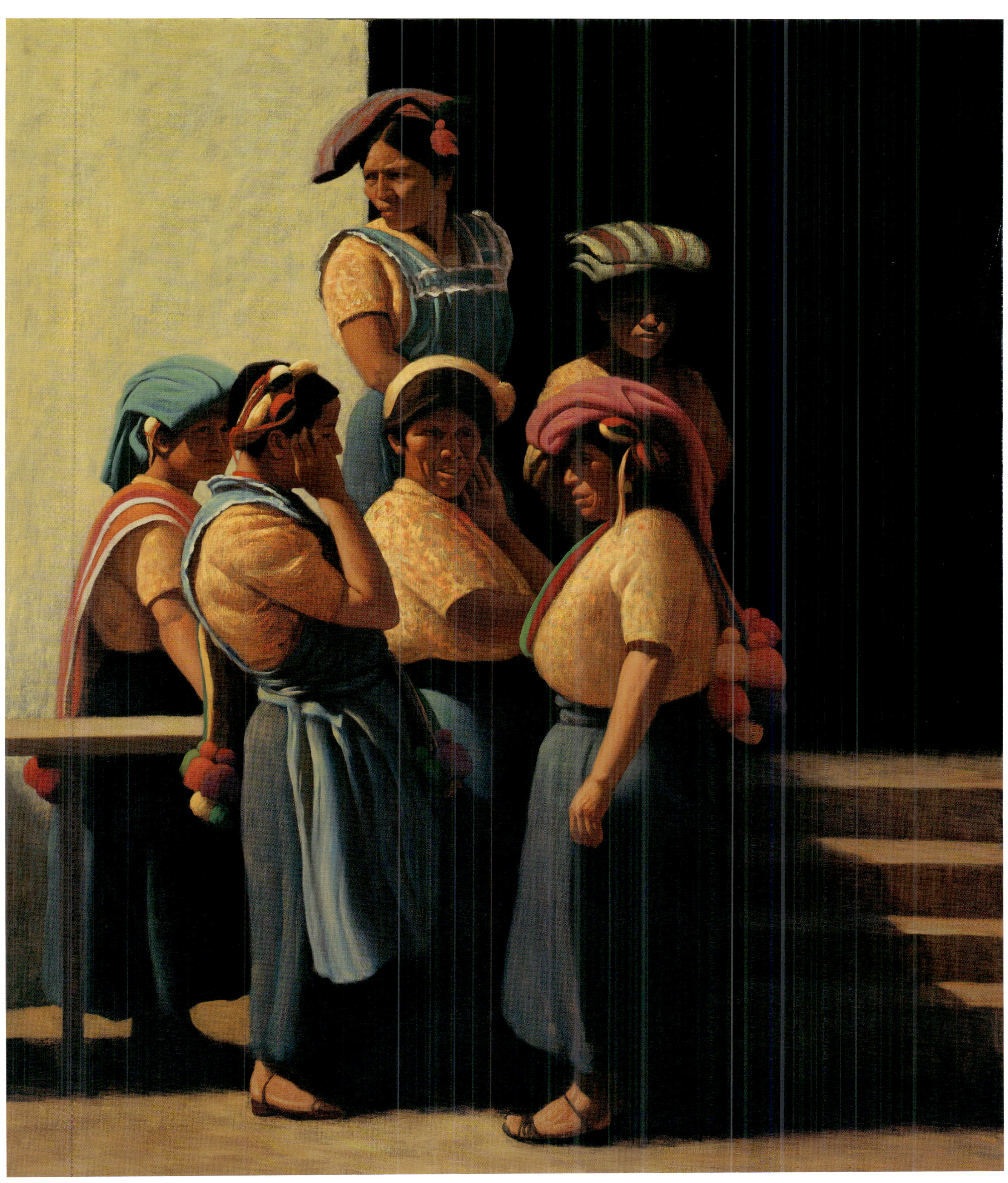

132. LAST LOOK
2000, oil on canvas, 80 × 68 inches

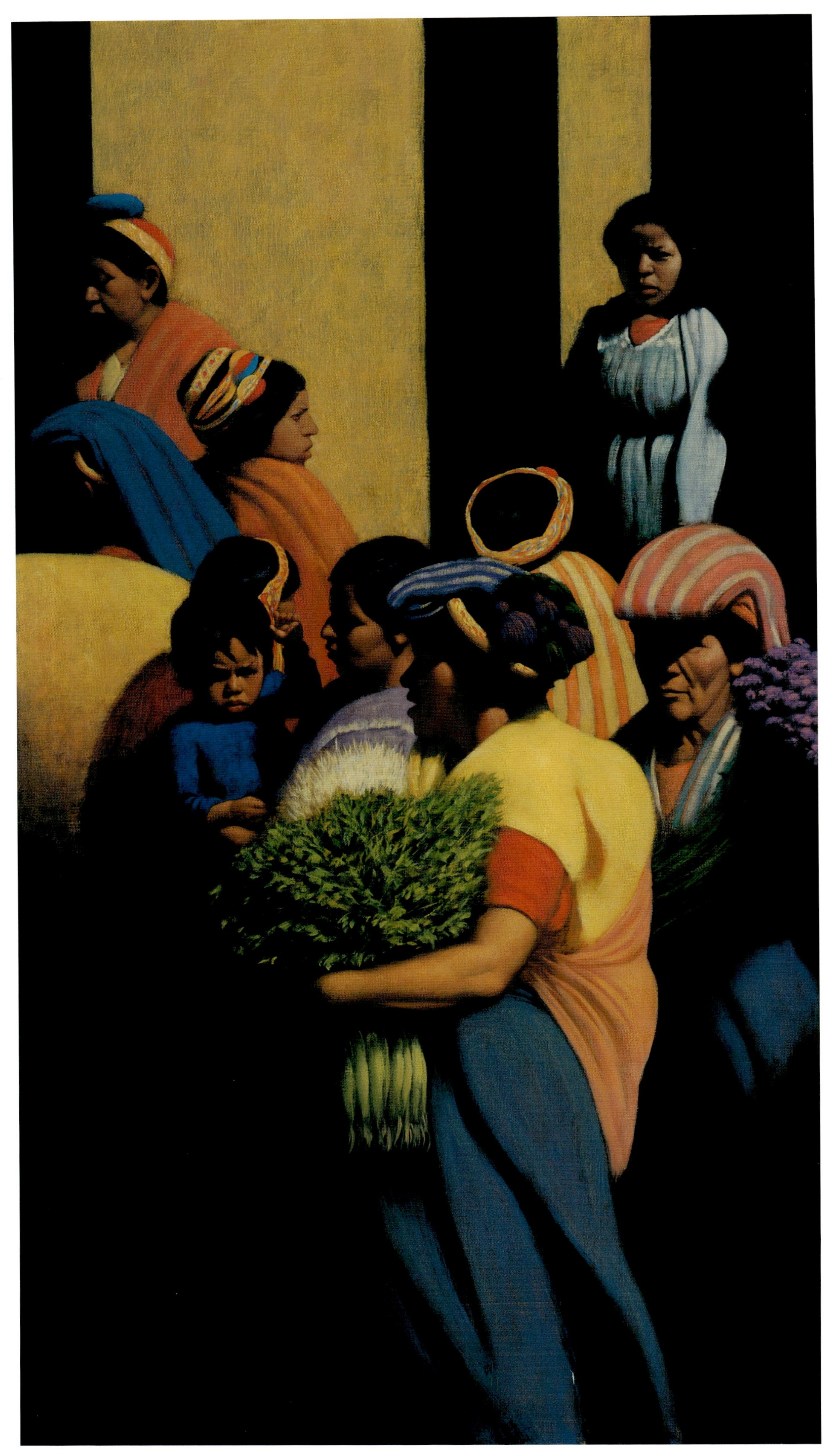

133. FROM THE SHADOWS

2000, oil on canvas, 72 × 40 inches

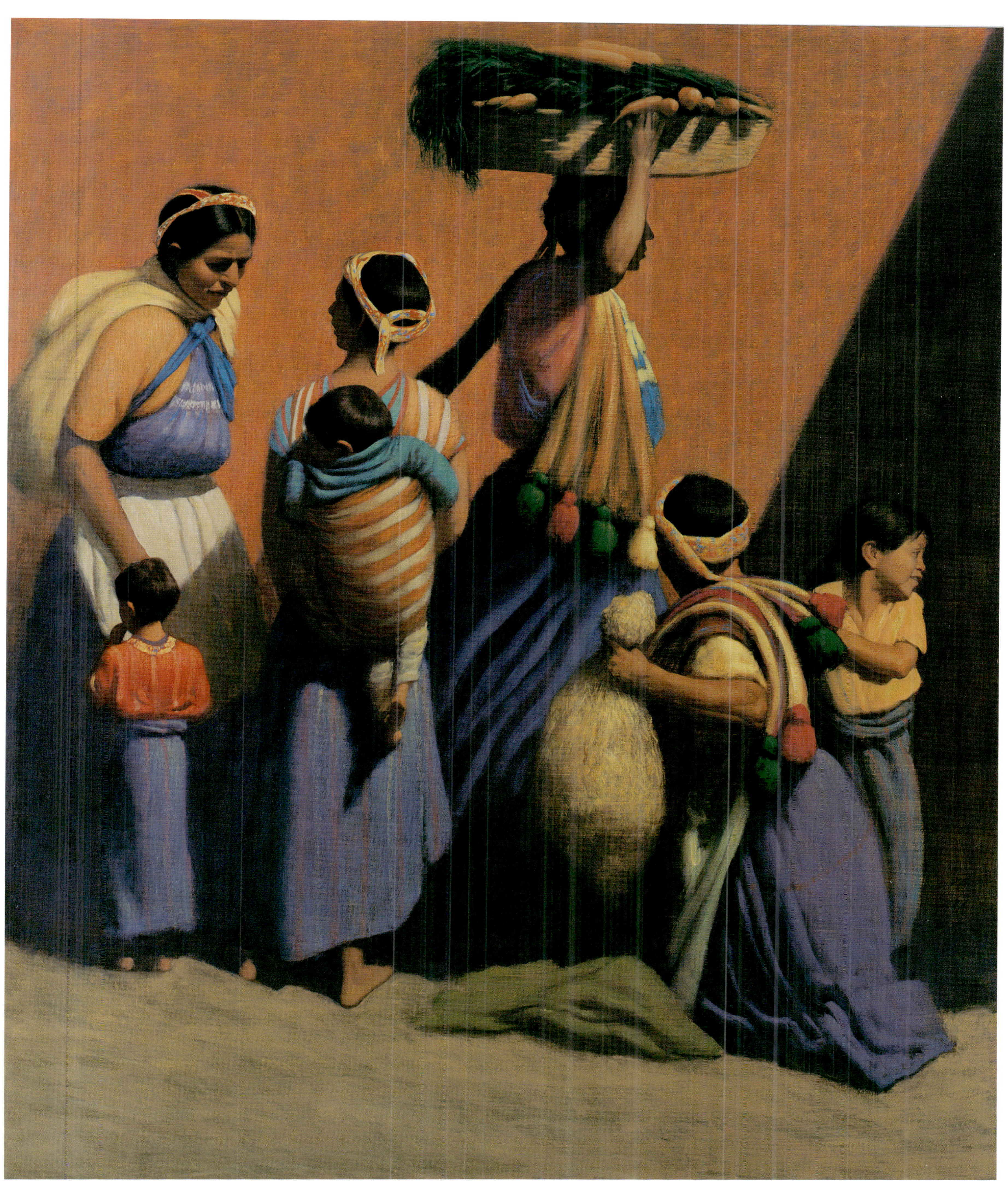

134. UNTITLED
2000, oil on canvas, 80 × 68 inches

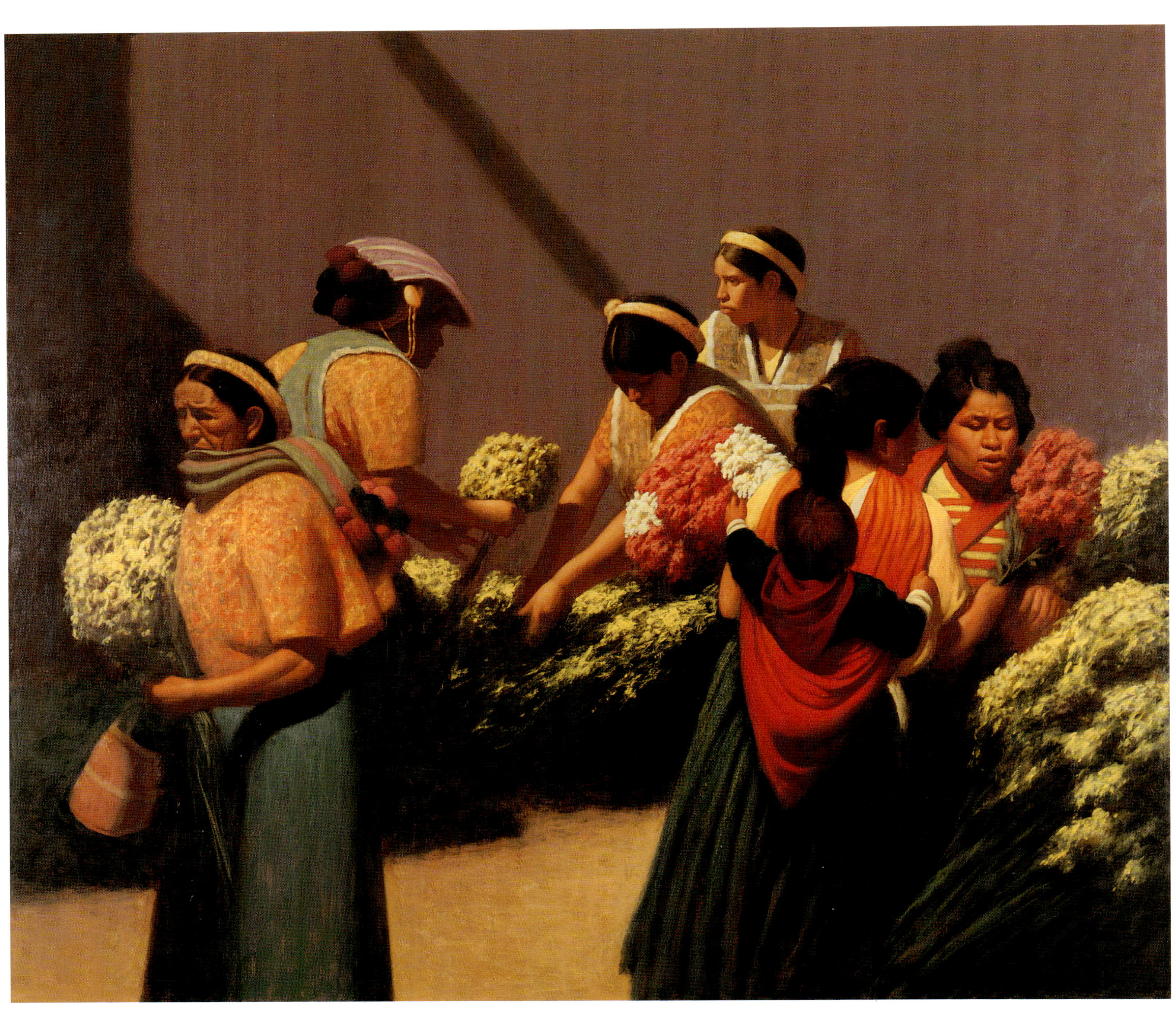

135. MARKET OF PROFUSION

2000, oil on canvas, 68 × 80 inches

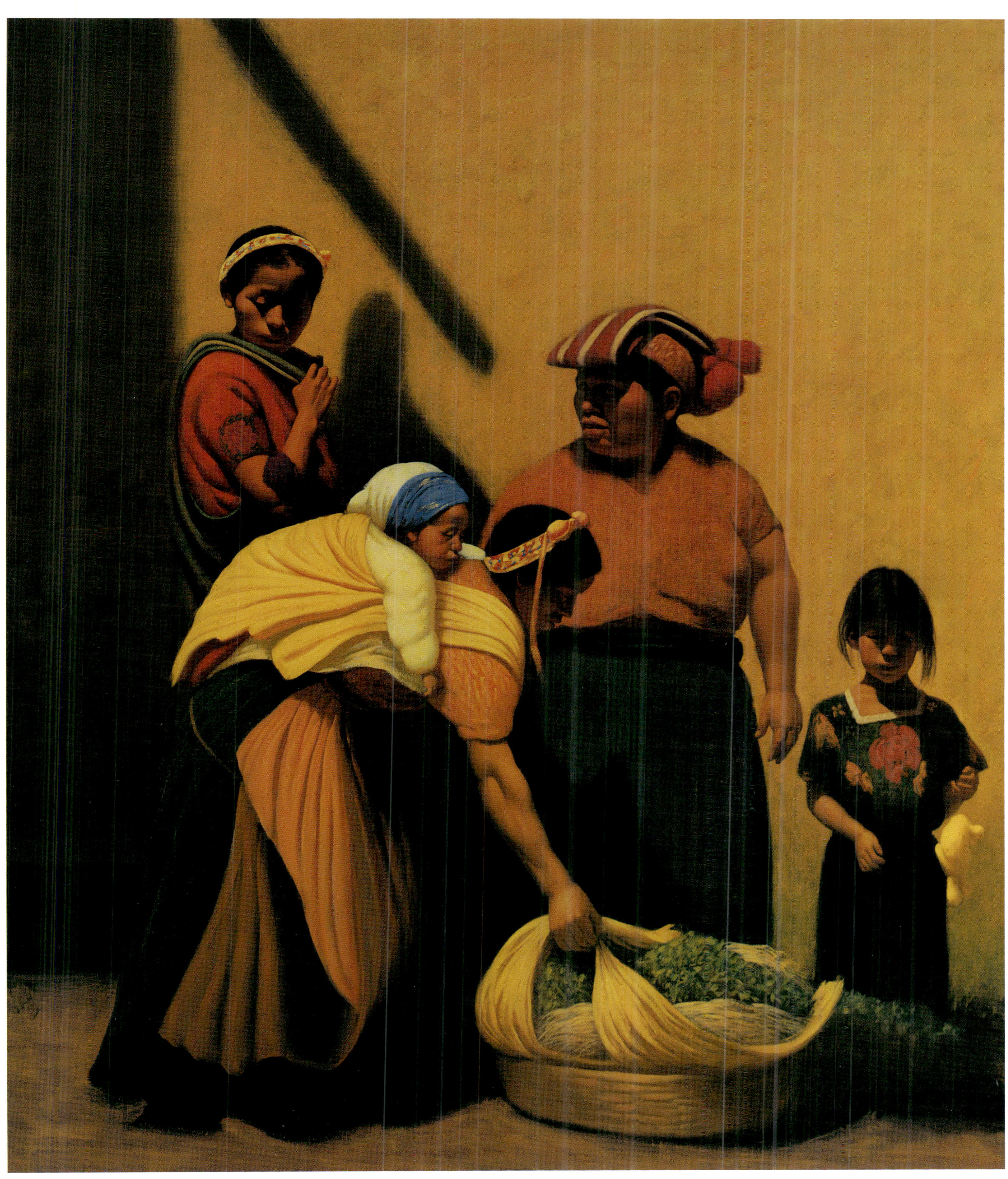

136. ANTE MERIDIAN

2000, oil on canvas, 80 × 68 inches

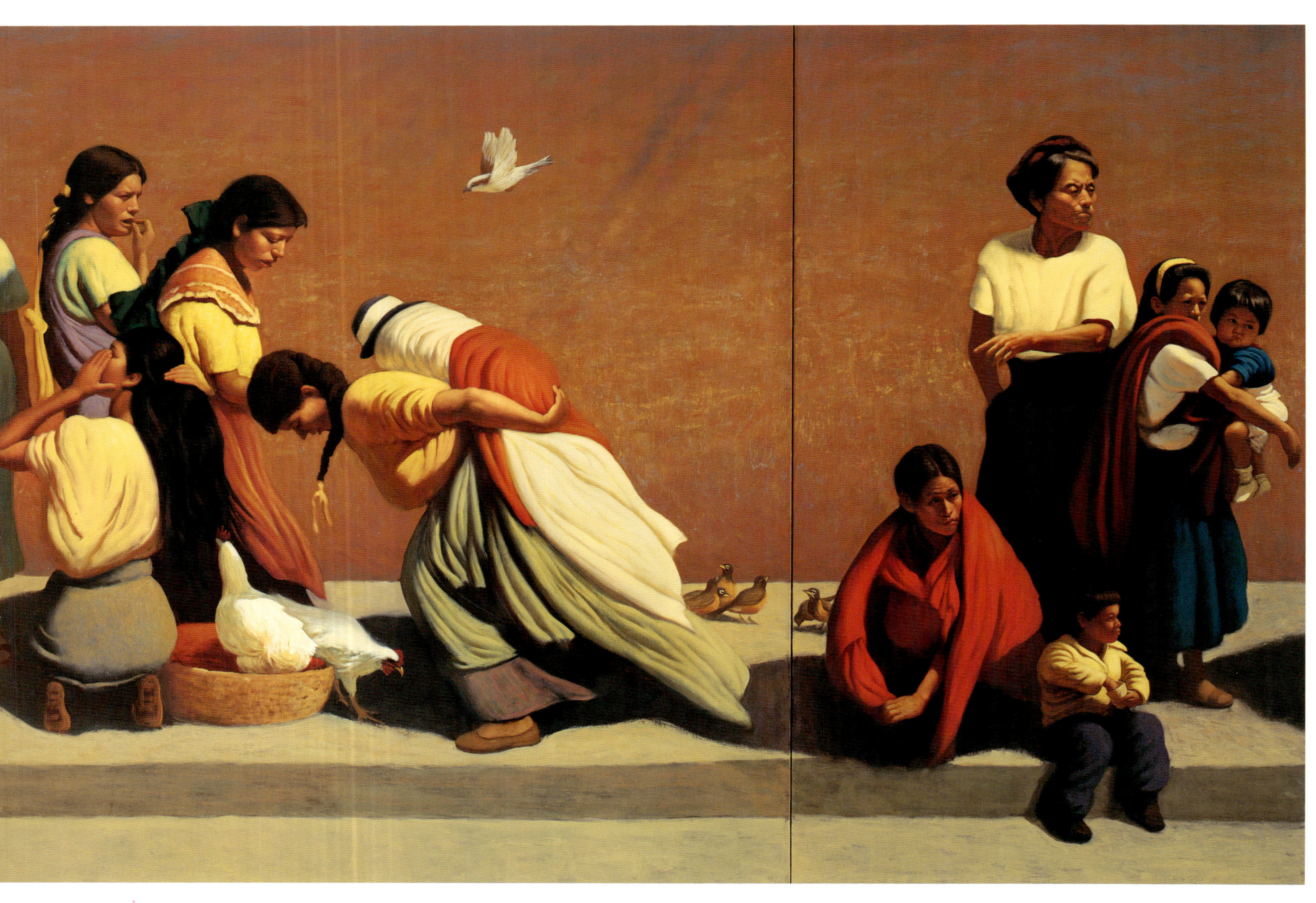

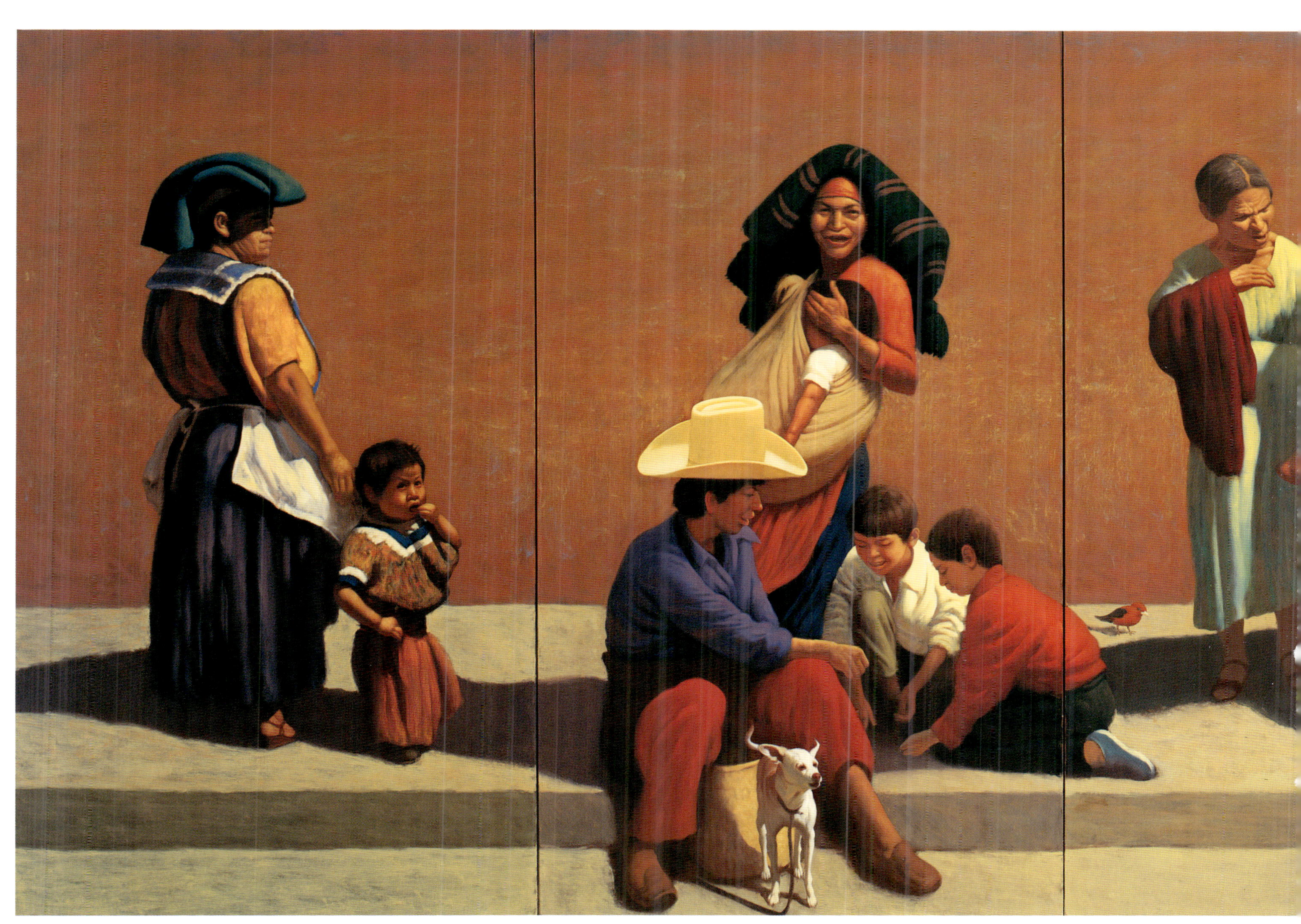

137. THE OTHER SIDE OF THE STREET (polyptych)
2000, oil on canvas, 84 × 480 inches

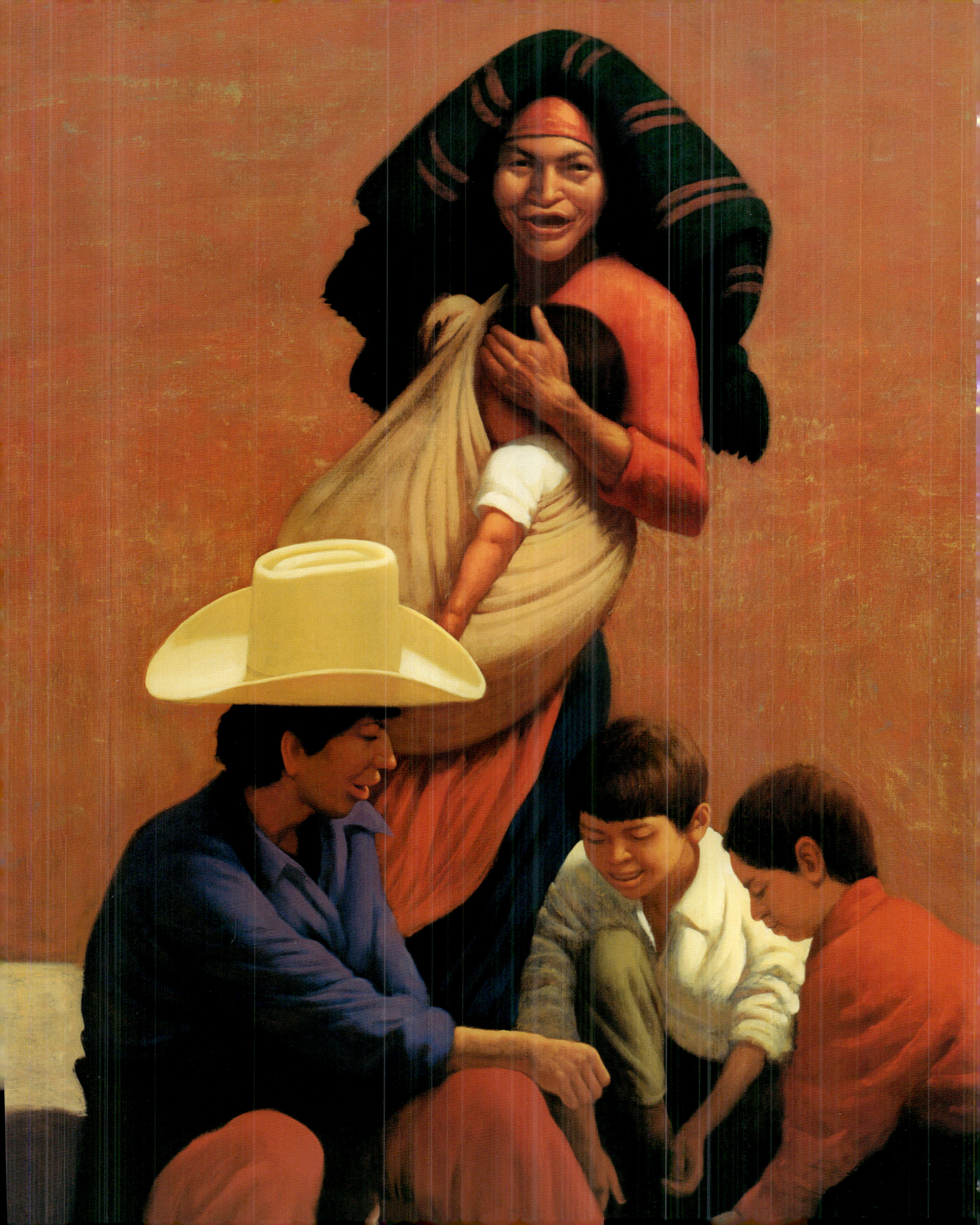

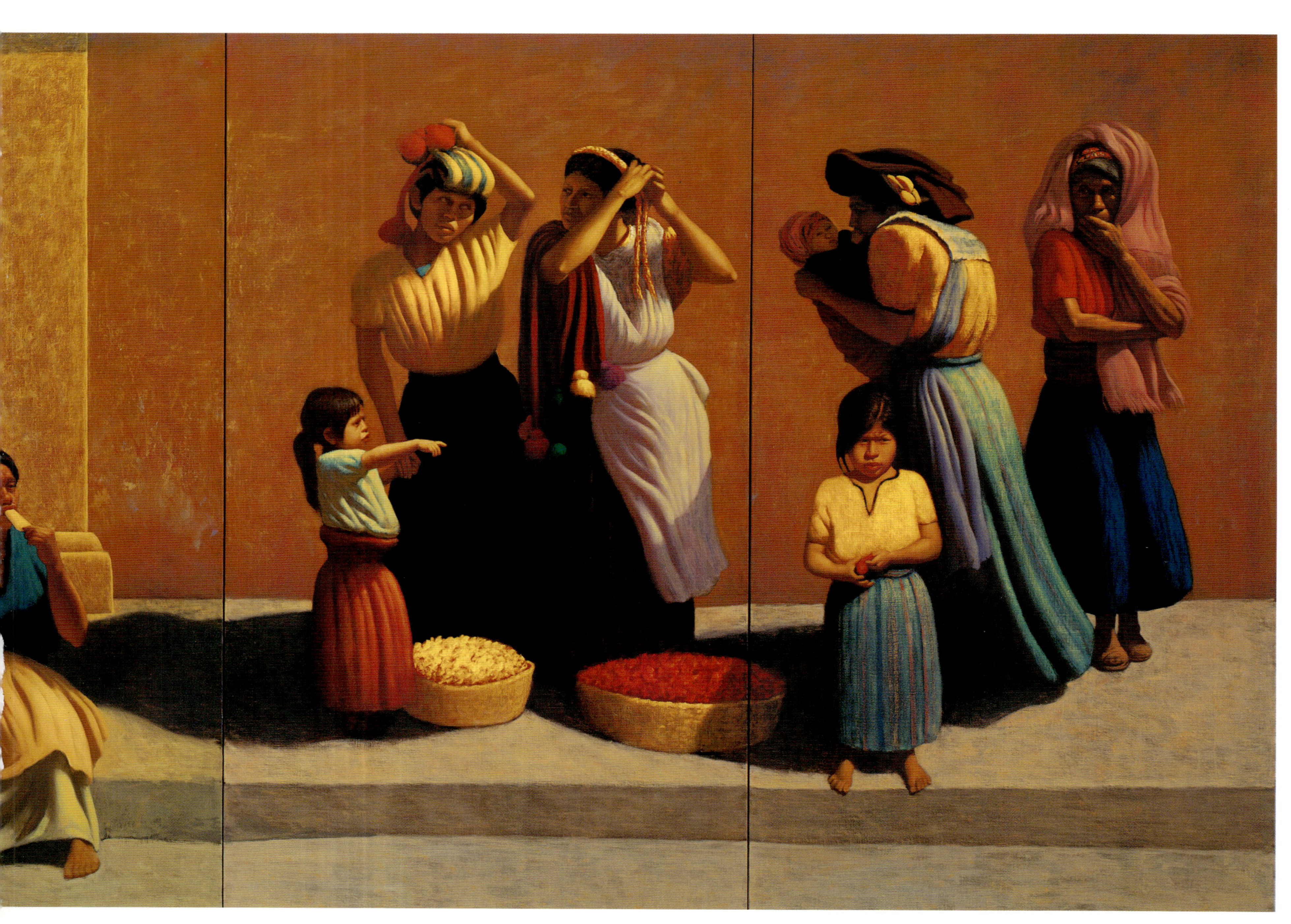

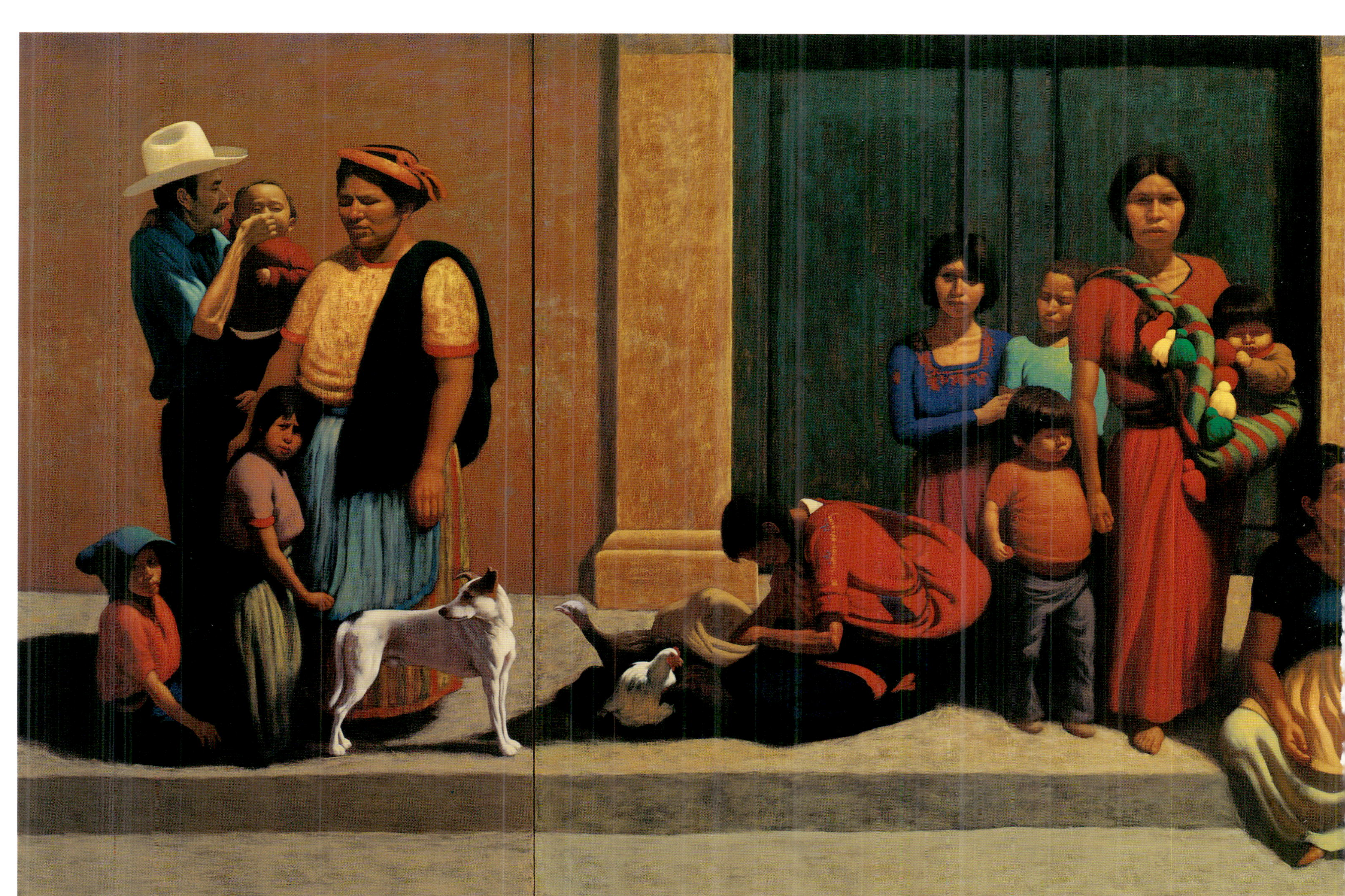

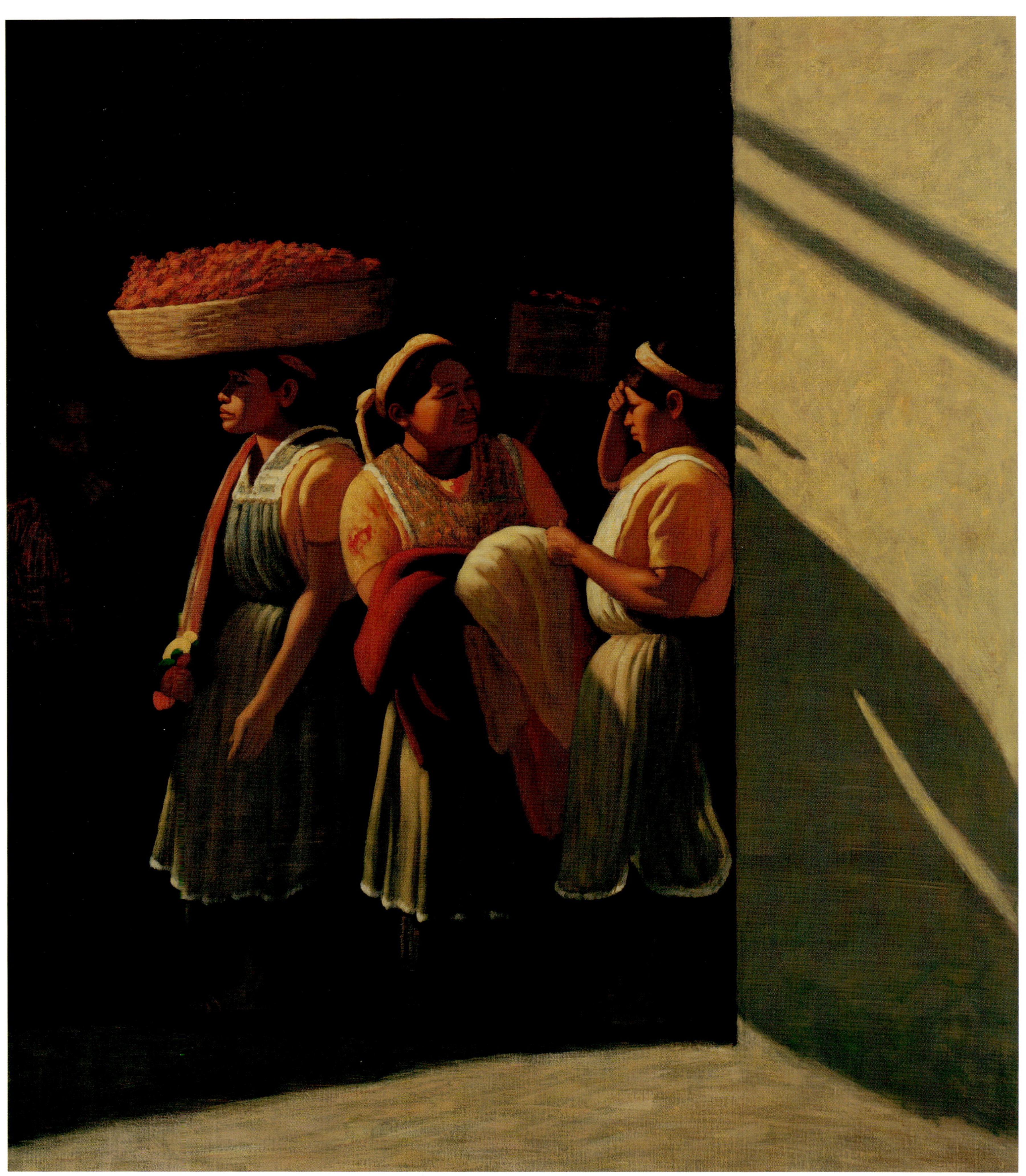

138. SUN AND SHADOWS
2000, oil on canvas, 80 × 68 inches

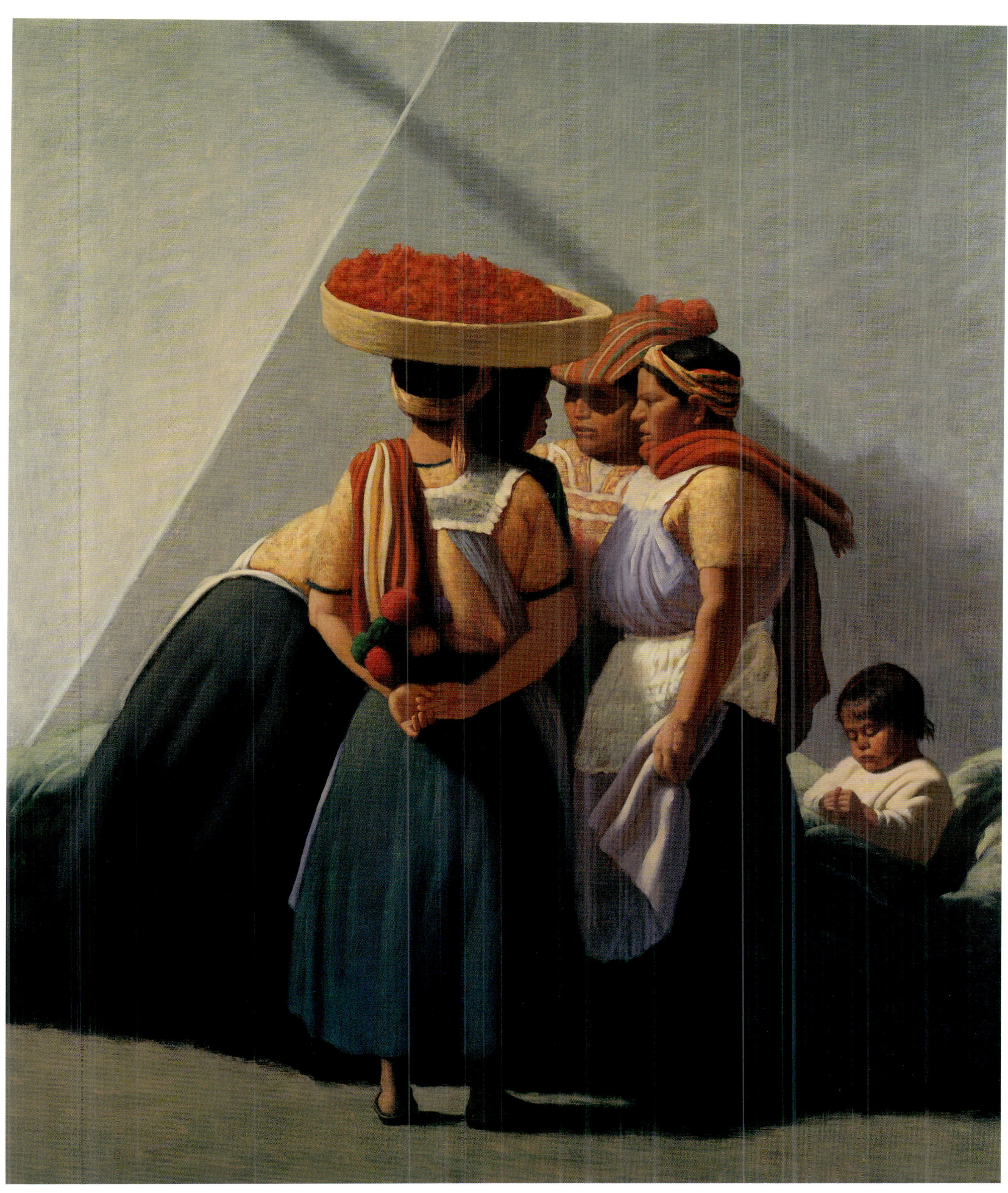

139. ISOLATED GATHERING

2000, oil on canvas, 80 × 68 inches

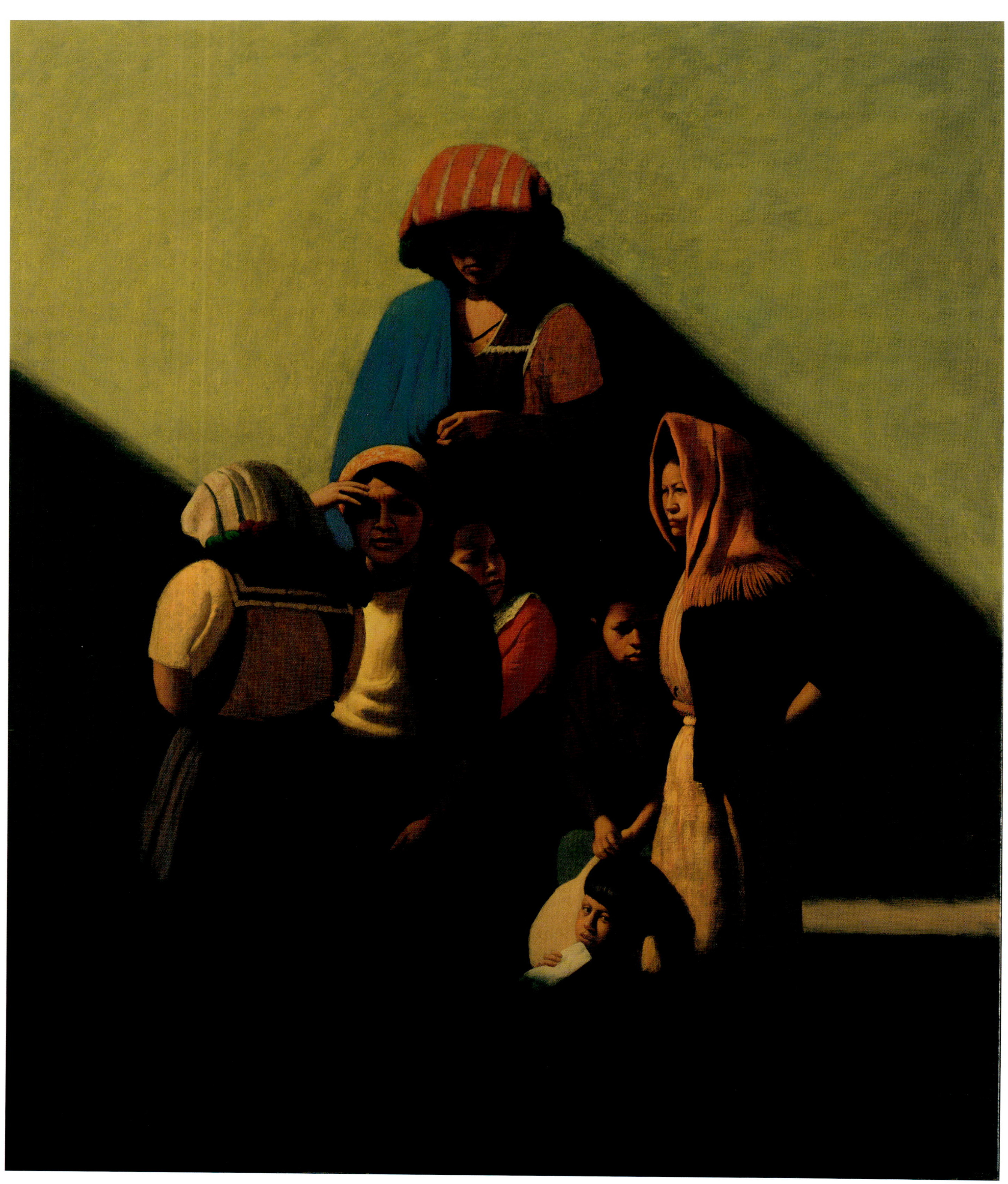

140. POST MERIDIAN
2000, oil on canvas, 80 × 68 inches

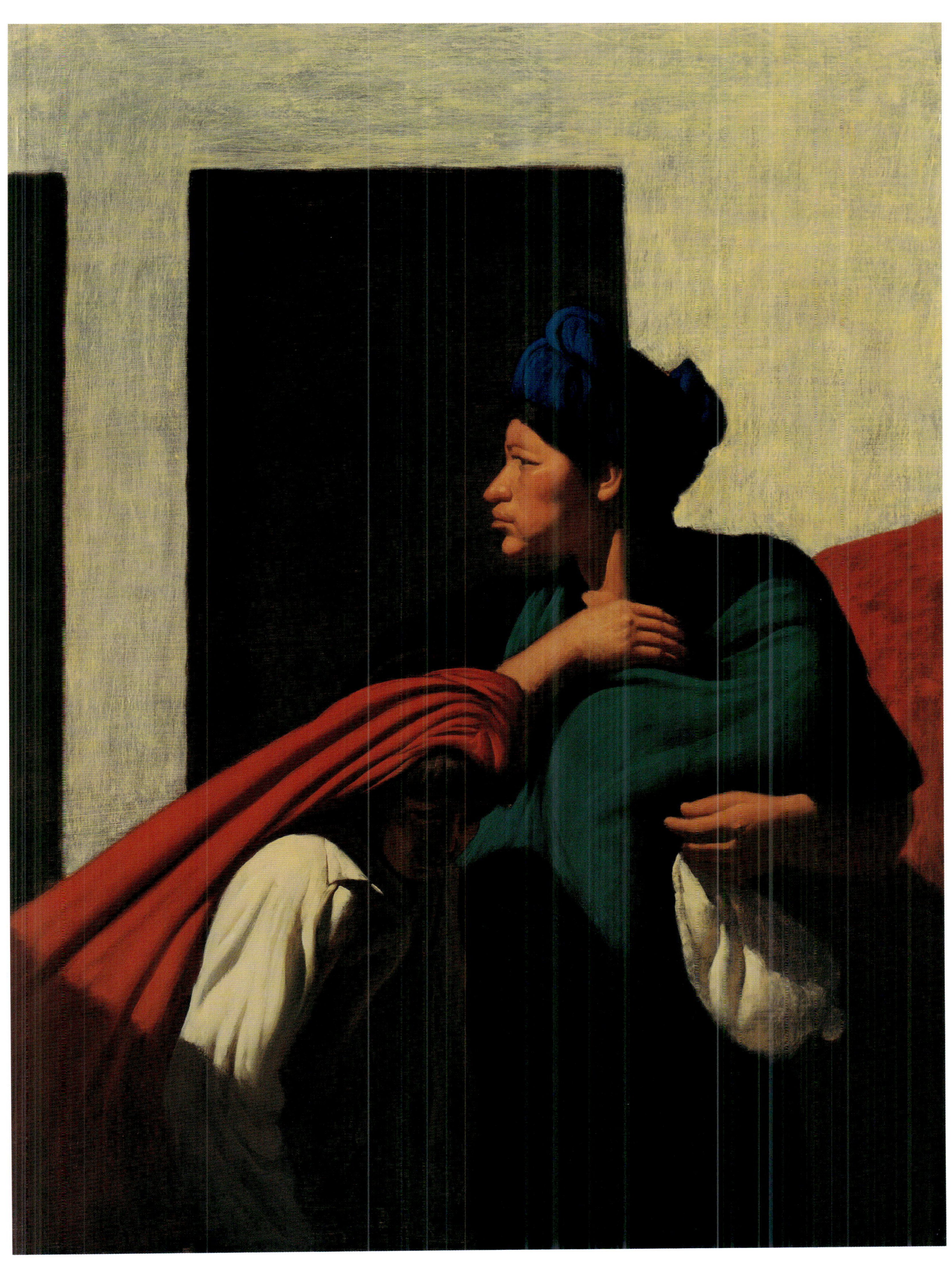

141. UNDER HER WING
2000, oil on canvas, 48 × 36 inches

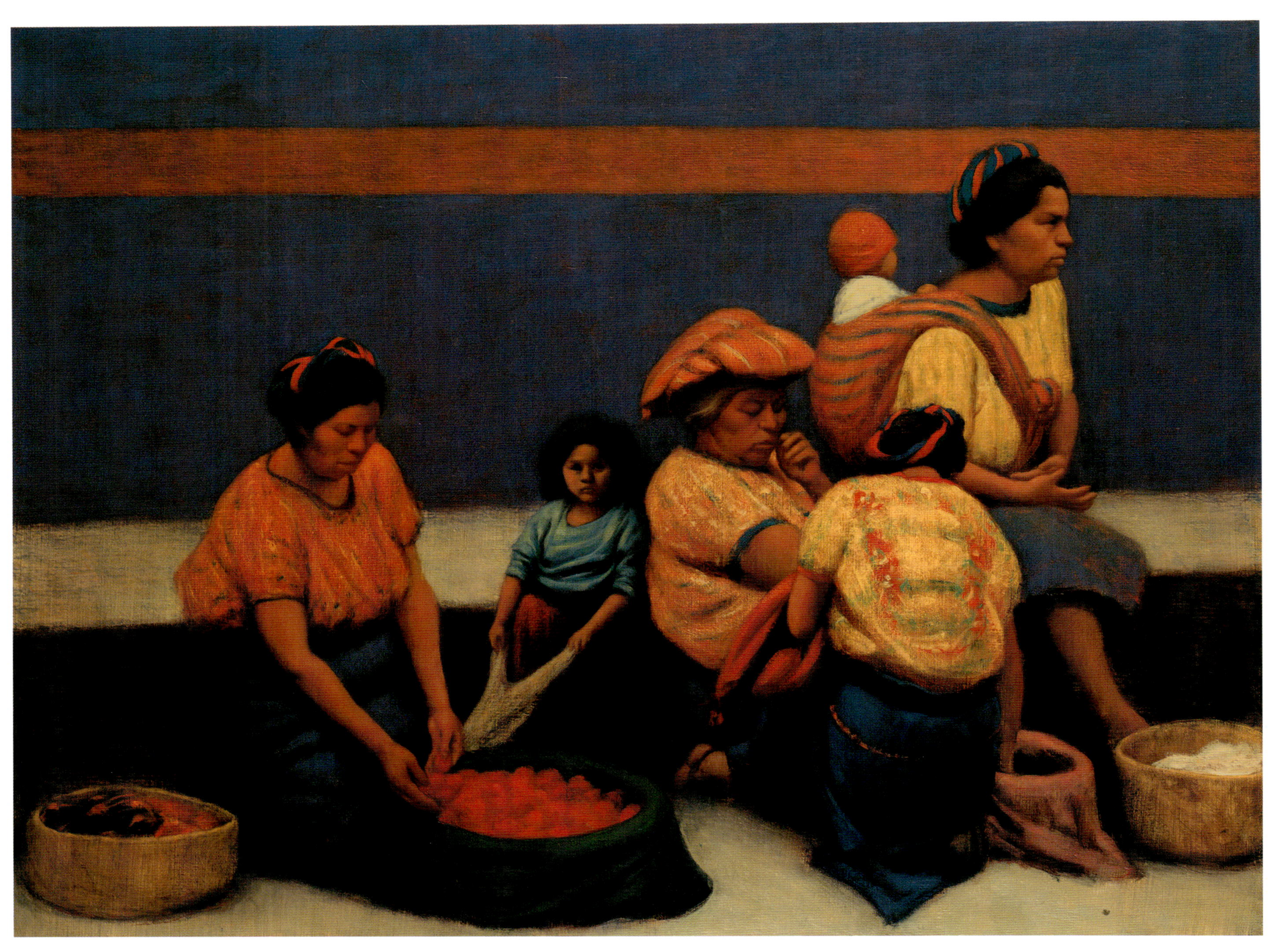

142. UNTITLED
2001, oil on canvas, 50 × 60 inches

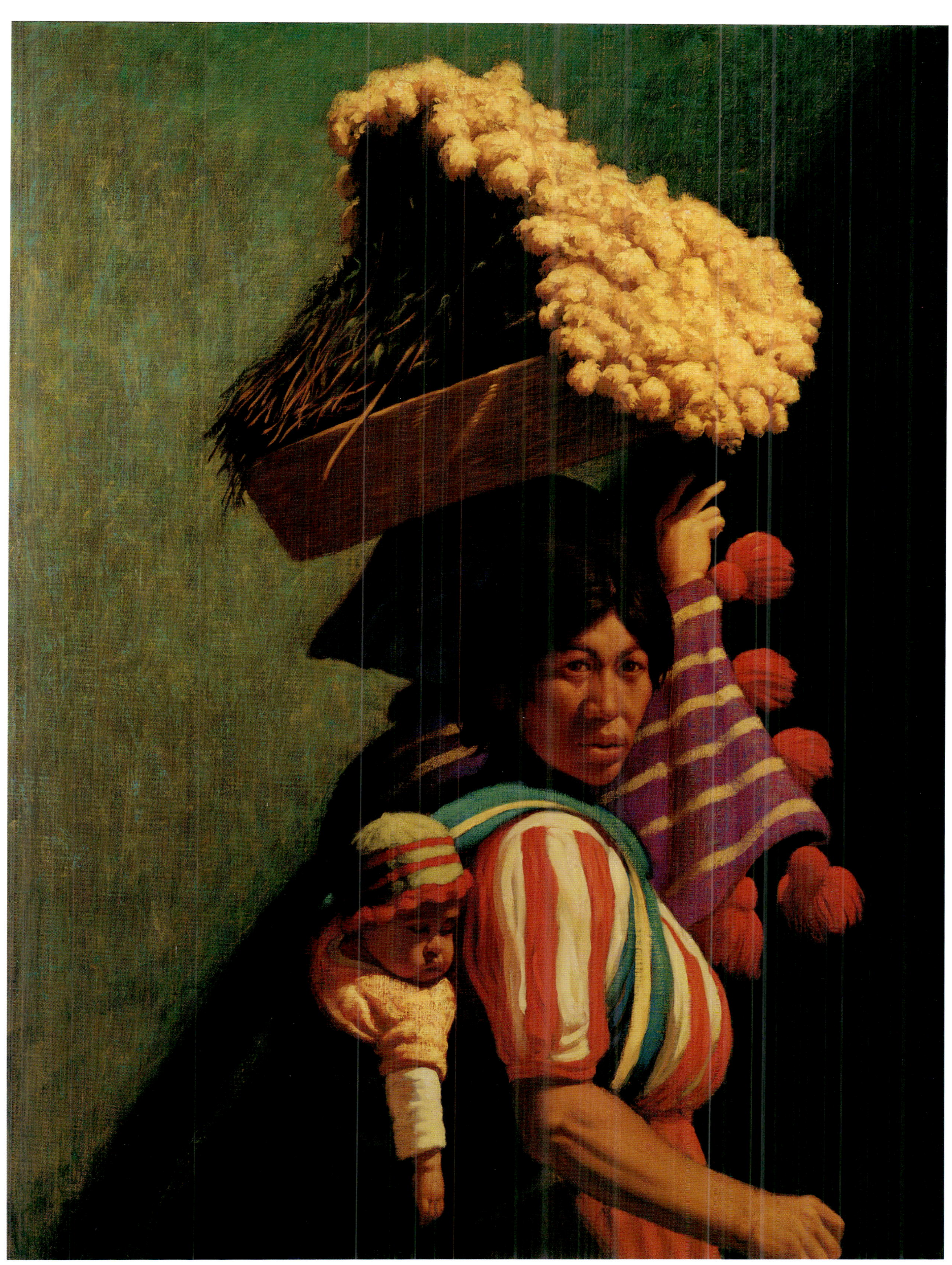

143. THE HUMAN BOUQUET
2001, oil on canvas, 48 × 36 inches

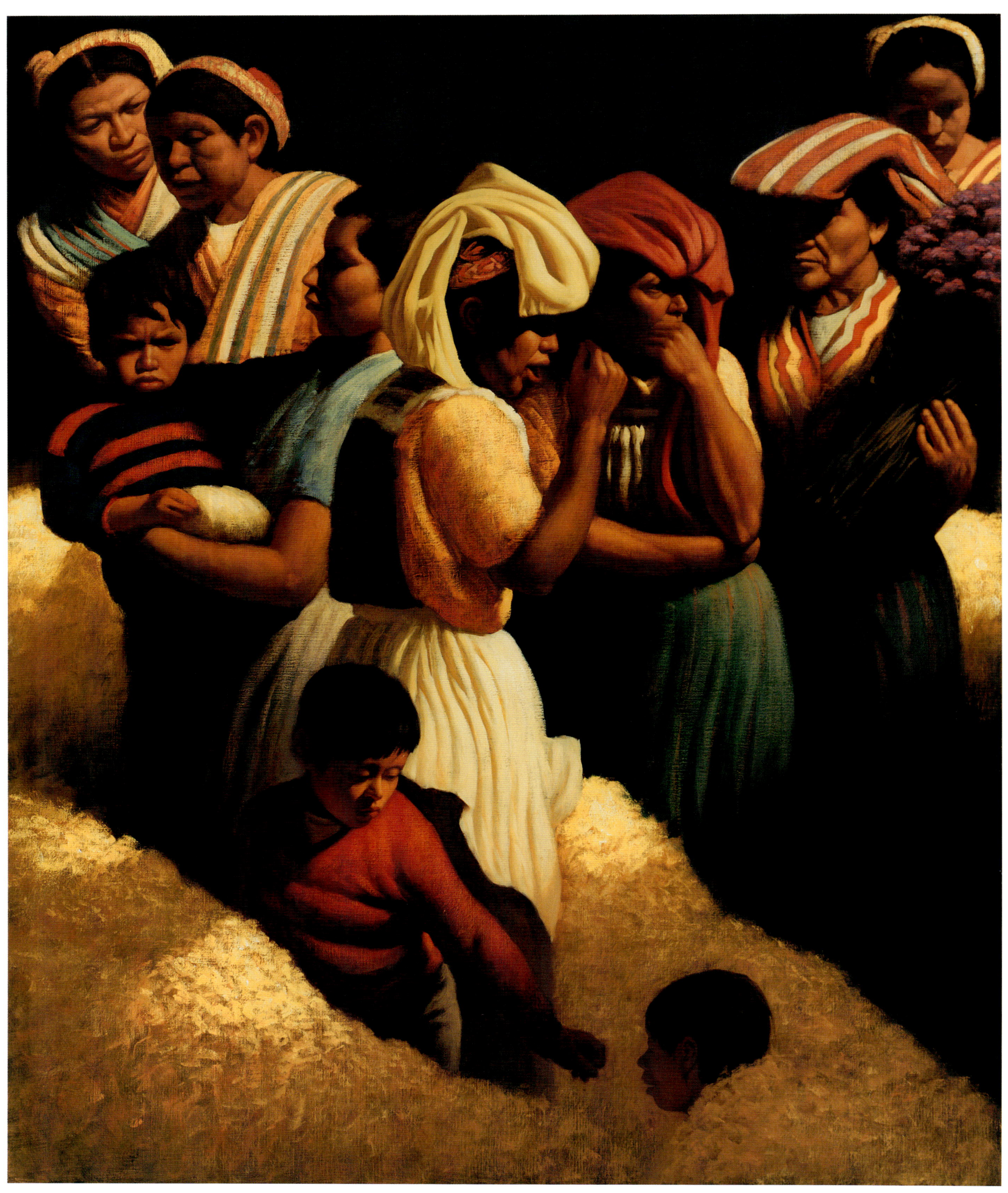

144. FLOWERS OF THE MIND #1

2001, oil on canvas, 60 × 50 inches

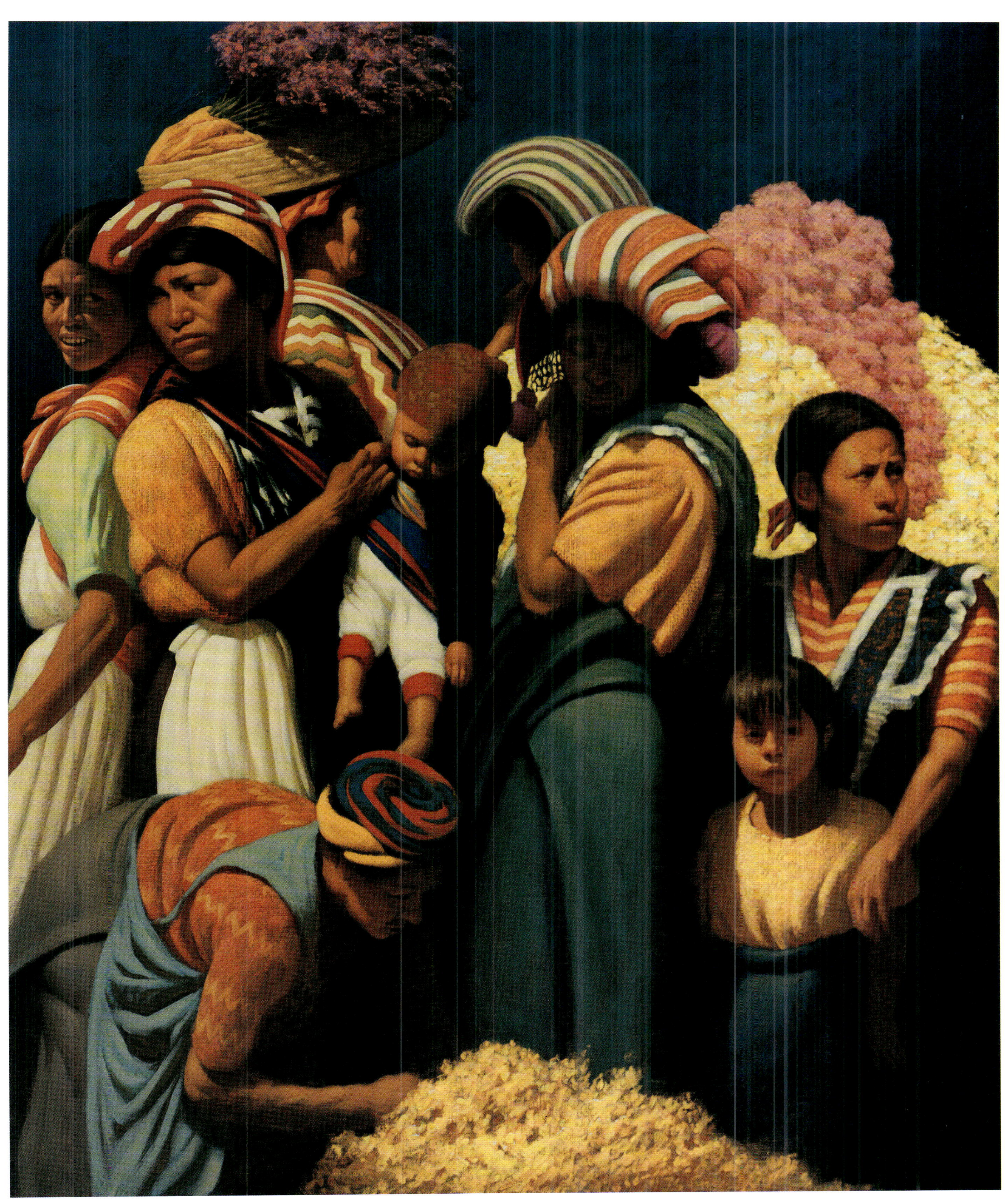

145. FLOWERS OF THE MIND #2

2001, oil on canvas, 60 × 50 inches

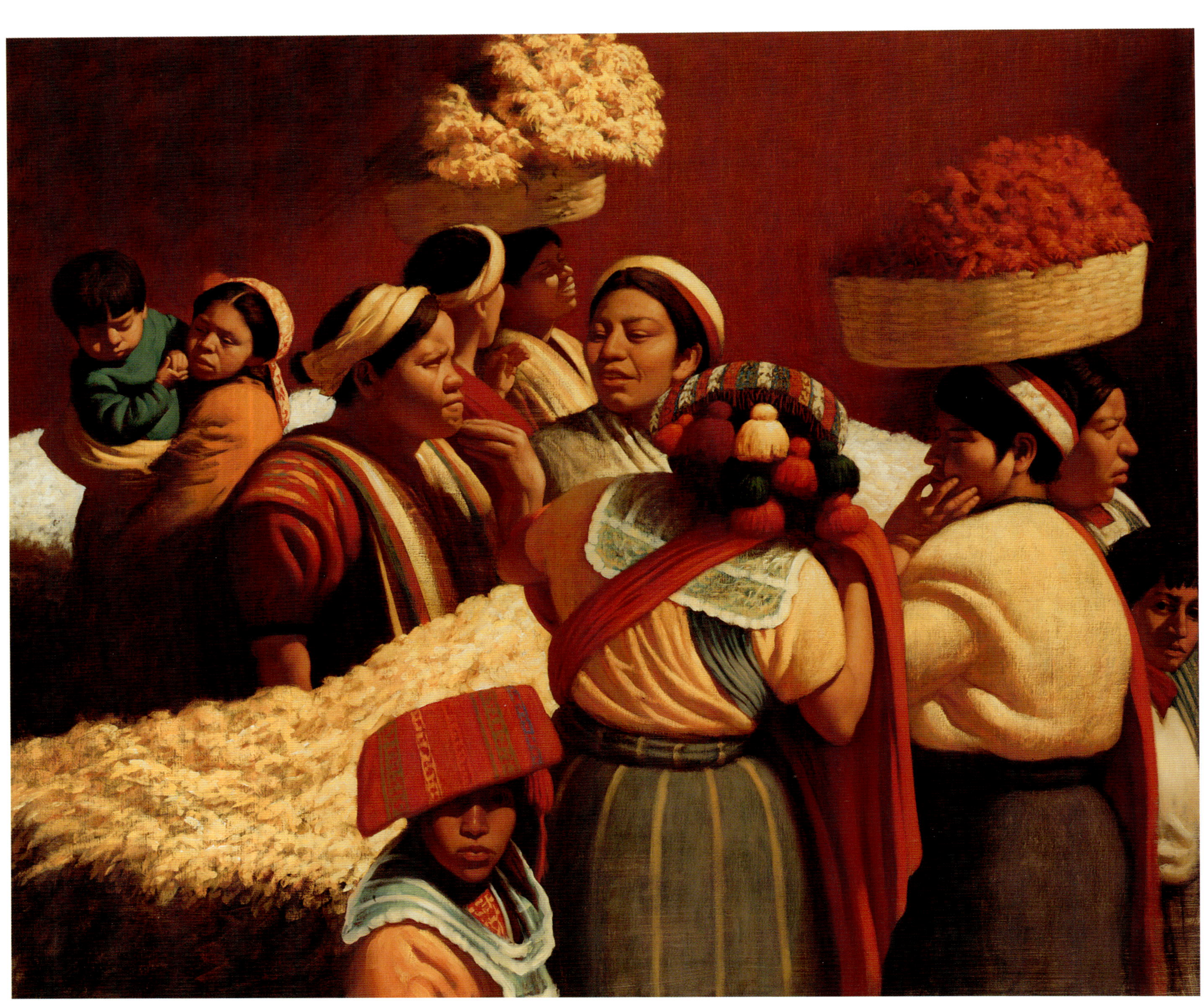

146. FLOWERS OF THE MIND #3
2001, oil on canvas, 50 × 60 inches

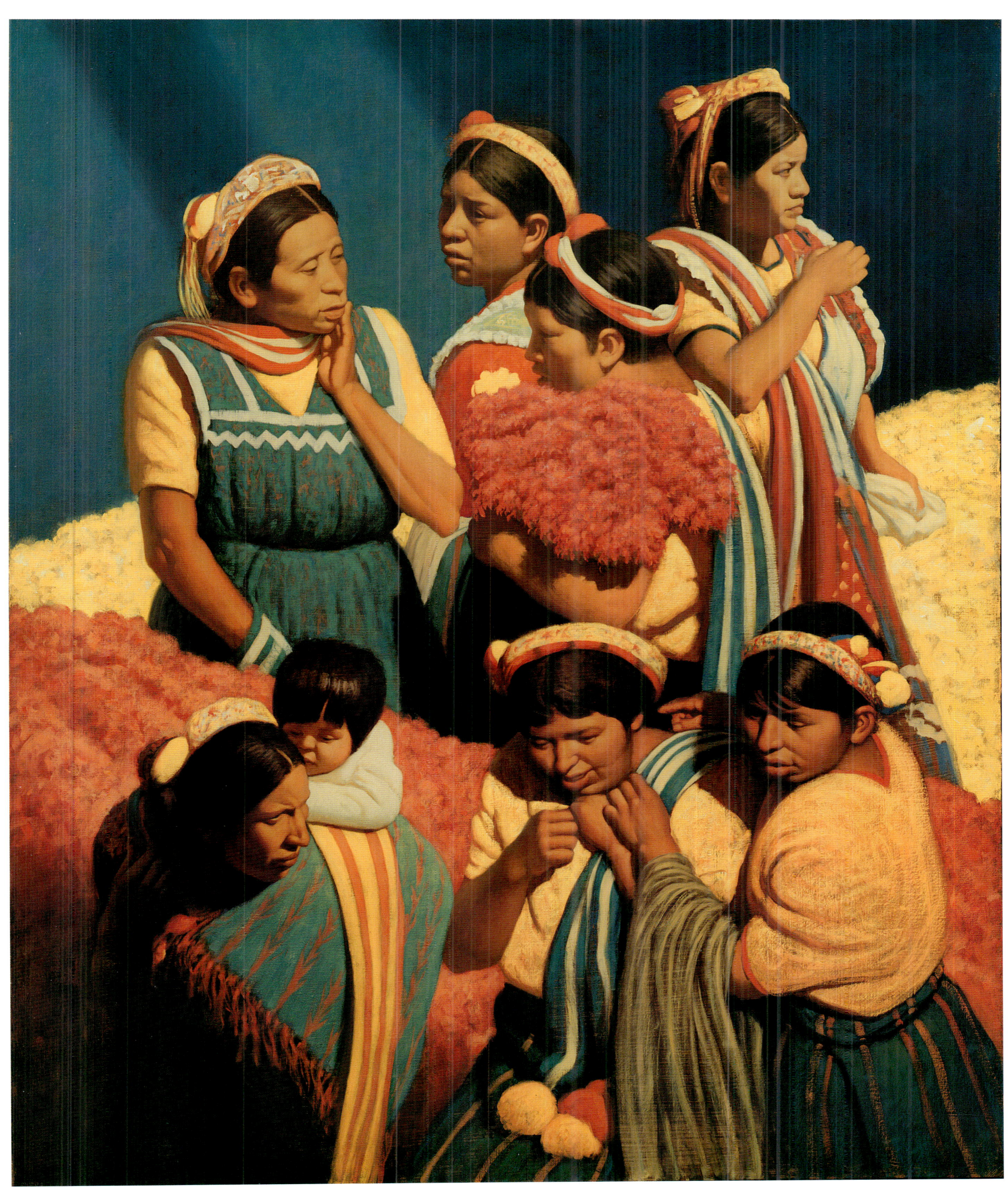

147. FLOWERS OF THE MIND #4

2001, oil on canvas, 60 × 50 inches

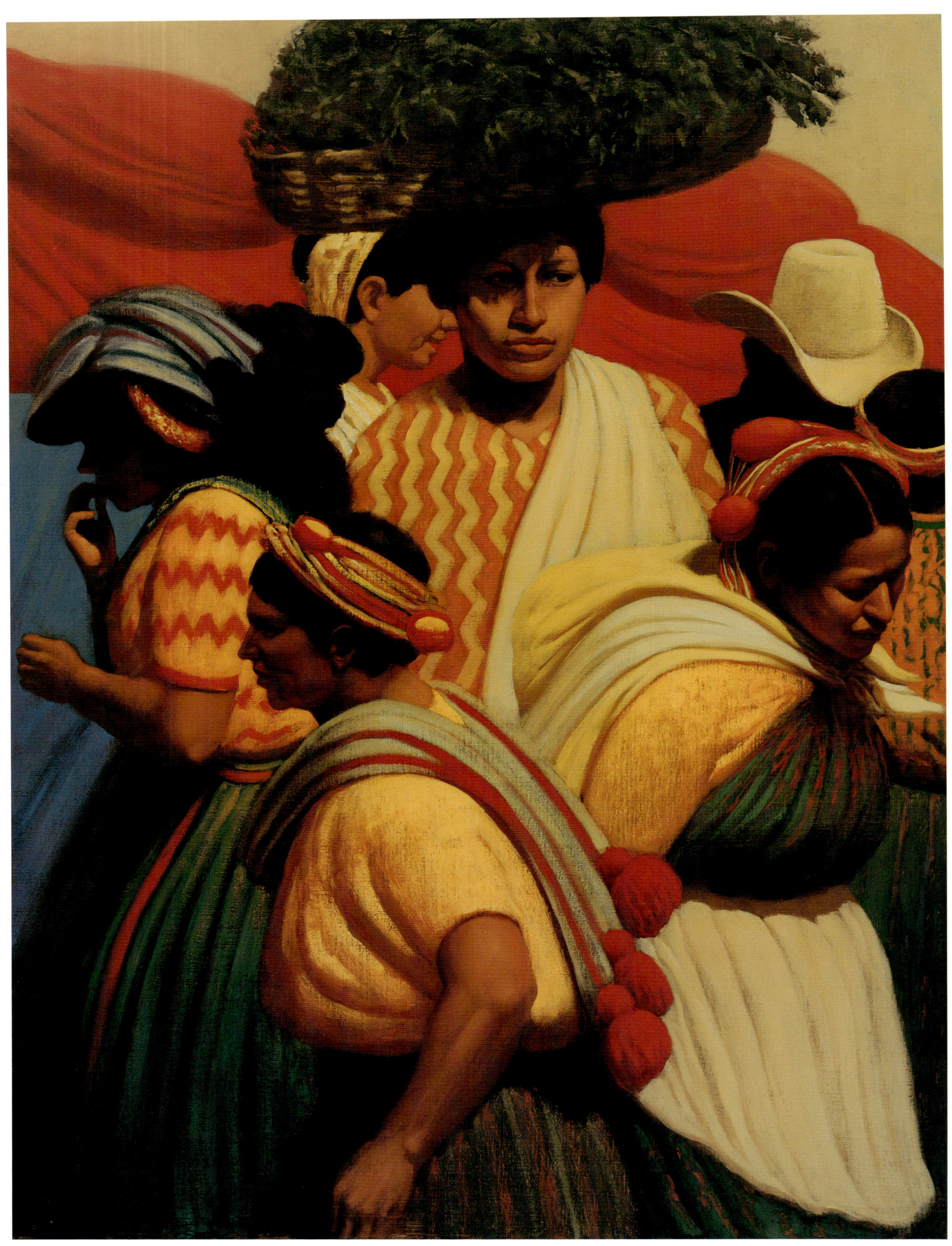

148. LIGHT OF THE MARKET

2001, oil on canvas, 40 × 30 inches

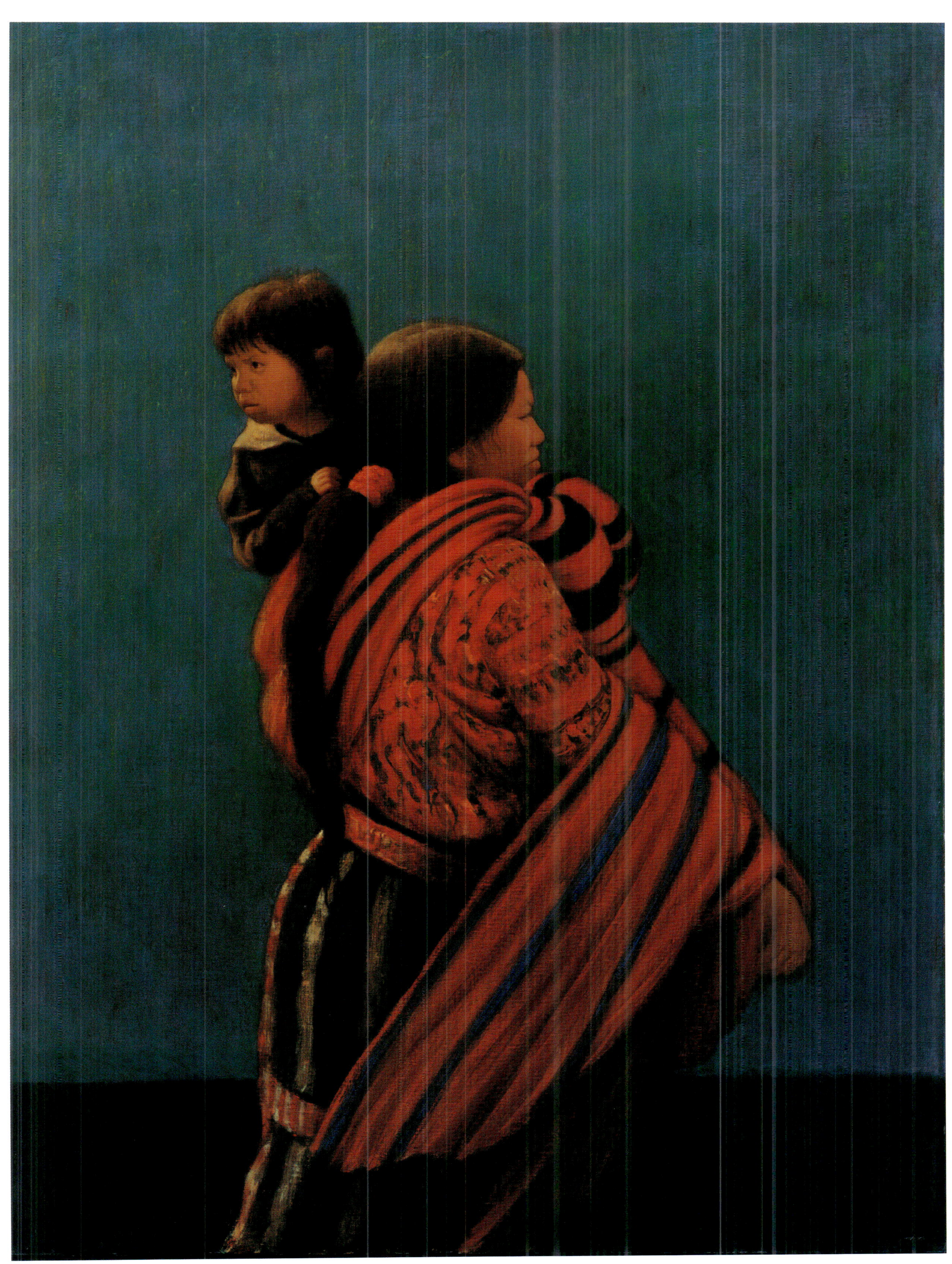

149. THE OBSERVER

2001, oil on canvas, 48 × 36 inches

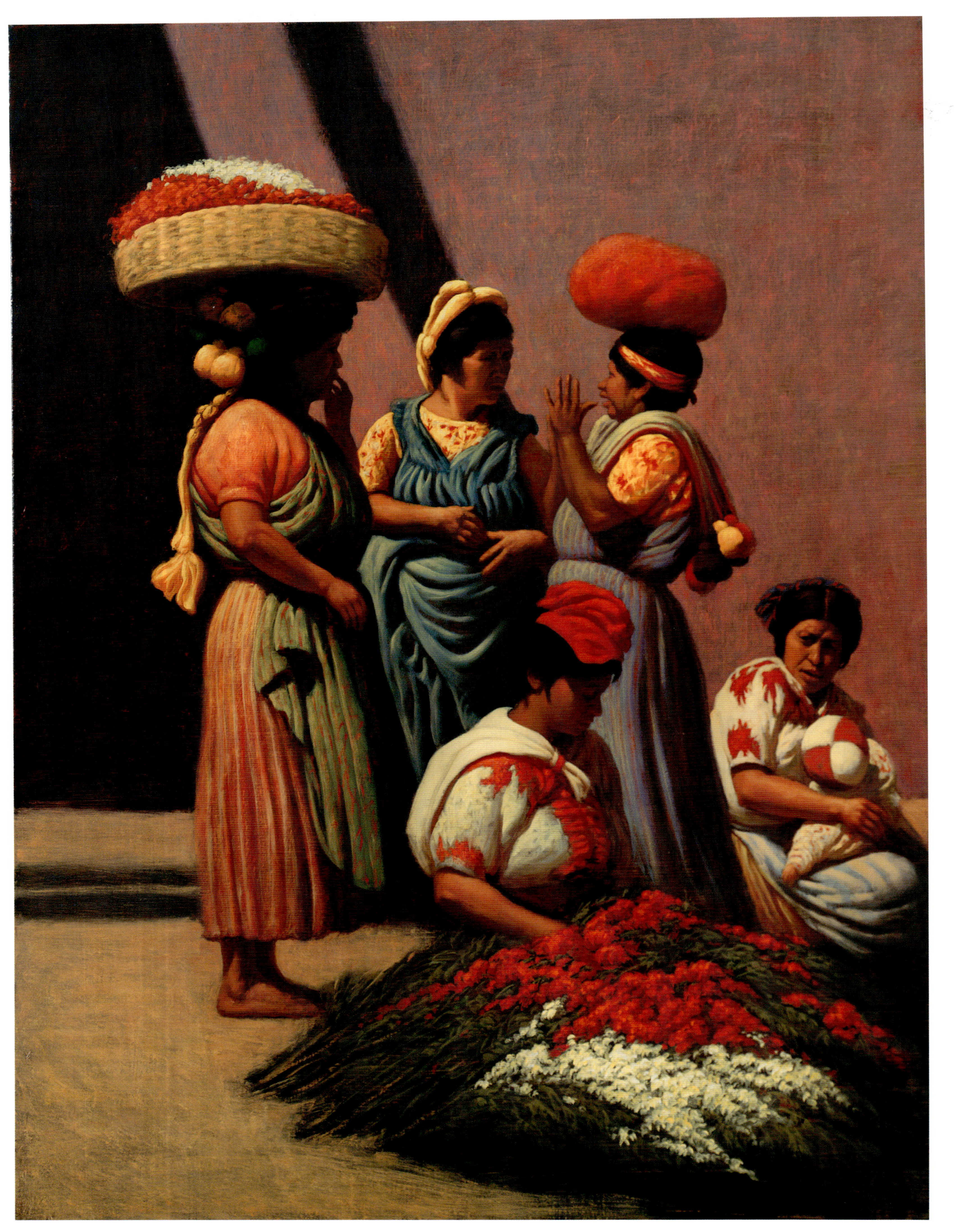

150. UNTITLED
2001, oil on canvas, 60 × 50 inches

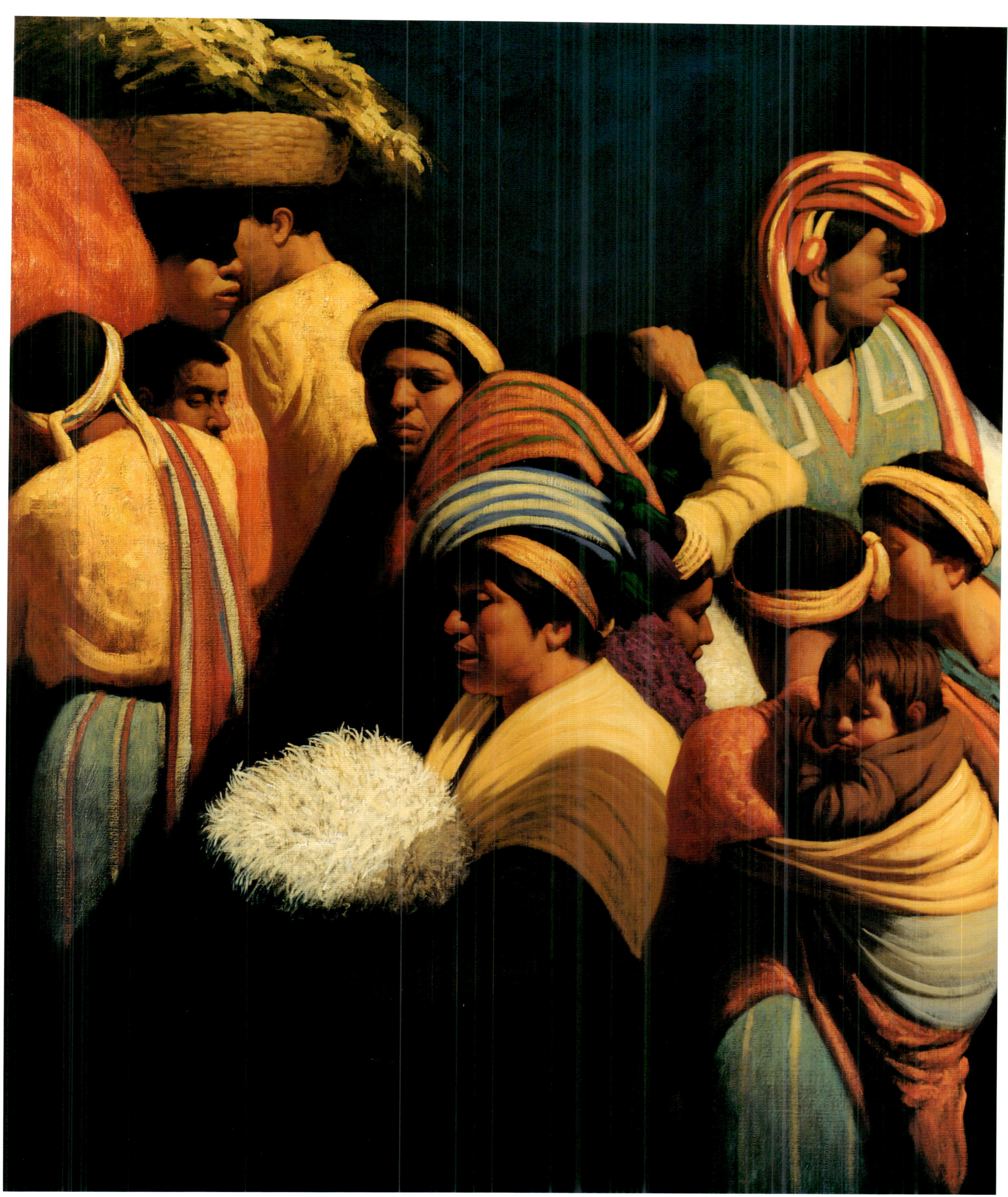

151. IN THE HEART OF THE CROWD
2001, oil on canvas, 60 × 50 inches

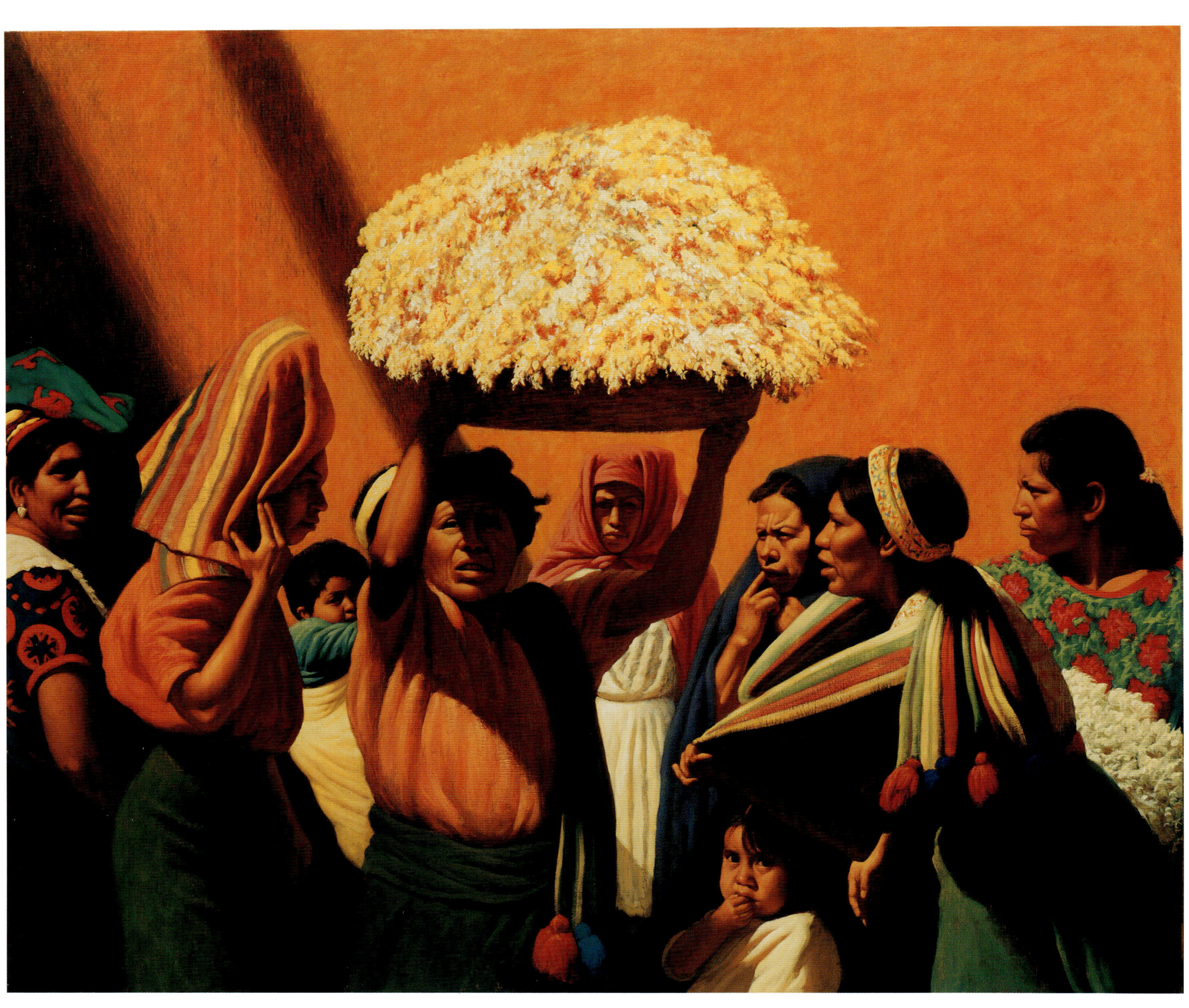

152. FLOWERS OF THE MIND #5

2002, oil on canvas, 50 × 60 inches

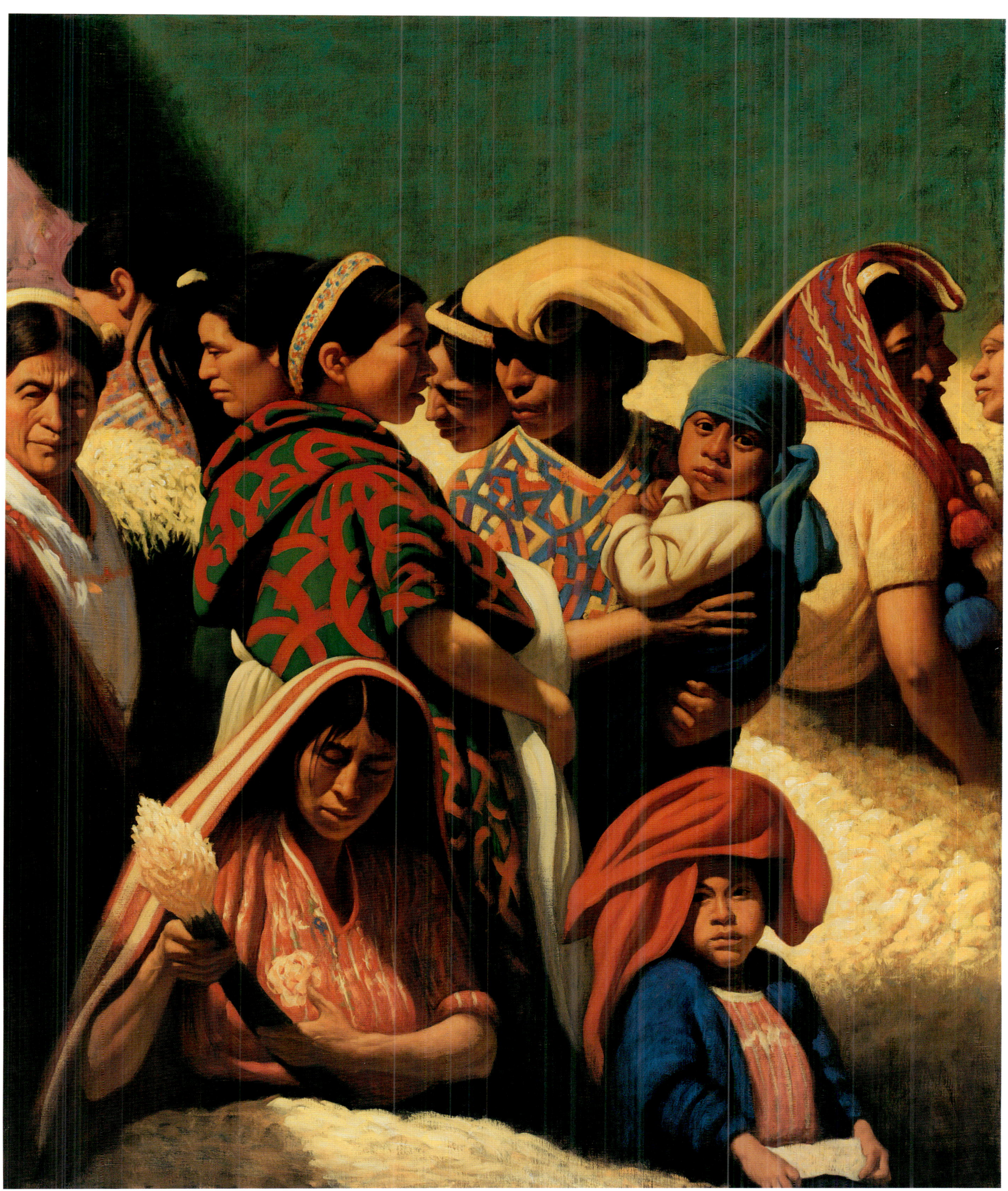

153. FLOWERS OF THE MIND #6

2002, oil on canvas, 60 × 50 inches

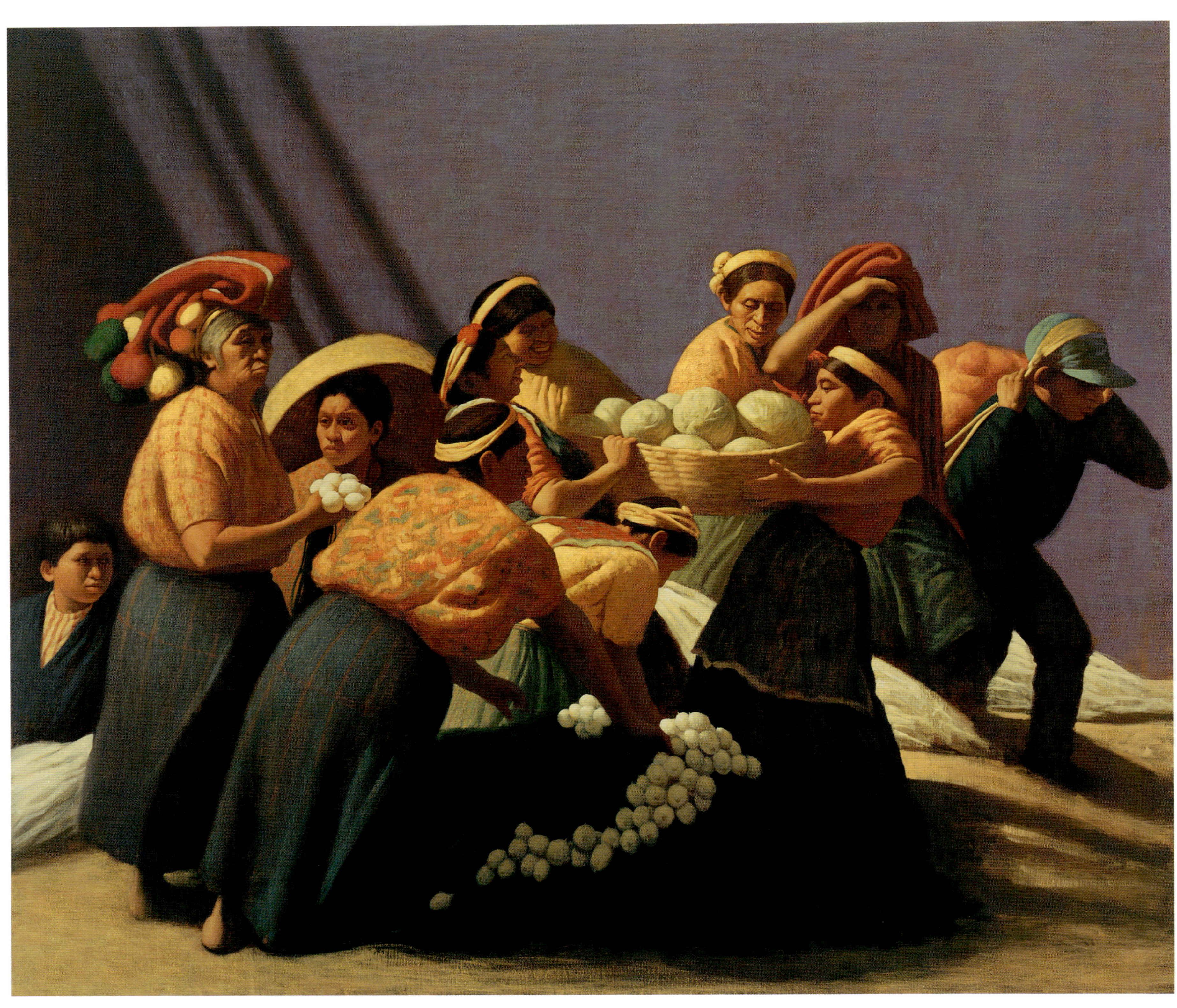

154. BASKET OF LIFE

2002, oil on canvas, 68 × 80 inches

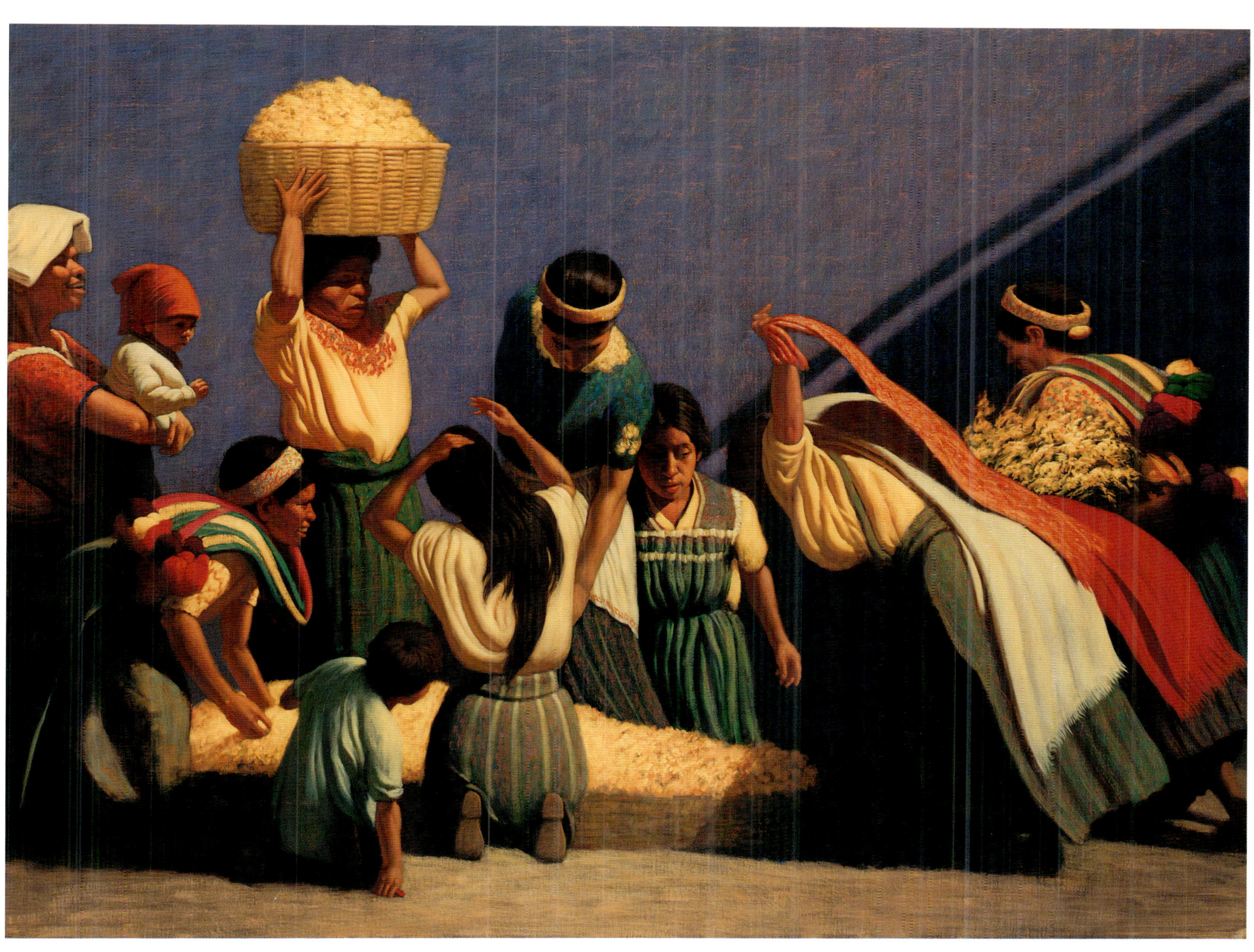

155. BASKET OF LIFE II

2002, oil on canvas, 60 × 80 inches

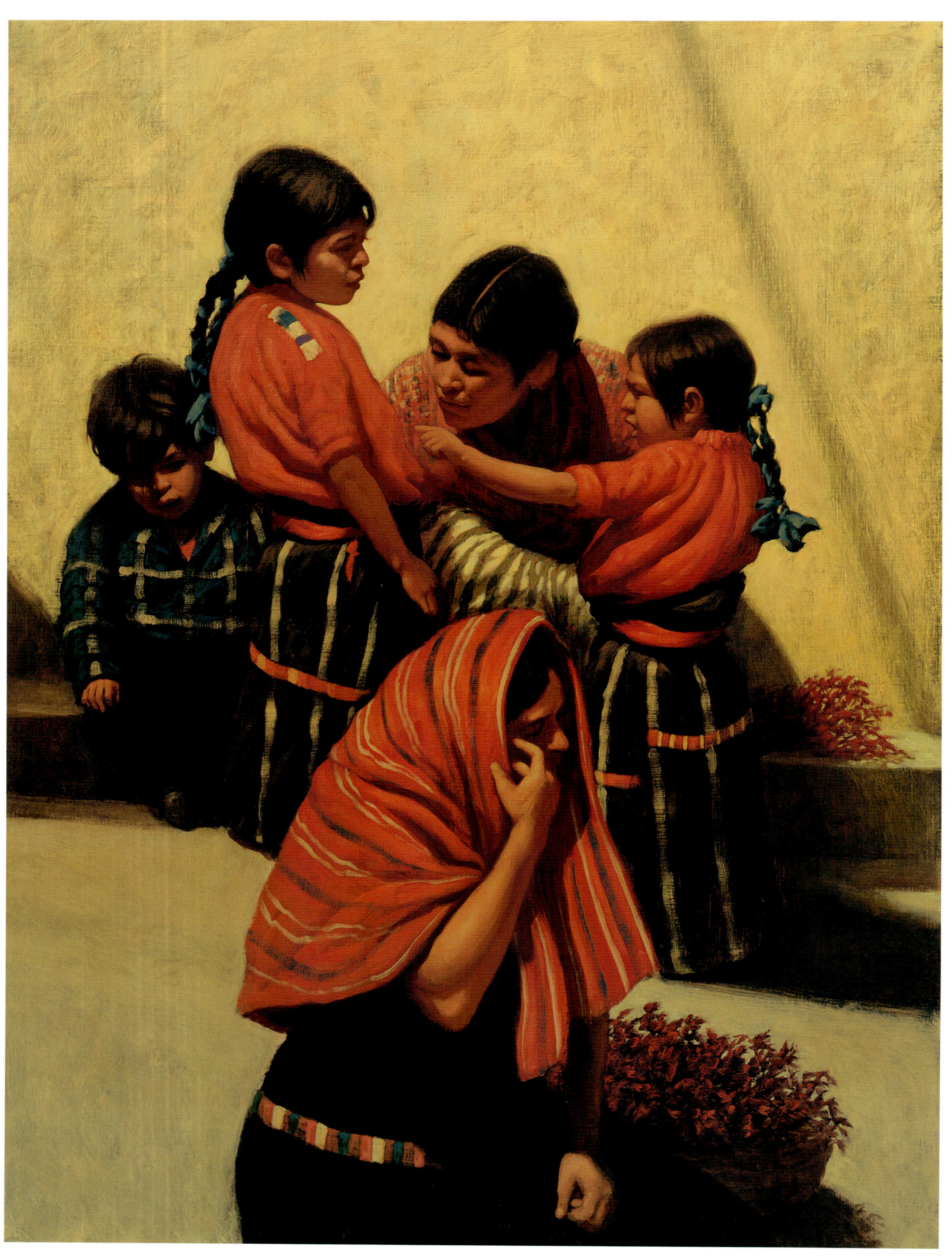

156. BOUNTIFUL STEPS
2002, oil on canvas, 48 × 36 inches

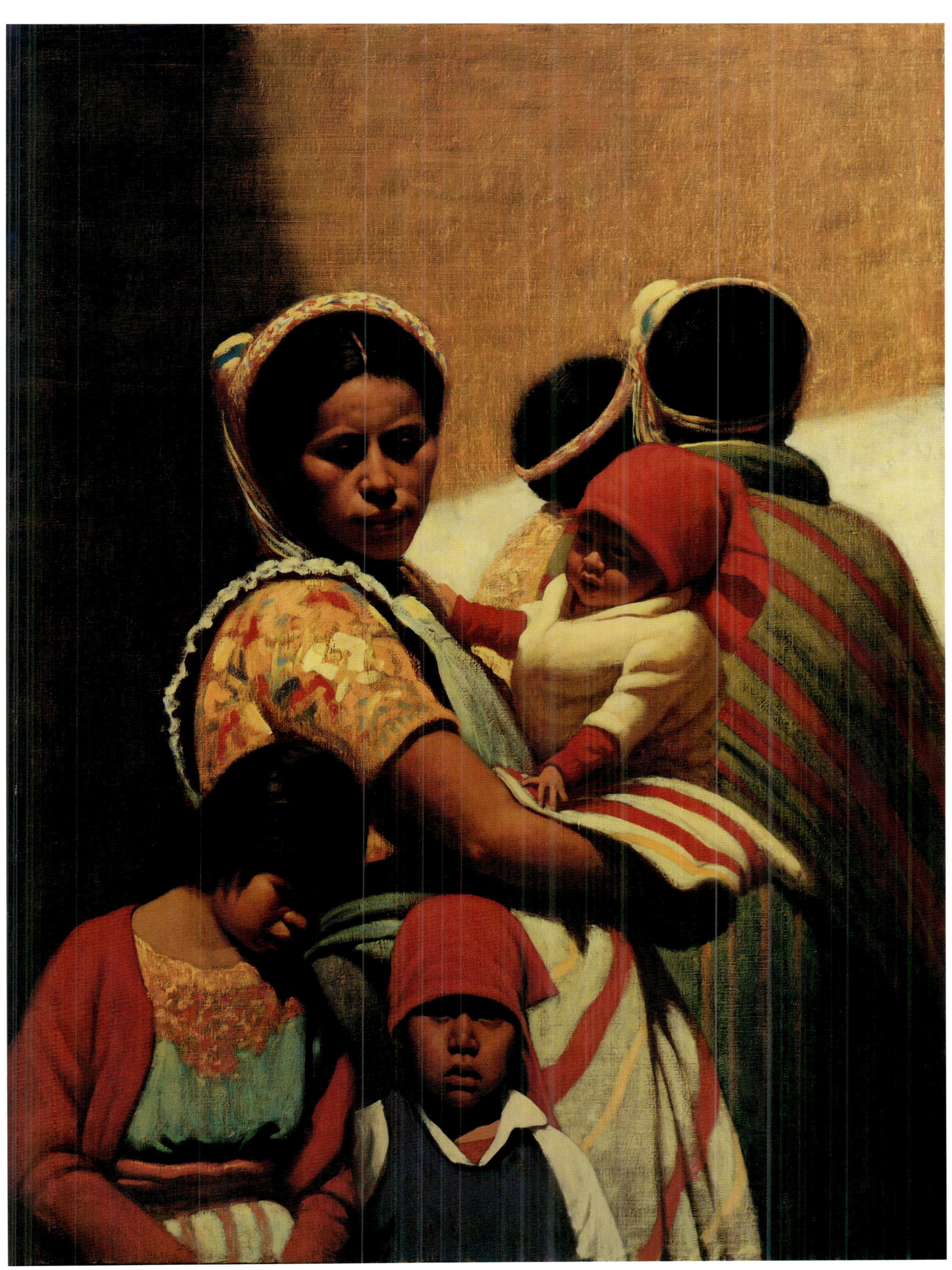

157. ALMOLONGA #1

2002, oil on canvas, 48 × 36 inches

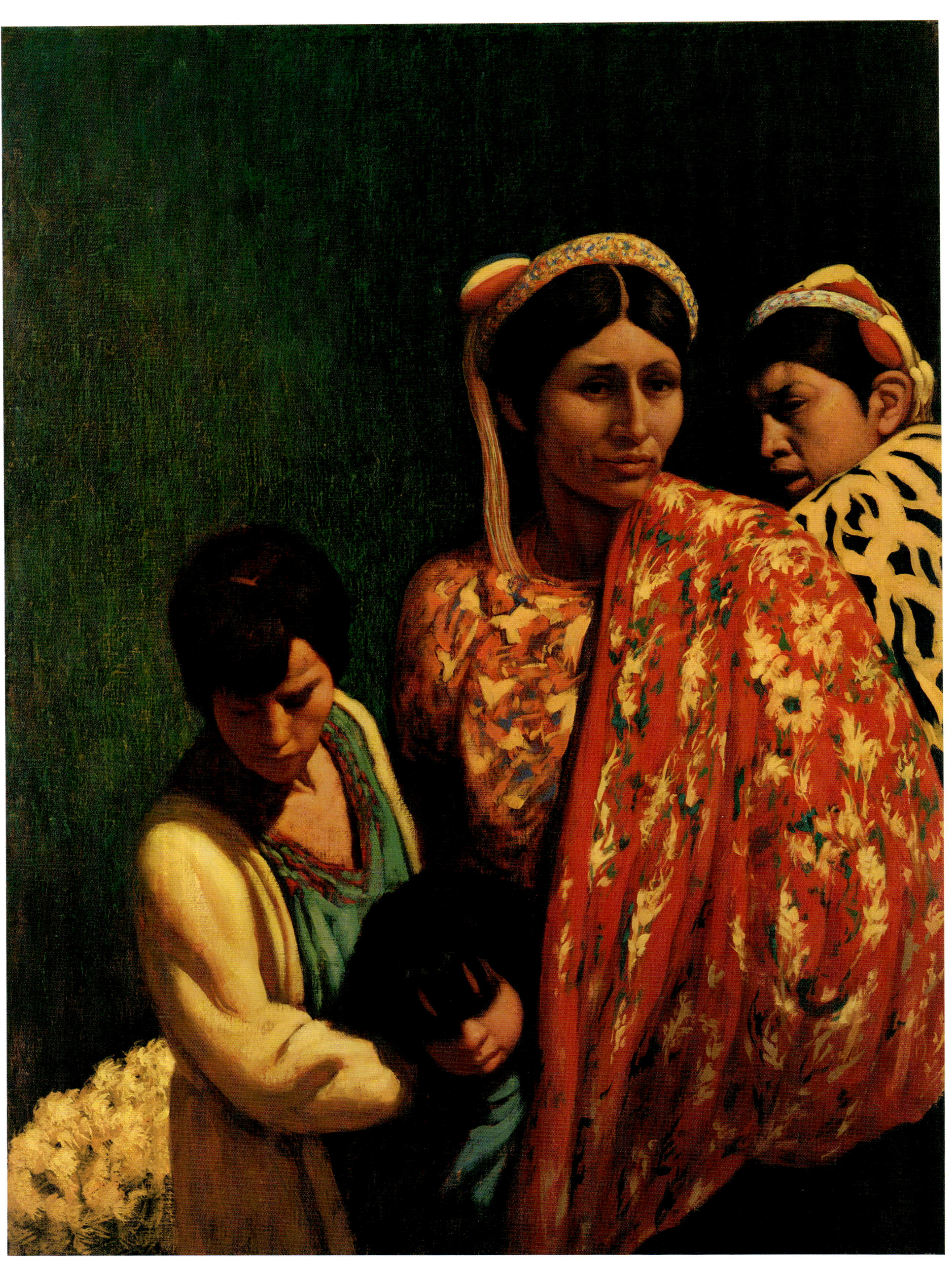

158. ALMOLONGA #2

2002, oil on canvas, 48 × 36 inches

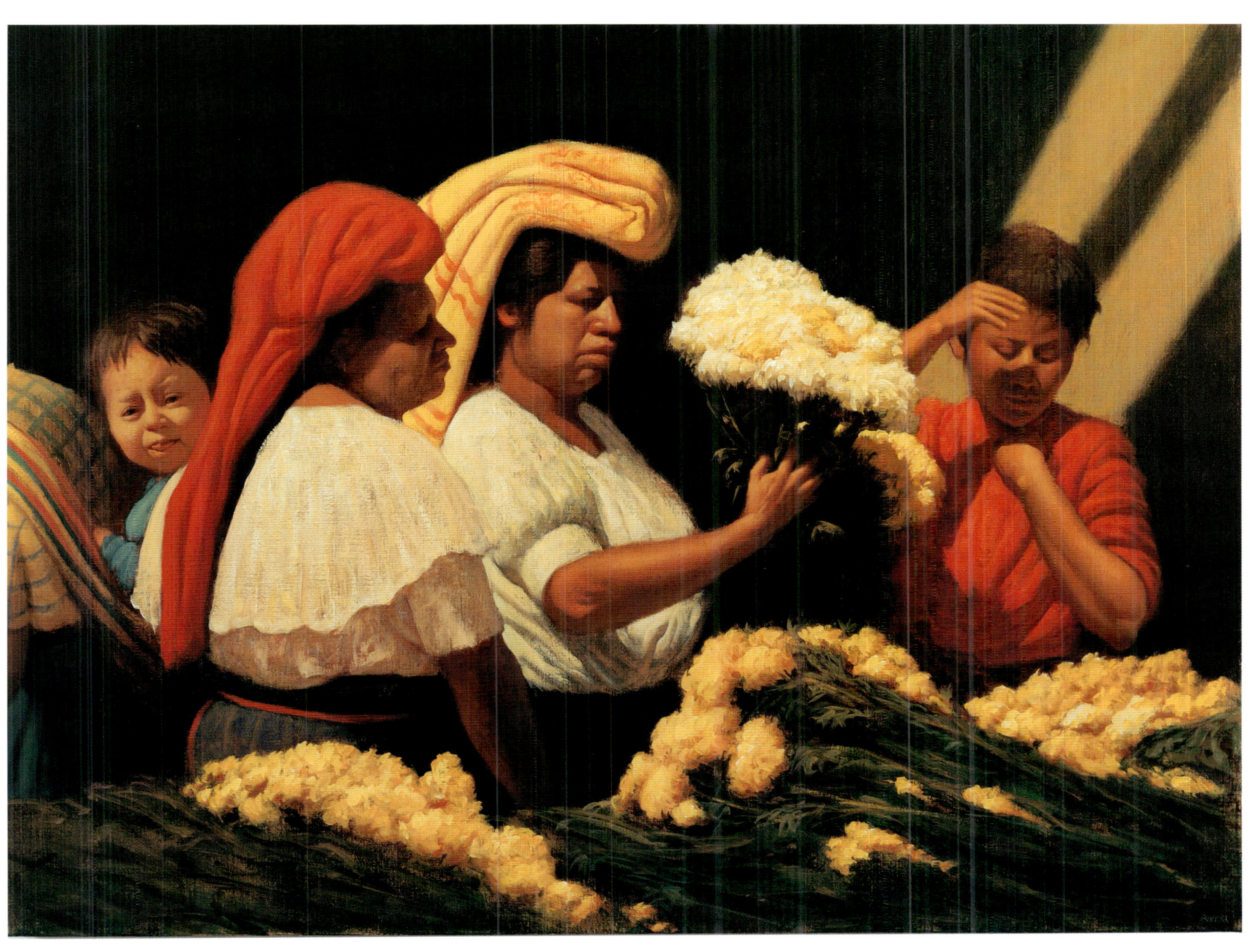

159. UNTITLED
2002, oil on canvas, 36 × 48 inches

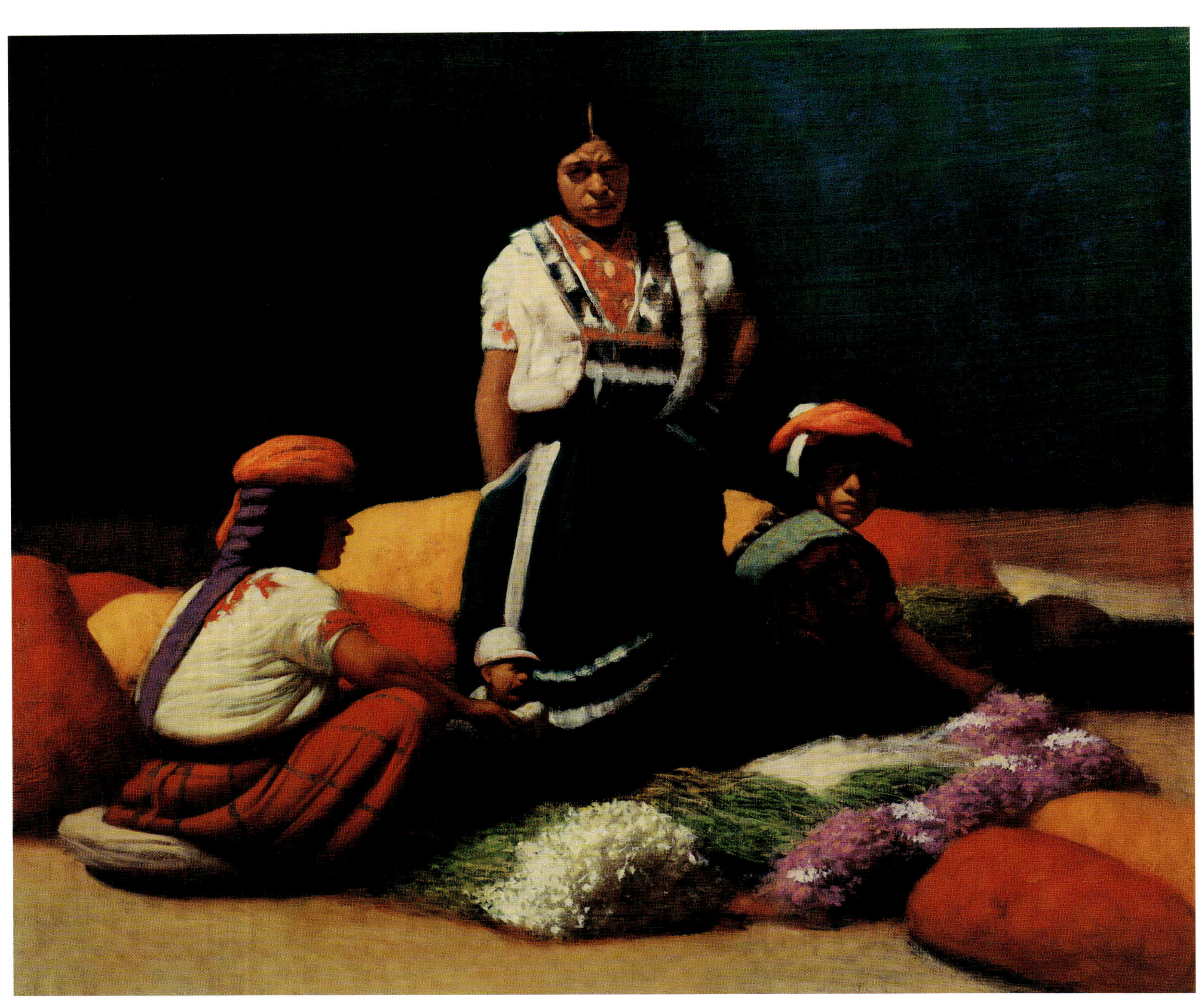

160. UNTITLED

2003, oil on canvas, 50 × 60 inches

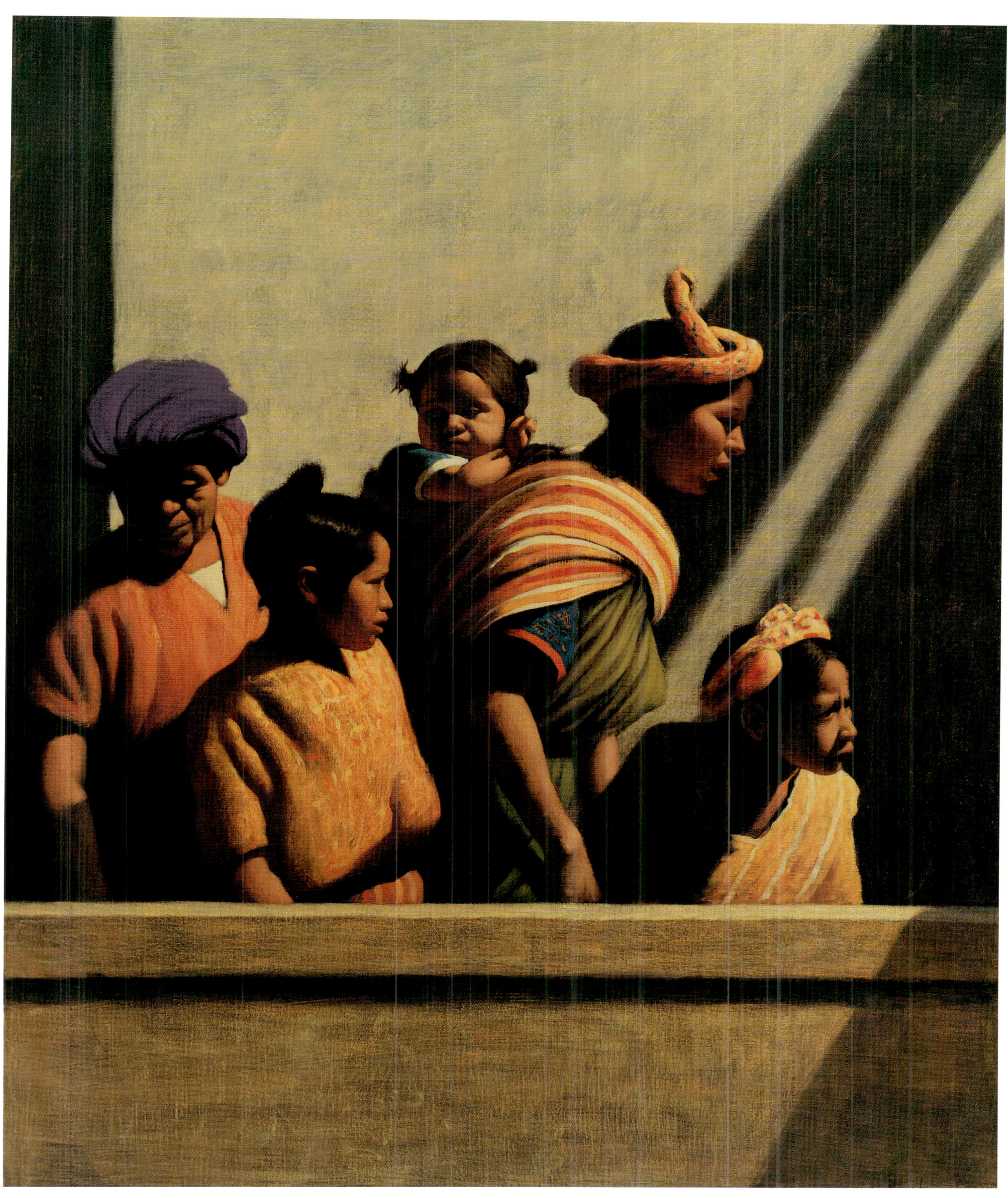

161. UNTITLED
2003, oil on canvas, 48 × 36 inches

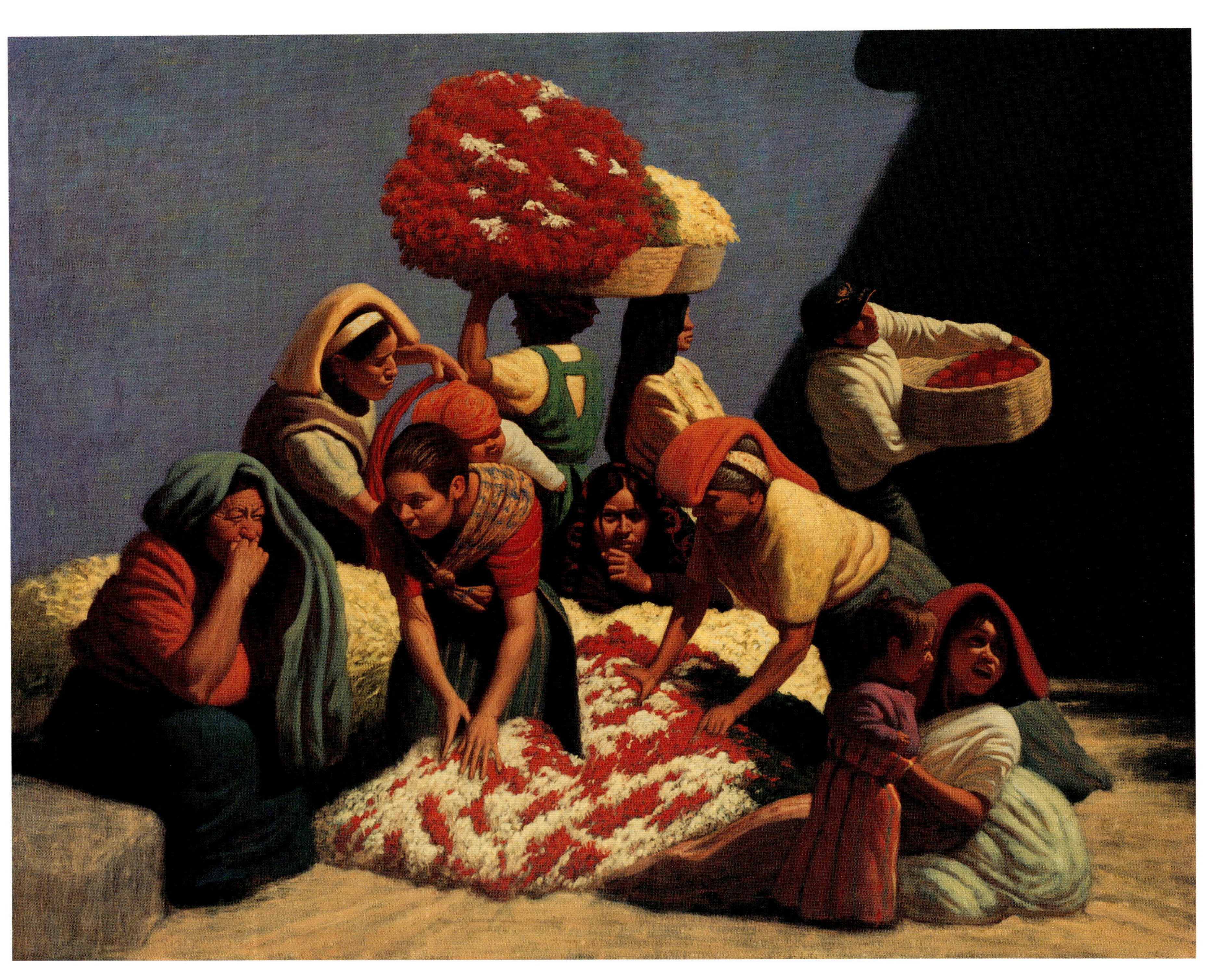

162. THE FLOWERS OF LIFE
2003, oil on canvas, 64 × 80 inches

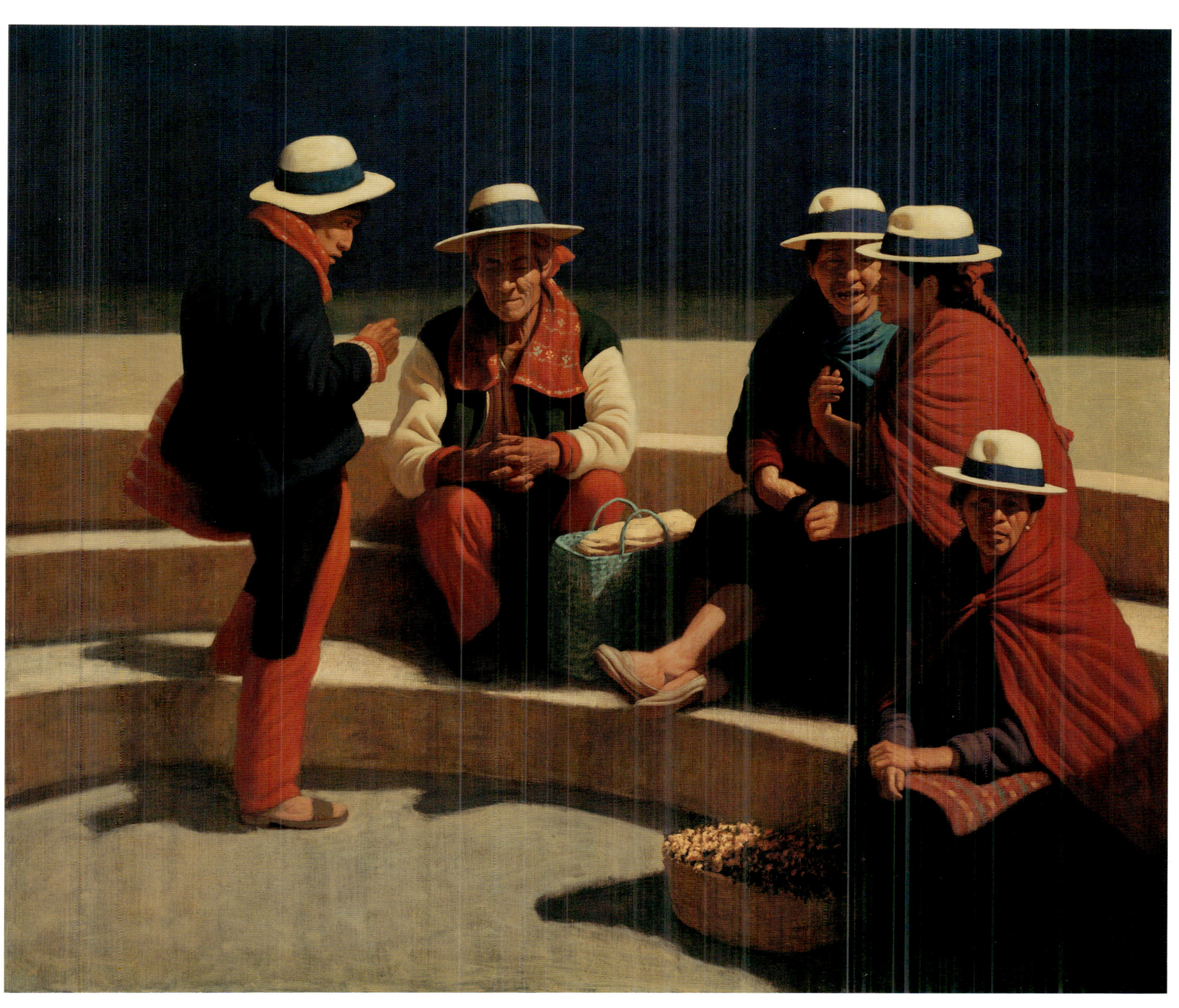

163. GATHERING AT DAWN

2003, oil on canvas, 68 × 80 inches

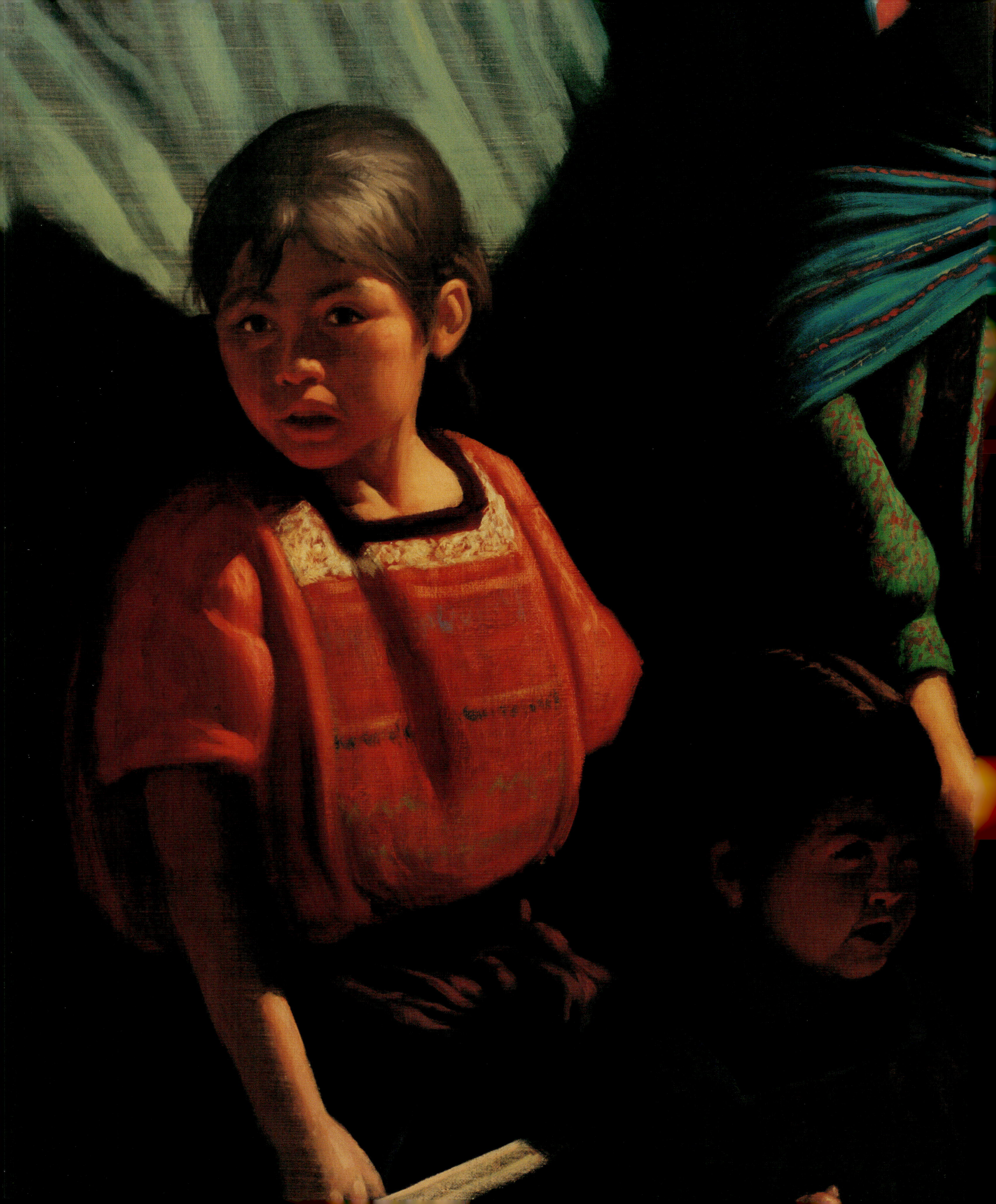

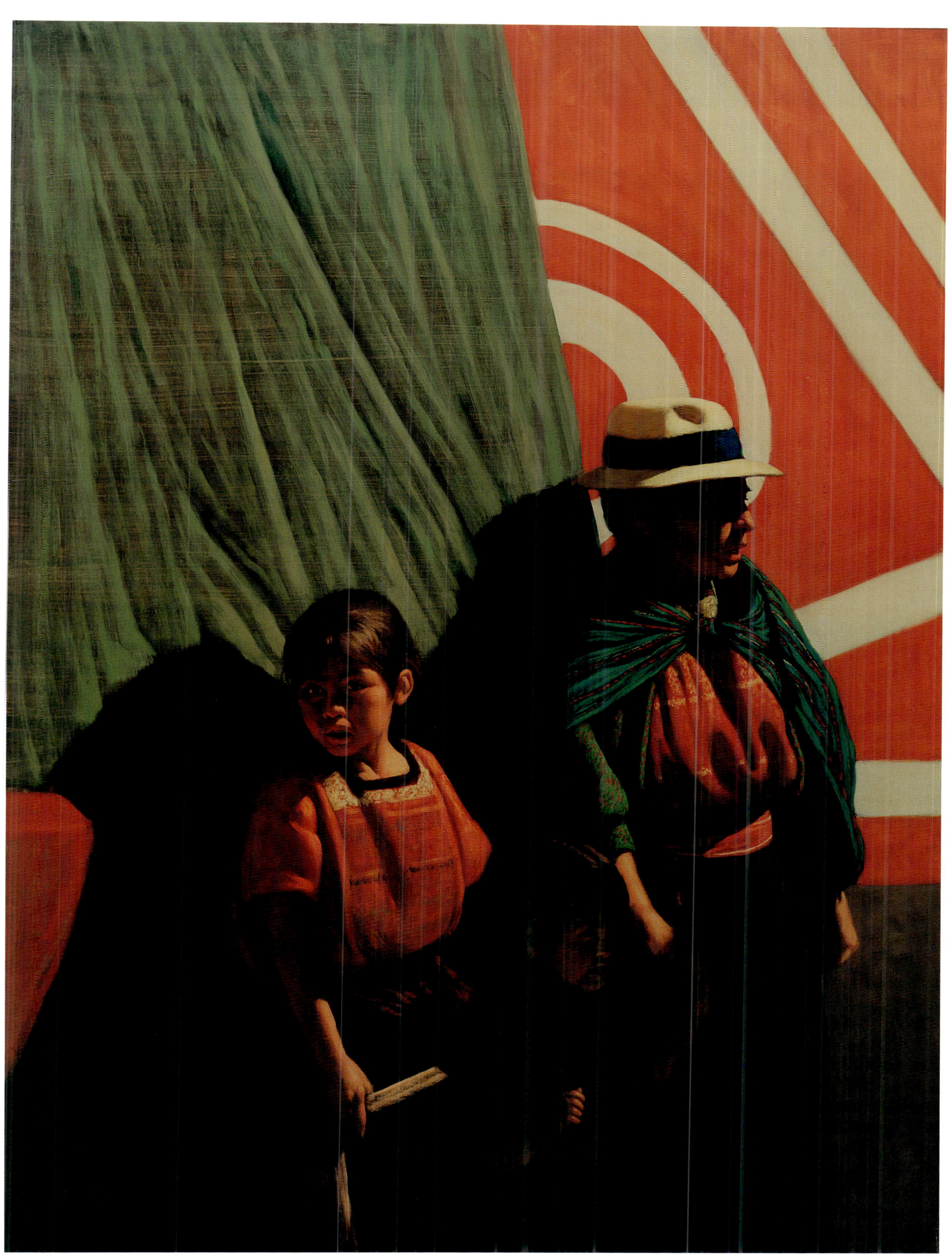

164. TRILOGY OF HOPE
2003, oil on canvas, 48 × 36 inches

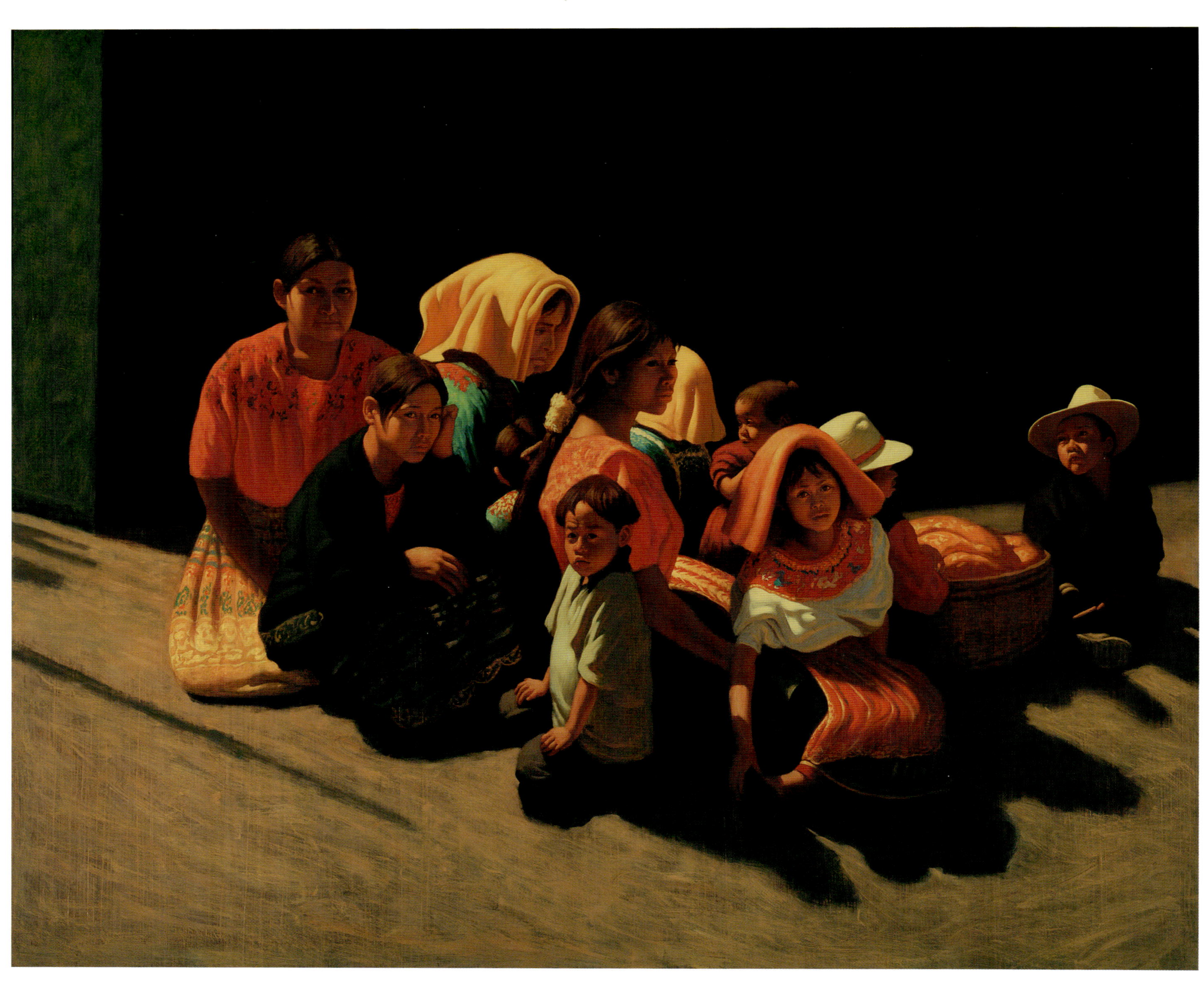

165. FIRST FAMILY
2003, oil on canvas, 68 × 80 inches

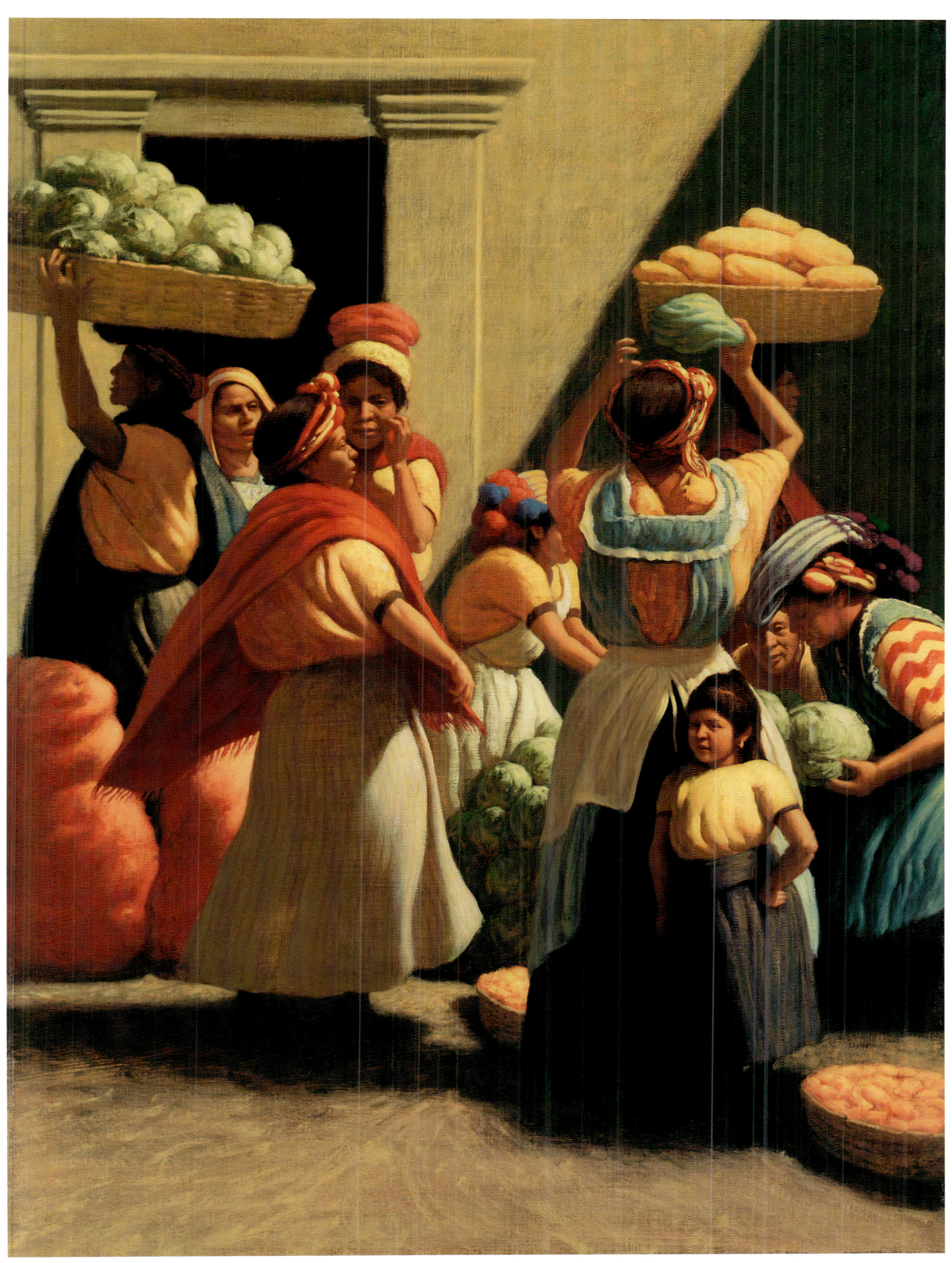

166. THE EARTH PROVIDES II

2003, oil on canvas, 48 × 36 inches

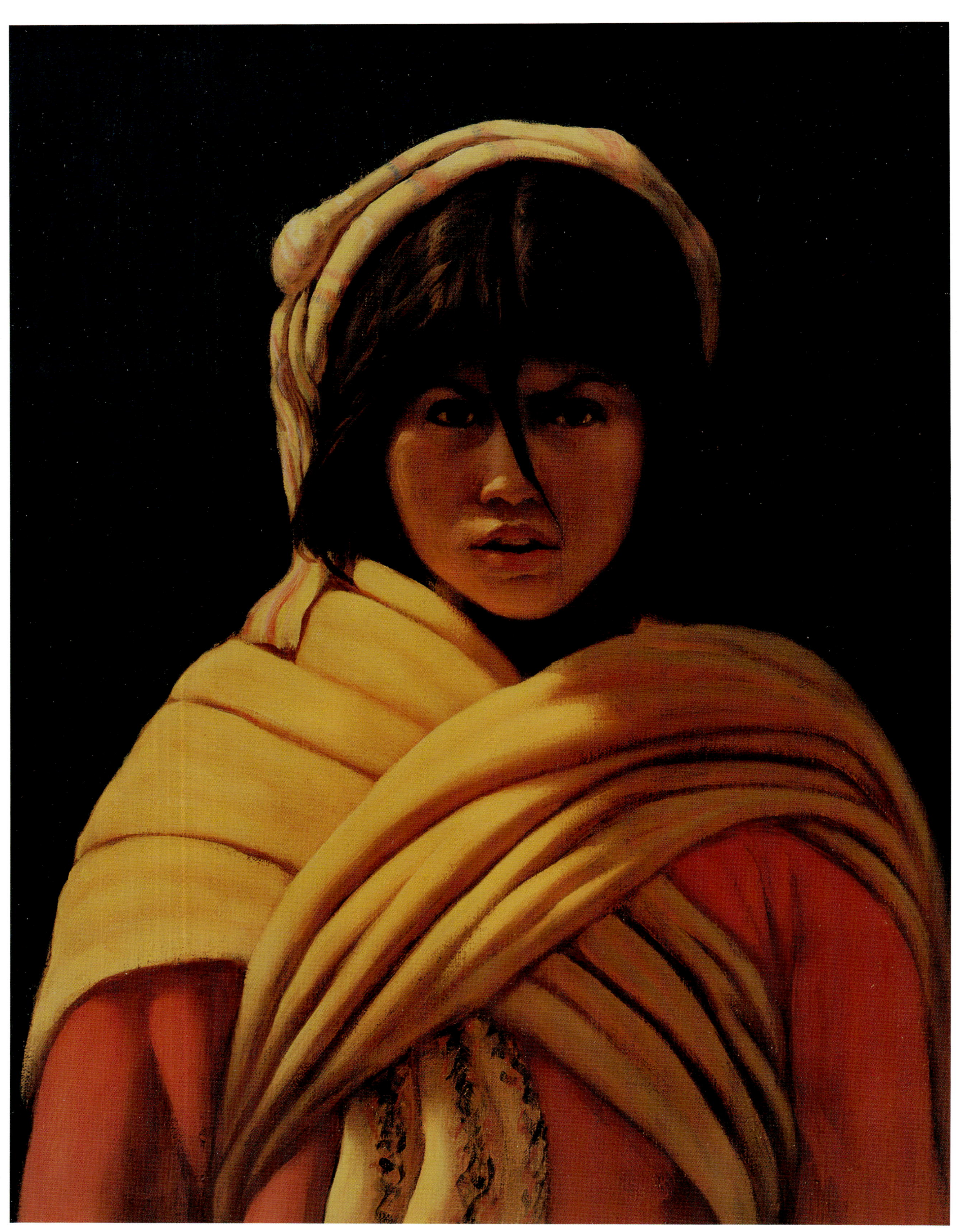

167. THE WATCHER

2003, oil on board, 12 × 10 inches

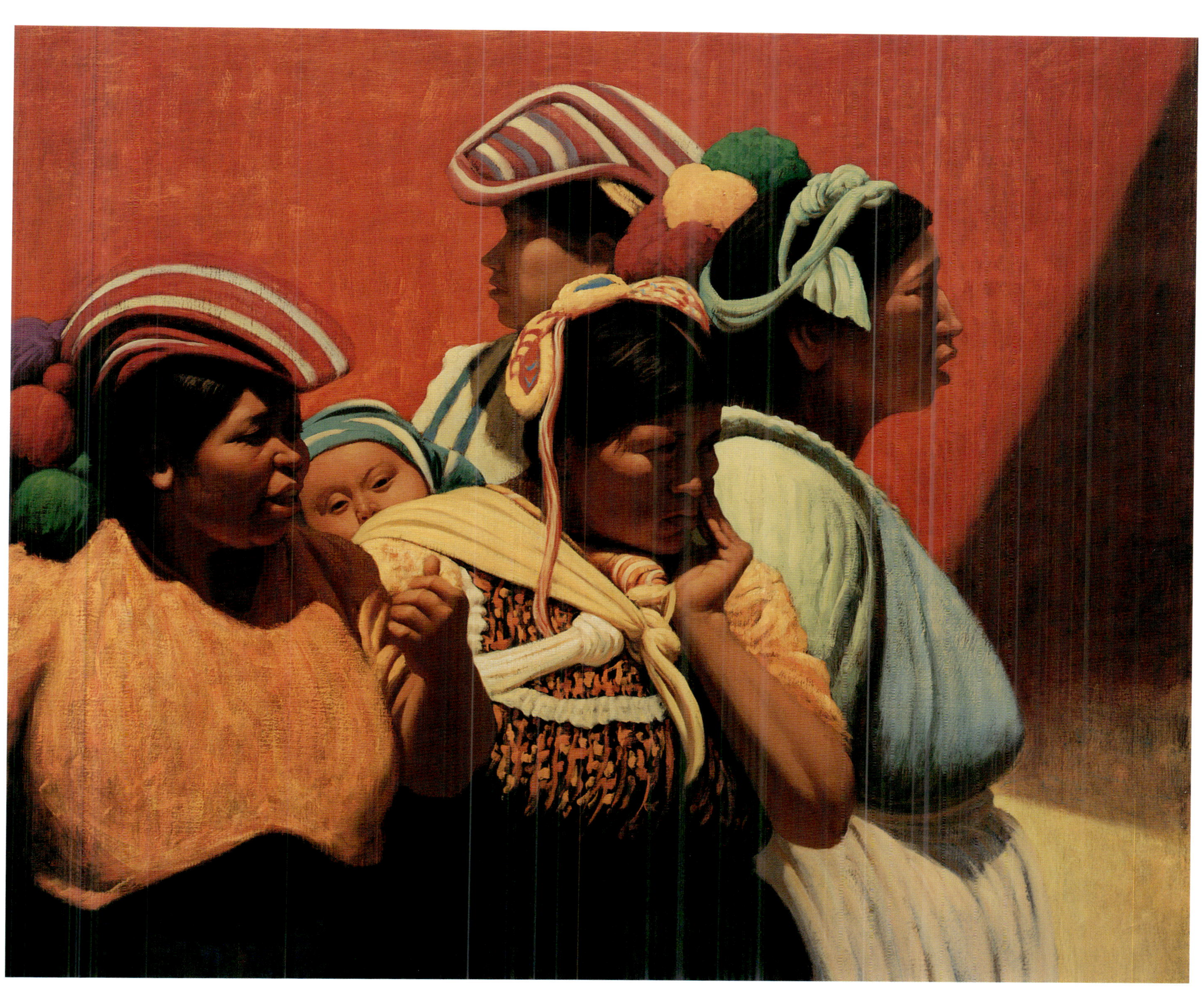

168. UNTITLED

2003, oil on canvas, 36 × 48 inches

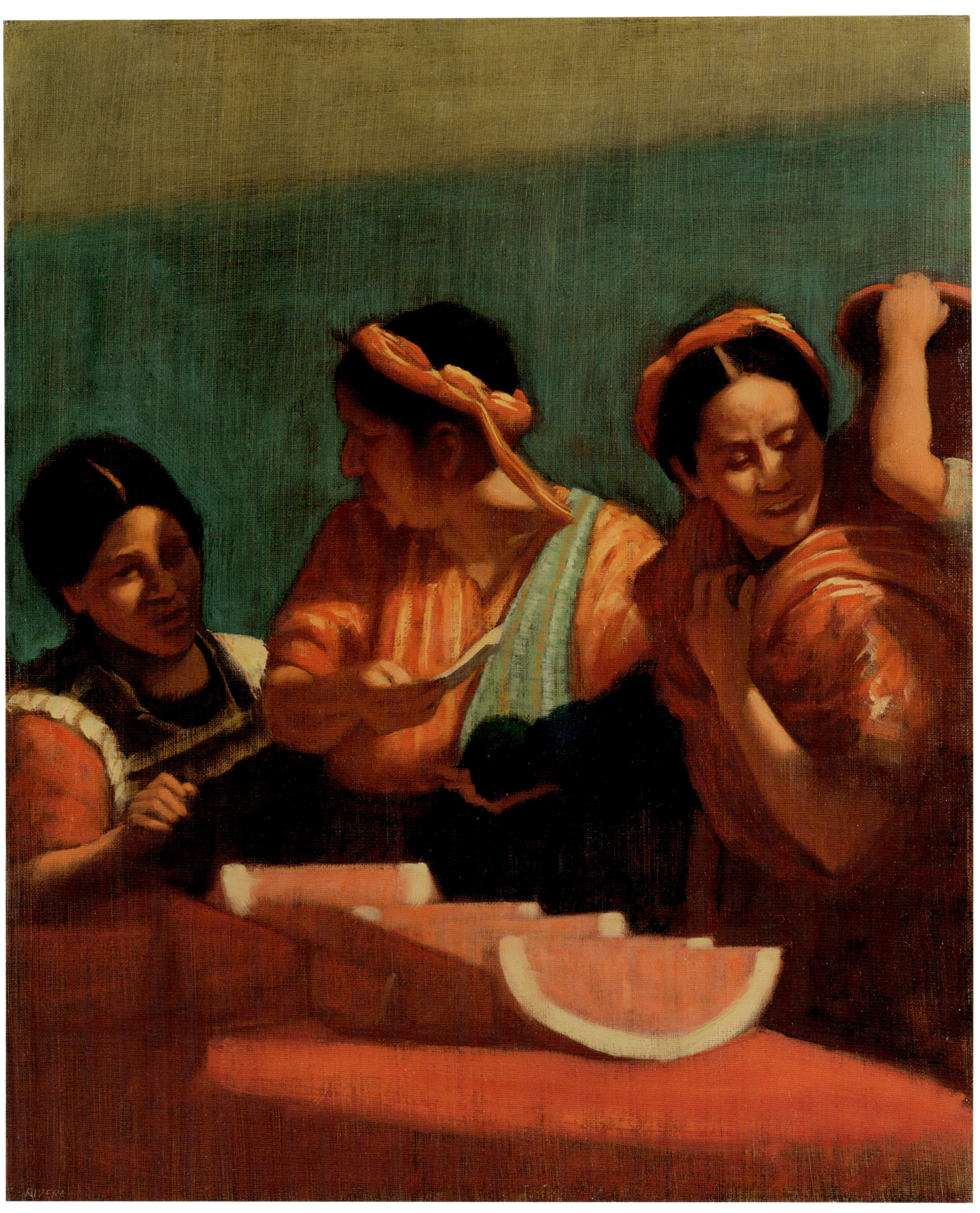

169. UNTITLED

2003, oil on board, 20 × 16 inches

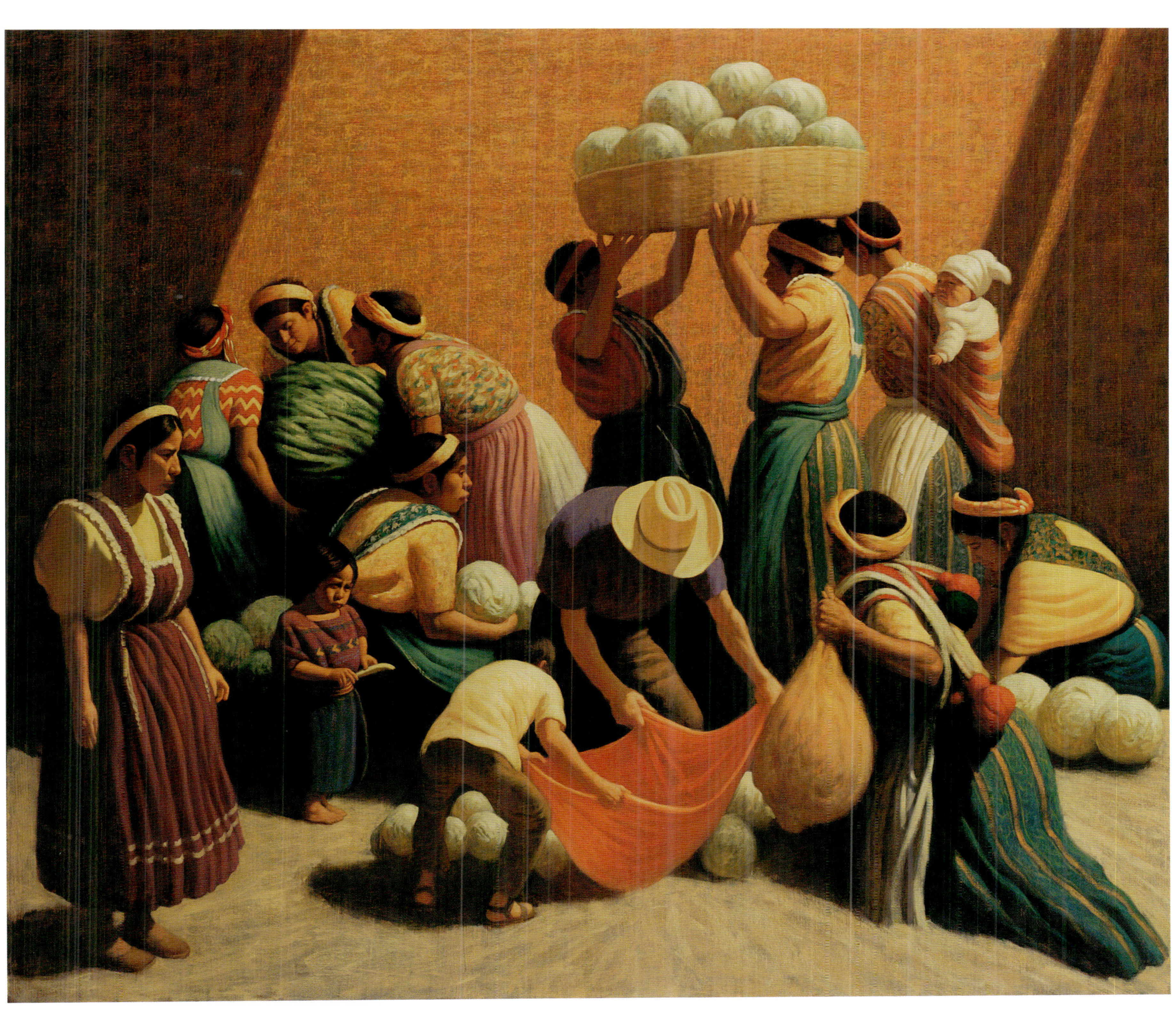

170. UNTITLED
2003, oil on canvas, 68 × 80 inches

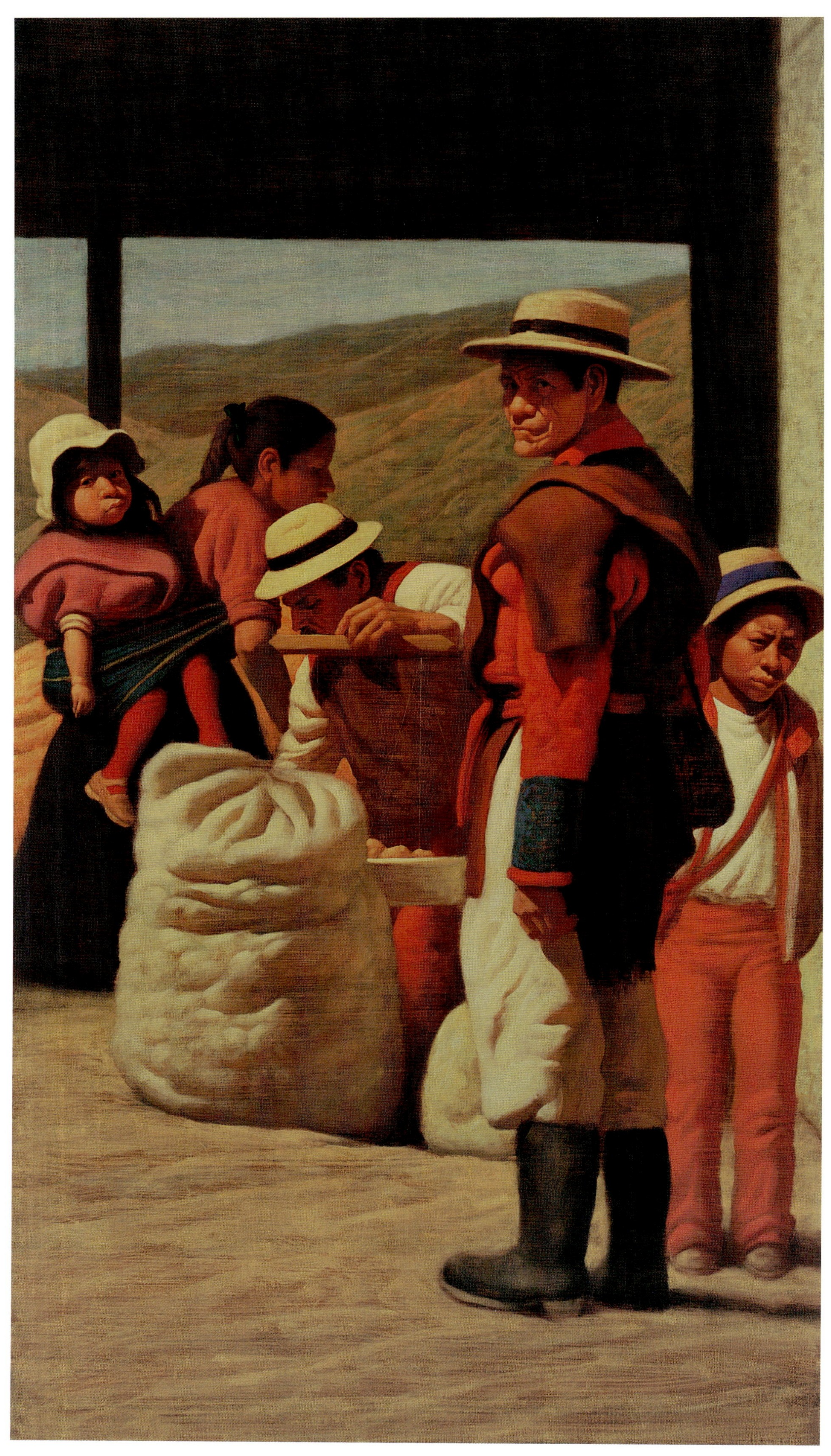

171. THE WEIGHT OF LIFE
2003, oil on canvas, 72 × 40 inches

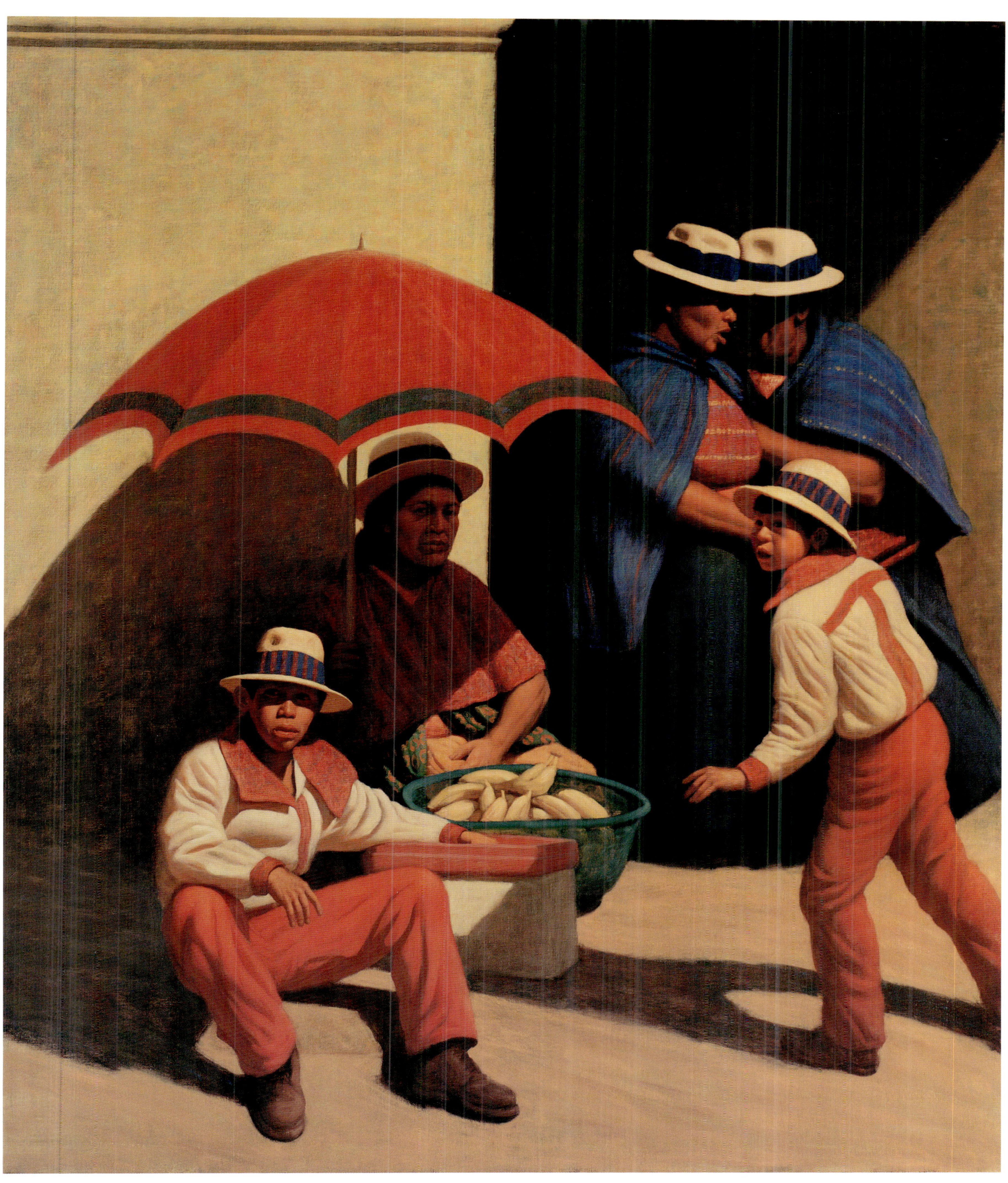

172. THE RED UMBRELLA
2003, oil on canvas, 80 × 68 inches

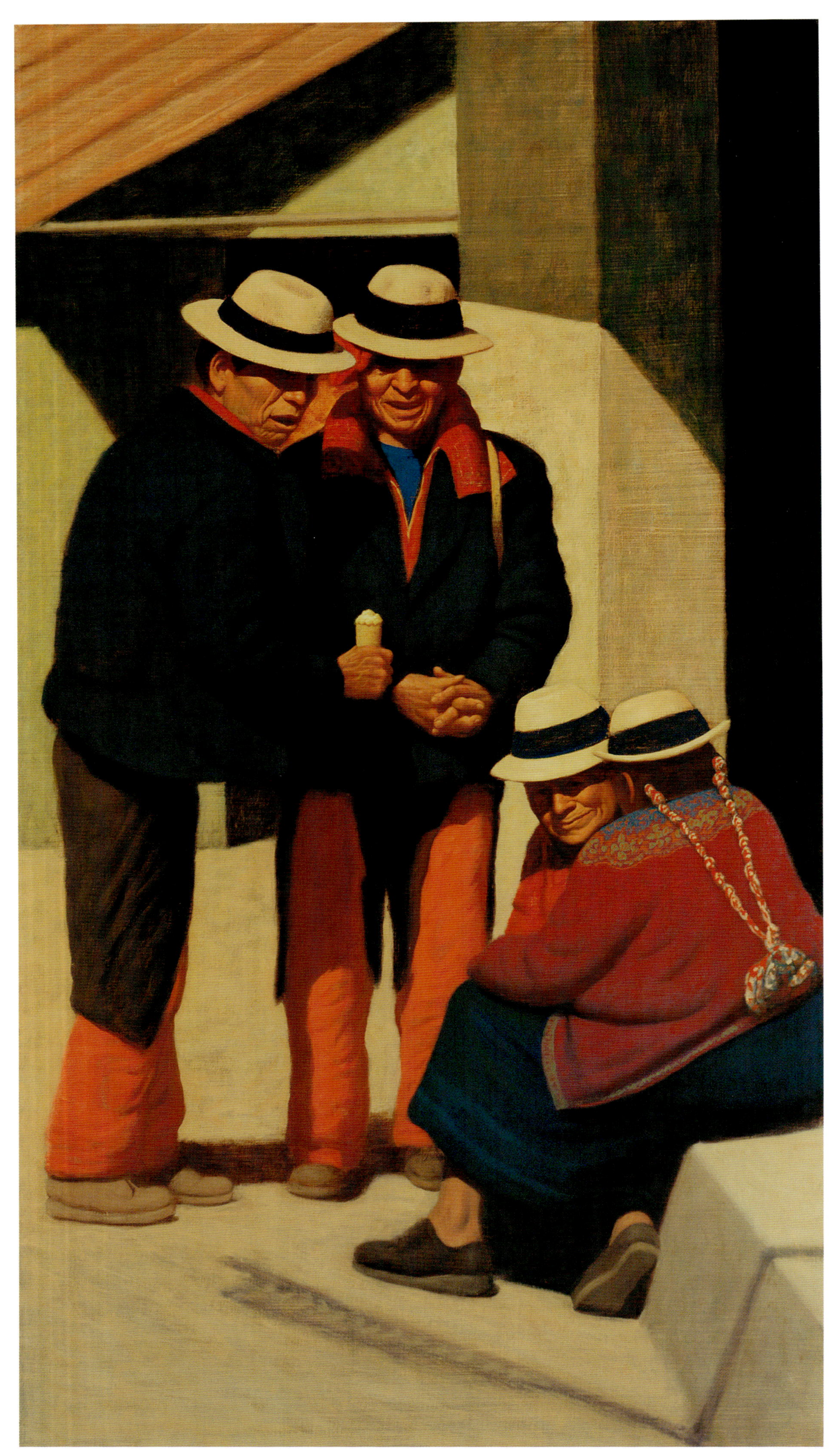

173. THE CONVERSATION
2003, oil on canvas, 72 × 40 inches

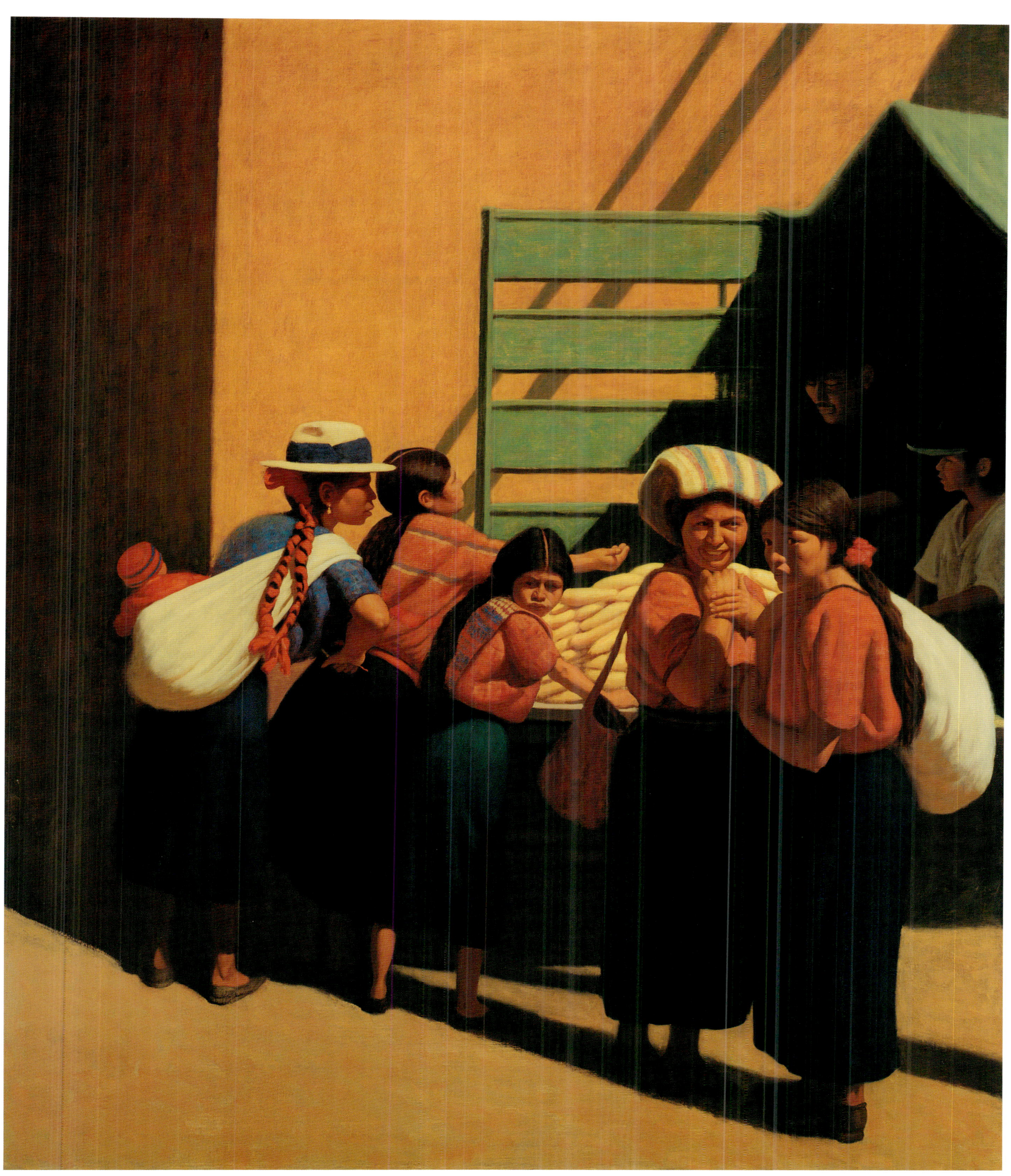

174. SUN AND SHADOWS II
2003, oil on canvas, 80 × 68 inches

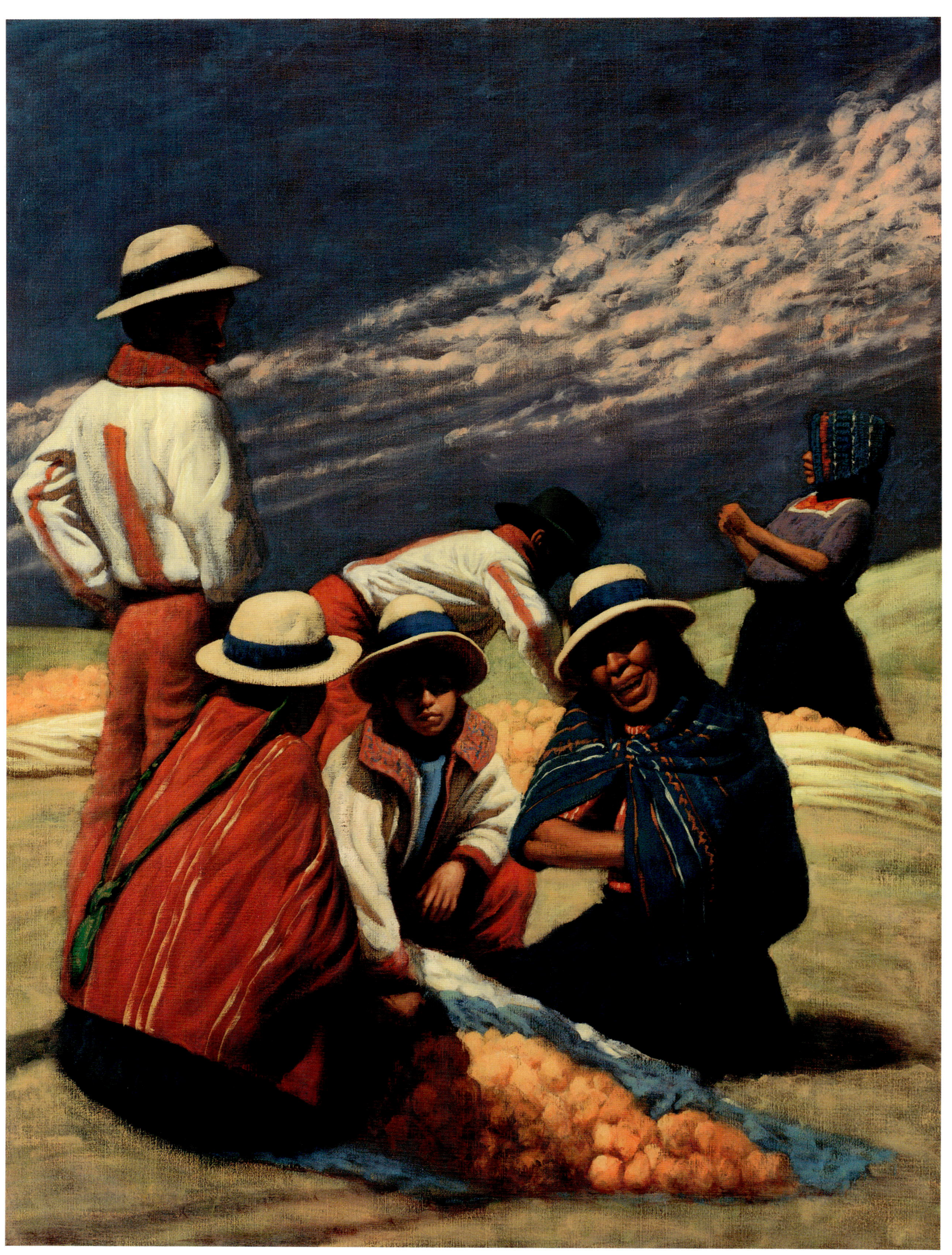

175. OUTDOOR GATHERING
2003, oil on canvas, 48 × 36 inches

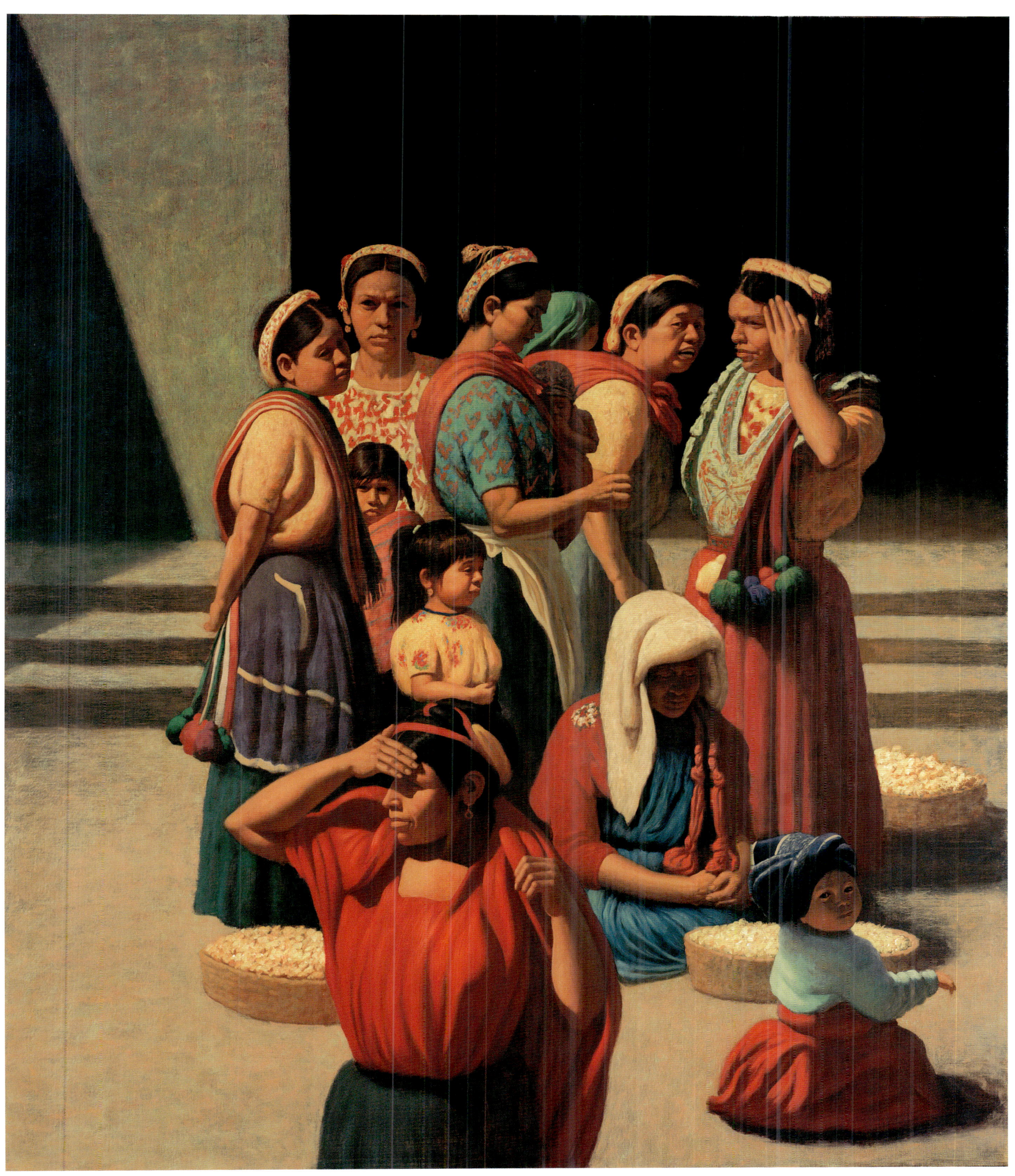

176. EVE'S APPROACH
2004, oil on canvas, 80 × 68 inches

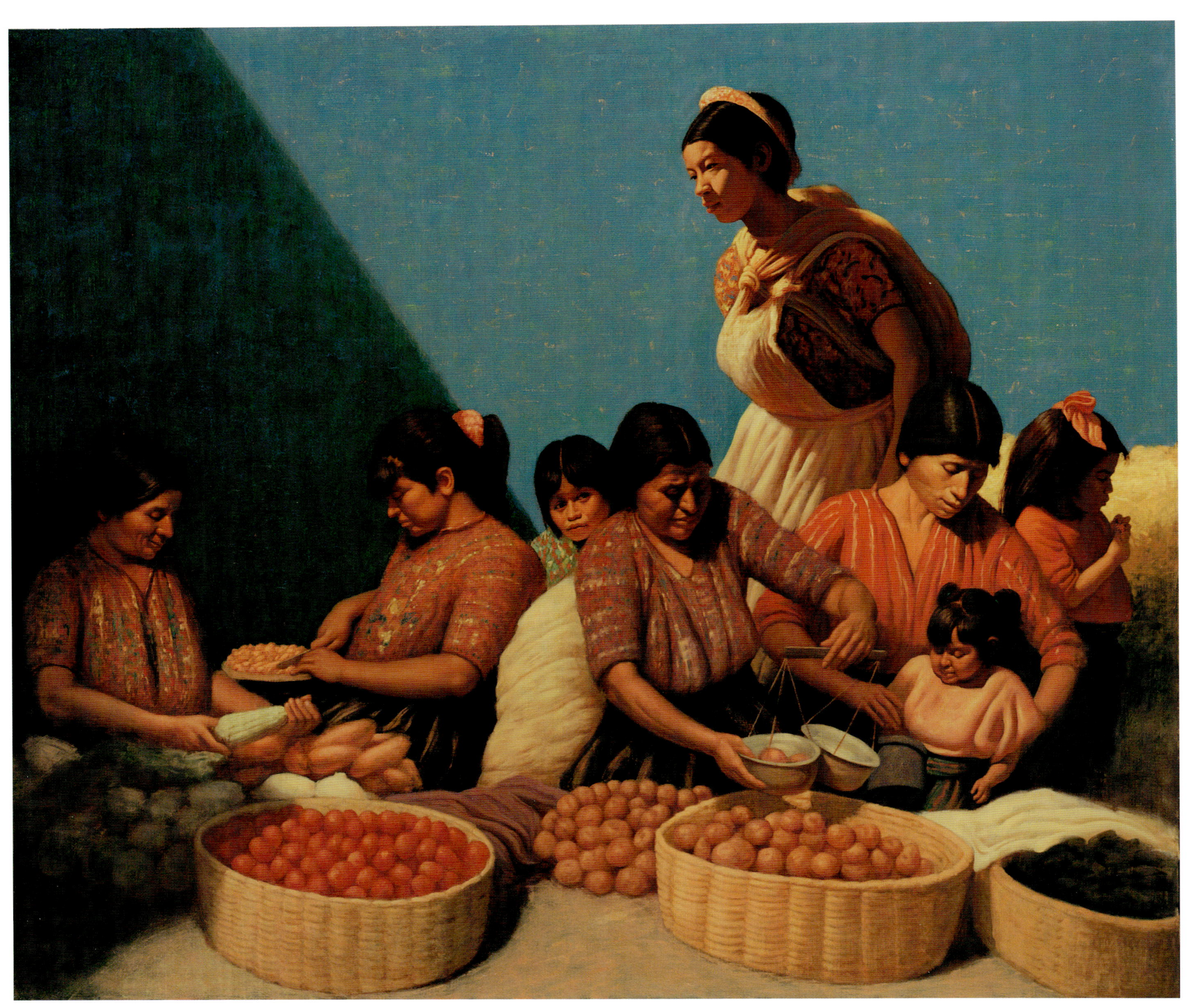

177. DAUGHTERS OF THE EARTH

2004, oil on canvas, 68 × 80 inches

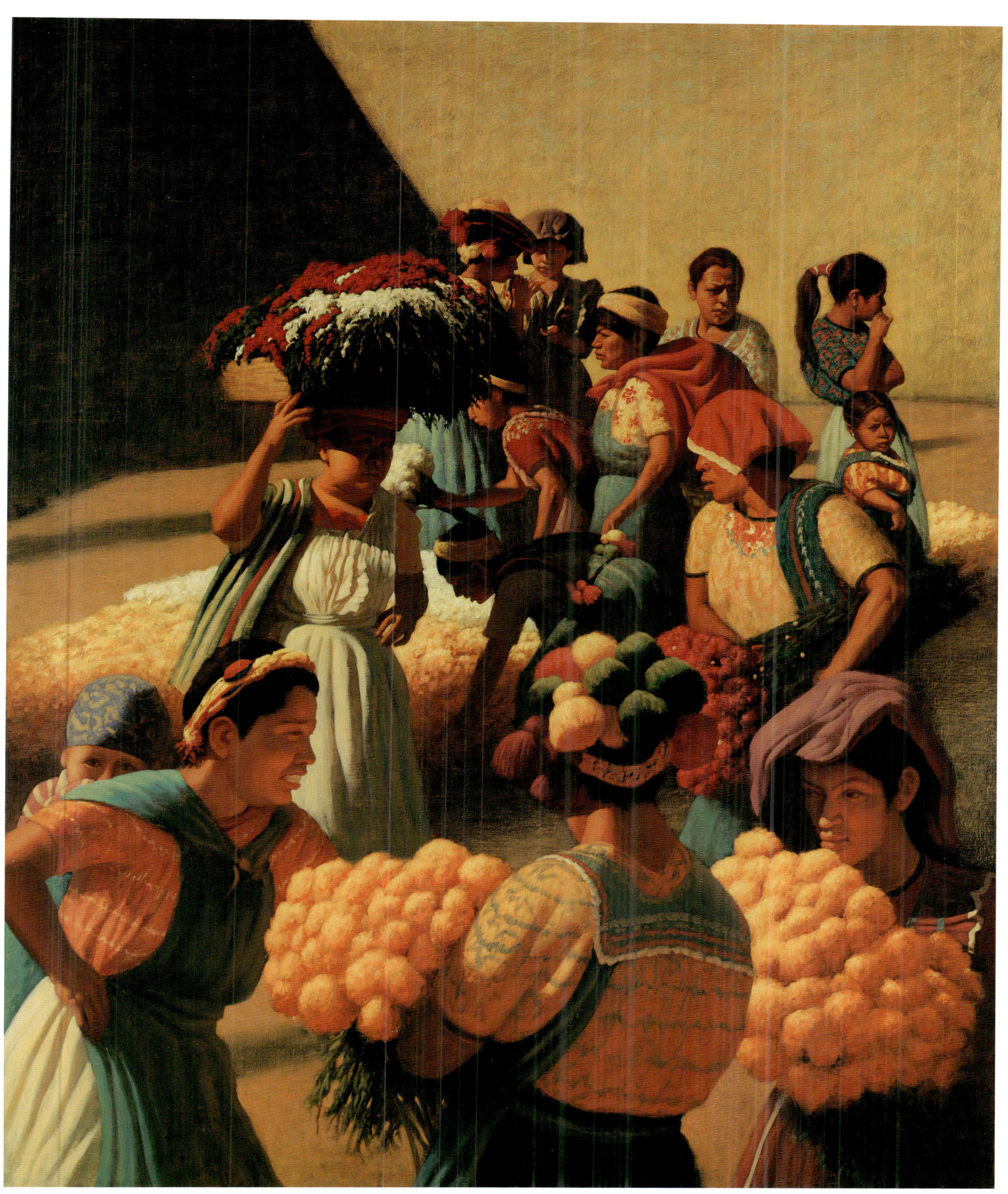

178. FLORAL ASCENSION

2004. oil on canvas, 60 × 50 inches

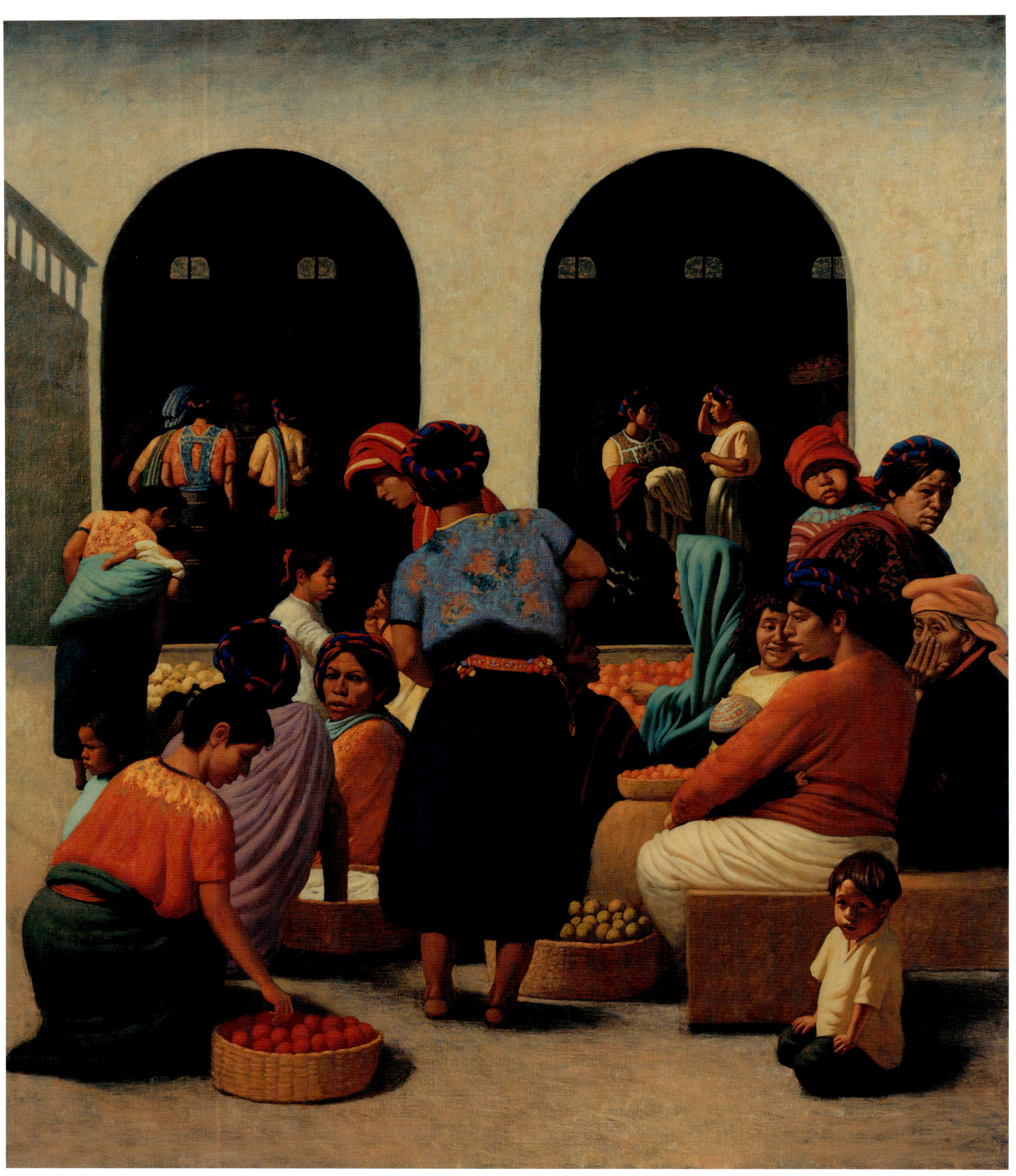

179. BEYOND THE PROSCENIUM
2004, oil on canvas, 80 × 68 inches

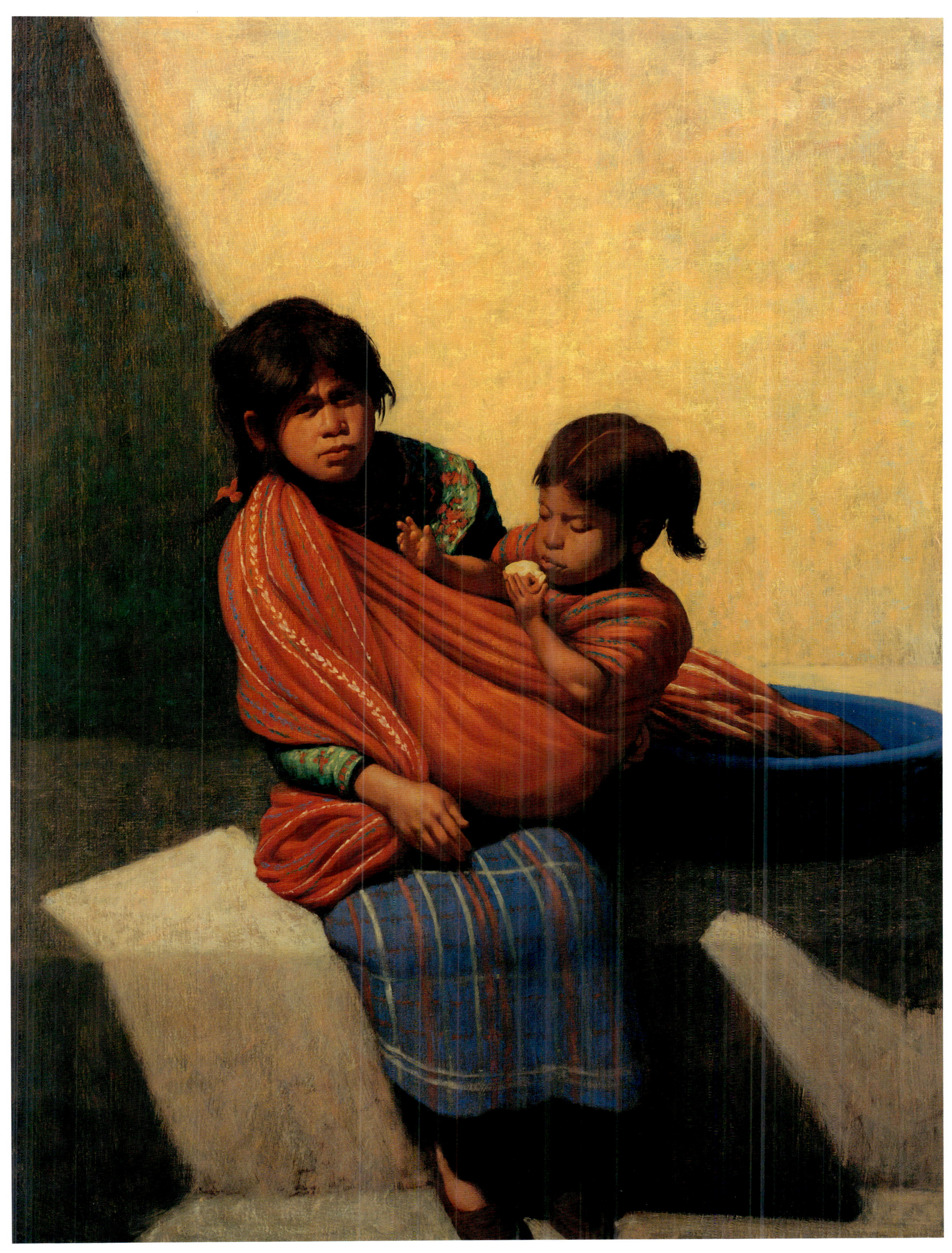

180. FRUIT OF THE EARTH
2004, oil on canvas, 48 × 36 inches

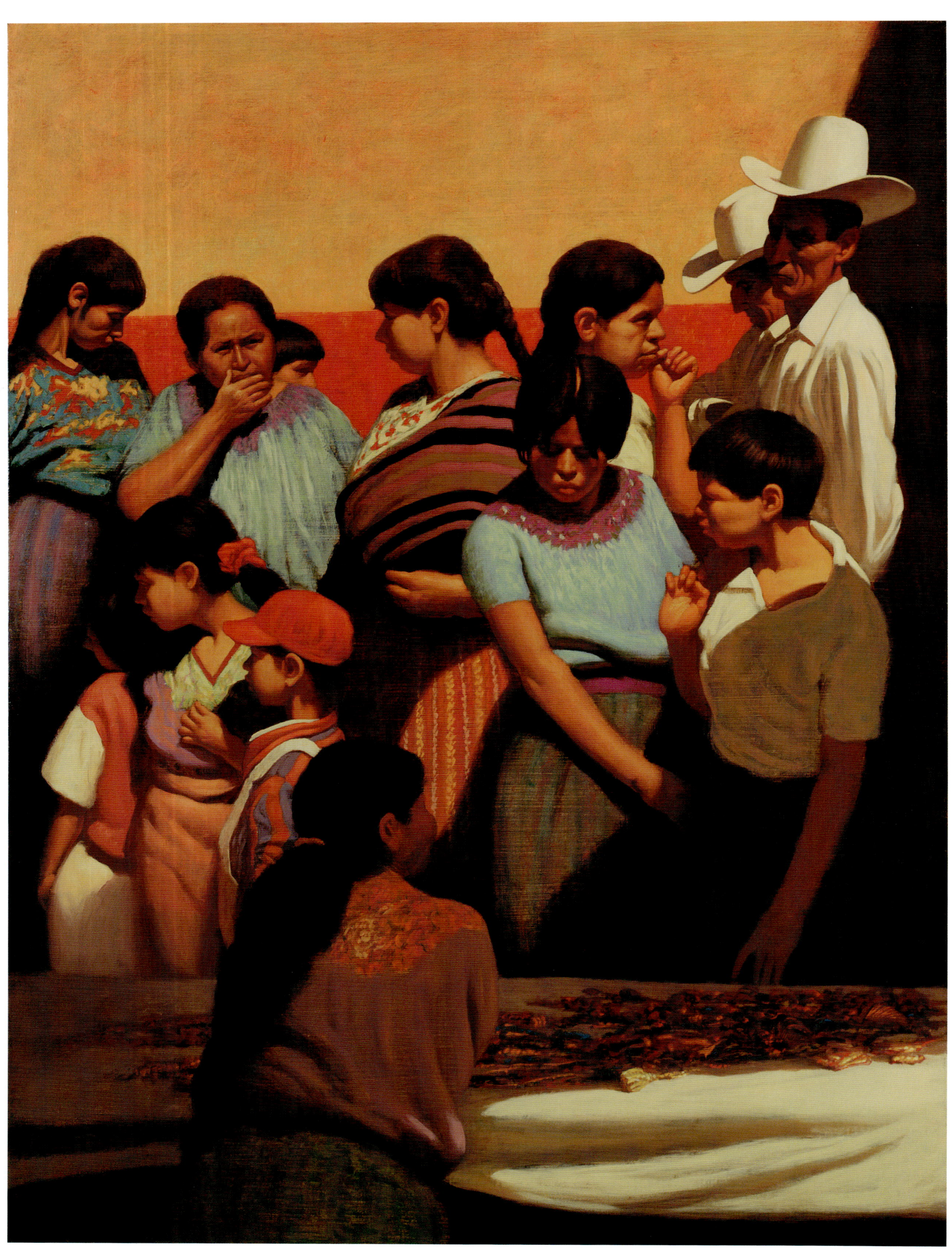

181. PASSAGEWAY

2004, oil on canvas, 48 × 36 inches

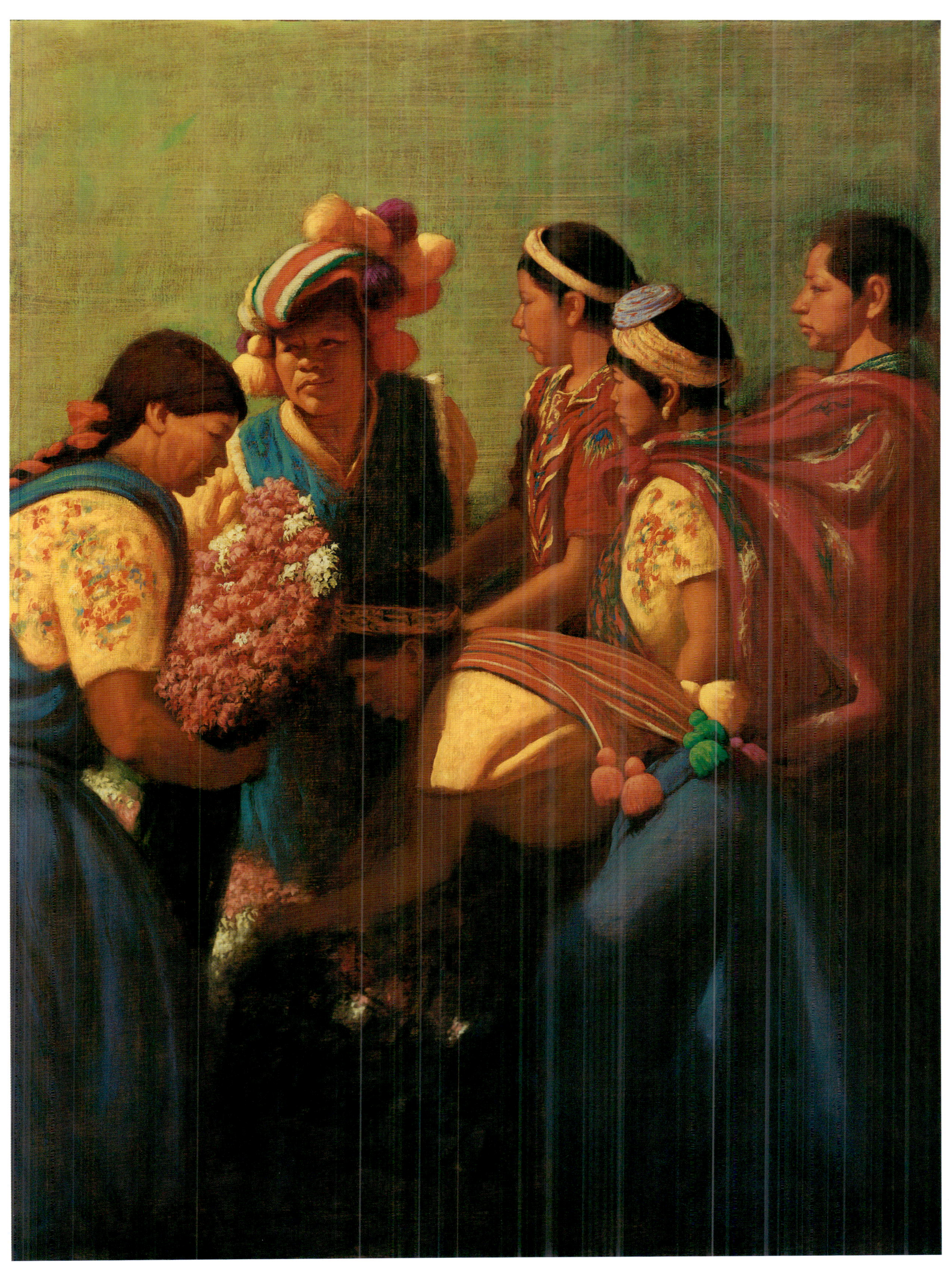

182. OPEN MARKET II
2005, oil on canvas, 48 × 36 inches

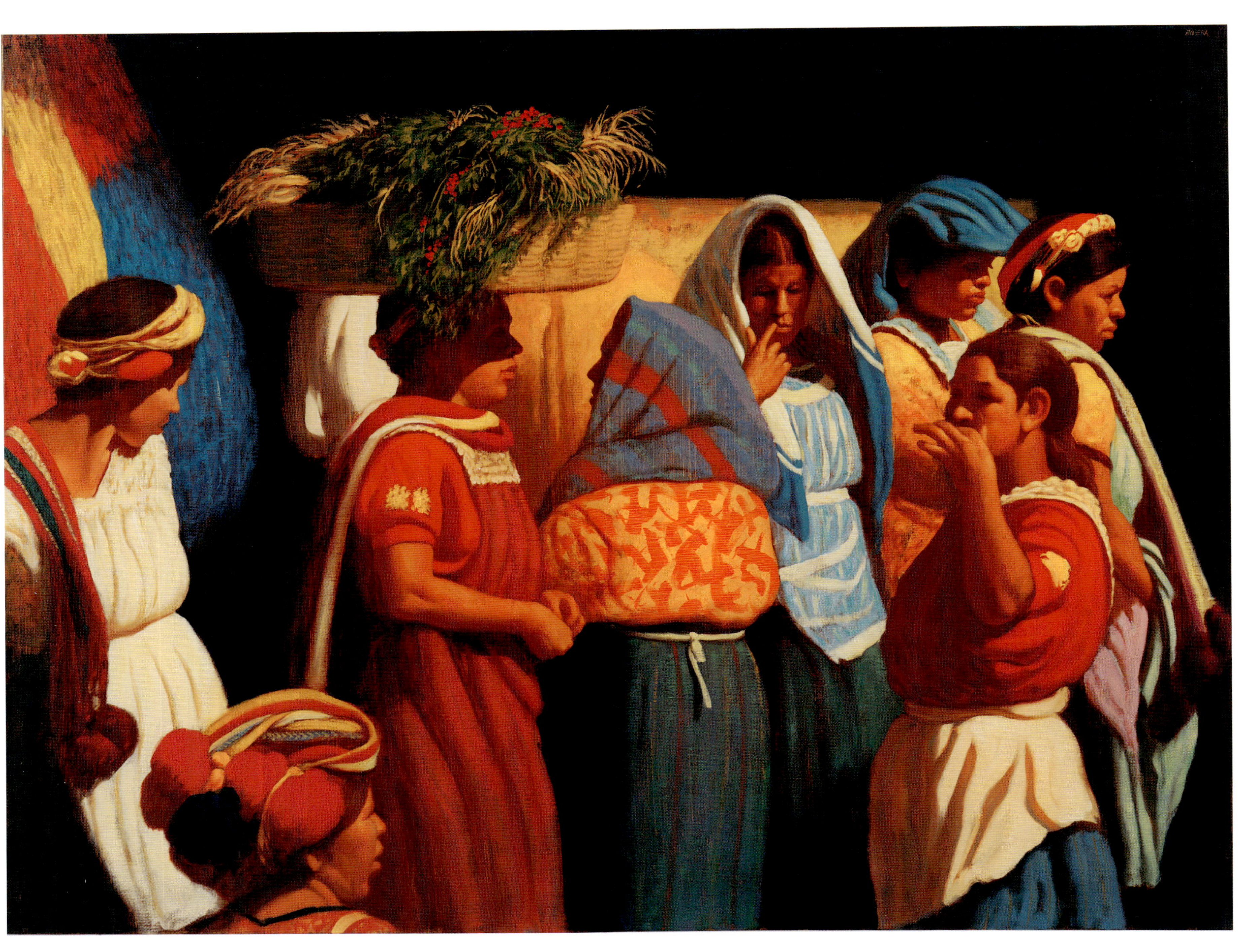

183. UNDER THE COVER OF LIGHT
2005, oil on canvas, 36 × 48 inches

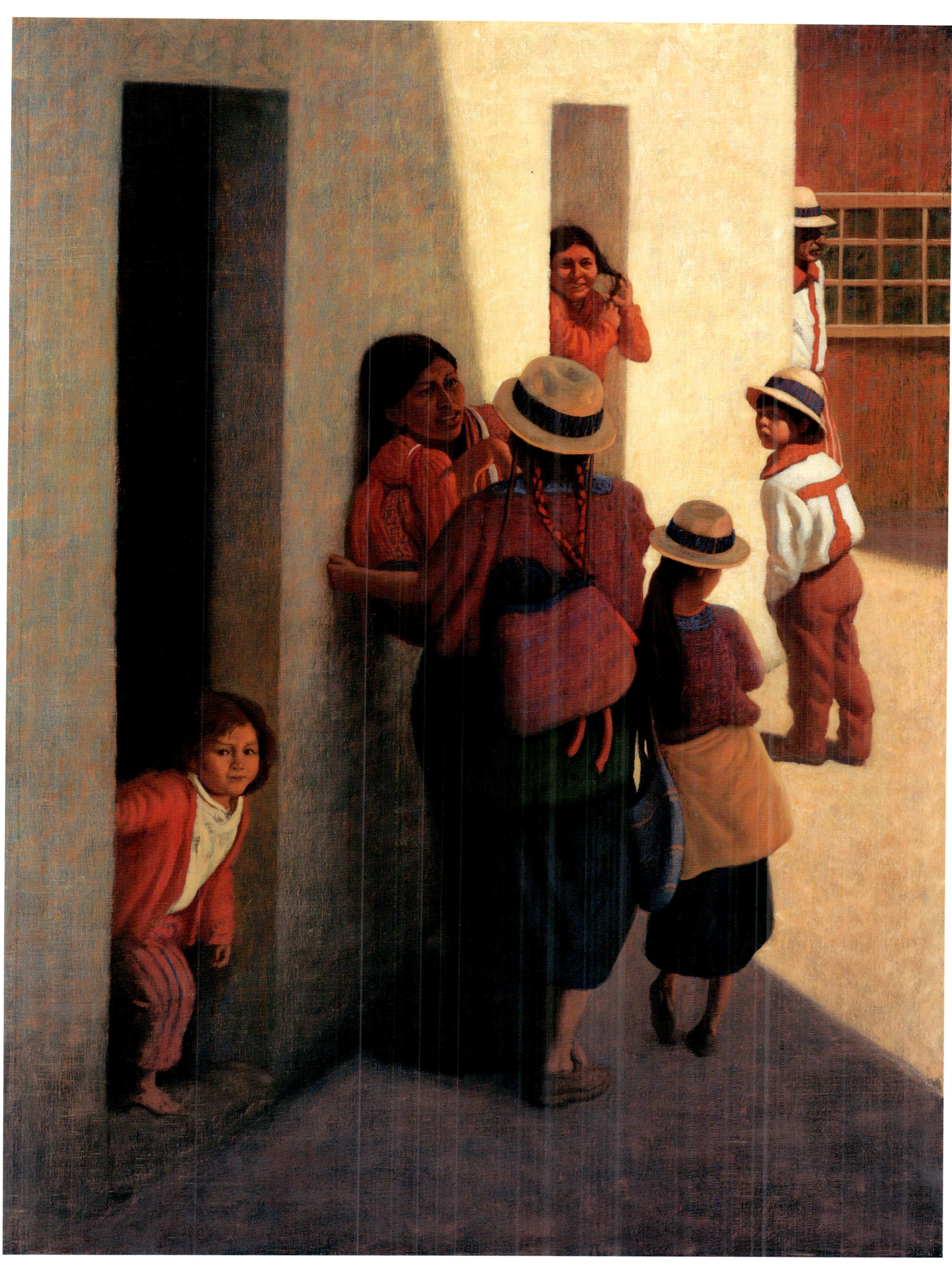

182. FROM THE SHADOWS II

2005, oil on canvas, 48 × 36 inches

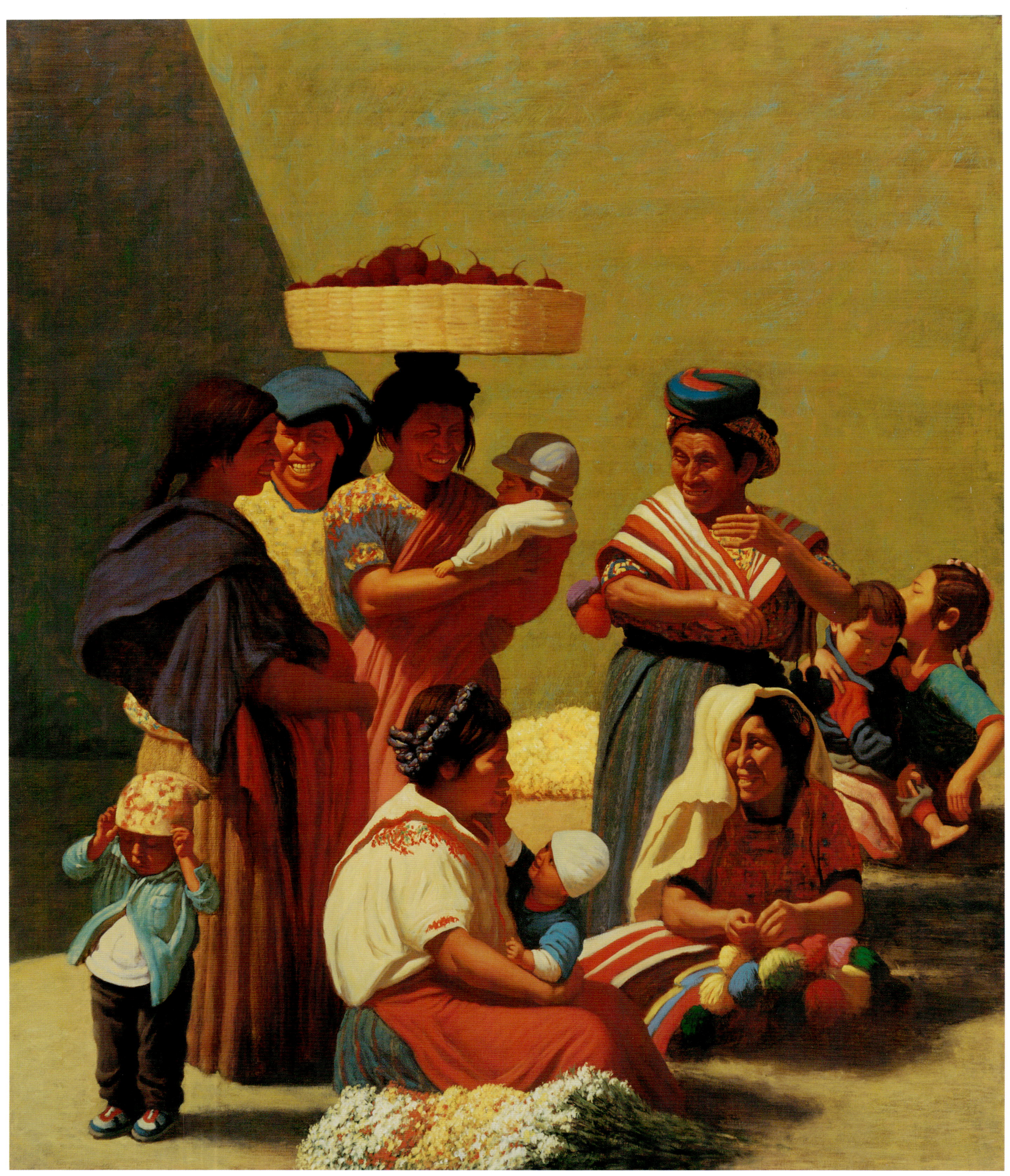

185. UNTITLED

2005, oil on canvas, 80 × 68 inches

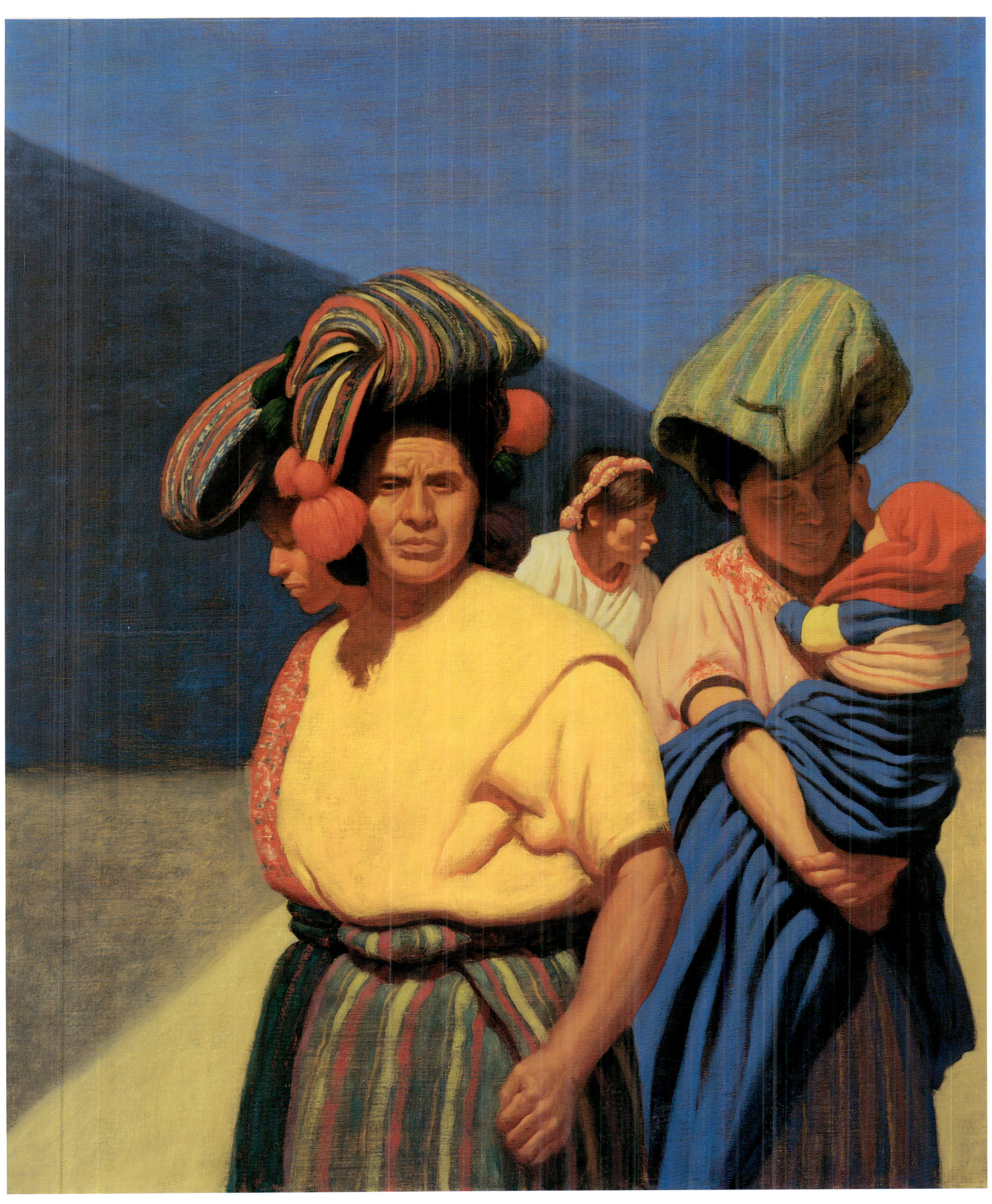

186. BEFORE THE PAST

2005, oil on canvas, 44 × 36 inches

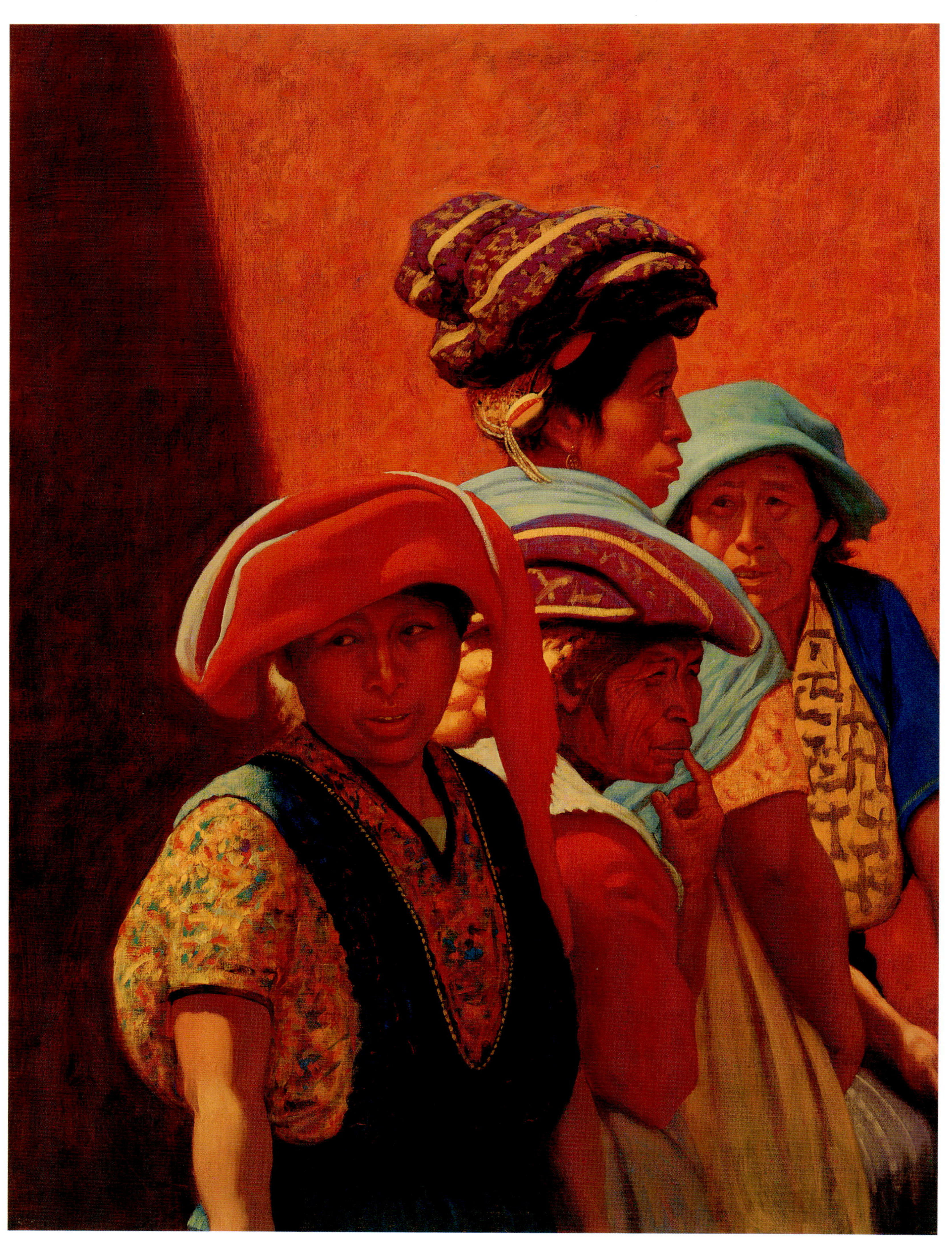

187. THE SECOND ACT

2006, oil on canvas, 48 × 36 inches

ACKNOWLEDGMENTS

I would like to express my gratitude to all those who have contributed to making this beautiful book. At Riva Yares Gallery, my representatives for nearly twelve years, I wish to extend my warmest appreciation to Riva Yares, Dennis Yares, Manuel Garcia, and Chee Ho. Many thanks go to longtime friend Stuart Ashman, as well as to the contributors to this publication: Mr. and Mrs. Hubbard Howe, Mr. and Mrs. Craig Ponzio, and Steve and Jane Messinger. Leslie van Breen, co-director of Hudson Hills Press, shepherded this project with great skill and David Skolkin is responsible for its wonderful design. I thank them both, along with their dedicated editor, Laura Addison. I am grateful to Gene Hackman, Governor Bill Richardson, and Edward Lucie-Smith for contributing their engaging texts to the publication.

This book represents a culmination of decades of work and the influence and friendship of many along the way. I would like to thank my most pivotal and important teacher, Frank Mason, for what he gave to me, both in inspiration and for opening up the magic of light. Steve Raffo, who privately taught me, introduced so much of the arts to me. I am grateful to my family of longtime friends, who have been encouraging and supportive countless times throughout the years: Lois Katz, Paula and Harry Tarzian, Richard and Irene Di Liberto, Cecile Moochnek, Karen and Michael Cuddy, and Joy and Dennis Derryck. A special note of thanks to a recently departed friend, Ed Davies. And a heartfelt thanks to dear Barbara Cleaver, who has a special understanding of my paintings, which I do so appreciate.

It is impossible to acknowledge all the special friends in Santa Fe. My greatest appreciation to Charmay Allred for introducing me to Guatemala and assisting in my career. I treasure her friendship. I am grateful to Albert Handell, a friend and fellow painter, for introducing me to beautiful Santa Fe, which I love so much. My thanks also to Edward Borins, as well as to David and Ruth Arthur for their support and for the superb documentary they created about my life and works.

Of course, I would not be anywhere if it were not for the graciousness of all those who have collected my works over the years: I am deeply and forever indebted.

Lastly, I want to thank my dear wife, Susan, for always being there. I treasure her insights to my paintings.

—Elias Rivera

CHRONOLOGY

1937	Born to Elias Rivera, Sr. and Anna Rivera in Bronx, New York.
1947–49	Lives in Puerto Rico with his uncle, Pepito Matias.
1950	Returns to New York.
1953–54	Enrolls in School of Industrial Arts in Manhattan.
1955–61	Attends Art Students League under the instruction of Frank Mason.

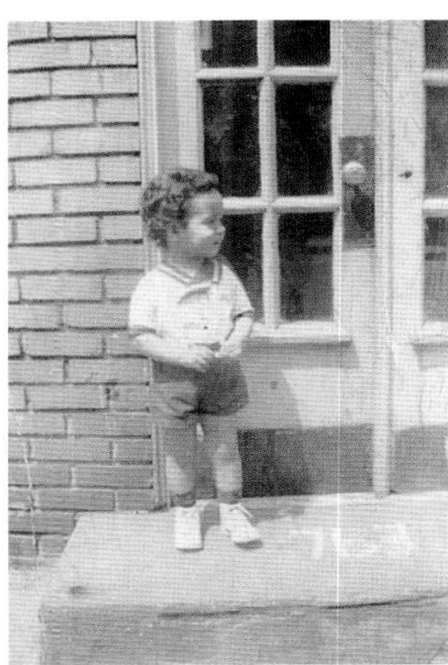

The Bronx, New York, 1940

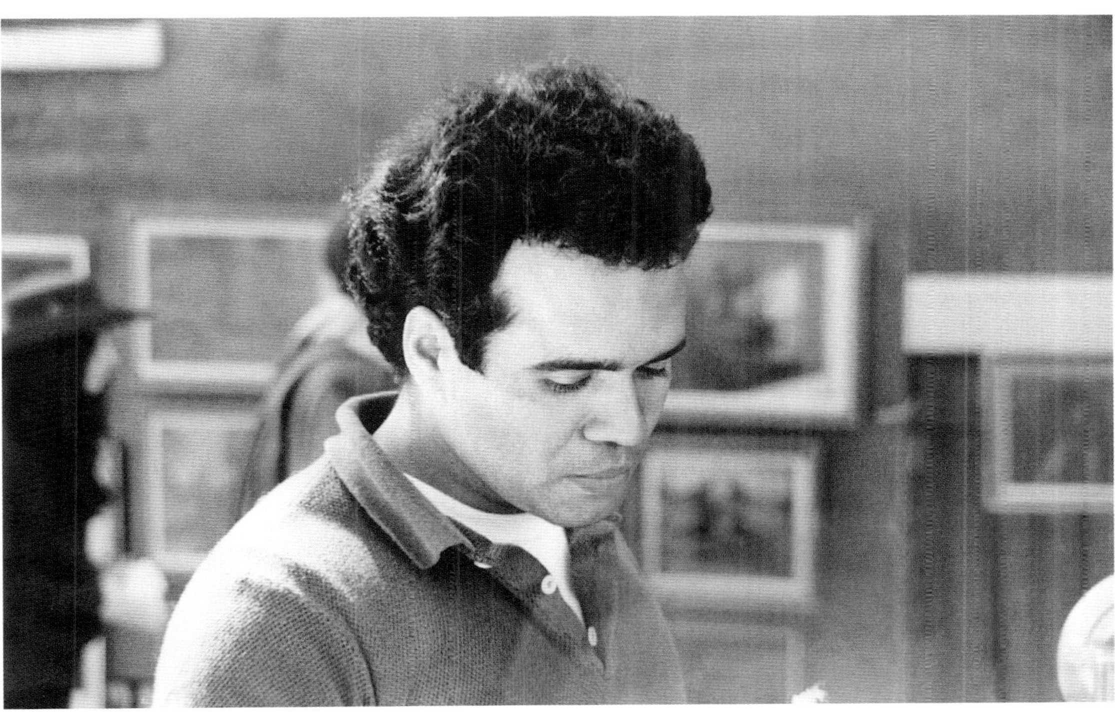

Outdoor Show, New York, 1960

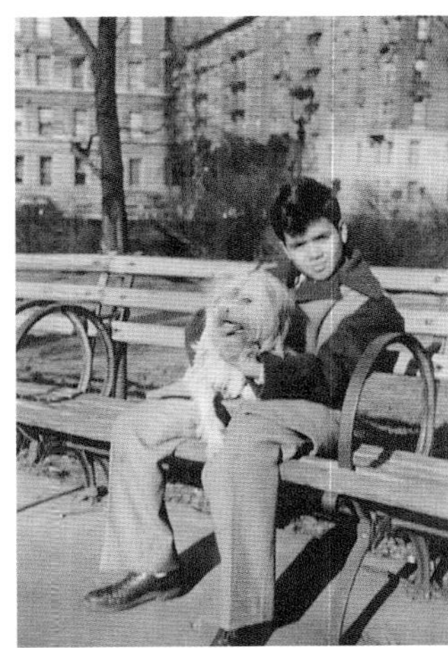

Central Park, New York, 1947

Outdoor Show, New York, 1960

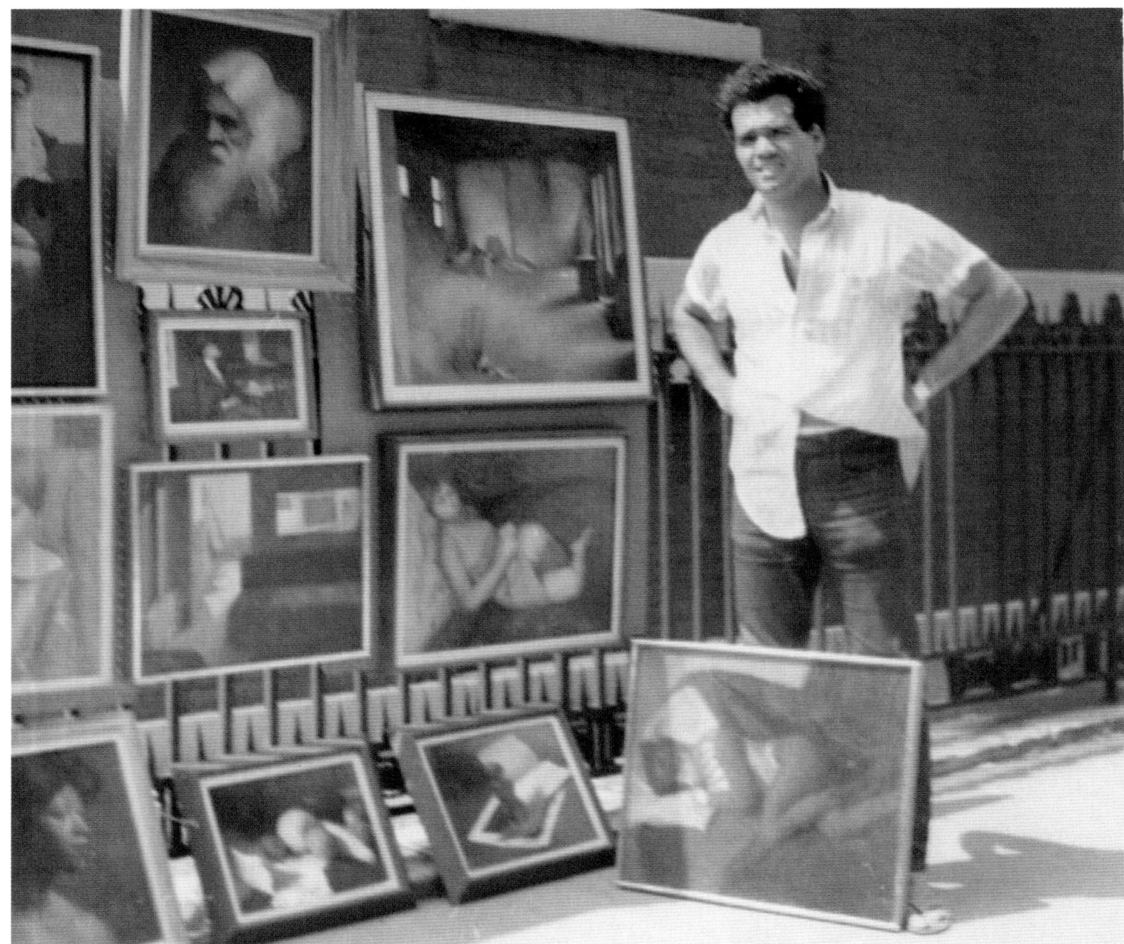

1961 Moves into an unheated railroad flat on 107th Street in Manhattan, which he gradually renovates and where he lives and works for nineteen years. From 1961 to 1964, he studies privately with his neighbor, artist Steve Raffo.

1965 Included in first gallery exhibition, at Lincoln Institute in New York.

1970 Has first one-person exhibition, at Harbor Gallery in Cold Spring Harbor, Long Island.

1972 Completes his first commissioned mural, for Banco de Ponce in Rockefeller Center.
Receives Best Painter Award from De Puerto Rico Institute in New York.
Completes a series of paintings for PBS portraying the Attica riots.

1973 Included in National Academy group exhibition, New York. Wins the Henry W. Ranger Purchase Prize.

1974 Awarded a Gold Medal for the painting *Men's Club* in a group exhibition at Allied Artists, New York.

1978 Awarded the Hassam and Speicher Fund Purchase Prize from the American Academy and Institute of Arts and Letters, New York, for the painting *Waiting*, which was presented by the Academy to the Georgia Museum of Art, Athens. Included in an Allied Artists group exhibition and he wins the David Humphrey Memorial Award.

1981	Exhibits work in a group show, *Crimes of Compassion*, at the Chrysler Museum in Norfolk, Virginia.
1982	Moves to Santa Fe, New Mexico. Meets future wife, artist Susan Contreras.
1983	Begins series entitled Under the Portal, depicting Native American subjects selling their wares under the *portal* of the Palace of the Governors on the Santa Fe Plaza.
1983–87	Travels to Oaxaca, Mexico, and all 32 surrounding villages. This trip becomes the inspiration for his signature works of peoples of Mexico and Central America.
1988	Commissioned to create a painting for the Albuquerque International Sunport.
1990–91	Visits Mexico's Copper Canyon. Paints series on the Tarahumara Indians based on this experience.
1991	Commissioned to create a painting for the Capitol Art Collection, Santa Fe, New Mexico, which remains on permanent display in the New Mexico State Capitol building.
1993	Travels to Antigua, Guatemala. The vivid colors and costumes and the charismatic people of Guatemala become his preferred subject matter.

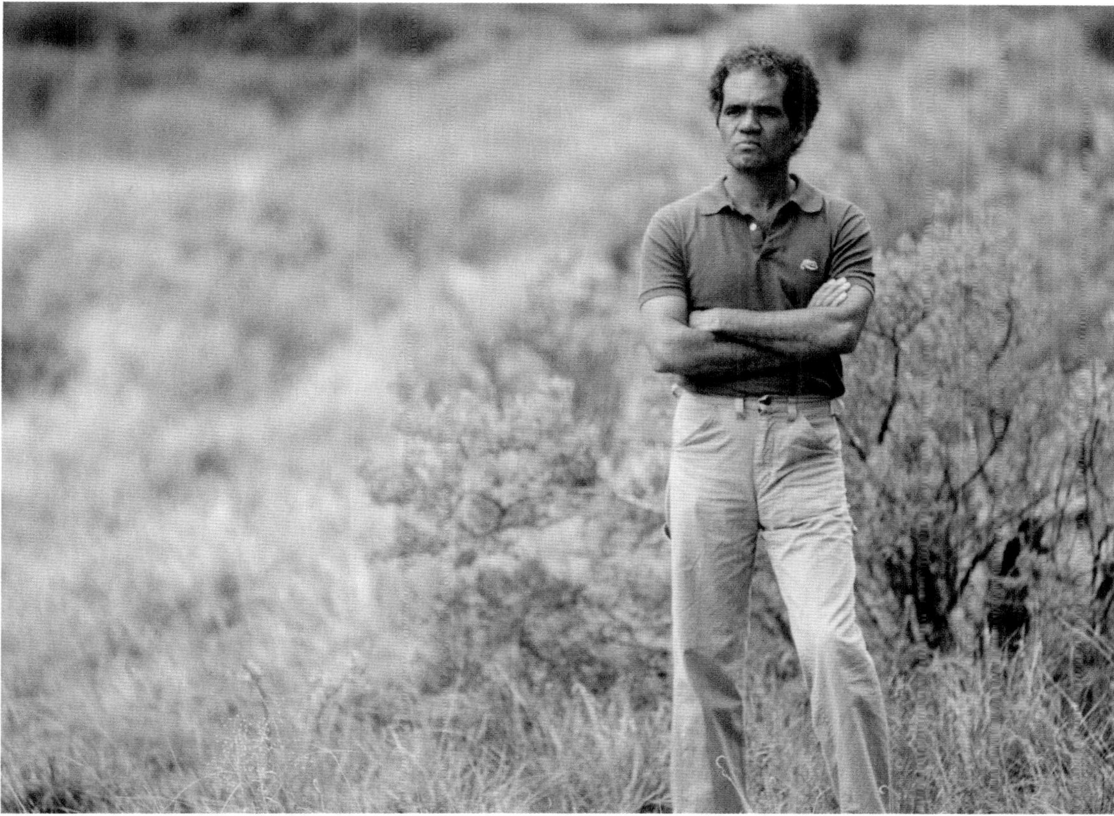

Santa Fe, New Mexico, 1982

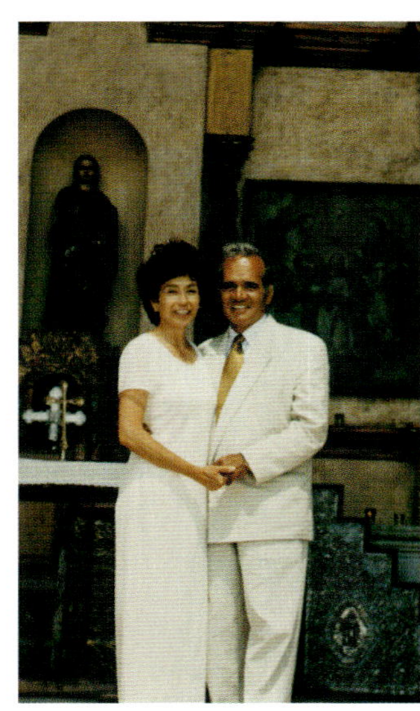

With wife, Susan Contreras, in Guatemala, 1998

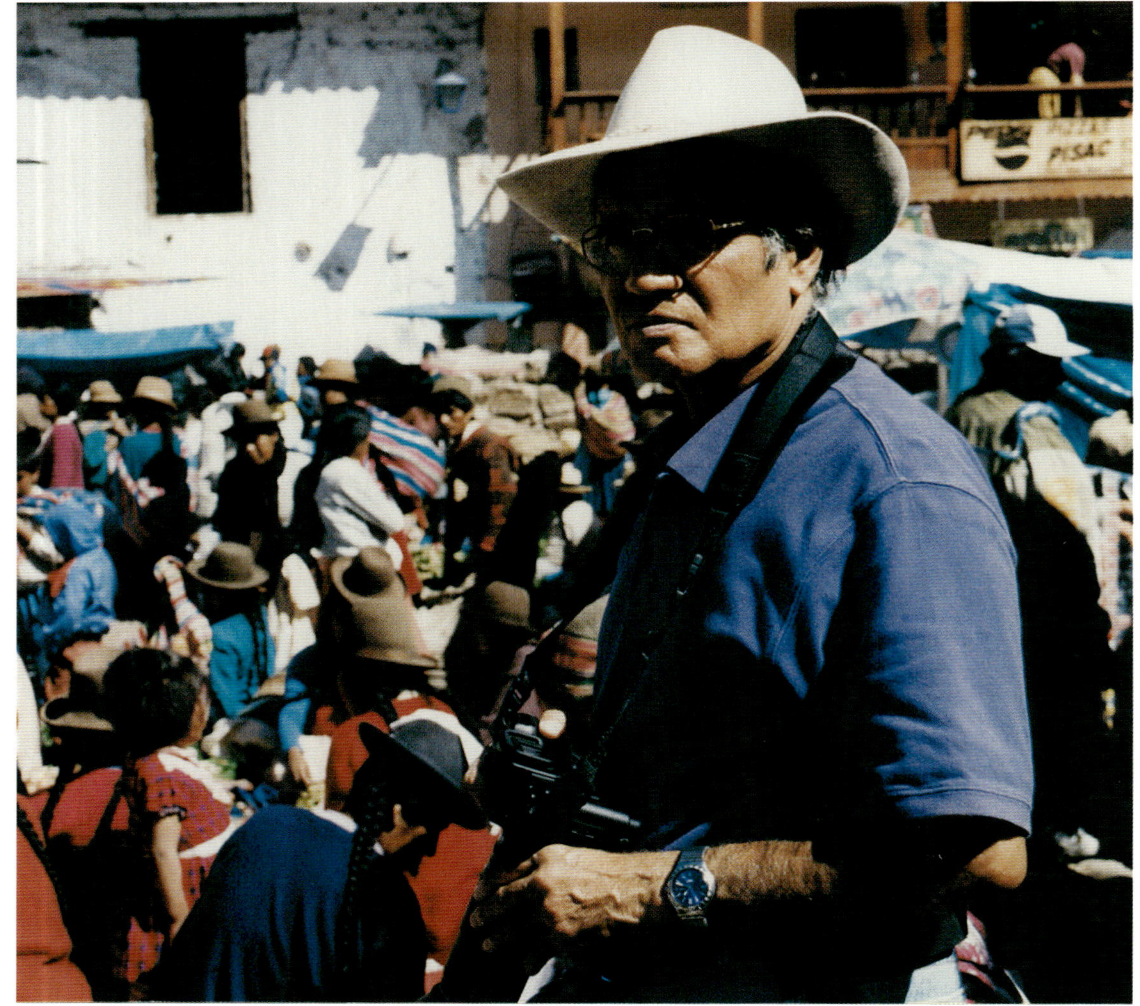

In the markets of Peru, 1999

1994 Returns to Guatemala, this time visiting Lake Atitlán and the village of Sololá, which becomes a favorite destination because of the lively market and the red and blue costumes typical of this Guatemalan village.

1995 One-person exhibition, *Visions of Sololá*, held at Riva Yares Gallery, Santa Fe, New Mexico, and Scottsdale, Arizona. Marries artist Susan Contreras.

1996 Travels to San Francisco el Alto, Guatemala.

1997 Exhibits *San Francisco el Alto* at Riva Yares Gallery, Santa Fe.
Travels to the western highlands of Guatemala.

1999 Visits Peru, with stops in Lima, Pisac, Cusco, and Machu Picchu. While he is awed by the landscape and the traditional technologies he experiences in Peru, the trip makes him realize that he has a stronger connection with the people of Guatemala.

2000 Exhibits *The Americas, Central & South* at Riva Yares Gallery, Santa Fe and Scottsdale.
Returns to the western highlands of Guatemala.

2001 Visits Paris, Belgium, and Holland, and has the opportunity to study Old Master paintings he has always loved.

2002 Travels to Verona, Italy, where he is included in the exhibition *Artists of the Ideal: Nuovo Classicismo* at the Galleria d'Arte Moderna e Contemporanea. Studies Venetian masters whom he has always identified as strong influences.

2003 Exhibits *Guatemala Revisited* at Riva Yares Gallery, Santa Fe, based on travels through Central America into Guatemala earlier in the year.
Invited by the University of Oklahoma to be a Distinguished Visiting Artist. The Oklahoma City Museum of Art organizes a one-person exhibition, *The Other Side of the Street.*

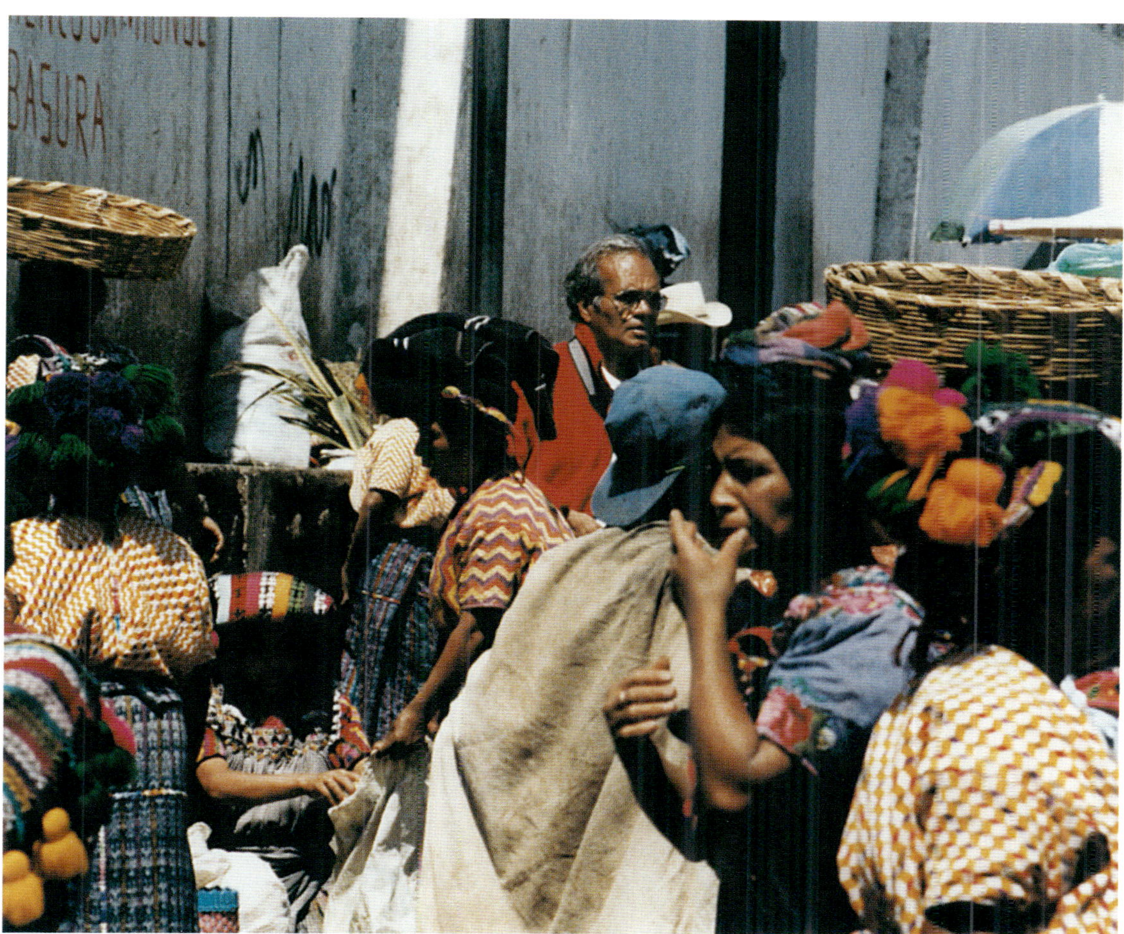

In the markets of Alomolonga, Guatemala, 2005

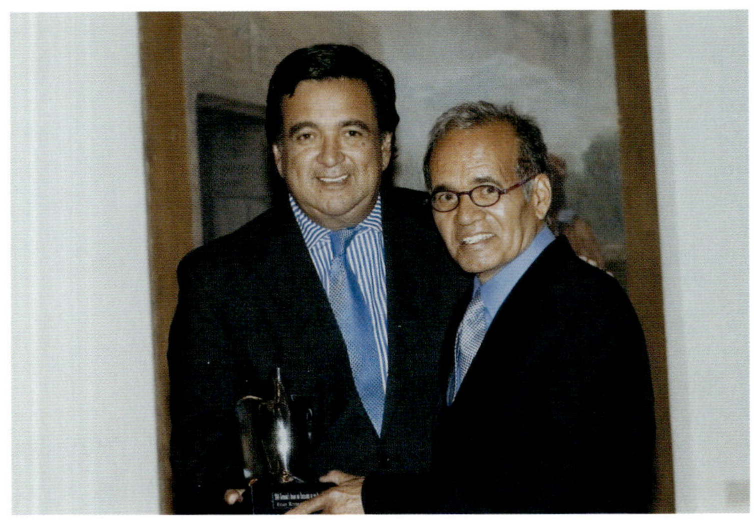

Receiving the Governor's Award for Excellence in the Arts, with Governor Bill Richardson, 2004

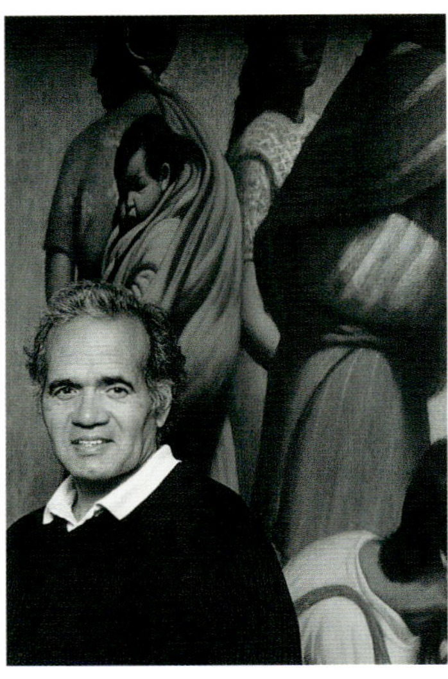

2004 Receives the Governor's Award for Excellence in the Arts, New Mexico.

2005 Travels to Guatemala.
The Rotary Foundation, Santa Fe, names him the Artist of the Year.
The documentary film "Elias Rivera: Through the Eyes of a Master" premieres at the Santa Fe Film Festival.

2006 Holds three one-person shows, at the Museum of Fine Arts, Santa Fe; the National Hispanic Cultural Center of New Mexico, Albuquerque; and Riva Yares Gallery, Santa Fe.

SELECTED EXHIBITIONS & COLLECTIONS

2006 Museum of Fine Arts, Santa Fe, New Mexico
National Hispanic Cultural Center, Albuquerque
Riva Yares Gallery, Santa Fe, New Mexico

2005 *Surface*, Exhibit 51, Albuquerque, New Mexico
National Small Format Invitational, Exhibit 51, Albuquerque, New Mexico
The Miniature Show, Albuquerque Museum, New Mexico
Cacciola Gallery, New York, New York

2004 *The Miniature Show*, Albuquerque Museum, New Mexico

2003 *Guatemala Revisited*, Riva Yares Gallery, Santa Fe, New Mexico
The Other Side of the Street, Oklahoma City Museum of Art

2002 *Artists of the Ideal: Nuovo Classicismo*, Galleria d'Arte Moderna e Contemporanea, Verona, Italy
Ahora: New Mexican Hispanic Art, National Hispanic Cultural Center, Albuquerque
The Miniature Show, Albuquerque Museum, New Mexico

2001 *The Miniature Show*, Albuquerque Museum, New Mexico

2000 *The Americas: Central & South*, Riva Yares Gallery, Santa Fe, New Mexico, and Scottsdale, Arizona
A New Mexico Influence, Art in Embassies, Madrid, Spain
The Miniature Show, Albuquerque Museum, New Mexico

1999	*The Human Fabric*, Riva Yares Gallery, Santa Fe, New Mexico *The City Series—Taos, Albuquerque, Santa Fe*, Cedar Rapids Museum of Art, Iowa
1997	*San Francisco el Alto*, Riva Yares Gallery, Santa Fe, New Mexico
1996	Syracuse University, New York [retrospective]
1995	*Visions of Sololá*, Riva Yares Gallery, Santa Fe, New Mexico, and Scottsdale, Arizona
1993	Cacciola Gallery, New York, New York *The Americas: A Latin Connection*, Nevada Institute of Contemporary Art *The Miniature Show*, Albuquerque Museum, New Mexico
1992	*Ventanas: Visiones Culturales / Contemporary Hispanic Art*, Plains Museum, Moorehead, Minnesota University Art Museum, Northrup Gallery, University of Minnesota *The Miniature Show*, Albuquerque Museum, New Mexico
1991	*The Miniature Show*, Albuquerque Museum, New Mexico
1990	Munson Gallery, Santa Fe, New Mexico Hispanic Invitational Show, Partners Gallery, Bethesda, Maryland Lizardi & Harp, Pasadena, California
1988	Munson Gallery, Santa Fe, New Mexico
1987	E. S. Lawrence Gallery, Taos, New Mexico
1986	Georgetown Gallery, Washington, D.C. Munson Gallery, Santa Fe, New Mexico
1985	Center for Contemporary Art, Santa Fe, New Mexico E. S. Lawrence Gallery, Taos, New Mexico
1984	Santa Fe Festival of the Arts, New Mexico Munson Gallery, Santa Fe, New Mexico
1983	Santa Fe Festival of the Arts, New Mexico
1980	Harbor Gallery, Cold Spring Harbor, New York
1978	American Academy and Institute of Arts and Letters, New York *Hassam and Speicher Fund Purchase Prize* Allied Artists, New York *David Humphrey Memorial Award*

1977	National Academy, New York Harbor Gallery, Cold Spring Harbor, New York
1975	Harbor Gallery, Cold Spring Harbor, New York
1974	Kenmore Gallery, Philadelphia, Penn. Allied Artists, New York *Gold Medal*
1973	National Academy, New York *Henry W. Ranger Purchase Prize*
1971	Quinata Gallery, Nantucket, Mass. Park Gallery, Brooklyn, New York Allied Artists, New York
1970	Harbor Gallery, Cold Spring Harbor, New York Cordiner Gallery, East Hampton, New York
1969	Brooklyn Museum, Community Gallery, New York Glaisek Gallery, Provincetown, Mass.
1968	Glaisek Gallery, Provincetown, Mass. Kenmore Gallery, Philadelphia, Penn.
1965	Lincoln Institute Gallery, New York Harbor Gallery, Cold Spring Harbor, New York

PUBLIC COLLECTIONS

Museum of Fine Arts, Santa Fe, New Mexico
The Capitol Art Collection, Santa Fe, New Mexico
Albuquerque International Sunport, New Mexico
Georgia Museum of Art, Athens
Northland College, Ashland, Wisconsin

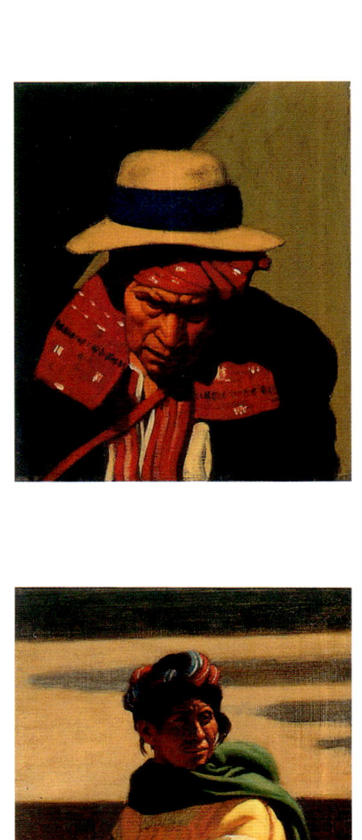
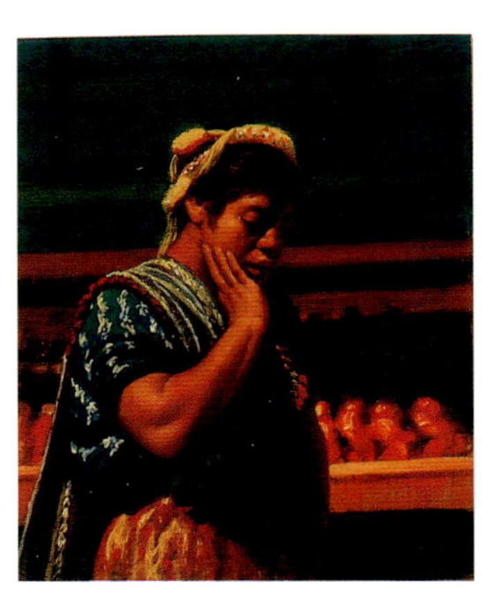
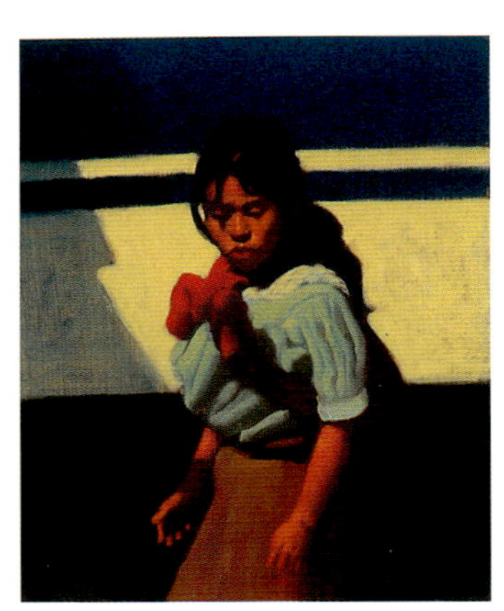
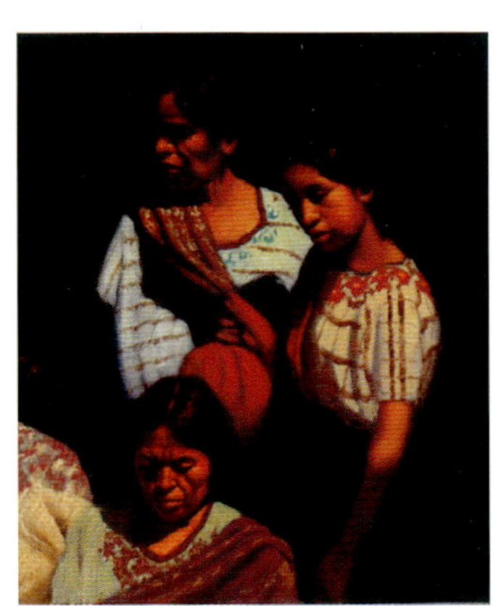
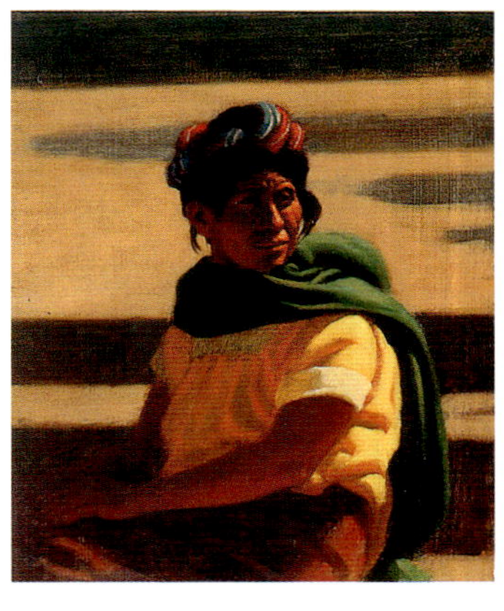
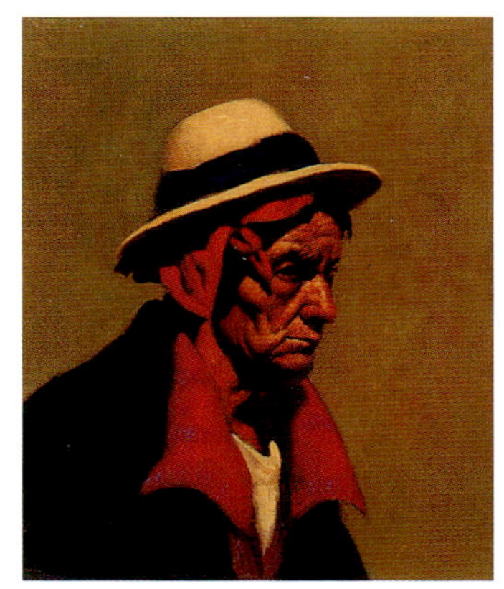
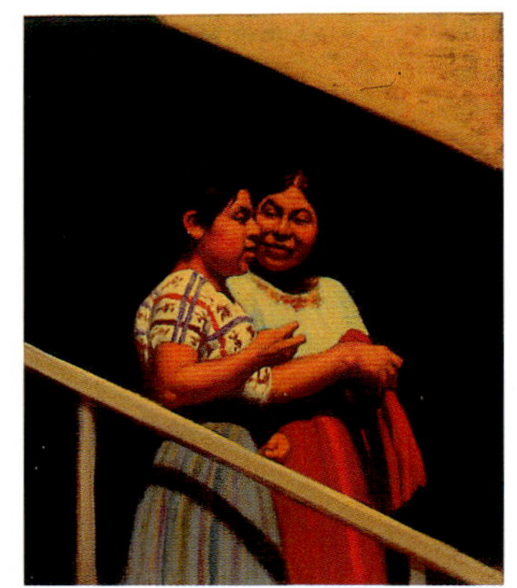
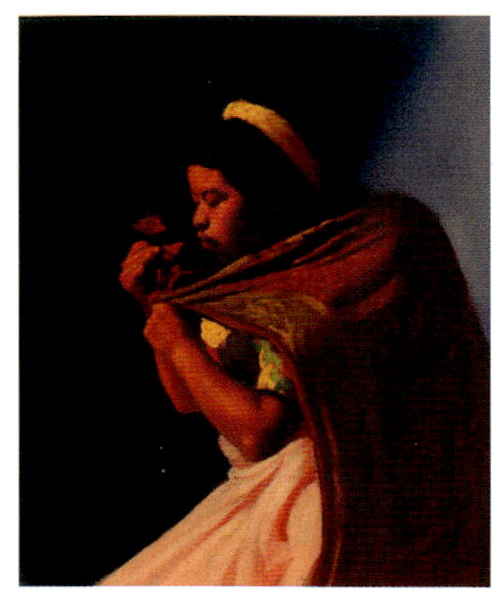
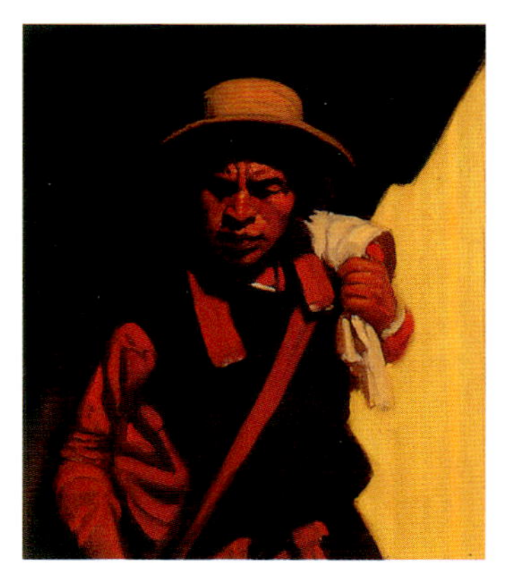
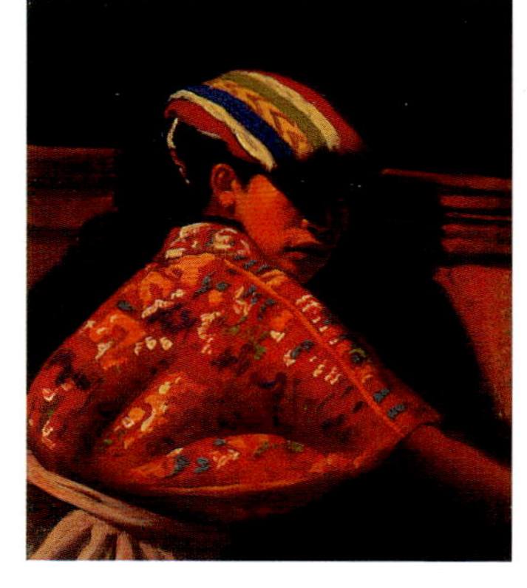
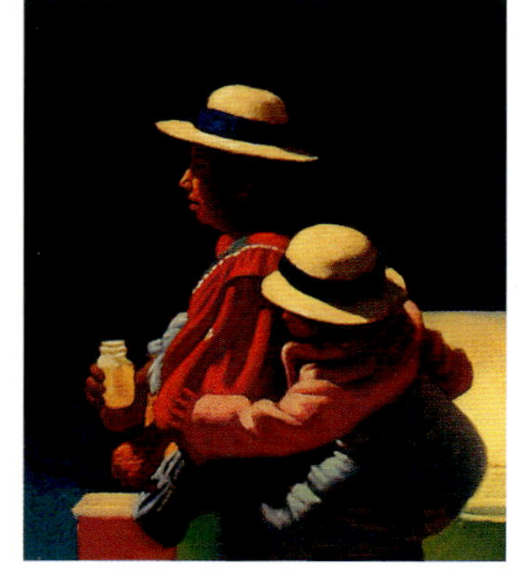
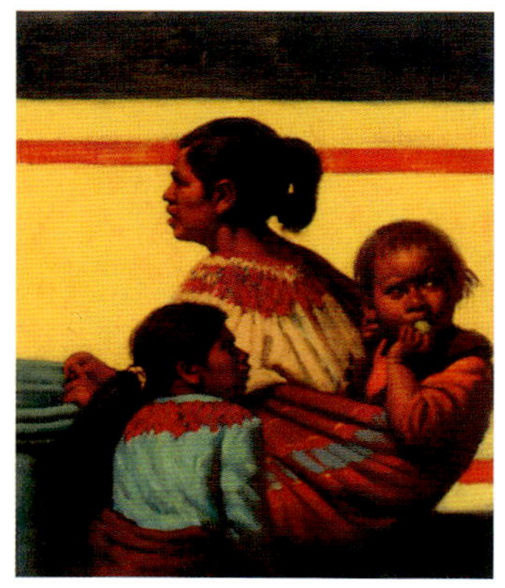
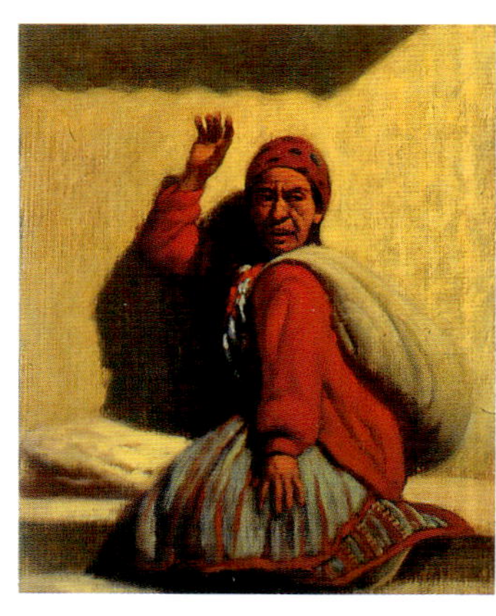
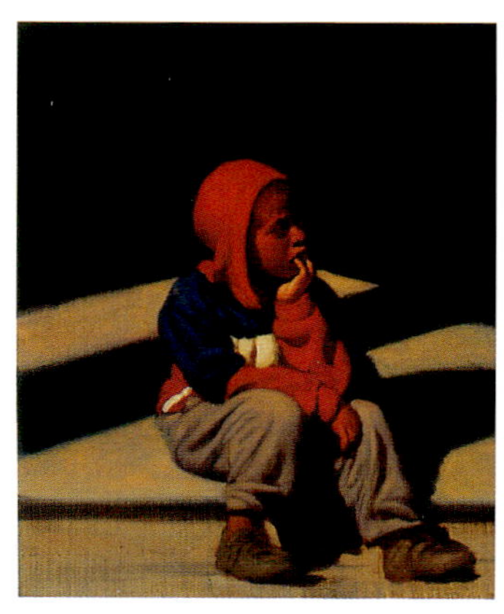
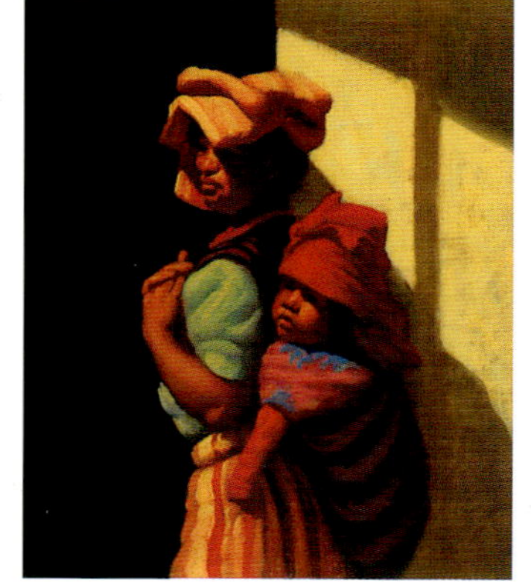
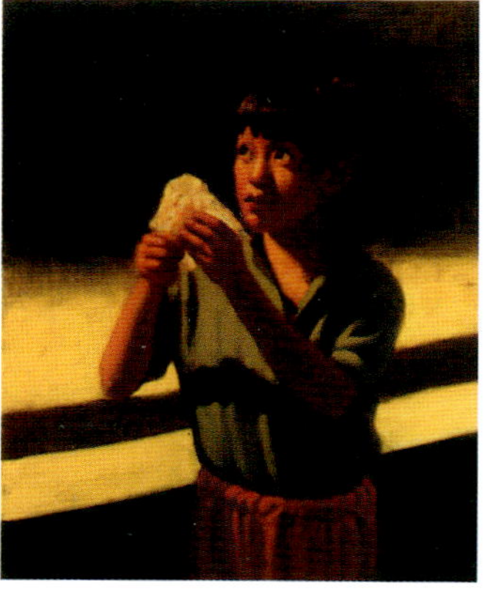

WINDOWS OF THE WORLD

2003, oil on board, 12 × 10 inches each

SELECTED BIBLIOGRAPHY

EXHIBITION CATALOGUES

Elias Rivera: The Americas, Central & South. Santa Fe and Scottsdale: Riva Yares Gallery, 2000. Essay by Edward Lucie-Smith.

Elias Rivera: San Francisco el Alto. Santa Fe and Scottsdale: Riva Yares Gallery, 1997. Essay by Edward Lucie-Smith.

Elias Rivera: Visions of Sololá. Santa Fe and Scottsdale: Riva Yares Gallery, 1995. Essay by Clayton C. Kirking.

Lucie-Smith, Edward. *Artists of the Ideal: Nuovo Classicismo*. Verona: Galleria d'Arte Moderna e Contemporanea, 2002.

ARTICLES AND EXHIBITION REVIEWS

"At E. S. Lawrence: Masters of Shadow and Light to Show." *Art-Talk* (October 1987): 54.

Baldinger, Jo Ann. "Colorful Calendar Artists Run the Spectrum." *New Mexico Magazine* (June 1991): 62, 66.

Bell, David. "Exhibition Is Auspicious Beginning for Art Center." *(Albuquerque) Journal North*, 1 May 1985.

Bell, David. "Faces in the Crowd." *Southwest Art* (April 1987): 70–77.

Bell, David. "Rivera Work Expresses Sensibility." *(Albuquerque) Journal North*, 24 November 1984.

Bell, David. "Rivera's New Work Shows His Mastery of Soft Light." *(Albuquerque) Journal North*, 17 August 1988.

Bensley, Lis. "Indigenous Splendors." *The New Mexican*, Pasatiempo, 8 August 1997, 36–37.

Berkovitch, Ellen. "A Beneficent Voyeur." *The New Mexican*, Pasatiempo, 4 August 2000, 44–45.

"Crimes of Compassion." *The Chrysler Museum* (newsletter) 11: 4 (April 1981).

Deats, Suzanne. "Heightened Reality." *Southwest Profile* (September/October 1987): 29–32.

Eauclaire, Sally. "Traditions: Cherishes and Challenges." *The New Mexican*, 29 July 1988.

"Elias Rivera." *Art-Talk* (February 1990): n.p.

"Elias Rivera—A People Painter." *Art-Talk* (November 1984): 33.

"Elias Rivera Exhibit on View at the Manhattan Art & Antiques Center." *Antiques and the Arts Weekly*, 8 February 1985.

Epstein, Pancho. "Capturing the Truthfulness of a Moment." *The New Mexican*, Pasatiempo, 10 August 1990.

Indyke, Dottie. "Magic Moments." *The New Mexican*, Pasatiempo, 26 March 1999.

Osburn, Annie. "Painting Slices of Life." *The New Mexican*, Bienvenidos, 21 May 1989.

Plett, Nicole. "Center Makes a Splash with 'Off the Wall' Art." *The New Mexican*, Pasatiempo, April 1985.

Preston, Malcolm. "Ordinary People." *Newsday*, 23 September 1980.

Preston, Malcolm. "A World of Sad Passivity." *Newsday*, 5 October 1977.

Roth, Michael R. J. "People Painter Captures Life's Drama." *The New Mexican*, 19 October 1983.

Sandrin, Kathleen. "A Painter's Steadfast Exploration of Humanity." *The New Mexican*, Pasatiempo, 9 June 1995, 24–26.

Scherch, Meg. "Theatrical Backdrops Keep Artist Off Balance." *The Taos News*, 3 October 1985, C5.

Terrell, Steve. "Artist's Inspiration: Santa Fe Selects Its Official Poster." *The New Mexican*, 18 August 1987.

"The Universe of Elias Rivera." *THE Magazine* (May 1994): 10–11.

Wilson, MaLin. "Rivera Captures the Spirit at The Downs: Show Traces Painter's Discovery of New Mexico Light." *The New Mexican*, Pasatiempo, 23 November 1984, 18.